"This new book is a must read for anyone involved with residential interventions! The focus on youth and family engagement is particularly exciting, as is the attention to current research and best practice. And, what sets this book apart, are the concrete strategies that can be implemented to take this service approach to the next level. I highly recommend this book!"
—**Johanna Bergan**, Executive Director, Youth MOVE National, USA

"Having effective strategies for maximizing relationships between residential providers and families is key to moving from principle to practice, achieving meaningful engagement and improving long-term outcomes. This publication provides real strategies and solutions and will inspire your journey to success."
—**Pat Hunt**, Executive Director, FREDLA, USA

"The authors are true champions for the well-being of children and families, never ceasing on their quest for best practices and clinical excellence. Their vision for partnership cannot be denied, with the ultimate partners being the children and families served through residential interventions. The voice of lived experience shines through like a beacon for authentic engagement, the only path forward."
—**Kari Sisson**, Executive Director, Association of Children's Residential Centers, USA

"Our nation is waking up to the importance of our nation's mental health system and that too many of our children and youth are facing significant behavioral and/or emotional challenges. Quality residential interventions are as important to a child or youth with behavioral and/or emotional challenges, and his/her family, as a quality cancer hospital is to a child being treated for cancer. This book is a must read for all professionals in the mental health, child welfare, juvenile justice and education fields who provide, fund and/or oversee residential interventions. The book shares practices and strategies about what it takes to ensure that all children and youth, and their families, receive the critical residential treatments and supports they need, within the context of their individual strengths and challenges, so that they can once again live together successfully in their homes and communities. This is our time!"
—**Susan N. Dreyfus**, CEO of Alliance for Strong Families and Communities and former Secretary of the Washington State Dept of Social and Health Services, USA

"The work of the Building Bridges Initiative and its two publications on residential interventions for children, youth and families has revolutionized our thinking and our understanding of best practice around supporting youth with serious emotional challenges and their families. This latest volume should be mandatory reading for anyone working with, overseeing and/or funding residential programs. This book crystalizes our understanding of how to support children, youth and families, translating the latest developmental research into practical methods that can be used with residential interventions, and defines the bar by which purchasers of residential interventions and families who are considering residential should judge residential programs. We can accept nothing less than the very best developmental opportunities for the emotional health of our children and youth, and their families. Bravo for this important contribution to the field!"

—**Tracey Feild**, former director of the Child Welfare Strategy Group of the Annie E. Casey Foundation, USA

"Over the past decade, the field of child welfare has made remarkable gains in the development of creative approaches to supporting children, families, and communities. This transformation has taken the form of greater integration of mental health services, enhanced community-based interventions, the expansion and diversification of wraparound approaches, and a greater focus on prevention and early intervention across all systems. As this paradigm shift has taken place, we have also begun to use residential interventions as a short-term tool for supporting successful reunification for youth and families, and helping youth achieve permanency. This book provides invaluable insights into the monumental transformation happening in the field today and is a must-read for practitioners who are working to create comprehensive systems of care that can flexibly and responsively serve children and families."

—**Ken Berrick**, Founder and Chief Executive Officer, Seneca Family of Agencies, USA

"Calling for the 2020s to be the 'Decade of Residential Practice,' this book sets a high bar for what is required to effectively integrate residential interventions into the network of community-based care and support for youth and families. With this second volume that includes practice innovations, policy approaches, planning and evaluation strategies, and first-person accounts, readers can gain practical information on how to infuse the Building Bridges framework of principles and practices into the way residential interventions are being implemented in their community. What is most apparent in this second volume, is the collective voice and purpose of the authors—families, youth, providers, policy makers, and researchers. They speak as one in their unified message of what it takes to implement quality residential interventions in a way that is affirming to all. The work of ensuring high standards and the principles and practices of the Building Bridges framework that are so eloquently laid out in this book is far from done. But this book provides tangible evidence that it can, and is, being done increasingly in communities across America. The 'Decade of Residential Practice' will require a strong commitment to continued dialogue, honest reflection, and strategic thinking. This second volume provides a roadmap for how to do just that."

—**Scott Bryant-Comstock**, President and CEO,
Children's Mental Health Network, USA

"The use of Residential Interventions in the United States is undergoing transformational change and just in time to impact how to think about the 'best use' of residential interventions is this new book by leaders in Systems of Care and Therapeutic Residential Interventions for youth and their families. Continuing on the ground-breaking work started by the Building Bridges Initiative, these thought leaders are challenging the field to focus on measurable outcomes for youth and families using residential interventions as a platform for recovery embedded in mature, community-based systems of care. A must read for anyone working with youth with significant behavioral health conditions and their families that may choose a period of out-of-home care."

—**Christopher Bellonci**, M.D., DFAACAP Vice President of
Policy and Practice Chief Medical Officer of Judge
Baker Children's Center; Medical Director of the National
Technical Assistance Center for Children's Behavioral
Health, Adjunct Associate Professor at Tufts University
School of Medicine, Member of the Faculty
of the Harvard Medical School, USA

"This book offers the most up-to-date, productive and constructive practice guidance for improving residential practices. It encourages readers to embrace change as an ongoing and evolutionary imperative given the significant impact of the service and support community on the lives of youth and families. The authors and editors all support the inevitable reality that everyone has a part to play in transforming residential interventions and advance clear direction on the roles we all must accept to ensure positive outcomes are achieved."

—**Jody Levison-Johnson**, President and CEO,
Council on Accreditation and President,
Building Bridges, Inc. Board of Directors, USA

TRANSFORMING RESIDENTIAL INTERVENTIONS

Transforming Residential Interventions: Practical Strategies and Future Directions captures the emerging changes, exciting innovations, and creative policies and practices informing ground-breaking residential programs. Building on the successful 2014 publication *Residential Interventions for Children, Adolescents, and Families*, this follow-up volume provides a contemporary framework to address the needs of young people and their families, alongside practical strategies that can be implemented at the program, community, system, and policy levels.

Using the Building Bridges Initiative as a foundation, the book serves as a "how-to manual" for making bold changes to residential interventions. The reader will learn from a range of inspired leaders who, rather than riding the wave of change, jumped in and *created* the wave by truly listening to and partnering with their youth, families, advocates, and staff. Chapters provide real-time practice examples and specific strategies that are transformational and consider critical areas, such as family and youth voice, choice and roles, partnerships, permanency and equity, diversity, and inclusion. These methods benefit youth with behavioral and/or emotional challenges and their families and will improve an organization's long-term outcomes and fiscal bottom line.

This book is for oversight agencies, managed care companies, providers of service, advocates, and youth/family leaders looking for an exemplar guide to the new frontier of residential intervention. In this era of accountability and measurement, it will become a trusted companion in leading residential interventions to improved practices and outcomes.

Beth Caldwell served as the director of the national Building Bridges Initiative since its inception and has years of experience consulting nationally and internationally to implement practices and policy changes that align with the research on improved outcomes for youth and families post residential discharge.

Robert E. Lieberman has over four decades of direct care, clinical, and organizational leadership in residential programs. He has written extensively and trains and consults nationally.

Janice LeBel is a board-certified psychologist with over 30 years' experience working in public sector youth and family services overseeing an array of services and promoting positive cultures of care.

Gary M. Blau is a clinical psychologist and the executive director of The Hackett Center for Mental Health, a Regional Program of the Meadows Mental Health Policy Institute. Prior to this he served as the chief of the Child, Adolescent and Family Branch at the Substance Abuse and Mental Health Services Administration.

TRANSFORMING RESIDENTIAL INTERVENTIONS

Practical Strategies and Future Directions

Edited by Beth Caldwell, Robert E. Lieberman, Janice LeBel, and Gary M. Blau

Routledge
Taylor & Francis Group
NEW YORK AND LONDON

First published 2020
by Routledge
52 Vanderbilt Avenue, New York, NY 10017

and by Routledge
2 Park Square, Milton Park, Abingdon, Oxon, OX14 4RN

Routledge is an imprint of the Taylor & Francis Group, an informa business

© 2020 Taylor & Francis

The right of Beth Caldwell, Robert E. Lieberman, Janice LeBel, and Gary M. Blau to be identified as the authors of the editorial material, and of the authors for their individual chapters, has been asserted in accordance with sections 77 and 78 of the Copyright, Designs and Patents Act 1988.

All rights reserved. No part of this book may be reprinted or reproduced or utilised in any form or by any electronic, mechanical, or other means, now known or hereafter invented, including photocopying and recording, or in any information storage or retrieval system, without permission in writing from the publishers.

Trademark notice: Product or corporate names may be trademarks or registered trademarks, and are used only for identification and explanation without intent to infringe.

Library of Congress Cataloging-in-Publication Data
A catalog record for this book has been requested

ISBN: 978-0-8153-9376-4 (hbk)
ISBN: 978-0-8153-9378-8 (pbk)
ISBN: 978-1-351-18747-3 (ebk)

Typeset in Minion
by Apex CoVantage, LLC

CONTENTS

About the Editors	xii
About the Contributors	xvii
Acknowledgments	xxiii
Preface	xxvi

1 Transforming Residential Interventions: A Practice Framework — 1
Robert E. Lieberman, Janice LeBel, Beth Caldwell, Joe Anne Hust, Julie Collins, and Gary M. Blau

2 Putting Families First: Strategies to Transform and Advance Family Engagement and Partnership — 8
Anne Kuppinger, Joe Anne Hust, Pat Hunt, Pat Mosby, Sherri Hammack, and Beth Caldwell

3 Youth Engagement and Empowerment Strategies — 31
Jammie Gardner, Lacy Kendrick Burk, and Raquel Montes

4 Advancing Equity, Diversity, and Inclusion in Residential Interventions — 54
Tanvi Ajmera, Julie Collins, Linda Henderson-Smith, Chandler Coggins, and Gary M. Blau

x Contents

5 Residential Transformation: Successful Strategies and Examples **75**
Janice LeBel, Martha J. Holden, Deborah A. Fauntleroy, Leticia Galyean, William R. Martin, and Carlene Casciano-McCann

6 Residential Intervention Strategies to Accelerate Permanency **94**
Christopher Behan, James Lister, Dianna Walters-Hartley, Lauren Frey, Evette Jackson, and Marlony Calderon

7 Residential Oversight Agencies: Successful Strategies and Examples for Residential Transformation **119**
Elizabeth Manley, Janice LeBel, and Kamilah Jackson

8 Establishing Partnerships to Improve Aftercare and Long-Term Outcomes for Youth and Families Served Through Residential Interventions **143**
Joe Ford, Debra Manners, Wendy Wang, Robert E. Lieberman, JuRon McMillan, and Beth Caldwell

9 Evidence-Informed Residential Programs and Practices for Youth and Families **168**
Sigrid James with Lacy Kendrick Burk

10 Understanding and Applying a Neurodevelopmental Approach in Residential Interventions **197**
Robert E. Lieberman, Tina Champagne, Emily Y. Wang, and Katie Rushlo

11 Measuring the Impact of Residential Interventions: A New Frontier **235**
Dana Weiner, Ronald Thompson, and Marvin Cain Alexander

12 Developing Fiscal and Financing Strategies for Residential Interventions **254**
Julie Collins and Sherry Peters

13 Residential Transformation: Taking Change to the Next Level 276

Gary M. Blau, Robert E. Lieberman, Joe Anne Hust, Janice LeBel, and Beth Caldwell

Index 285

ABOUT THE EDITORS

Beth Caldwell, MS, was honored to serve as the director of the national Building Bridges Initiative (BBI) from the time of its inception in 2005 to October 2019, when she retired from the directorship. She continues part-time with BBI as its Lead Expert Consultant. Ms. Caldwell has been the principal consultant with Caldwell Management Associates since 1980, a group dedicated to supporting organizations who serve individuals with complex needs and their families. Ms. Caldwell served as teaching faculty for the National Association of State Mental Health Program Directors' Office of Technical Assistance Center and co-authored the Six Core Strategies© evidenced-based curriculum on preventing restraint and seclusion and promoting trauma-informed care. Through the previously mentioned work, Ms. Caldwell has provided training, consultation, and/or on-site reviews for oversight agency and/or program staff in all 50 states and several countries on residential best practices that align with the research on improving long-term outcomes for youth and families post-residential discharge. The focus areas of this work included trauma-informed care, resiliency and recovery, family-driven and youth-guided care, and preventing aggression and the need for coercive interventions, specifically restraint, seclusion, and police calls. Ms. Caldwell started her career working in several residential programs, moving from direct care to Director, and she worked overseeing child- and family-serving residential and hospital programs for the State Office of Mental Health in New York State.

Well versed in the literature on effectiveness in the fields of mental health, substance abuse, child welfare, juvenile justice, and education and using state-of-the-art training and consultation practices, Ms. Caldwell has been called upon frequently to provide technical assistance and to develop written documents related to topical issues. She has multiple publications, and she has received both national and state recognition and awards for her tireless work to ensure that compassionate, respectful, and effective services are provided to children and families. She and her funny, thoughtful, and loving husband, Bob, are blessed with four wonderful adult children (Carey, Oliver, Maggie, and Lia), a much-appreciated son-in-law and daughter-in-law (Chris and Katrina), and three adorable grandchildren, Sophia, Amara, and Aidan.

Robert E. Lieberman is a licensed professional counselor who has worked with young people facing serious emotional and behavioral challenges and their families for over 45 years. He is President of the Lieberman Group, which provides training and consultation supporting organizations and communities in understanding and implementing trauma-sensitive, evidence-informed/-based practice. He holds certifications from: The National Board of Certified Counselors, Think:Kids at Massachusetts General Hospital as a trainer in Collaborative Problem Solving®, and ACE Interface as a Master Trainer of NEAR (neuroscience, epigenetics, adverse childhood experiences, resilience).

Mr. Lieberman was a founder and for 29 years served as Chief Executive Officer of Kairos (formerly Southern Oregon Adolescent Study and Treatment Center—SOASTC), an intensive treatment services agency for children, youth, young adults, and their families. Over his 40 years at the organization, he helped it achieve national acclaim for its innovation, quality, accountability, and leadership in implementing best practices. Kairos was featured as one of twelve exemplar agencies in *"Implementing Effective Short-Term Residential Interventions—A Building Bridges Initiative Guide."*

During the course of his career, Mr. Lieberman has been integrally involved in advancing public policy for children, youth, and families. He was a founding member of the Building Bridges Initiative Steering Committee and has chaired or co-chaired the BBI Outcomes Workgroup since its inception. He served as President and for 12 years Public Policy Chair of the Association of Children's Residential Centers and is editor and lead or co-author of its "Redefining Residential" papers. He has had national appointments to: The Outcomes Roundtable for Children and Families of the Center for Mental Health Services, SAMHSA; the Professional and Technical Advisory Committee of the Joint Commission; and the Child Welfare League of America Advisory Committee on Best Practices in Behavior Management (Restraint and Seclusion Initiative).

In Oregon Mr. Lieberman served for ten years on the Oregon Commission for Children and Families, one of several gubernatorial appointments. He also co-chaired the Oregon Children's System Advisory Committee, Statewide Wraparound Advisory Committee, and the Oregon Planning and Management Advisory Council.

Mr. Lieberman has been the recipient of many awards, including: The Lifetime Achievement Award (Association of Children's Residential Centers), Children's Mental Health Advocate of the Year (Oregon Council of Child and Adolescent Psychiatry), the Heart of Change award (Youth MOVE Oregon), the Oregon Mental Health Award of Excellence, The Asante Spears Healthcare Award, and the Josephine County Asset Builder Award.

He has authored over 30 papers, invited chapters, and journal articles; co-edited the first book on residential interventions; and made hundreds of presentations to professional and civic groups. Mr. Lieberman operates his own practice as a professional counselor for youth and families. He received his MA from Southern Oregon University in 1985. He is happily married to Kerrie Walters and deeply appreciative of two wonderful and accomplished children, Maggie and Aaron.

Dr. Janice LeBel is a licensed, board-certified psychologist with more than 35 years' experience in the public sector working primarily in mental health but also with other populations. She is Director of System Transformation for the Massachusetts Department of Mental Health and oversees a statewide system of inpatient, secure care, and community-based residential services for youth. Dr. LeBel leads the Massachusetts Department of Mental Health's nationally recognized Restraint/Seclusion Prevention Initiative and an Interagency Initiative with the same focus involving seven child-serving state agencies and the public and private special education schools in the state. For this work, she was awarded the Governor's Manual Carballo Award for Excellence in Public Service, the National Alliance for the Mentally Ill's Gloria Huntley Award, the Substance Abuse Mental Health Service Administration's first Restraint/Seclusion Reduction Award, as well as the Herbert J. Hall Award for outstanding contribution to the field of Occupational Therapy and the Cutchins Center for Youth and Families' award for Transformational Leadership.

Dr. LeBel was a principal architect of a large-scale, statewide transformation effort implementing the Building Bridges' Initiative platform in a residential re-procurement for both mental health and child welfare services representing $250M worth of annual purchased service. In this capacity, she helped to implement new roles for youth and families and amplify the important role of occupational therapy in residential interventions.

Dr. LeBel is a founding member of the National Association of State Mental Health Program Directors' Office of Technical Assistance Center's teaching faculty and co-authored an evidenced-based curriculum on R/S Prevention. She has lectured and taught extensively across the United States and internationally on preventing conflict, violence, and the use of restraint and seclusion; creating culture change; and implementing trauma-informed, youth-guided, family-driven care. Dr. LeBel also serves as a faculty member for the Building Bridges Initiative. She has provided expert testimony at Congressional Briefings and served as an expert witness in several legal proceedings. She has researched and published on trauma-informed care, consumer-inclusion, and restraint and seclusion-related issues and authored more than 40 professional publications.

Dr. LeBel has provided consultation to more than 60 residential programs, inpatient facilities and health care systems in the United States and other countries including: Canada, Australia, New Zealand, Finland, and the United Kingdom. She has also presented at many national and international forums and serves as a peer reviewer for more than a dozen journals. Dr. LeBel received her dual-concentration doctorate in leadership/administration and counseling psychology from Northeastern University in 1987. She was blessed to be married to her extraordinary husband, Dick, for 32 years until his passing in 2019. As a formerly anonymous egg donor, she is grateful for meeting and joining the family of her biological sons, Neil and Ryan, who along with their parents, Benny and Connie, give her endless joy.

Gary M. Blau, PhD is a licensed clinical psychologist, and Executive Director of The Hackett Center for Mental Health, the first Regional Center of the Meadows Mental Health Policy Institute (MMHPI). Prior to this, Dr. Blau served for 15 years as Chief of the Child, Adolescent, and Family Branch at the federal Substance Abuse and Mental Health Services Administration (SAMHSA) where he provided national leadership for children's mental health and created "systems of care" across the United States. He also served for ten years in senior management positions with the Connecticut Department of Children and Families (DCF) and as Director of Clinical Services for the Child and Family Agency of Southeastern Connecticut.

Dr. Blau has been the recipient of numerous awards; most notably, in Connecticut, he received the Governor's Service Award for his outstanding contribution to children's mental health, the Phoebe Bennet Award for outstanding contribution to mental health services for Connecticut's children and families, and the Making a Difference Award presented by the Connecticut's Federation of Families for Children's Mental Health. And, upon the occasion of his leaving Connecticut, the Governor proclaimed December 12, 2003, as "Dr. Gary Blau Day."

For his national work, Dr. Blau was the recipient of the HHS Secretary's Award for Meritorious Service for his national leadership in children's mental health. He was also the first recipient of the Rock Star Award, presented by Youth MOVE, National for "being a true champion for the youth movement and advocate for youth voice." This award has now been named the "Dr. Gary Blau Award" and is given yearly to a mental health professional who has distinguished themselves as a voice for youth. Dr. Blau was also the recipient of a SAMHSA Administrator's Award for "unparalleled and

xvi About the Editors

innovative leadership in children's mental health" and the HHS Spirit Award for being "an outstanding HHS employee who is making a real difference in the Department."

Dr. Blau has over 70 publications and is the editor of eight books. He received his PhD from Auburn University (Auburn, Alabama) in 1988, and he has been happily married since December of 1982 to his best friend, Gwenn Blau, and they are incredibly proud of their wonderful children, Jennifer; her husband, Riley (and their sons, Logan, Evan, and Elliot); and Andrew and his wife, Kristina (and their daughter, Ophelia).

ABOUT THE CONTRIBUTORS

Tanvi Ajmera has a master's in clinical psychology and is a public health advisor at the Substance Abuse and Mental Health Services Administration (SAMHSA) where she manages a portfolio of grant programs, with the goal of providing support and technical assistance to ensure that children, youth, young adults, and their families receive high quality mental health services.

Marvin Cain Alexander, PhD, LICSW is a professional educator, clinical social worker and human services leader in the United States of America. His work includes provision of behavioral health services for children, youth, and families who are multi-systemically involved; youth rights advocacy; and transformative system leadership at the local, state, and national levels. Marvin is recognized across the country for his ability to integrate lived experience into academic research, clinical practice, leadership, and advocacy.

Christopher Behan, MSW, MPA, is Senior Associate with The Annie. E. Casey Foundation's Child Welfare Strategy Group. Before coming to Casey, Chris directed several programs at Sweetser, a child- and family-serving provider in Maine, and he practiced as a family therapist.

Lacy Kendrick Burk, MS, MBA, is the Chief Strategy Officer with Youth Era. Lacy is an internationally recognized expert on youth engagement and has led the nation in several innovative youth-led programs. Over the last 15 years, Lacy's work has impacted more than 250,000 individuals across 40+ countries.

Marlony Calderon, age 19, spent five years in different types of child welfare placements, including residential, most recently at Plummer Youth Promise.

He graduated from high school in 2018 with an award for outstanding achievement in biliteracy. Marlony hopes to work as a barber or as an interpreter. His kind disposition and genuine smile will be assets no matter what career he chooses.

Carlene Casciano-McCann, MA; CAGS; LMHC, is Executive Director of St. Mary's Home for Children in Rhode Island, which provides comprehensive residential and community-based services for youth and families. Carlene and her team have partnered with the Parent Support Network to operationalize the Building Bridges Initiative principles and practices and have transformed their services by implementing trauma-informed approaches, decreasing physical management, and increasing youth and family engagement.

Tina Champagne, OT, OTD, FAOTA is Chief Executive Officer of Cutchins Programs for Children and Families in Northampton, MA. She is an occupational therapist and an international consultant on sensory processing, trauma, and attachment informed care. Dr. Champagne is also a professor for American International College's OT post professional doctoral program.

Chandler Coggins is a licensed clinical social worker associate, and currently works as a clinician on an Assertive Community Treatment (ACT) team in North Carolina. Previously he worked as a child behavior therapist and case manager, and was an intern at the Substance Abuse and Mental Health Services Administration (SAMHSA). Mr. Coggins has also served on the board of the Jacksonville chapter of NAMI.

Julie Collins, MSW, LCSW, is Vice President of Practice Excellence, CWLA and a BBI expert consultant. She has over 36 years of experience in child welfare, behavioral health, and managed care. She provides training and TA on various topics with public and private agencies and has authored or co-authored many publications.

Deborah A. Fauntleroy, MSW, was a social worker and a parent of a young adult with a history of mental health challenges. She was a trainer for the Massachusetts Department of Mental Health's Caring Together initiative and workforce development efforts and served as a family member expert consultant for the Building Bridges Initiative. Deborah held a variety of leadership positions focused on children's mental health. She was a graduate of the Columbia University School of Social Work and resided in Dorchester, MA before her death in April 2019.

Lauren Frey, MSW, LICSW, is the Director of Permanency Practice Leadership at Plummer Youth Promise, providing training, consultation, and coaching to public and private child welfare organizations. Previously, Lauren was a director at 3P Consulting and Casey Family Services. She is an adoptive parent of young adults who aged out of the foster care system.

Joe Ford, MA, has worked with youth and families for 36 years and is currently Senior VP of Programs for Hathaway-Sycamores in Pasadena, California. He serves to cultivate hope and resilience to enrich the well-being of children, adults, families, and communities. Joe is the current president of the Association of Children's Residential Centers.

Leticia Galyean, MSW, LCSW, is Chief Operating Officer at Seneca Family of Agencies, based in Oakland, CA. Throughout her time at Seneca, Ms. Galyean has helped to design, launch, supervise, and evaluate family-focused programs serving over 17,000 families annually throughout California and the state of Washington.

Jammie Gardner, AA, is Chief Operations Officer of Youth Era and Director of Youth Program Builder. Jammie has received numerous awards for her work in the family and youth field. Jammie has trained over 100,000 people across the nation over the last 20 years serving communities.

Sherri Hammack is National Coordinator for the Building Bridges Initiative, with over 40 years' experience leading systems transformation within the health and human service field. In Texas, Ms. Hammack has served as a state leader guiding public policy and best practices, including serving as the state's system of care leader and the principle investigator for federal grants.

Linda Henderson-Smith, PhD, LPC, is Director of Children and Trauma-informed Services at the National Council for Behavioral Health. She has over 18 years of clinical and administrative experience, including with the Georgia Department of Behavioral Health and Georgetown University. As a trauma survivor herself, she brings a unique perspective and passion to the field.

Martha J. Holden, MS, Director of the Residential Child Care Project at the Bronfenbrenner Center for Translational Research at Cornell University, is the author of the book "*Children and Residential Experiences (CARE): Creating Conditions for Change,*" an evidence-based program model and is the lead developer of the Therapeutic Crisis Intervention System.

Pat Hunt is Executive Director of the Family Run Executive Directors Association. Pat's experience as a parent has informed her work to direct a statewide family-run organization, lead family efforts to impact local and

xx About the Contributors

national public policy, and provide corporate leadership within managed care for children, youth, and families.

Joe Anne Hust is a national consultant and has been involved in activities related to improving services, supports, and reducing stigma for children with mental health challenges and their families for more than 20 years. She is currently the BBI Family and QIC Coordinator.

Evette Jackson, MHA, is Senior Associate with The Annie E. Casey Foundation whose career in child- and family-serving systems informs her work. Evette brings a track record of management expertise and cross-agency collaboration to improve child outcomes to Casey's Permanency for Older Youth strategy team.

Kamilah Jackson, MD, MPH, is Deputy Chief Medical Officer, Children's Services at Community Behavioral Health in the Department of Behavioral Health and Intellectual Disability Services in Philadelphia.

Sigrid James, PhD, MSW, is Professor in the Department of Social Work and Social Welfare at the University of Kassel in Germany. Previously, she was a full professor at Loma Linda University in California and Editor-in-Chief of *Residential Treatment for Children & Youth* (2015–18). Her primary research focuses on residential programs and interventions.

Anne Kuppinger, MED, is Senior Research Coordinator with the Community Technical Assistance Center at New York University where she works to increase the availability of family and youth peer support services, promote family-driven and youth-guided practice, and support providers as they adapt to changes in the healthcare environment.

James Lister, MBA, is Executive Director of Plummer Youth Promise in Massachusetts. In James's 14 years with Plummer, he has led the transformation to become a permanency-driven organization and overseen significant expansion and growth. He has authored several papers and presented many workshops and webinars.

Elizabeth Manley, MSW, LSW, is Clinical Instructor for Health and Behavioral Health Policy for the Institute for Innovation and Implementation; she provides technical assistance with specific focus on innovative approaches in children's behavioral health and developmental disabilities. Previously, Elizabeth was Assistant Commissioner for NJ's Children's System of Care.

Debra Manners, LCSW, is President and CEO of Hathaway-Sycamores, responsible for clinical and administrative oversight of all agency programs.

She has worked as a child care worker, clinician, supervisor, and program director, and she brings lived experience as a parent of a child with mental health challenges to her professional endeavors.

William R. Martin, MHSA, is Executive Director of Waterford Country School, a non-profit agency offering four types of residential treatment programs and five other non-residential programs including education and foster care. He also works part time for the Cornell University Residential Child Care Project doing training, research, and conference presentations.

JuRon McMillan, MBA, serves as the project manager for the Building Bridges Initiative, which focuses on improving outcomes for youth and families post-residential discharge. McMillan received his MBA in 2015 and has had a successful career in fostering culturally sensitive trauma-responsive environments that empower youth, family, and community voice and choice.

Raquel Montes, MSW, is Program Supervisor and Clinician at Casa Pacifica Centers for Children and Families. She brings her personal and professional experience across foster care, mental health, and juvenile justice systems to equip others in providing compassion, healing environments, and positive connections for those who have endured adversity in their lives.

"Pat" Mosby is a family member with lived experiences. She currently serves as Lead Family Supervisor at Montgomery County Federation of Families in the state of Maryland and as a BBI expert consultant for family voice, choice, and roles. She is a retired system of care family coach and trainer and has several national certifications. Pat is a single mother of three children and a grandmother of four.

Sherry Peters, MSW, ACSW, was formerly Director of the PRTF Waiver Initiative at Georgetown University's National Technical Assistance Center for Children's Mental Health. Sherry spent 21 years in Pennsylvania state government working on children's mental health policy and program development after working as a therapist in residential and community settings.

Katie Rushlo, BS, uses her personal and professional background in the child welfare and mental health systems to implement best practice change for youth being served in residential interventions. She is the national Youth-guided Care consultant for the Building Bridges Initiative and serves on many other national projects and initiatives.

Ronald Thompson, PhD, is Managing Member, RT Consulting, LLC., and retired Vice President and Director, National Research institute for Child

xxii About the Contributors

and Family Studies, Boys Town. He has published more than 100 papers and book chapters about therapeutic residential care, clinic- based and in-home intervention with children and families, and program implementation.

Dianna Walters-Hartley is a data specialist with Plummer Youth Promise and an independent child welfare consultant. Dianna brings to Plummer a wealth of knowledge and expertise as founding member of Maine's Youth Leadership Advisory Team and over a decade of local, state, and national systems change efforts with the Jim Casey Opportunities Initiative.

Emily Y. Wang, PhD, MSc, MA, is Executive Manager of Advancement and Integration of Trauma Informed Practice at Hull Services in Calgary, Alberta, Canada. She has a wide range of clinical and training experience and is a fellow with the Child Trauma Academy and a specialist in Infant Parent Mental Health.

Wendy Wang, MPP, is Vice President overseeing Public Policy and Advocacy for Hathaway-Sycamores. A champion with policymakers on mental health and child welfare issues, Wendy has been a member of the Los Angeles Mayoral Administration, Library Commissioner in Pasadena and Torrance, and President of the USC Price School Alumni Board.

Dana Weiner, PhD, is Policy Fellow at Chapin Hall at the University of Chicago, where she provides analytic and implementation consultation to child welfare systems across the country. Dr. Weiner's work applies rigorous research methods to generate evidence for complex systems interventions and support strategic system transformation with science.

ACKNOWLEDGMENTS

As with our first book, completing this second volume was a labor of love and could not have happened without the passion and commitment of so many people along the way. Our authors and contributors had to endure a rigorous and multi-layered editorial process; it is their collective experience and expertise that makes this volume meaningful. We also would like to offer our gratitude to JuRon McMillan, who organized many details of the project and kept us on track.

We want to especially thank and acknowledge the youth and family member co-authors and contributors who, based on their lived experience, provided their expertise, ideas, and feedback—some by serving as lead or co-authors, some by reviewing draft materials, and some by helping shape the principles and practices that comprise this book. In the creation of this second book, we tried to model partnership and collaboration, and we hope we were successful.

This book would also not have happened were it not for the knowledge, skill, passion, and hard work of the many residential stakeholders from across the country involved with the Building Bridges Initiative (BBI)—especially the countless hard-working staff who every day operationalize BBI principles into practices in their programs. The commitment of the professionals, advocates, families, and youth involved in BBI has contributed in so many ways to make this book a reality.

The editors would also like to personally acknowledge each other, our family members, and the many authors and contributors who made this book possible. Beth is blessed to have had a team of co-editors who are dedicated, hard-working, collaborative, committed to ensuring high quality standards, and who did not complain about requested changes—again and

xxiv Acknowledgments

again and again. She would like to give deep thanks and big hugs to these co-editors and to all the chapter authors and contributors to this book. Each of them bent over backwards to make this book happen.

As with the first book, Beth would like to also thank the children, adolescents, young adults, and family members whom she has worked with over the years and whom the Building Bridges Initiative has worked with. It is truly the lessons learned from these strong people, who have overcome so many challenges, that are reflected throughout this book.

Beth would like to dedicate this book to her husband, Bob, who fed her and other family members and friends, ran errands for her, carried more than his share of house responsibilities, and was the best co-grandparent in the world throughout the writing of this book. She would also like to dedicate this book to her three wonderful grandchildren, Sophia, Amara, and Aidan, for the laughter, love, and fun they bring to our lives. And finally, she would like to acknowledge her four children (Carey, Oliver, Maggie, and Lia) and her son-in-law and daughter-in-law (Chris and Katrina) for being such good human beings; she is proud of and thankful for each of them.

Bob would like to offer deep thanks to his wife Kerrie for her enduring patience with his many professional commitments and long hours and for her support and perspective on tough issues he has faced throughout his career. His children, Maggie and Aaron, are credits to the planet, solid human beings following their passions, skilled, responsible, and compassionate. Bob often reflects upon and is profoundly grateful for the start he received in life from his parents, Reuben and Sara, who raised him and his two brothers to have confidence in themselves, to believe in people and have empathy for their circumstances, to value the arts and human expression, to stand up in support of those who are downtrodden in any way, and to "repair the world" by advocating and working for social justice, equity, equality, and peace.

Bob is deeply thankful for the countless youth and families who have taught him so much over the years, and he is in awe of their courage and resilience. He is also greatly appreciative for the many great thinkers, researchers, clinicians, and scientists who have done such monumental work to advance our understanding of the human condition and how to help improve it. He highly values the co-editors, who have been amazing to work with, forging consensus decisions focused on yielding a product of the highest quality with integrity to the science, research, principles, and practice. Finally, influenced by a quote from Albert Einstein that has been a touchpoint throughout his career, Bob believes that his outer and inner life and work is built upon the labors of countless others, known and unknown, living and dead, to whom he stands in deep gratitude.

Janice would like to thank her co-editors for extending the invitation to participate in the development of this book and sharing their wisdom and talent so generously. She also extends much gratitude to all the co-authors, contributors, and her colleagues at the Department of Mental Health for their contributions, innovations, and dedication to pushing the field forward. Finally, Janice has unending love and appreciation for her wonderful husband, Dr. Richard A. LeBel, a talented psychologist, educator, and leader who offered his incisive intellect, keen sensitivity, fabulous humor, and endless love and support to this and all of Janice's work until he passed away in March 2019. She dedicates her effort on this book to him and feels blessed and honored to have had such a remarkable partner in life.

Gary wants to thank the co-editors of this volume for their hard work and dedication to this transformational project. His appreciation and friendship is everlasting. And, as written in the final chapter, may the 2020's truly become the "Decade of Residential Best Practice." Gary also wants to thank the talented authors and contributors. It is their knowledge, skill, and experience that rings loud throughout this volume, and they have made this a definitive "go-to" tool. In addition, Gary wants to thank the professionals, advocates, policymakers, families, youth, and everyone who are working to make lives better, communities better, and systems better. You embody the Building Bridges Initiative passion, commitment, and caring, and you have been Gary's inspiration for his over 30-year government and clinical career. And, you will remain his inspiration as he embarks on new adventures.

And, finally, Gary wants to thank his family for their unconditional love and support. His amazing wife and best friend of 36+ years, Gwenn and their children and grandchildren; daughter, Jennifer; her husband, Riley; and their three fantabulous sons, Logan, Evan and Elliot; and Andrew, his wife, Kristina, and their lovable and charming daughter, Ophelia. He is so proud of his family and loves them all so very much.

As shared with our first book, we can think of no greater calling than a career dedicated to improving the lives of children, adolescents, and families. If this is your calling, this book is dedicated to your ongoing efforts.

Beth Caldwell, Robert E. Lieberman, Janice LeBel, and Gary M. Blau

PREFACE

In 2014, The Building Bridges Initiative (BBI) organized and produced a long-awaited book to share emerging, advanced, and best practices being implemented by residential programs across the country. The pent-up demand for and success of this eye-opening book illustrated the need and desire within the field to learn more, know more, and do more—differently. The book focused on meeting the needs of youth and families-served and on helping organizations implement residential interventions and community services and supports that are efficient and effective; with sustained positive outcomes. In short, the book helped to plant the seeds for substantive transformation . . . *and transformation has arrived.*

With many states, counties, oversight agencies, and funders/managed care organizations now carrying the mantle for change by adopting BBI principles and practices and new federal legislation that shifts how child welfare dollars are spent to closely mirror the BBI framework, more pragmatic help is needed for the field to deliver the rising standard of practice expected from residential interventions. Some of the new expectations include: Shorter lengths of stay; actively engaging youth and families in new ways; respecting diversity in all its forms through humility, competency, and continual learning; and using data and objective and subjective measures to provide effective service and shape the ongoing refinement of residential intervention.

Readers of this new book will discover innovations in:

- New and creative fiscal strategies and approaches to support residential intervention advancement and redesign;
- potent permanency practice strategies as a core residential intervention, with the demand for urgency in ensuring meaningful life-long permanency connections for every youth;

- pragmatic methods for engaging "families first" as an essential practice of residential intervention—far more than the new legislation of the same name requires;
- specific steps that oversight agencies have taken to push the bounds of contracting, elevate new standards of practice, and create new service lines to promote positive sustained outcomes—and pay for them;
- how powerful, active partnerships can "build bridges" across and within systems to accelerate and integrate transformation; and
- neurodevelopmental and sensory based approaches that promote healing, learning, and recovery and shift the work of residential intervention from being "trauma-informed" to trauma-responsive . . . and so much more.

If you think this next volume reflects only modest change from Book One . . . think again. This book is a template for transformation. This book highlights experts and their first-hand experiences leading transformation along with their contact information, perspectives of cutting-edge researchers and industry leaders, powerful insights from youth/family experts, practical resources and tools, and specific strategies to move your organization forward into the new era of accountability for residential intervention. Read. Learn. Go forth and do wonderful work for youth and families. They deserve no less.

Beth Caldwell served as the director of the national Building Bridges Initiative at its inception and has years of experience consulting nationally and internationally to implement practices and policy changes that align with the research on improved outcomes for youth and families post-residential discharge.

Robert E. Lieberman has over four decades of direct care, clinical, and organizational leadership in residential programs. He has written extensively and trains and consults nationally.

Janice LeBel is a Board-Certified Psychologist with over 30 years' experience working in public sector youth and family services overseeing an array of services and promoting positive cultures of care.

Gary M. Blau is a clinical psychologist and is currently Executive Director of The Hackett Center for Mental Health. Prior to this he served as the chief of the Child, Adolescent and Family Branch at the Substance Abuse and Mental Health Services Administration.

Disclaimer Statement

As a former federal employee, Gary M. Blau did not accept any royalties for this book. As a state employee, Janice LeBel did not accept any royalties for this book either. Beth Caldwell and Bob Lieberman will donate their respective royalties to youth serving organizations so they can continue to engage and empower youth across America. Also, please note that the views

xxviii Preface

and opinions in this book do not necessarily reflect those of the Center for Mental Health Services, the Substance Abuse and Mental Health Services Administration, or the Department of Health and Human Services. Nor do the views and opinions of this book necessarily reflect the views and opinions of the Massachusetts Department of Mental Health or the Massachusetts Executive Office of Health and Human Services.

1

TRANSFORMING RESIDENTIAL INTERVENTIONS

A Practice Framework

Robert E. Lieberman, Janice LeBel, Beth Caldwell, Joe Anne Hust, Julie Collins, and Gary M. Blau

A Parent's Reflection

"*Providers were lined up on either side of the foyer. I was standing alone, off to the side of the room, feeling extremely uncomfortable. It was June 2006, and I was in Omaha, Nebraska for a summit. I had been cautioned about the long-standing disagreements between residential and community-based providers and as I eyed the crowd, it seemed apparent to me that the lines had been drawn. It was reminiscent of an eighth-grade dance with boys and girls lined up on side walls so they could size up the other side. I wondered who would succeed as champion. I also questioned why I was there, as a parent. Fast forward to 2019, and I asked a colleague the other day if he remembered how he and another residential provider pulled me aside at the summit and asked me if I could talk to the other parents to 'calm them down' so the providers could get on with the agenda and business of the summit. He replied, 'You mean the day the parents took over and the next day when the youth did the same?' It wasn't exactly the response I was looking for, but it was accurate. The tensions were definitely palpable. If that parent and youth 'takeover' had not taken place, I sincerely doubt we would have the Building Bridges Initiative today. It was a day of reckoning for both residential and community-based providers. Services and interventions cannot be designed successfully without a genuine partnership with youth and families. Partnership is the foundation for the Building Bridges core principles.*

Today, I am no longer that uncomfortable parent. I am still involved with Building Bridges and leading three states in BBI Quality Improvement Collaboratives. As you read through this second book and wonder how you might integrate BBI practices, I urge you to embrace partnerships with families and youth, and you will be halfway to home."

—(J. Hust, personal communication, July 25, 2019)

The practice of what has historically been called "residential treatment" has evolved and improved significantly over the past decade. This has been in response to a number of practice, policy, and financing factors; emerging research; and, perhaps most importantly, because of the engagement and empowerment of families and youth who have experienced this level of intervention. Collectively, these factors, experiences, and lessons learned have been the impetus to improve long-term outcomes post residential discharge for youth and families. Progress has also been made by re-conceptualizing how services are delivered, a greater emphasis on data collection and outcomes measurement (particularly post-discharge outcomes), and transformational changes at the provider, managed care, and oversight agency levels.

Five years ago, the book *Residential Interventions for Children, Adolescents, and Families: A Best Practice Guide* highlighted the emerging knowledge about the core components of successful residential programs and a redefined role for residential interventions in communities. The volume asserted the importance for residential providers to be part of community systems of care and addressed the tensions between residential and community providers, payers, and families and youth. As demonstrated in the title and opening paragraphs, the book offered the new term—*residential interventions*—encompassing all different types of residential programs. This intentional shift in language was a way to move the residential field away from the mindset of placement/a place for youth to live and receive treatment within the program to that of a short-term intervention, with a primary focus on engaging and supporting youth and families in their homes and communities, using a range of culturally and linguistically competent, family-driven and youth-guided, trauma-informed, best, evidence-based, and evidence-informed practices to address their needs and strengths. The new term has broad implications, as reflected in the compendium of strategies identified in the 2014 book and the changes in the field since. "Treatment" becomes something that happens through the practices and strategies available for both youth and their families—in the program and in their homes and communities—through strong partnerships with community services and supports. "Care" is available to the youth from their family, extended family, advocates, and residential and community staff. And honoring all cultures and diverse backgrounds equally—with equity, diversity, and inclusion—becomes more the norm than the exception.

The 2014 volume identified key themes: Using and disseminating the new terminology and mindset; creating and sustaining partnerships between all involved in the life of a youth and family; ensuring the essential role of family members and youth as drivers, through voice and choice in individual and organizational planning; understanding and implementing the vital significance of trauma-sensitive practices; embedding the importance of cultural and linguistic competency; and defining and measuring outcomes, especially post-discharge, long-term. The book provided a foundation from which to develop and implement best practices and offered multiple starting points for those who may feel overwhelmed at the task of change and transformation, invoking Lao-Tsu: "A journey of a thousand miles begins with one step"(Blau, Caldwell, & Lieberman, 2014, p. 226).

The Current Terrain

The 2014 book was an important factor in galvanizing the support needed and training required to implement transformational changes in delivery of residential interventions, and the past five years have been witness to several significant shifts in the expectations, policies, and vision that govern residential programs. Examples include:

- Residential providers are beginning to: Understand the necessity of shorter lengths of stay, recognize the importance of preventing and striving to eliminate restraint and seclusion, value and pursue partnerships, realize and respond to the impact of overwhelming stress and trauma, and believe in the importance of measuring post-discharge outcomes and impact;
- national associations are adopting the term "residential interventions";
- state and county oversight agencies (17 thus far) are adopting the national Building Bridges Initiative (BBI), a framework for implementation of the strategies and practices identified in the book, to support alignment of residential practices with research on improving long-term outcomes post-residential discharge. These agencies have implemented formal and comprehensive residential transformation initiatives via policy, regulatory, and/or fiscal mechanisms, incorporating BBI principles and practices and/or research into their work. A number of other states have adopted BBI principles and materials to improve residential practices and/or oversight agency mechanisms to support improved youth and family outcomes post-residential;
- new federal law (2018), the Families First Prevention Services Act (FFPSA)[1] is establishing expectations and requirements for "Qualified Residential Treatment Providers (QRTP)," consonant with the spirit—and in some cases, the specifics—of the themes described previously. The FFPSA marks a turning point in the evolution of the residential field, as for the first time stringent residential requirements are explicitly detailed in national law. While it technically applies to a subset of residential programs—those that receive Title IV-E dollars through the state or tribal Title IV-E agency—the new law sets a bar that, by proxy, extends to all residential interventions. A bi-partisan product of extensive stakeholder negotiation and collaborative compromise, FFPSA builds on established mechanisms that assure a baseline of quality (accreditation that includes a focus on quality improvement, presence of medical personnel, and

initial and ongoing assessment with a utilization review process) while also specifying practices that reflect the latest knowledge and evidence regarding what produces sustained positive outcomes (family-driven and trauma-informed care, provision of appropriate clinical services, shorter lengths of stay, focus on permanency, post-discharge support and services/family based aftercare, and outcomes/impact measurement).

The FFPSA thus brings together infrastructural elements that were historically available to the field of child welfare with newer transformative practices and shifts the historic tensions noted earlier to more nuanced and potentially productive challenges, e.g., embracing a transformational mindset, redefining the goals of a residential intervention, engaging family members whenever possible—even when there have been significant challenges in the household, involving youth in their family and permanency team to inform decisions about their own lives, designing efficient measurement systems to know when youth and families have the supports and skills to live together safely and successfully at home, and impact measurement to prevent cost shifting to the juvenile justice system.

Building Bridges Initiative

BBI was identified in the previous book as a "key driver," providing the guiding principles and framework for operationalizing new practices and strategies. The principles and framework have driven policy change in dozens of states and practice changes in hundreds of provider organizations, impacting thousands of individuals. BBI is not a model or a prescription; rather, it provides a framework and a foundation for residential transformation and articulates the values, principles, strategies, and practices that are consistent with research on improving long-term outcomes for youth and families post-residential discharge.

The BBI principles, as identified in its formative document, the Joint Resolution, bear repeating.

Table 1.1 Building Bridge Initiative Joint Resolution Principles

- Youth-guided;
- Family-driven;
- Culturally and Linguistically Competent;
- Comprehensive, Integrated, and Flexible;
- Individualized and Strength-Based;
- Collaborative and Coordinated;
- Research-Based;
- Evidence- and Practice-Informed;
- Sustained Positive Outcomes

For each of these there is a growing set of resources available on the BBI website (www.buildingbridges4youth.org) that help guide dialogue and decision making for youth, family members, residential and community providers, advocates, oversight agencies, and payers. When these resources and guides are used and incorporated into daily practice, the successes and lessons learned advance the body of knowledge and pragmatic experience in ways that compel transformation of residential and community interventions in an integrated fashion that leads to improved lives.

Purpose

This second volume is intended to capture the emerging changes, exciting innovations, creative policies and practices, and latest advances in the science, research, and evidence informing the work. This book aims to build on the previous text, serving as an extension of that work, and an update on lessons learned. The specific purpose is to address the key themes from the first book noted previously and highlight transformational approaches at the individual level (youth, family, staff, and advocates), the program level (residential and community providers, family and youth-run support organizations), and the system level (government oversight and financing, including managed care companies). It goes beyond the first by focusing on broader policy, financing, and system change factors to improve residential interventions; examining strategies to incorporate meaningful evidence and outcomes measurement; exploring brain science and its connection to the BBI framework; and taking a closer look at the critical importance of permanency and equity, diversity and inclusion.

In seeking to foster the wider and deeper changes needed at all levels of the system, the book is organized into chapters that examine and provide essential elements for residential and system transformation. Each chapter provides a discussion of the pertinent issues and offers guidance, tips, strategies, and resources, along with references to the science, research, and evidence and, for many chapters, contact information that may be useful on a transformational journey. Of course there remains much more to explore than this volume can cover in the effort to continually identify and refine best practice strategies, in areas such as: Workforce retention, transformation for oversight agencies, social justice, services for rural youth and families, education, sibling supports, families formed by adoption, addressing the different types of individual challenges parents and families face, and specialty services, including for youth who are LGBTQ, sexually trafficked, hearing and visually impaired, substance using, intellectually disabled and/ or on the autism spectrum, and their families. With more progress to come, perhaps a third volume will follow!

Each chapter has one or more youth or family members as co-authors or contributors, in keeping with the BBI value of ensuring family and youth are

6 Robert E. Lieberman et al.

at the table, their presence respected, their voices heard, and their recommendations given primary attention. In working toward diverse representation, the editors have also striven to ensure that the chapters have lead or co-authors and contributors representing a marginalized community and/or that experts in equity, diversion, and inclusion and cultural and linguistic competence have provided input.

Terminology

Once again it is important to make mention of the terminology used in the book. The term "youth" essentially is meant to include children, adolescents, and young adults, unless the context indicates a more specific age referent, or the more generic "young people." The term "residential interventions" remains as defined in the first book. This continues to be a more appropriate term that reflects many different types of treatment and support approaches. The term residential treatment, for example, can be misinterpreted as something that happens only in a residential setting, when in fact, best residential practices occur in the home and community as well as in the program. When referring to something that occurs within a residential setting, the term "residential program" instead of "facility," "organization," or "center" is typically used.

How to Use This Book

This book is meant to stand alone or as a companion to the first volume. And, while this volume can be used by itself, it is recommended that the reader become familiar with the first book to have the full benefit and understanding. Between the two volumes, residential providers and their community counterparts, advocates, funders and oversight agencies, and youth and families have resources, strategies, practices, and directions that have emerged in the past decade.

At any level, this book can be used to stimulate discussion, dialogue, and innovation.

- Youth and family members can gain ideas to share with policymakers, payers, and providers in requesting system or practice change;
- providers can ask their staff to read a chapter, identify one strategy that could conceivably be implemented in their organization that can then lead to quality improvement, and work together to implement this strategy;
- agency leaders can use the resources and references to support their efforts to improve policies, practices and strategies;
- policymakers and payers can refine and revise their regulatory and contractual requirements to expect and incentivize transformational practices.

As you read this book, think strategically about how to implement the core principles, strategies, and practices. How do we effectively engage families with complex challenges? What are important components of effective aftercare practices? What does it take to more deeply understand equity, diversity, and inclusion and to ensure we're competent in practicing it? How can we shift our thinking and practice to make permanency a priority? How can the workforce be expanded and enhanced through hiring of family and youth partners/advocates? What more can be done to hire and retain a committed and culturally diverse workforce—representing the diversity of the youth and families served at all levels of an organization? How can the science about the brain be used to change how staff interact with youth and families? How can the community and residential leaders and staff come together differently to improve services and outcomes? How can one measure outcomes post-discharge? How can the field of residential intervention adopt a "high reliability" approach (e.g., aviation industry) that commits to service delivery in which failure is not an option?

The co-editors of this volume hope and expect that you will generate your own thoughts and ideas as you critically examine the ideas, research, and examples provided throughout this book. Please share your thoughts within your organization and community to foster the ongoing growth so critical to "Advancing Partnerships and Improving Lives."

Thank you for your effort in this critical life-changing work—and happy reading!

Note

1. The Family First Prevention Services Act, Division E, Title VII of the Bipartisan Budget Act of 2018, Public Law 115–123. February 9, 2018.

Reference

Blau, G. M., Caldwell, B., & Lieberman, R. E. (Eds.). (2014). *Residential interventions for children, adolescents, and families: A best practice guide.* New York:Routledge.

2

PUTTING FAMILIES FIRST

Strategies to Transform and Advance Family Engagement and Partnership

Anne Kuppinger, Joe Anne Hust, Pat Hunt, Pat Mosby, Sherri Hammack, and Beth Caldwell

Why Family Engagement and Partnership?

Engaging families as partners is essential to achieving long-term positive outcomes for youth and families involved with residential interventions (Blau, Caldwell, & Lieberman, 2014). Every aspect of the National Building Bridges Initiative (BBI) underscores the importance of family engagement, and the Family First Prevention Services Act, new federal child welfare legislation that became law in 2018, requires Qualified Residential Treatment Programs (QRTPs) to put a strong focus on engaging families. Support from family is critical to shortening lengths of stay, increasing community connections, improving behavioral health outcomes, and sustaining success in the community post-discharge (McKay & Bannon, 2004; BBI, 2007; Walters & Petr, 2008). Although every youth has a family and each youth's family is an invaluable resource, for some providers it has been challenging to successfully engage families (Acri, Gopalan, Chacko, & McKay, 2017).

The first book in this series, *Residential Interventions for Children, Adolescents, and Families: A Best Practice Guide* (Blau et al., 2014), provided readers with foundational concepts and strategies to support family engagement. After a brief review of these concepts, this chapter will emphasize the critical importance of hiring Family Partners and then discuss examples of how residential providers shifted their approach to work in partnership with families.

Residential leaders who are focused on long-term positive outcomes postdischarge have found that they must work in partnership with families.[1] Meaningful partnership goes beyond simple family involvement. Partnership involves shifting beliefs about the potential of families even if they have serious and complex challenges. It means investing in families as a child's most important resource—including identifying permanent family resources for children if their parents are not able to care for them. It means adopting a broad array of direct-care, clinical, and practice strategies that engage and strengthen families (BBI, 2017; Dalton, 2011; Kohomban, 2011; Leichtman, Leichtman, Cornsweet, & Neese, 2001; Martone, 2010; Hust, 2010).

Principles and Fundamental Approaches to Support Family Partnership

"I remember dreading the intake call from the new residential program for my son. When the intake coordinator called, she said 'Hello' and asked me what I wanted to be called. She asked when a good time would be for us to interview their program—not us being interviewed by them. I felt empowered and wanted to work with her."

—Family Member who wishes to remain anonymous

Family-Driven Care: Family-driven care is a set of principles and practices that stem from the belief that interventions will be respectful, relevant, and effective when parents are empowered to make decisions about their child's services and valued as true partners in their child's care (Spencer, Blau, & Mallery, 2010). A full definition states, in part, that "families and youth, providers, administrators, and policymakers accept and support willingly and enthusiastically shared decision-making and responsibility for outcomes" (National Federation of Families for Children's Mental Health (FFCMH), 2016). For an organization to make a meaningful shift toward family partnership, leadership must "carry the banner" of family-driven care and make a public commitment to families and their staff that the organization will be "family-driven." As a part of this effort, organizations can evaluate policies and implement a range of practices to ensure parents are partners in all decision making and actively involved in the day-to-day lives of their children throughout their time with the residential program.

A nationally recognized expert in family-driven care, with extensive experience supervising parent partners working for residential programs, identified the following foundational elements for engaging families when their child is receiving a residential intervention (Hust, 2019):

1. Provide parent peer support by hiring parents as change agents. They will change agency culture faster than any evidence-based research—not just to provide peer support but to change the agency environment.
2. Provide a strong focus on the cultural and linguistic competence of staff who work with families.
3. Treat parents with dignity and respect and do not judge them. Judgment only allows blame and blurs professionals' capacity to evaluate their own practice especially when their help is not effective.

4. Expect parents to be the parent. Involve them in every possible opportunity to parent their child and include them in all decisions about their child.
5. Ask parents for their opinion. They know what has been tried, what works, and what doesn't work. They know their child best.
6. Provide hope to parents for their children's future and help them adjust to their "parenting reality."
7. Insist on a sense of urgency to return/reunite children with their families. Every day spent in care is another day the child is away from their family.
8. Do not accept "there is no family" as a reason to slow things down or keep a youth in a residential program longer. Find and engage family.
9. Understand that youth and families may make statements that seem harsh during treatment. It is the professional's job to hold the hurt, help heal the family, and put hearts back together.
10. Take every opportunity to work in the family's home and in the community. A focus on "youth in the milieu" is only teaching the youth how to live in congregate care. Go into family's homes to provide a valuable lens through which to learn how to modify or personalize helping interventions and to help the parent, siblings, and extended family equip themselves with new techniques that they can use in real time without back-up staff.

Clinical Engagement Principles: Families who are involved in residential interventions often have had multiple past experiences in which they have felt blamed, marginalized, and/or left without enough support to care for a child with complex needs. To engage, families need to feel valued and hopeful. Sexton, Rios, Johnson, and Plante (2014) outline six universal principles of engagement, summarized here:

1. *Work from respect*: Acknowledge the family's struggles, that they are doing the best they can, and provide help that "fits" for them.
2. *Build balanced alliance*: Work toward a shared understanding of goals and tasks that incorporates each family member's point of view.
3. *Focus on the concerns of both the youth and the family*: Work with family members to collaboratively define the issues and prioritize goals.
4. *Maintain a strength focus*: Draw upon and build up individual and family strengths. Recognize progress.
5. *Be empathetic*: Demonstrate that you can see the world as family members see it and relate to what they are feeling.
6. *Provide hope*: Recognize effort and progress and help the family see their capabilities.

Approaches to Foster Partnership in Residential Interventions

Knowledge about which clinical practices contribute to positive residential outcomes is still developing (please see Chapter 9 for further detail). However, there is ample evidence from practice models used primarily in the community to indicate that positive steps forward will happen when families are respected, engaged, and confident that their providers can help them meet their family's priority needs (Ontario Centre, 2016; Osher, Osher, & Blau, 2008).

In addition to broad principles, there are specific therapeutic approaches that are built around the belief that both families and providers have expertise and that working in partnership is the only pathway to positive outcomes. Clinical approaches that support family engagement are described in a previous volume on best residential practices (Blau et al., 2014), in the chapter *Clinical Strategies for Engaging Families* (Sexton et al., 2014). These approaches provide a framework and staff skills for successfully engaging families and for producing positive outcomes post-discharge. Some of the approaches are: Motivational Interviewing (Miller & Rollnick, 2002), Functional Family Therapy (Alexander, Pugh, Parsons, & Sexton, 2000; Functional Family Therapy, LLC, n.d.), Multisystemic Therapy (Multisystemic Therapy Systems, 2019; Cunningham & Henggeler, 1999), Family Centered Treatment (National Child Traumatic Stress Network, 2019), and Structural Family Therapy (Minuchin, 1974; Minuchin & Fishman, 1981). See the resource section of this chapter for more information.

Also, context matters. Family members with complex challenges have valuable knowledge of their child, their family's culture, their community, and what has and has not worked in the past. One of the reasons that BBI focuses on residential staff working with families and children in their homes and communities as often as possible, is that this builds family members' repertoire of practical strategies that work for them.

> "*The paradigm shift of viewing parents as the source of the problems to active partners . . . has changed clinical work.*"
>
> (Spencer et al., 2010, p. 176)

The Importance of Family Partners

Good things happen when parents receive encouragement, support, information, and linkage to resources through other parents with similar lived experience (Center for Healthcare Strategies, 2013)—and *nowhere* is this approach needed more by families than during a residential intervention.

Families whose children receive residential interventions often feel confused, isolated, embarrassed, hopeless, and disappointed. They may have become fearful for their child's future and concerned about their siblings; their family may have endured blame, shame, and traumatic events. Families who interface with a residential program are long overdue to be greeted and supported by a parent who understands their feelings, alleviates their uncertainty, translates their experience to inform program practices, links them to new information and opportunities, provides hope and guides them throughout the entire residential intervention, and continues to provide support post-discharge (BBI, 2012).

Families care about having a say in their child's treatment plan (Tambuyzer & Van Audenhove, 2013) and are more likely to feel satisfied with services when they participate in service planning (Koren, Paulson, Yatchmonoff, Gordon, & DeChillo, 1997). Research suggests that families are likely to disengage—or entirely withdraw from services—if they feel excluded by service providers, particularly when they perceive a lack of helpfulness or support (Gopalan et al., 2010; Thompson, Bender, Lantry, & Flynn, 2007) or feel that the provider is biased or judgmental. Conversely, families who experience a personal bond or collaborative relationship with the service provider are much more likely to engage in and benefit from services (Gockel, Russell, & Harris, 2008; Saxe, Ellis, Fogler, & Navalta, 2012; Thompson et al., 2007). While engaging and involving families is everyone's responsibility, the family is better supported to partner with the help of a Family Partner who has a deep understanding of their experience and who is equipped with a repertoire of strategies to ensure they are actively involved.

One of the most important roles Family Partners (also known by other names, such as parent peer partner, parent partner, family advocate) play is that of nurturing meaningful partnerships between families and their child's providers. Family Partners work with parents to ensure they have a voice in all decisions that impact their family—from planning treatment goals to day-to-day decisions in the life of their child—while they and their child receive residential interventions. With the support of Family Partners, parents are empowered to share their own expertise on their child and family. Parents move from participating with caution to offering ideas and contributing time and energy. They take on an active role in making positive changes. This spirit of reciprocity brings a different level of energy and acknowledges parents, staff, and policy makers as partners in improving services for families.

Family Partners work individually with families and as part of a team supporting a family. Some Family Partners are hired and supervised through a family-run organization to work primarily with one or more residential programs; others are hired (either as an employee or on a contractual basis) by the residential program itself. In either case, they should be full partners on the residential team, involved with families from before the residential intervention begins and well after discharge to ensure continuity.

As a family makes the decision for their child and themselves to receive residential interventions, the Family Partner can prepare them for a new experience, welcome them to the program, and create a comfortable environment for them by sharing program nuances, answering questions, and giving them an opportunity to talk about their feelings. As treatment and support plans are being developed, the Family Partner can support them to engage with the Child and Family Team to help them understand their child and family's strengths, needs, and goals. The Family Partner can support families to collaborate with staff throughout the treatment and support process and develop new skills and strategies to help them care for their child at home. They can also help families and program staff speak a common language and support families to express any concerns they have, so solutions can be explored.

Family Partners also work in the community with families. If the family lives some distance away from the residential program, Family Partners may collaborate with a local family support program as well. The goal of this community work is to help the family strengthen their network of community support and lay the groundwork for long-term support when their child returns home.

Family Partners are essential for ensuring that family-driven care is embedded within the organization; they work daily with all program staff and need to have a direct line to administration to facilitate meaningful agency-wide shifts in practice. Family Partners provide a family's perspective and work to translate family experiences into items for training, supervision, quality improvement, evaluation, practice and program implementation, physical environment enhancement, and policy change.

As demonstrated by the following residential program examples, Family Partners play a critical role in many residential programs.

Recommendations From Program Leaders and Their Peer Family Partners

Residential leaders across the country are shifting their primary focus on working with youth to a primary focus on working with youth *and* their families. Many leaders have underscored the critical importance of learning from others who have already made this important change in approach. Using this recommended learning strategy, this section highlights insights and strategies from leaders and family partners, using their own words, from six residential programs and one community program. Community provider partners need the same best practices and staff skills to provide seamless services for youth and families. Each of these programs is at a different stage on their journeys to successfully engage families and implement family-driven care practices. There are many more programs across the country that could also be highlighted for their good work; it is recommended that cross program fertilization occur in all communities so that the field of residential practice specific to successfully engaging and supporting families can continue to advance.

Damar Services (IN): Jim L. Dalton, President and CEO; Denise Lyons, Parent Partner; Angel Knapp, Clinical Director

Like other providers of children's residential services, Damar's historical post-discharge outcomes (first 35 years) were bleak. In Indiana, historical recidivism rates for children placed in residential programs were estimated to be greater than 75%—with some as high as 86% (Holstead, Dalton, Horn, & Lamond, 2010). Because of these poor outcomes, Damar considered abandoning residential interventions and moving to services with more promising and longer-term positive impacts. However, in 2006, Damar became involved with BBI and decided to fully endorse the BBI principles. With top leadership and staff motivated to improve outcomes for youth and families, Damar used BBI principles to create new ways to engage and serve youth and families with intensive needs. Damar made the decision to focus on family and youth engagement in their own communities as the primary mode of residential intervention, and conducted research to identify a set of best practices (Holstead et al., 2010).

In 2007, Damar also made the commitment to fully engage Parent Partners. Parent Partners serve on all internal committees, approve all policies, supervise outcome data collection, provide training, respond to family concerns, and facilitate parent information and support groups. Parent Partners also conduct training, participate in hiring interviews, and serve as advocates and parent liaisons. In addition to incorporating Parent Partners, Damar's family engagement practices and principles include:

- Outcome measures direct practices; family engagement is one of the most important variables most strongly correlated with long-term sustained outcomes (Walters & Petr, 2008), so it is measured and reported. Families are contacted for five years post-discharge to track the efficacy of Damar's work, and recidivism (i.e., youth do not experience additional out-of-home interventions/placements after formal discharge) has been reduced to less than 9% in 2018;
- barring Court Orders or imminent risks of safety, Damar's leadership encourages family time in the program and the family home and

commits to full accommodation. Spending time with family is *never* contingent on behavioral progress or earned. It is needed at high dosages for effective outcomes (Holstead et al., 2010; Lyons, McCulloch, & Hamilton, 2006);

- treatment goals are established with the family and include variables leadership had found, based on their understanding of the literature and evidence within the organization, to be associated with long-term sustained outcomes, including specific measures of family engagement, association with prosocial peers, school attendance, self-efficacy, skill building, generalization of gains, and number of medications at discharge;
- the most efficacious treatment setting is the family's home and community. While interventions conducted on campus can result in behavioral improvements, there is little evidence that progress in a residential intervention correlates with long-term sustained outcomes (Landsman, Groza, Tyler, & Malone, 2001). Interventions and skill building that occur in the family home and community are most efficacious and most strongly related to positive outcomes. Walking alongside families in their own communities as a primary way of supporting progress and crisis management are especially potent;
- Damar restricts residential interventions to families that reside within 30 miles of the main campus, based on its experience that access to families and communities increases the likelihood of family engagement and positive outcomes;
- Damar changed the way it categorizes "critical incidents" to be more consistent with the goals of long-term outcomes. The "critical incident" that has the most impact on long-term outcomes is a youth's lack of face to face contact with his/her family. If 24 hours pass and a youth does not have family or community engagement, this is considered a highly critical incident; it is documented, reviewed, corrected, and monitored; significant effort is given to avoid such incidents—thereby increasing family engagement;
- families and staff act as co-experts together; Damar provides as many training opportunities for families as for staff so that families can increase their expertise;
- Damar posts and publishes the organization's values and commitment to engage and respect families and provide formal and informal ways for parents to provide feedback. This promotes trust, transparency, and clear staff and family expectations;
- respectful and empowering language is ensured by consulting with family members on preferred language (i.e., children do not visit their own homes, so use terms such as "home time" or "time at home" versus home "visit" or "pass");

- families work closely with the Human Resources Manager and participate fully in interviews, vetting processes and the final selection and approval of staff hired to support their family;
- Damar uses several workforce practices to support staff:
  - Staff and clinicians are assigned to families, not residential units; they move with the family if the child and family move from one program to another;
  - for direct care staff to feel comfortable and confident in moving from residential to the family home and community, robust and practical training occurs, as well as intensive coaching and supervision;
  - Damar's residential clinicians are positioned and focused in the community, traveling to the residential organization when needed; this makes family engagement and providing ongoing supports in the community more probable;
  - work hours are based on family needs. Traditional "shifts" in the residential industry (i.e., 3 to 11) are based on organizational needs, not family needs. Matching staff member supports with the needs of the family's schedule is a far better outcome-enhancing practice than families fitting their schedules to those of the organization.

Damar's top recommendations to achieve family engagement include having the CEO and Board make the commitment to strong family engagement practices and ensuring the significant needed changes in polices, processes, budgeting, and personnel occur to match this commitment. Focus on direct care staff; they are the most potent change agents specific to effective family engagement. Finally, track outcome data three to five years post-discharge and rigorously use this data to inform practice improvement (Dalton, 2014).

Upbring Krause Children's Center (TX): Jason Drake, Regional Director; Amanda Martin, Executive Director; Amshur Dunn, Youth

Upbring provides a range of services and supports throughout Texas. Krause is the agency's residential program serving teenage girls and their families. Krause began using the BBI framework in 2016. They are committed to a family system's approach in their work with youth and families (Hansen, 1995; Goldenberg & Goldenberg, 2007). Krause uses several trauma-focused and evidence-based clinical models, including Family Systems Trauma (FST), to support operationalizing their family systems approach. Krause employs a variety of different practices to engage families, including conducting preplacement interviews, involving families in the development of each youth's plan for support and crisis de-escalation, and providing family therapy. Krause also provides financial assistance to ensure families and youth can spend time together at home and at the program. Through their use of FST, family engagement practices, and other evidence-based practices, Krause created a culture of collaboration with families and youth that has resulted in several positive outcomes, including increasing family engagement and significantly reducing restraints from 504 restraints in 2015 to only two restraints during the first two quarters of 2019.

Pressley Ridge (PA; OH; MD; DE; VA; WV): Alex Cameron, Senior Director of Clinical Services and Patti McCloud, Family Support Coordinator

Pressley Ridge provides services and supports for children and families across six states, including numerous residential programs. The Family Engagement Initiative at Pressley Ridge was formally implemented in 2015 with the generous support of the Richard King Mellon Foundation. Through this initiative, Pressley Ridge implemented an agency-wide culture shift where family-based treatment is ingrained in all operations and programs. In order to support this effort, clinical leaders who had family engagement expertise were put into regional roles as Family Engagement Consultants, a Family Support Coordinator was added to the team, and a Family Engagement Tracer Methodology was developed. This methodology is a mechanism to gather information about programs to determine how a family member might experience the program and provide feedback to staff on the integration of family engagement in the program.

Pressley Ridge is also currently developing a family engagement training curriculum that will be shared internally and externally. In 2015, they changed their logo and rebranded from "All Children, Always" to "Strong Families, Strong Communities." This is more than a slogan or a strategic initiative—it's a call to action to ensure that family engagement is embedded in their culture.

The Children's Village (NY): Takisha Wright, Parent Advocate; Mona Swanson, Chief Program Officer; Warren Kent, Vice President; Jessica Grimm, Executive Director, Brave Hearts.

The Children's Village represents one of the earliest documented examples of mandated residential care for children, grounded in the belief that children were best served when removed from "troubled families." Fortunately, today, there is growing consensus that children do best when they are with and/or close to their families and communities. And, families who were once viewed as damaging and dangerous to their children are recognized more accurately as families burdened by poverty; disadvantaged by their minority racial status; and, while limited in resources, deeply committed and loving toward their children. The

Children's Village was an early innovator in realigning the residential philosophy and approach to better engage families.

Over the past 15 years, Children's Village's has found that the overwhelming majority of the families they meet love their children and struggle very hard to bring good things into their lives. Similarly, Children's Village has never met a child who doesn't yearn for family. Family is defined broadly: One appropriate, willing adult capable of providing a child with unconditional belonging. Children's Village is not perfect, however, today at Children's Village families are welcomed, involved, respected, and heard.

The shift to a focus on families was not easy. Despite willingness, families had no reason to trust that this would actually happen. Hiring family members 15 years ago as Parent Advocates with full salary and benefits was an early game-changer. Parent Advocates have the freedom to challenge leadership and help make improvements; they have direct lines of communication to the CEO and COO. Parent and Youth Advocates now serve as full members on all agency teams. Parent Advocates' access to leadership very quickly led to an open-door policy and encouraging parents to call any agency leader any time. Most importantly, when parents call, leaders are determined to provide them with a response that is open and transparent. Parent Advocates developed the Parent Leadership Council; they train staff in customer service and orient and support new families. All of this has improved collaboration, reduced misunderstandings, and led to enhanced treatment and clinical experiences for youth and families.

In addition to the collaboration between leadership and Parent Advocates, Youth Peer Advocates, known as the Bravehearts, helped leaders and staff build trust with young people. Bravehearts, also noted in Chapter 3, is an independent, peer-led organization that provides pragmatic peer mentorship and youth advocacy for youth served by Children's Village.

With an almost 200-year history of speaking badly about families and describing them in the worst possible ways, undoing this mindset required showing the workforce that families love their children and that youth can be successful. Family Finding (Landsman, Boel-Studt, & Malone, 2014) has been a tool to help dispel the idea that youth in residential have no family members who care. With Family Finding, deep digging occurs in looking for family members "lost" to the child. This has led to exciting outcomes where teens with very lengthy residential involvement and limited family involvement are surprised to learn that they have interested family (Shklarski, Madera, Bennett, & Marcial, 2017). Family Finding also allows staff to begin valuing the role that family can play in providing youth hope.

A culture has been built at Children's Village in which leadership provides the most visible example of what is expected. Seeking to recruit and hire committed people who want to change the world requires acculturating them to Children's Villages' values. Staff must be around leaders who often remind them of these values and help them find success in this difficult work of residential intervention. Children's Village leaders continue to be humbled, not always understanding about generations of substance abuse issues, and finding that working with families who are afraid to engage with the program or the system due to the current political climate or social injustice, poverty, or race, can be challenging. Change happens when leadership commits to a new philosophy of engagement, valuing family and reminding the organization that residential is not a destination anymore. The job of leaders is to find a family member who loves each youth unconditionally and supporting that to become a reality.

Warwick House (PA): Jeffrey M. Friedman, Clinical Director; Dan and Melyssa Blanchard, Parents who, with their child, were served by Warwick House.

Warwick House serves children (ages 5–14) and families struggling to live safely together. Their primary objectives are: 1) facilitating permanency for children; and 2) actively working with families to create a comprehensive plan for community-based aftercare services. Warwick has developed a unique residential version of Attachment Based Family Therapy (Diamond, Diamond, & Levy, 2014; Liddle, 2013). Warwick's family-driven care model redefines the family's role, making the family, not only the child, the primary recipient of residential interventions. Staff-family relationships are defined by the concept of partnership, a transformational approach that engages family members equally, creating shared responsibility for growth and change. Family engagement occurs in three concurrent stages:

Orientation and Assessment:

- Parents and children meet with staff, past and current residents, and family members; do a tour; and decide whether this is the treatment program they are committed to;
- at admission, the family is warmly welcomed; each family member is asked to identify a treatment goal for themselves and their needs for growth and change;
- the reality of the brevity of residential intervention is made explicit to ensure families understand that time is limited and that the program is focused on stabilizing children, with the understanding that there will be ongoing work once their child is discharged. The program purposely communicates to parents that their focus is to reduce the time the child

spends outside of the family home, not address every concern before discharge;

- families are treated as experts on their child's needs, behaviors, strengths, and challenges;
- families commit to high levels of involvement, and staff maintain respect for the family schedule and preference for frequency of contact on a day-to-day basis;
- power is shared with families to provide opportunities for them to work with the team to explore strategies they can use to provide consistency and security for their child so they can be successful;
- family time spent at Warwick is carefully planned yet flexible, so families can be with their child at any time and participate in programming;
- youth time at home occurs often and begins early, providing an opportunity to better understand family interactions and provide the support needed to set the stage for long-term success when their child returns home;
- treatment goals are strategic and primarily focused on key permanency barriers.

Treatment and Training:

- All extended family members are included in the permanency quest (e.g., siblings, aunts, uncles, grandparents, even custodial and non-custodial parents with considerable conflicts);
- economic barriers are addressed: Transportation or funds for travel are provided. Families can stay at the program overnight. Parent work obligations are the primary consideration when making staffing decisions and scheduling therapy;
- supervised, high-quality family therapy is provided with frequency and intensity individualized to the family's needs. Additional work is done by telephone or video conference; strategic use of media allows parents to be involved alongside the residential staff as they work with their child;
- frequent time at home focuses on the "transfer of training." Staff encourage parents to use interventions they have practiced with success at Warwick;
- on-call accessibility for crisis intervention is provided 24 hours a day to families;
- concurrent planning may be necessary, involving both birth parents and prospective foster or adoptive families, kinship, or alternative family resources.

Discharge and Aftercare:

- Aftercare planning "begins on day one." Family treatment, planning, and implementation of important community support systems for the family occurs from the beginning;

Family Engagement and Partnership **21**

- knowledge is power and providing up to date information about resources, both formal and informal, in the community is one method used to empower families. Hierarchy of needs determines the right community supports, e.g., baseline needs for economic and psychosocial survival must be addressed first;
- families and staff co-create a detailed aftercare plan; the same degree of planning as used for residential interventions is required for developing formal and informal community supports, school, financial resources, workplace, and respite;
- regarding crisis intervention, parents must be empowered by the certainty that they will not be faced with situations where they are forced to manage the unmanageable;
- solutions are designed to address gaps in the families' ability to provide supervision for the child.

Warwick has found several workforce strategies to be important, including providing staff training on family-based residential treatment and on family support; in addition to improving skills, attention to these areas challenges potential staff's existing beliefs and assumptions that may impede partnership and permanency. Warwick leaders also teach staff to use strength-based treatment planning that targets key barrier behaviors and issues that impede permanency and optimum family relational health. Most importantly they teach and support staff in mobilizing courage and respect when confronted with hard family truths, e.g., child abuse, alcoholism, poverty, mental illness, or criminal behavior.

Warwick's recent outcomes show that lengths of stay are, on average, five months and that youth require lower levels of care post-discharge, with 80% returning to a stable permanent family. Their top recommendations to improve family engagement include: 1) Ensure strong leadership messaging that a shift in purpose, family relational health, and reduced length of stay, will occur, why, and how it will benefit children and families; 2) retain the strengths of staff's expertise in ensuring a safe and trauma-informed residential program while expanding staff capacities to teach and support families in their homes; and 3) strongly emphasize developing community partnerships that ensure services sufficient to support the family's ongoing process of growth and change post-discharge.

> "It was very valuable to have therapists and staff interact with us who were also interacting with our son on a day-to-day basis. This kept us informed and made me feel like they 'got' the challenges we were facing in living with him. Through this process we felt validated and encouraged to try new ways of parenting with both of our children."
>
> (Family Member served by Warwick)

Stanford Youth Solutions (CA): Laura D. Heintz, CEO; Ebony Chambers, Director of Family and Youth Partnerships

A national leader in family and youth engagement strategies, Stanford Youth Solutions (Stanford), after 106 years of running congregate care programs, transformed their business model to be 100% home and community based in the Northern California region; partnering with a wide range of residential programs to support successful transitions of youth into family homes. The mission of Stanford is to inspire sustainable change for youth and their families and empower them to solve serious challenges together. Family-centered practice is embedded into every aspect of Stanford. Their Family and Youth Partnership program serves to ensure strong advocacy for families and youth and considers the whole family in system planning. No matter the service delivered, the youth and their family are at the center of the work. Child Family Teams (CFT) are the forum for decision making, treatment planning, and accountability. To ensure that the clinical team does not make decisions without the youth and family in the center, each youth and family is paired with peer advocates. There are four key functions of peer advocates at Stanford, working in collaboration with other staff: 1) Ensure families (parents, other caregivers, and youth) are equal partners—*if not leaders*—in the development and implementation of their plans; 2) represent the needs and perspectives of youth/families to internal and external stakeholders; 3) ensure that youth/families have access to a comprehensive array of prevention and support services; and 4) work together with leadership and all staff to ensure that services are family-centered; easily accessible; respectful of cultural, ethnic, and other community characteristics; and stigma free.

Stanford has found that engaging families in service delivery promotes the safety, permanency, functioning, and overall well-being of youth and is central to a comprehensive and effective system of care. Of those youth who transitioned home through the Stanford child family teaming process, 78% have achieved family stabilization (Stanford Youth Solutions, 2018). Stanford's top recommendations for improving family engagement include hiring family and youth advocates, ensuring robust Child and Family Team Meetings, building family and youth partnership practices into new project proposals, ensuring culturally competent and trauma-informed care practices, and becoming an outcome-driven organization. Finally, Stanford recommends building an organizational culture that is reflective of staff honoring and respecting the family as experts of their own family to create a sense of partnership and shared responsibility.

Family Engagement and Partnership **23**

Three Rivers Clinically Intensive Residential Treatment Program / Cutchins Program for Children and Families (MA): Rob Terreden, Program Director; Amy Breton, Family Support Coordinator

"Knowing that I was getting to practice and working with someone in my home was not only valuable but life changing. Staff were able to help back me up and help strengthen my parenting skills. Having people in my home at first made me feel standoff-ish. I did not want to be judged. Three Rivers never made me feel judged for having a child with mental health issues."

(Family member served by Cutchins)

The Three Rivers Program is a "Clinically Intensive Residential Treatment" program serving children ages 6–12, committed to trauma-informed care and family engagement, with the mission of returning children safely to the community and their families. One of the most important strategies Cutchins uses to improve successful engagement of families is to employ a full-time parent partner with the title of Family Support Coordinator. In partnership with the Family Support Coordinator, four basic principles guide the implementation of family-driven practices:

Principle 1: Belonging. Despite whatever diagnosis a child may have, know that they are a person who needs to feel they are important to someone, belong in the world, and are lovable. Cutchins has taken several steps to keep children connected with their loved ones:

- Changed the job titles of direct-care staff to Family Support Counselors so that staff understand their work is with the whole family and often in families' homes;
- established that the criteria for children spending time at home is that staff and family feel it will be safe. If staff need to go home with the child to reach this threshold, it happens. There are no policies that inherently limit how soon or how often a child can go to their home following admission; it happens as quickly as possible. Increments of independence, i.e., having the staff go "hang out" at the town library to be available to the family if needed but give families space to build confidence, are built in;
- ensured that different disciplines of staff work in families' homes, not just clinicians;
- changed language: Family Support Counselors use "Counseling for Success" in the homes (i.e., transferring what was learned about supporting

a child in the program to their home/community). Along with the obvious practical benefits of these processes, the partnership and trust that is fostered has tremendous value;

- provided travel funding: Parents submit travel vouchers as employees do, to bring their child home and to attend treatment events. Staff provide transportation to take children home or pick them up. This happens *every weekend*;
- ensured children go home every week: Team meetings include creative problem-solving to ensure children get home each week. In one situation, it was clear that, although a child would probably never again live with her mother, she and her mother loved each other, and that connection was vital to this girl's sense of connectedness and need for a loving relationship. Despite great distance and without regard to expense, staff made sure she spent time at home, and they believe that contributed to her success in treatment.

Principle 2: Accessibility and Approachability. Staff consciously make the style of conversations with families informal and unpretentious. Parents can talk with anyone (e.g., janitor, office manager, program director). There are no visiting hours. Parents are always welcome at the program and invited to join meals. Pre-admission/admission strategies focus on welcoming, including providing families with welcome gifts (i.e., gift bags containing handmade mugs, hand sanitizer, lotions, stress balls, and thank you notes "for letting our program be part of their family's healing process"). There is focus on being sensitive to how scary admission to a residential program can be for families and recognition that the last thing any parent wants is to have their child be in a residential program and sleep away from home. Program staff work hard to call and meet families before admission; this provides a familiar face/voice during the admission. Staff also check in with families within 48 hours post admission. The Family Welcome Packet was rewritten based on family feedback to have simple and clear language; it includes contact information for every staff member as well as a staffing schedule. There is a strong focus on providing creative family supports, for example: Having a staff member go on a weekend vacation with a family (child welfare required this type of supervision for the child to go on vacation); having a staff member fly with a child to Florida so the child could spend time with pre-adoptive grandparents; and having a staff member spend the night at a child's home on Thanksgiving, with the program's therapy dog in tow.

One recurring obstacle for treatment has been when families lose their housing. The team works closely with families alongside housing authorities, child welfare supports, and social service providers to look for housing solutions. Through these efforts, which take considerable time, determination, and creativity, 95% of these families succeed in securing housing. It is worth the effort as children then can practice living with their family and feel the hope of that possibility.

Principle 3: Non-Judgmental. Recognize that families have lives that include other kids, jobs, neighborhoods, illnesses, etc. Leaders emphasize being non-judgmental and have found that engaging, encouraging, and empowering, with authenticity, is the most important intervention. Staff make accommodating schedules of parents a priority. The program provides childcare for other children to support family participation in meetings, family training, and therapy sessions. With compassion and without judgement, staff support family members with obtaining needed community resources for their own needs (i.e., substance abuse or mental health treatment).

Principle 4: Support Direct-care Staff. Various strategies are used to ensure that direct-care staff are supported (e.g., they are included in weekly Team meetings; the psychiatrist checks in with them regarding medication decisions; treatment decisions are informed by what they observe). Leadership endeavors simply to treat staff at all levels with sincere respect and appreciation. Supporting the morale of direct care staff results in such things as a parent going out to her car and finding that a staff went out before her and cleaned off the snow. This parent shared *"this gesture made me certain my child was in a good place."*

> *"The in-home work we have done with the team . . . included the clinician, family partner and different staff. We were afraid that our son would never be able to come home and if he did, I would feel unsafe. Although things were not magically better overnight, the transformation has been significant. My son is home with us and integrated into our family and community again. We have support 24/7 and can call for assistance at any time. They speak with him or me on the phone and we can work through things together. Then we are able to process the event in family therapy. This approach has helped our family make significant gains. We are so thankful for the dedication of everyone to help make our family whole again."*
>
> (Family member served by Cutchins)

Conclusion

Whether your program is planning, as part of Family First, to begin your focus on successfully engaging families; has recently begun your journey; or has already established solid family-driven care practices, the strategies highlighted throughout this chapter are intended to support you and your team to further improve successful family engagement strategies and broaden the array of family-driven care practices used in your program.

Contact Information

Damar Services (IN)/www.damar.org
Jim L. Dalton, President and CEO/jimd@damar.org
Denise Lyons, Parent Partner/dlyons260@gmail.com
Angel Knapp, Senior Director of Youth and Family Engagement/angelkr@damar.org
Pressley Ridge (PA)/www.pressleyridge.org
Patti McCloud, Family Support Coordinator/Pmccloud@pressleyridge.org
Alex Cameron, Senior Director of Clinical Services/acameron@pressleyridge.org
Stanford Youth Solutions (CA)/www.youthsolutions.org
Ebony Chambers, Director of Family and Youth Partnership/echambers@youthsolutions.org
Laura D. Heintz, Chief Executive Officer/lheintz@youthsolutions.org
The Children's Village (NY)/www.childrensvillage.org
Warren Kent, Vice President; Mona Swanson, Former Chief Program Officer/Retired; Takisha Wright, Parent Advocate; Jessica Grimm, Executive Director/Brave Hearts
All contact info through: JKohomban@childrensvillage.org
Three Rivers Program (MA)/https://cutchins.org/programs/three-rivers/
Amy Breton, Family Support Coordinator/abreton@cutchins.org
Rob Terreden, Program Director/rterreden@cutchins.org
Upbring Krause Children's Center (TX)/www.upbring.org
Jason Drake, Regional Executive Director/jason.drake@upbring.org
Amanda Martin, Associate Executive Director/amanda.martin@upbring.org
Warwick House (PA)/www.warwickfamilyservices.com
Jeffrey M. Friedman, Clinical Director/jfriedman@warwickfamilyservices.com

---

Resources

Documents to Support Engaging Families:

The National Building Bridges Initiative (BBI) website, www.buildingbridges4youth.org, includes many resources for engaging families; some are available in Spanish.

- Supporting Fathers: www.youtube.com/watch?v=UfV4Ykntipw
- Supporting Grandparents: www.youtube.com/watch?v=dIvs5COV9z0

Examples of Clinical Practice Models for Engaging Families:

- Multisystemic Therapy: www.mstservices.com/
- Functional Family Therapy: www.fftllc.com/

Family Engagement and Partnership **27**

- Motivational Interviewing—Network of Trainers: https://motiva tionalinterviewing.org/
- Structural Family Therapy: https://familybasedtraining.com/treatment-philosophy/ and www.minuchincenter.org/structural_family_therapy

National Family Organizations/National Organizations Promoting Family Support:

- Family Run Executive Director Leadership Association (FREDLA) www.fredla.org
- List of Family Run Organizations www.fredla.org/wp-content/ uploads/2019/02/FRO-List-At-a-glance-2_2019.pdf
- National Federation of Families for Children's Mental Health (NFFCMH) www.ffcmh.org
- Mental Health America—www.mentalhealthamerica.net/about-us
- National Alliance on Mental Illness (NAMI)—www.nami.org/ About-NAMI
- National Family Support Network—www.nationalfamilysupport network.org/

Documents to Support Use of Family Peer Partners:

- **Building Bridges Initiative:** Examples of family peer job descriptions/job postings: www.buildingbridges4youth.org/sites/default/ files/Job%20Descriptions.pdf
- **FREDLA** has several documents on their website (www.fredla.org)
- **Best Personnel Practices in Parent Support Provider Programs:** https://docs.wixstatic.com/ugd/49bf42_9982b967a517484dbfe71 5c8b44f4ce2.pdf
- **Parent Partner Program Manual Sample Policies and Procedures:** https://library.childwelfare.gov/cwig/ws/library/docs/gate way/Blob/107662.pdf?w=+NATIVE%28%27recno%3D107662% 27%29&upp=0&rpp=10&r=1&m=1

Note

1. For the purposes of this chapter, a child's parent/family may include biological, adoptive, step-parent, extended (siblings, grandparents, and relatives), fictive kin, tribal, or a permanent foster family or legal guardian who will serve as the permanent lifelong family for the child.

References

Acri, M., Gopalan, G., Chacko, A., & McKay, M. (2017). Engaging families into treatment for child behavior disorders: A synthesis of the literature. In J. Lochman &

W. Mathys (Eds.), *The Wiley handbook of disruptive and impulse-control disorders.* New York, NY: Wiley.

Alexander, J. F., Pugh, C., Parsons, B, F., & Sexton, T. (2000). Functional family therapy (Book Three: Vol. II). In D. S. Elliott (Series Ed.), *Blueprints for violence prevention: Institute of behavioral science.* Boulder, CO: Regents of the University of Colorado.

Blau, G. M., Caldwell, B., & Lieberman, R. E. (Eds.). (2014). *Residential interventions for children, adolescents, and families: A best practice guide.* New York, NY: Routledge.

Building Bridges Initiative. (2007, March). *Innovative practices for transformation.* Unpublished Internal Workgroup Document Summarizing Webinar Comments Offered by Mark Courtney.

Building Bridges Initiative. (2012). *Engage us: A guide written by families for residential providers.* Retrieved from http://www.buildingbridges4youth.org/sites/default/files/BBI%20-%20Engage%20Us%20-%20Family%20Engagement%20Guide.pdf

Building Bridges Initiative. (2017). *Implementing effective short-term residential interventions: A building bridges initiative guide.* Retrieved from www.buildingbridges4youth.org/sites/default/files/BBI%20Short%20Term%20Residential%20Intervention%20Guide.pdf

Center for Healthcare Strategies. (2013). *Family and youth peer support literature review.* Trenton, NJ: Center for Healthcare Strategies.

Cunningham, P. B., & Henggeler, S. W. (1999). Engaging multiproblem families in treatment: Lessons learned throughout the development of multisystemic therapy. *Family Process, 38*(3), 265–286.

Dalton, J. (2011, August). *Modernizing residential treatment: Indiana & Damar services* [PowerPoint slides]. Presentation presented at the New Hampshire's Transition to Permanency for Youth Project Kick-Off Event, Concord, NH.

Dalton, J. (2014). Creating organizational culture change. In G. M. Blau, B. Caldwell, & R. E. Lieberman (Eds.), *Residential interventions for children, adolescents, and families: A best practice guide* (pp. 182–194). New York, NY: Routledge.

Diamond, G. S., Diamond, G. M., & Levy, S. A. (2014). *Attachment-based family therapy for depressed adolescents.* Washington, DC: American Psychological Association.

Functional Family Therapy, LLC. (n.d.). *Functional family therapy clinical model.* Retrieved from www.fftllc.com/about-fft-training/clinical-model.html

Gockel, A., Russell, M., & Harris, B. (2008). Recreating family: Parents identify worker-client relationships as paramount in family preservation programs. *Child Welfare, 87*(6), 91–113.

Goldenberg, H., & Goldenberg, I. (2007). *Family therapy, an overview* (6th ed.). Belmont, CA: Thompson Books/Cole. ISBN-13: 978-0495097594

Gopalan, G., Goldstein, L., Klingenstein, K., Sicher, C., Blake, C., & McKay, M. M. (2010). Engaging families into child mental health treatment: Updates and special considerations. *Journal of the Canadian Academy of Child and Adolescent Psychiatry, 19,* 182–196.

Hansen, B. G. (1995). *General systems theory beginning with wholes.* Downsview, Ontario: Routledge Taylor & Francis. ISBN 1-56032-346-9

Holstead, J., Dalton, J., Horn., A., & Lamond, D. (2010). Modernizing residential treatment outcomes. *The Damar Pilot: Child Welfare, 89*(2), 115–129.

Hust, J. (2010). *Hathaway-Sycamores residential transformation: A parent's perspective—changing the metaphor of help* [PowerPoint slides]. Presentation presented at the Massachusetts Interagency Residential Provider Forum, Marlborough, MA.

Hust, J. (2019). *Foundational elements for engaging families when their child is receiving a residential intervention.* Unpublished workgroup document, Building Bridges Initiative.

Kohomban, J. (2011, May). *The children's village: Keeping children safe and families together* [PowerPoint slides]. Presentation presented at the Massachusetts 11th Annual Provider Forum on Restraint & Seclusion Prevention, Shrewsbury, MA.

Koren, P. E., Paulson, R. I., Yatchmonoff, D., Gordon, L., & DeChillo, N. (1997). Service coordination in children's mental health: An empirical study from the caregiver's perspective. *Journal of Emotional & Behavioral Disorders, 5*, 162–173.

Landsman, M. J., Boel-Studt, S., & Malone, K. (2014). Results from a family finding experiment. *Children and Youth Services Review, 36*, 62–69.

Landsman, M. J., Groza, V., Tyler, M., & Malone, K. (2001). Outcomes of family-centered residential treatment. *Child Welfare, 80*, 351–379.

Leichtman, M., Leichtman, M. L., Cornsweet, B. C., & Neese, D. T. (2001). Effectiveness of intensive short-term residential treatment with severely disturbed adolescents. *American Journal of Orthopsychiatry, 71*(2), 228–235.

Liddle, H. A. (2013). Multidimensional family therapy for adolescent substance abuse: A developmental approach. In P. Miller (Ed.), *Interventions for addiction: Comprehensive addictive behaviors and disorders* (Vol. 3). San Diego, CA: Academic Press.

Lyons, J. S., McCulloch, J. R., & Hamilton, J. (2006). Monitoring and managing outcomes in residential treatment: Practice-based evidence in search of evidence-based practice. *Journal of the American Academy of Child and Adolescent Psychiatry, 45*(2), 247–251.

Martone, W. (2010, October). *Hathaway-sycamores child and family services* [PowerPoint slides]. Presentation presented at the Massachusetts Interagency Residential Provider Forum, Marlborough, MA.

McKay, M. M., & Bannon, W. M. J. (2004). Engaging families in child mental health services. *Child and Adolescent Psychiatric Clinics of North America, 13*(4), 905–921. [PubMed] [Google Scholar].

Miller, R., & Rollnick, S. (2002). *Motivational interviewing: Preparing people for change* (2nd ed.). New York, NY: Guilford Press.

Minuchin, S. (1974). *Families & family therapy.* Cambridge, MA: Harvard University Press.

Minuchin, S., & Fishman, H. C. (1981). *Family therapy techniques.* Cambridge, MA: Harvard University Press.

Multisystemic Therapy Systems. (2019). *Multisystemic therapy® (MST®) research at a glance short version: Published MST outcome, implementation and benchmarking studies.* Retrieved from https://cdn2.hubspot.net/hubfs/295885/MST%20Re design/Marketing%20Collateral/Marketing%20Kit%20Collateral%20Digital%20 Files/Case%20Study%20and%20Reports/2019%20R@@G%20Short%20Version %208pg.pdf

National Child Traumatic Stress Network. (2019). *FCT: Family centered treatment [PDF]*. Retrieved from www.nctsn.org/interventions/family-centered-therapy

National Federation of Families for Children's Mental Health. (2016). *Definition of family driven practice*. Retrieved from https://docs.wixstatic.com/ugd/eeeef8_88b 094b359a74a018affa486bc55043d.pdf

Ontario Centre of Excellence for Child and Youth Mental Health. (2016). *Evidence insight: Best practices in engaging families in child and youth mental health*. Retrieved from www.excellenceforchildandyouth.ca/file/9169/download?token=D1vYdkSP

Osher, T. W., Osher, D., & Blau, G. (2008). Families matter. In T. Gullotta & G. Blau (Eds.), *Family influences on childhood behavior and development evidence-based prevention and treatment approaches* (pp. 39–61). New York, NY: Routledge.

Saxe, G. N., Ellis, B. H., Fogler, J., & Navalta, C. P. (2012). Innovations in practice: Preliminary evidence for effective family engagement in treatment for child traumatic stress—trauma systems therapy approach to preventing dropout. *Child and Adolescent Mental Health, 17*, 58–61.

Sexton, T. L., Rios, G. O., Johnson, K. A., & Plante, B. R. (2014). Moving toward family-driven care in residential. In G. M. Blau, B. Caldwell, & R. E. Lieberman (Eds.), *Residential interventions for children, adolescents, and families: A best practice guide* (pp. 182–194). New York, NY: Routledge.

Shklarski, L., Madera, V. P., Bennett, K., & Marcial, K. (2017). Family finding project: Results from a one-year program evaluation. *Child Welfare, 94*(6), 67–87.

Spencer, S., Blau, G., & Mallery, C. (2010). Family-driven care in America: More than a good idea. *Journal of Canadian Academy of Child and Adolescent Psychiatry, 19*(3), 176–181.

Stanford Youth Solutions Quality Improvement and Research. (2018). *Annual operating plan: Process metrics-outcomes, activities and measurements FY17–18 internal report*. Sacramento, CA: Vroon.

Tambuyzer, E., & Van Audenhove, C. (2013). Service user and family carer involvement in mental health care: Divergent views. *Community Mental Health Journal, 49*, 675–685.

Thompson, S. J., Bender, K., Lantry, J., & Flynn, P. (2007). Treatment engagement: Building therapeutic alliance in family-based treatment. *Contemporary Family Therapy, 29*, 39–55.

Walters, U. M., & Petr, C. G. (2008). Family-centered residential treatment: Knowledge, research, and values converge. *Residential Treatment for Children and Youth, 25*(1), 1–16.

3

YOUTH ENGAGEMENT AND EMPOWERMENT STRATEGIES

Jammie Gardner, Lacy Kendrick Burk,
and Raquel Montes

Youth-guided care has been a pillar of transformational practice in residential interventions over the past decade, propelled in large measure by the Building Bridges Initiative (BBI). "Becoming a Youth Guided Residential Program," a chapter in *Residential Interventions for Children, Adolescents and Families: A Best Practice Guide*, introduced beginning steps to understand what it means to be "youth-guided," provided resources to assist organizations, identified clinical practices that support youth-guided peer support, and offered ideas for implementation (Lulow, Harrington, Alexander, & Kendrick Burk, 2014). This chapter takes a more in-depth look at these concepts and strategies, focuses on a diverse set of ways to develop a peer workforce and engage youth, and introduces the concept of "youth-driven" as an evolutionary next step from youth-guided.

Why Youth Engagement?

When working with children and adolescents (hereafter referred to as "youth"), it is all about engagement; among youth and their family, youth and their community, staff and family, staff and youth, program and youth, and youth with peers. With effective engagement and support, a young person is more likely to develop and grow, and a residential intervention will likely have positive outcomes. (Lulow et al., 2014)

The United Nations Convention on the Rights of the Child stipulates that the active participation of youth in their lives and society is a fundamental human right and one that every child should have. Article 12 of the Convention states, "when adults are making decisions that affect children, children have the right to say what they think should happen and have their opinions taken into account" (Committee on the Rights of the Child, 1992). This applies to all children, regardless of race, nationality, culture, country, class, gender, language, sexuality, family, or health status, and the statement absolutely extends to youth receiving residential interventions.

As an initial step, it is essential to understand what "youth engagement" means, as its prevalence in youth-serving systems and across the youth development field continues to expand. "Youth engagement" refers to the connection a young person feels toward a particular person, activity, or place. Although the term has more recently become a buzzword of sorts, engagement in this context has been a focus of youth development, public policy, and social change movements for at least the last 40 years (Pittman, 2017).

A study by Strangler and Shirk (2004) defined youth engagement as involving youth in their own future planning. This definition means that young people should be involved in all aspects of their treatment planning and that adults should support the development and utilization of their voice for advocacy. This sentiment is best summarized by youth who said, "Nothing about us without us" (Oliveras, Cluver, Bernays, & Armstrong, 2018). It is a process that offers meaningful participation for youth—that is, participation with passion—and opportunities for youth to take responsibility and leadership while working in partnership with caring adults who value, respect, and share power with them (Ontario Trillium Foundation, 2007).

It is common to think of youth engagement as something providers do to increase youth agreement with treatment plans or when seeking a young person's ideas for an event, but it is much more than that. Quality youth engagement functions to ensure that youth and adults are working together in ways that are mutually beneficial and ideally in equal partnership (ACT for Youth, 2019). Involving youth voice at every level, from treatment to the hiring of young adults with lived experience and other staff, not only facilitates deeper engagement but will improve both residential interventions and the system of care overall.

Of multiple models for facilitating youth engagement, Positive Youth Development (PYD) offers an excellent comprehensive framework for outlining the supports all young people need to be successful in life. Zarret and Lerner (2008), developmental scientists, have suggested that positive youth development encompasses psychological, behavioral, and social characteristics that reflect what they call the "Five C's": Competence, Confidence, Connection, Character, and Caring/Compassion.

Youth peer support is also a foundational approach to increasing youth engagement in services. This chapter emphasizes the importance of youth peer support specialists in helping with youth engagement and empowerment and their critical role in youth-guided/driven care. While the engagement strategies highlighted can be implemented by the traditional professional staff of a residential intervention, programs that incorporate youth peer support to engage their participants demonstrate a level of cultural responsiveness that leads to faster buy-in, better overall satisfaction with services, and greater commitment to recovery. Peer support providers counteract the impact of trauma by helping youth see coping strategies instead of "symptoms" and create safe spaces to consider new ways of coping (SAMHSA, 2017). In fact, SAMHSA has identified peer support as one of the ten fundamental components of recovery (SAMHSA, 2014).

Casa Pacifica Center for Children and Families provides an array of services for youth and families throughout the California's central coast. In 2010, its CEO introduced new objectives for the agency-improving service quality and respect for youth and families, reducing restrictive interventions, and training and empowering staff as the main priorities. This "top to bottom" approach was instrumental in shifting the culture to listening, engaging, and empowering youth and families. Casa Pacifica began implementing youth-guided practices after familiarizing itself with the Building Bridges Initiative. Peer and family advocates were hired and joined the leadership team of Directors.

Engaging the Lived Experience Workforce

A Youth Peer Support Specialist (YPSS) is a young adult worker who utilizes lived experience to engage youth in services. Lived experience describes any participation in human-serving systems including receiving services as a child, youth, or young adult, as well as any experience currently or formerly living with a mental health or substance abuse diagnosis (Kendrick Burk et al., 2013). Lived experience can also include other adverse life experiences such as (but not limited to) discrimination, oppression, poverty, trauma, and addiction. The term "lived expertise" is used to describe the application of lived experience as a professional skill set (Kendrick Burk & Sikes, 2018). Lived expertise is what makes these positions unique and so valuable for engaging youth. Through shared experience, respect, and empowerment, YPSSs connect with youth on a deeper and often more personal level. YPSSs foster hope and recovery by supporting youth through their challenges and sharing their own experiences when appropriate.

Residential interventions have options when it comes to employing YPSSs. Many communities have peer support available by contracting through entities separate from the residential program; other organizations have elected to employ their own peer support workforce. Research shows that peer support is effective for supporting recovery and behavioral health conditions (Davidson et al., 1999). Benefits include: Increased self-esteem and confidence, increased sense of control and ability to make personal changes, higher empowerment scores, increased sense that treatment is responsive and inclusive of needs, increased sense of hope and inspiration, increased empathy and acceptance, increased engagement in self-care and wellness, increased social support and social functioning, decreased psychotic symptoms, reduced hospital admission rates and longer community tenure, and decreased substance use and depression.

The most common mistakes agencies make when employing youth peers are not understanding the role and scope of the position and not providing adequate support. Agencies have a responsibility to educate their team about the position and how the job functions, utilize the role for collaboration between system partners, and create a plan to sustain the role and support their employees' ongoing success. Clarity and open communication can drastically increase support and reduce tension and conflict that can arise from role confusion and generational miscommunication among employees. Issue and strategies specific to hiring Youth Peer Support Specialists are addressed in this section.

Organizational Readiness and Culture Shift for YPSSs

Before hiring YPSSs, the program must be ready, as these positions require a shift in the agency's culture if they are to be successful; YPSS's needs are different than staff in traditional positions. The first step toward initiating a cultural shift of this magnitude is to broaden the agency's understanding of youth culture and commit to learning how to best support peers in the workplace. Utilizing a transformative learning theory approach helps put the focus in the organization on mindset change, rather than limiting it to behaviors, skills, or actions. "If we think differently, we do differently, including the way we think about ourselves and do for ourselves" (Kendrick Burk, 2019). A useful resource is the "Pillars of Peer Support," a set of 25 principles that guides the peer support specialist workforce. Developed through a consensus process, the pillars represent guidelines that will help guide success. The Pillars include: Clear job descriptions and related competencies, a robust recovery and peer delivered services training program, availability of employment related certification, ongoing continuing education, professional advancement opportunities, networking, peer workforce development, peer Code of Ethics/Code of Conduct, culturally diverse peer workforce, and competency based peer supervision, among others (Carter Center, 2009).

Understanding the Peer Role in the Services
Array for Residential Interventions

The primary duties of a YPSS include listening and supporting youth through their challenges, advocating, resource referral, building natural supports, setting goals, and strategically sharing their lived experience. These roles are intended to help bridge gaps between youth and the systems that aim to serve them. The position complements but does not duplicate other roles. Above all, YPSSs maintain authentic support relationships built on trust, so critical because, when youth have access to trusting support relationships, they are more willing to engage in other formal supports when referred.

Transition Support for YPSS

"Change happens. And it happens to everyone. . . . Transition, on the other hand, is the process that happens inside your head, heart, and gut as you adjust and become familiar with change."

—(Ecke et al., n.d.)

As we consider the pool of applicants for our young adult lived experience workforce, we must consider the context required for effectively utilizing lived expertise. Not only are potential YPSSs developmentally young adults new to the workforce; with the added overlay of lived experience, they have multiple training and development needs. YPSSs are uniquely qualified to provide peer support services *because* they have experienced involvement in a system or are currently living with a diagnosable mental health condition. Many of the applicants could have even been youth in the program who have potentially served in advocacy roles and still likely are learning how to best manage their own mental health conditions as they transition to adulthood. They have specific training needs including general peer support practices, trauma stewardship, and leadership development, and they require unique generational considerations for Millennials and Generation Z as well as retention and burnout prevention practices.

Transition support is necessary to help YPSSs gain understanding of professional roles in general and in the context of the larger clinical team, boundaries, and how to use their experience in direct services. YPSSs bring life experience as a skill set and are still navigating their own transition to adulthood, including normal developmental processes such as meeting basic food, shelter, and transportation needs; identity development; managing existing mental health systems; and recovery from effects of adverse childhood experiences and/or complex trauma. At the same time, YPSSs are expected to check that at the door once they are hired and show up as professionals with established skill sets and understanding of professional etiquette norms, when often the peer support role may be the first professional job these young adults have had. Therefore, it is important to meet the YPSS workforce where they are, offer reasonable accommodations, take a coaching and professional development approach to supervision and support if we are to help them be successful, and in turn expand our capacity to reach the families and youth we serve (Delman & Klodnick, 2017). (Figure 3.1 shows

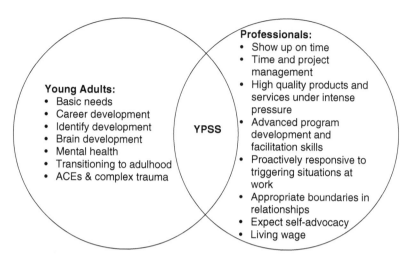

Figure 3.1 Transition from Young Adult to Young Professional (Kendrick Burk, 2019)

the transition from young adult to young professional and the overlap that YPSSs experience.)

As the young adults become grounded in the YPSS role and comfortable with their talents and interests, they may then transition further, assuming more of an advocacy role and using their voice to motivate change in systems as well as individuals. Some may decide to continue a career in systems advocacy and services, while others may leave advocacy and integrate into non-human service settings, i.e., medical field, teaching, mechanical jobs, etc. Unique skill sets and resources are required at each stage of this transition. The guide *Youth Advocates to Advocates for Youth* provides an overview of this transition with resources appropriate for each stage (Kendrick Burk et al., 2013).

Hiring and Managing the YPSS Workforce

There are five phases when hiring a YPSS: Application, interviewing, preparation, supervision, and ongoing professional development.

> ***Recruitment***: Agencies should consider collaborating with youth being served in developing their applications and job descriptions. Begin by informing the youth about the intention to recruit a YPSS. They may decide to share opinions and concerns that may not have otherwise been considered. Try hosting a youth focus group to identify the essential qualities and skills of a YPSS. Remember, a YPSS will not have the "traditional" work experience or history. Consider allowing atypical application questions that allow young adults to showcase transferable skill

sets, such as technical and leadership competencies, accomplishments, or community involvement. Invite youth to participate as part of the group responsible for developing the peer support job description and application. Before posting the job announcement and application, be sure to have youth take a final look and provide feedback.

Interviewing: When interviewing, it's important to remember that skills and experiences may be quite different compared to traditional job searches. At a minimum, a prospective peer support specialist should have lived experience and be able to model recovery. Try conducting a youth focus group to identify what interview questions to include and involve a few of the youth to participate as interviewers; this will promote positive development for the youth and facilitate authentic youth engagement at all organizational levels. Be sure to debrief with the youth at the end of each interview to gather feedback on the candidates. For the candidates, consider providing them with the interview questions ahead of time to ensure adequate preparation. Once the interviews are complete, give the candidates who were not offered the position positive and constructive feedback.

Preparation: Once the YPSS is hired, they must go through training and, if available in the state or community, certification training. Seek professional peer delivered services training from local, statewide, or even national entities. It's important to remember that this job is brand new for the youth so their needs may look different than someone with years of experience. This may be the peer specialists' first "professional" job, so they will likely require support, along with guidance for their professional development. Be prepared to support the YPSS as they develop professional etiquette and other critical interpersonal skills.

Supervision: Supervision should be provided by a peer delivered services professional. This may involve a clearly defined collaboration between an agency supervisor and a local peer delivered services organization or even telephonic support. Program supervisors must understand and see value in the YPSS role and also have a voice and perspective that is valued within the organization. It is important to understand at the onset that YPSSs may require more frequent support, both personally and professionally. To do this, supervisors should maintain an open-door policy and use a coaching approach in their supervision. One-on-one supervision should occur at least weekly and can slowly taper down to biweekly once the YPSSs have acclimated to their positions and begin to show an increase in their technical competencies.

Ongoing Professional Development: For many young adults, this workforce is unlike anything they've ever experienced. Often this is their first step down a career path rather than a traditional young adult job, like fast food or retail. Additionally, it bears the risk of triggering memories of their own lived experience and creating confusion, burnout, and low overall well-being. Other challenges include lack of support in the workplace, cultural misalignment in organizations, limited professional development opportunities, and not receiving a livable wage (Kendrick Burk & Sikes, 2018). As a result, YPSS can experience high turnover and retention challenges. This increases the critical importance of ongoing professional development.

Often YPSS need additional support, including coaching, to ensure transfer of knowledge from training and implementation of learned skills. YPSSs also require ongoing, dedicated, confidential support beyond technical competencies. Isolation can be a primary cause of turnover. Networking and opportunities to connect with other YPSSs are vital to young professionals feeling connected and empowered through shared inspiration. YPSSs should be supported to attend conferences and other professional development events where other young professionals with lived experience are present. YPSSs should also have a professional development budget to continue growth in skills and competencies as a professional, particularly in the Millennial generation, as lack of development opportunities are cited as the number one reason for Millennial turnover across industries (Chopra, 2018; Fry, 2018, April 11). Don't fire young professionals for the same reasons you hired them; provide adequate opportunities and support to build an effective workforce.

Challenges and Approaches for Positive YPSS Workforce Development

In a national survey, young adults and their supervisors identified key challenge areas that need to be addressed to ensure success for young professionals (Kendrick Burk & Sikes, 2018). The challenge areas included: Isolation, boundaries, productivity and time management, burnout prevention and self-care, professional etiquette, conflict management, strategic sharing and public speaking skills, networking, facilitation skills, program development skills, and leadership skills. The study also identified organizational phenomena compounding the challenges: High turnover rates, limited professional development support for YPSSs, role confusion among peer and non-peer staff, limited reasonable accommodations, and cultural misalignment of young professionals and the organizations by which they are employed.

Fortunately, there are many approaches that organizations can take to mitigate the aforementioned challenges. Training and retreat experiences can build skills capacity and equip young professionals to address challenges

Youth Engagement and Empowerment Strategies **39**

in complex youth-serving positions, reduce isolation, improve well-being, help make meaning of experiences, and "develop autonomous thinking" (Mezirow, 2003, p. 5). Coaching can ensure application of skills learned in training, promote YPSS retention through wellness support and burnout prevention, and provide a safe space outside of the organization for reflection, visioning, goal setting, empowerment, and conflict resolution (Coates, 2013). Connection to peers through shared experiential learning can help to find solutions to common problems YPSSs face and reduce isolation (Rossiter & Socho, 2018). Leadership development for young professionals AND organizational colleagues can increase leadership competencies in working with others, i.e., conflict management, confronting direct reports, managing and measuring work, composure, listening (Coates, 2013).

Attention to key resilience factors facilitates training and coaching: 1) Youth resilience, building on strengths; 2) social connections that promote trust and belonging; 3) knowledge of adolescent development and best practices; 4) concrete support and self-advocacy in time of need; and 5) cognitive and social emotional competence, including executive functioning, future orientation, persistence, etc. (Browne, Notkin, Schneider-Munoz, & Zimmerman, 2015, pp. 34–35).

A useful guide for professional development of Youth Peer Support Staff is the Young Adult Peer Mentor Practice Profile. It frames YPSS work as "peer mentoring" and identifies six core elements: 1) Practicing Cultural Responsiveness; 2) Building Relationships and Collaboration; 3) Supporting Young Adult Vision and Goals; 4) Role Modeling; 5) Promoting Self-Care; and 6) Demonstrating Safe, Professional, and Ethical Behavior. For each there are specific practices categorized as "Ideal," "Developmental," and "Insufficient." For example, for Addressing Cultural Misunderstandings:

IDEAL: Invites and supports youth to address cultural misunderstandings with providers.

DEVELOPMENTAL: Struggles to know when or how to address cultural misunderstandings.

INSUFFICIENT: Avoids discussion of cultural misunderstandings. * Takes sides behind the scenes in addressing misunderstandings. (The Young Adult Peer Mentor Practice Profile Workgroup, 2017)

At Casa Pacifica, hiring peer support (peer advocates) was one way of establishing youth-guided practices and advancing the agency's commitment to youth-guided and family-driven care. All new staff were trained on youth-guided and family-driven practices in order to sustain this culture.

Throughout the years it collaborated closely and receptively with youth to come up with the detailed roles peer advocates play in their lives. After they learned more about the advocacy needs of youth, they developed a peer advocate manual. The manual went over training, role descriptions, and procedures uniquely developed for this role. Supervision and maintenance of the peer advocate role was a crucial element in ensuring its success. Leadership collaborated and informed staff about this role and the importance of youth-guided practices repeatedly to improve the acceptance of it agency-wide. Peer advocates focused on various tasks such as: Relationships, skill building with youth, county and state advocacy, TAY support, and various trainings on hot topics (CSEC, AB 12, etc.).

In the last 12 years, Casa Pacifica has hired over ten advocates. Each advocate has been critical in strengthening youth-guided practices, brought an expertise of their own on how to make positive changes, and positively impacted the staff perceptions of young people. This has become evident across the board, from recipients of a service to individuals with enough insight and knowledge to help direct their own treatment and lives. The peer role has changed and improved the work. Specifically, there has been reduction of coercion and restraints, increased involvement with family members, more time at home, and the development of new lines of service for transition aged youth.

Youth Engagement Strategies

Youth engagement begins at the time of referral and continues throughout the residential intervention including post-discharge. There are many specific strategies that can be implemented by Youth Peer Support Specialists, family members, and staff to promote engagement, organized in the following sections as per the phases of the intervention identified on the BBI Self-Assessment Tool: Entry, during, and post-residential intervention.

Entry/Initial Engagement

For residential interventions, the entry phase is key to initiating sustainable engagement and ensuring buy-in from youth and their families. Many families and youth may be entering residential interventions in a state of trauma, grief, and exhaustion, so being present, attentive, attuned, and responsive (Perry, 2019) is important to help them manage the transitions they are going through. Ideally a youth peer currently in the program or Youth Peer Support Specialist (YPSS) is able to demonstrate a level of connection and responsiveness that leads to faster buy-in, deeper engagement, and support.

It is strongly recommended that all residential programs hire YPSSs. Until programs develop the foundation to hire youth peers as staff it is also appropriate to contract this work through a community peer organization if they have youth who can comfortably assume leadership roles and support the process. This can occur through a "buddy" or "ambassador" type of system, introducing the young person to other peers, the environment, and the program routines. This has a positive impact at entry for both parties, helping the new person experience support while building the skills related to positive youth development (confidence, compassion, connection, character, and caring) for the "buddy" or "ambassador".

> Casa Pacifica involved peers and peer advocates in the intake process, having them facilitate tours, welcoming new residents, and prepare them for meetings. This set the tone of shared partnership in decision making. This was one of the easiest changes the organization made and one that yielded immediate results; youth reported feeling safe when their peers positively endorsed the living environment, making the transition less scary.

While the implementation of such strategies may result in an intake process that looks very different from how many programs currently function, this is not to minimize the role of the rest of the staff. Ideally, the entry phase of a youth-guided program also involves a meeting between the youth and family and a staff member. This initial meeting serves as an opportunity for the staff to start building a support relationship focused on mutual understanding and trust. During intake, the youth and staff can also engage in youth-focused activities, take a tour, and discuss the youth's goals, dreams, and hopes for their life and their strengths, fears, and concerns about their current transition to the residential intervention. Well-trained staff engage quickly, ease fears and anxieties, foster hope, and discover what youth and families want from their time in the program.

Like youth, family members also find that talking to their peers results in a reduction in stress and trauma symptoms (Donnelly, Baker, & Gargan, n.d.). See Chapter 2 for information about how Family Support Partners support family members receiving residential interventions. In tandem, youth and family peer roles can support residential staff in achieving successful family and youth engagement.

The "During" Phase

The staff, ideally including a YPSS, works with the youth and family to create a plan of care that reflects their goals, hopes, and dreams. Their goals should

42 Jammie Gardner et al.

not be limited to the youth's time receiving in-program residential supports and services; rather goals should encompass all of the young person's life domains, including a focus on the time spent with family at home and in the community during the residential intervention and during transition back into the community. It is critical that youth are supported to express their voice and needs and to participate meaningfully in developing their plan. After all, it is THEIR plan. To be successful the team must focus on youth and family strengths and identify opportunities for skill development that connect to the stated goals. They must also approach each youth and family individually, commit to solving problems collaboratively, and work to find consensus with all involved adults. This approach provides youth with opportunities to actively address challenges and find solutions, and fosters the development of social-emotional skills rather than relying solely on program rules.

An even more powerful strategy to support and engage each youth's voice is to empower him/her/them to lead the team meeting. This involves help in identifying their goals in advance and skills training in conducting a meeting.

> At Casa Pacifica, much of the skill building work was focused on using voice and choice at meetings by leading and/or co-leading their team decision meetings. Treatment plans were based on the youth's own goals and youth were provided with opportunities to be involved in everyday decision-making about their care.

Throughout the "during" phase of the residential intervention, several strategies can help develop the "5 C's" that promote positive youth development and youth engagement (Family and Youth Services Bureau, 2012).

Competence: Offering many opportunities for youth to make decisions supports building competence. Examples include: Providing alarm clocks for youth to get themselves up in the morning; allowing them to make decisions about what time to go to sleep and awaken, thus helping them to learn to plan ahead to get the right amount of sleep and have enough time to be ready for school in the morning; supporting youth in choosing what activities of daily living to participate in and when (i.e., they choose whether to shower in the morning or evening, whether to shower every day, how often to wash their hair); giving choices about their responses to programming ("Do you need a little more time to finish up or do you think you will be ready at 3pm?"); asking them to decide what community or school groups they want to join; and encouraging them to talk about pros and cons before making decisions.

Confidence: Finding opportunities to support self-efficacy builds confidence. For example: Ask the youth to create a list of things they do well; ask them to teach a skill to another youth; train them to orient new youth to the program; engage them in helping create outreach materials; have the youth accompany staff to go meet a youth and family considering the program or before intake to put them at ease; notice and reinforce prosocial skills ("I appreciate how you asked everyone to clean up after dinner so respectfully. This way of communicating will make people want to listen to you").

Connection: Building connections supports broader engagement and fosters resilience (Masten, 2001). Allowing youth to engage in prosocial activities helps to build connections as a byproduct of their involvement. Think beyond the residential walls and into the community—can a youth who loves animals volunteer at a local animal shelter where they will create new natural supports and build their skills? Work to have every youth engaged in activities, groups, and clubs in the community that match their individual strengths and talents with pro-social peers. Can you provide opportunities where peers can help peers in groups or teaching small lessons? Ensure that youth spend time with their family members at home regularly and frequently, as well as with coaches/staff of home community activities they are/have been involved with and with their home community friends approved by the family if necessary, so they are continuing to build connections and new memories with the people who will be there beyond the residential intervention. Additionally, restricting home and family visits should never be used as a means of behavior modification, consequence, or punishment.

Character: Engage youth through character affirming and building strategies. For example: Assist young people in identifying their strengths and how they have utilized them in their life—then connect their strengths to program, home, and community opportunities. If they play the guitar would they be interested in co-teaching a group of youth at the local "Y" who would like to learn, or teaching or providing entertainment to youth in the program? Are they a good listener and support person? Provide them with opportunities to provide support for younger youth in the program. Have them participate in a mentoring program in their home community for younger youth. Are they a writer? Ask them how they might contribute their talent by leading the production of a book for other youth about the program or written materials for youth who are new. Provide multiple opportunities for leadership development in the program and in their home community. Provide roles for youth during group meetings (planner, supporter, note taker, clean up, resources manager); ask each youth to identify two solutions for every problem they bring to the table; train youth to co-facilitate meetings or activities; involve youth in hiring committees; provide avenues for self-discovery and awareness, such as journaling, art projects, slam poetry nights, or methods to learn about their culture; begin meetings with a ritual such as each youth sharing the following: "One way that I helped another person today was by . . ."

Caring/Compassion: Opportunities for caring and compassion toward oneself and others create relational connections that foster engagement. For example: Teach youth skills to care for themselves by setting boundaries and practicing self-care and self-advocacy; help youth learn how to resolve conflict with understanding and compassion; support youth in helping animals and/or people in the community through community service projects; role-play real scenarios that youth have faced at home, at school, and in the community and debrief the role-play; notice and reinforce when youth are treating their family members, siblings and community friends, and other youth in a kind/caring manner; build empathy by starting conversations in difficult situations with empathy (ex: "It seems like this situation is hard for you—can you help me know what is going on? Can I share what I'm thinking?"). Consider empathy workshops for youth.

> Casa Pacific shifted its priority to increase youth voice and choice to establish a positive peer culture. Many youth had not been feeling engaged or active in being part of their solution, leaving them feeling disempowered and isolated. Looking back, this new objective challenged the paradigm of youth coming in to participate in a service, shifting it instead to partnering with them to shape what the service entails. Viewing young people as partners promoted youth engagement. What was helpful was to provide youth with specific outlets to express their needs including changes in the agency's policies and procedures.

Youth Advisory Councils (YAC) provide a unique and powerful opportunity for engagement during the residential intervention that also prepares for ongoing community engagement post-discharge. Youth Advisory Councils value the youth voice and create ways for youth to become full participants in all of the decision-making processes within a program (Adolescent Health Initiative, 2013). In setting up YAC's it is critical to ensure that they are addressing issues important to the youth and that their advice is taken seriously. Connection of the YAC with leadership, up to and including the CEO and Board of Directors, empowers and engages the youth. Kairos, an agency in southern Oregon, established a chapter of Youth Move National for its agency wide YAC. Youth MOVE Kairos made recommendations for changes in policy and focus to the Executive Council and Board, spoke at the Oregon state capital every year for Children's Mental Health Awareness Day, and made presentations at local service clubs and agency functions, using video and Impact Theater, regarding the challenges faced by young people in the system. Upbring, in Texas, also recently developed a Youth MOVE chapter in their Krause residential program. Youth Development Institute (YDI) in Arizona credits its YAC as an important factor in its not having any restraints in its large organization for nearly 800 days (and counting at the time of the writing of this chapter). Members of its YAC are part of every hiring committee for new staff and must explicitly approve each staff to be hired.

Casa Pacifica's implementation of youth advisory councils was instrumental in helping develop a positive peer support culture. Youth advisory council members represented and advocated for the perspectives of youth in the program and brought suggestions to the leadership regarding areas in need of improvement, new initiatives, and ideas for change. Youth were presented with opportunities to highlight areas of concern in their living environment, program policies, and procedures. Initially peer advocates provided the agenda and were liaisons between youth and staff but as staff "proved themselves" through shared respect and power, youth began to seek support from them directly as needed. An example was when a young person requested a meeting with all directors to advocate for a change in their program procedures. Although youth were part of the same community, they hadn't been allowed to spend leisure time together in the evenings. This conflict created an opportunity for most youth to "break the rule" and created a very hostile environment. A council representative was successful in communicating the need. In his words, all youth were part of a community and the connections increased their motivation, networking post-residential, and hope. Youth were able to seek the changes they wanted, and the Directors heard them, implementing a program change to allow "social time" every evening. Once these changes occurred there was a decrease in elopements and restraints.

Post-Discharge/Full Community Engagement

The goals, hopes, and dreams of the youth and their family should always drive treatment and support goals, as well as transition planning. For example, programs in Massachusetts meet with families and youth prior to admission to start engagement earlier, ease angst, and formulate agreed upon treatments and post-discharge planning before youth walk in the door.

Planning that begins at admission engages the youth and family in creating hope and a vision for the future and generates ongoing invaluable supported opportunities to identify and practice the skills necessary to achieve their vision within the real life setting of their communities. It's particularly critical that youth maintain their relationships with family, friends, and supports throughout the intervention with ongoing time at home, with the family, and in the community (Hamilton, 2019). Relationships have a significant impact on "long-term outcomes, including social skills, emotion regulation, conscience development, trust in others, and general psychological well-being" (Li & Julian, 2012, pg. 158).

Youth will leave the residential intervention to go back and live in their community with friends and family—maintaining and strengthening these relationships while the youth has support is critical. In situations in which this appears to not be feasible, permanency-focused planning, described in Chapter 6, creates opportunities for the youth to build new permanent relationships in the community with relatives or individuals they regard as family. Person-centered planning templates can be used to support the journey from the pre-admission discharge vision to post-residential discharge strategies (NC Dept. of Health and Human Services, 2013).

Opportunities for youth to work toward community engagement in their home communities may be improved when they have had previous involvement in a Youth Advisory Council. Youth are able to use their leadership skills developed in the YAC on committees, councils, and workgroups in their home communities. These may be tied to local systems of care, mental health or foster care groups, state or local level advisories where young people are being asked their opinions on issues, service clubs, and other civic opportunities. Other options are in arenas that a youth is interested in; for example, for a youth who is passionate about animal welfare, getting them involved with a local rescue or issues around the protection of animal rights may be a great option. Youth interested in sports can be encouraged and supported to participate in local teams through schools, Boys and Girls Clubs, etc. Enrolling or maintaining the connection between the youth and a local mainstream school can create opportunities to join school clubs and activities.

All of these options can and ideally do begin at admission and occur throughout the residential intervention, providing ongoing connections for each youth to his/her home community and continuing post-discharge. Because real life experience helps build skills (Gaskill & Perry, 2017), it is vital that residential interventions look beyond traditional in-program treatment and provide community opportunities and connections for youth during and post the residential intervention. In particular, all youth, including youth in transition, need permanency and consistent and reliable links to providers and other caring adults so they can access help when they need it.

> Casa Pacifica established an Alumni Association which is a network of peers who have stayed connected with the agency over the last 20 years. This association gathers throughout the years and offers the agency input and guidance, which inspires youth and staff to keep pushing through adversity. Alumni support seems to provide a certain amount of credibility through shared lived experience, creating a foundation of trust which is critical to the collaborative work the program aims to achieve. Peers and peer advocates who have graduated from their programs help improve the young people's overall satisfaction with the service. Peer support requires a shift to embracing youth-driven and collaborative effort within departments to hold the value of youth representation and better outcomes.

The Role of Family in Youth-Guided/Driven Care

Engaging family members throughout every phase of residential interventions is crucial to help facilitate the youth's positive development at home and in the community. Establishing permanency, as addressed in Chapter 6, promotes sustained long-term positive outcomes. The residential intervention offers a prime opportunity to validate and educate families regarding the importance of youth voice and thereby improve outcomes for the youth and themselves as well. Understanding and implementing youth-guided care practices, including peer support, generates new opportunities to come alongside family members in their efforts to support their youth at home. Acknowledging a family member's fears for their child's future and/or concerns about past trauma will help them heal and become better prepared for the next part of their journey (Brach, 2015; Warren & Moses, n.d.).

As youth mature and become teenagers and the family shifts away from a primarily family-driven model to a model driven by youth and guided by the family, it is important to educate family members and others supporting the youth what this normative transition means. One family member explains:

> *"For a long time, I controlled every aspect of my child's care. One day I realized I was doing a disservice to my teen by not shifting from family-driven and youth-guided to youth-driven and family-guided. I knew then that I had a few years to support him as he learned to make decisions, lead his meetings, have a voice in his treatment and essentially grow into an adult. I took on the role of support to my youth as he learned how to manage his care while working toward his dreams and goals. I realized that despite my fears, I couldn't force my 14-year-old to take his meds, comply with treatment and in general do what I thought was best.*
>
> *This was a big shift for me as I had to release control and work through my fears while learning how to assist my son in gaining skills and moving*

toward his goals. Now he is a young adult, living on his own and working in a field that he finds joy in most days. I don't believe he would be doing as well if I hadn't shifted my thinking and focused on assisting him to learn, grow, celebrate his failures and ultimately find his strength, resiliency, and success. Once we shifted our perspective, we experienced less stress, fear, arguing and fighting; our family dynamics improved, as did sibling relationships. I wouldn't have done it any other way!"

(Anderson, 2019)

As shared earlier in this chapter, Family Support Partners are a valuable asset to help family members move from a place of fear and frustration to one of acceptance. Family Support Partners coordinate with YPSSs to ensure consistent language and understanding regarding the importance of youth-guided and driven supports. At Children's Village in New York, the Parent Leadership Council and Parent Advocates coordinate with an external Youth Peer Support organization, known as the Bravehearts (M.O.V.E New York Bravehearts), which provides pragmatic peer mentorship and youth advocacy.

Family members should have access to learning about Positive Youth Development (PYD) and Search Institute's 40 Developmental Assets, which can help provide a framework for the skills they are helping their child to build. When they understand these concepts their efforts to assist their children in developing skills, attaining assets, and achieving their goals improve tremendously. Once families make this transition, it becomes the youth's responsibility to take the steps necessary to achieve their goals. This supports youth-guided care at home as part of the overall residential intervention.

Some residential interventions include or are somehow linked with foster care. Although working toward permanency should be the most urgent focus for youth with no identified permanency resources, there is a need to assist foster parents and educate them when youth will be returning to them temporarily or permanently post-residential discharge. Foster parents face challenges that are unique to the child welfare system. Helping foster parents and, perhaps more importantly, the foster care system, understand and embrace youth-guided care can improve outcomes. Helping engage and empower youth as partners in foster home decision making can reduce the stresses faced by the young people and the foster family.

Youth Engagement: From Youth-Guided to Youth-Driven Care

Youth engagement, when applied to youth voice in systems and residential interventions, is a central component of youth-guided care. To become a youth-guided residential program necessitates a foundational understanding of several key concepts outlined herein and in the first volume in this book series (Blau, Caldwell, & Lieberman, 2014). These are encompassed in the definition of "youth-guided" by the Substance Abuse and Mental Health Services Administration (SAMHSA): "Youth are engaged as equal partners in creating systems change in policies and procedures at the individual, community, state and national levels" (SAMHSA, 2014, para. 5). While the term "youth-guided" is still very much used, recently "youth-driven" has begun to be used when referring to systems and programs for older youth (ages 14+), especially when those programs are committed to ensuring that youth are driving services and systems.

Deepening the Commitment

As has been noted throughout this chapter, advancing youth voice through meaningful participation requires youth engagement throughout the residential intervention and input at multiple levels to support their development and their integrated involvement in the agency's programs and structures (Lulow et al., 2014). Program leadership must remain committed to and invest time and resources in moving toward an implementation that begins with meaningful youth advisory committees to an integration that fully invests in the strategic planning for and implementation of youth voice at all levels. Full implementation means amplifying the voices of youth participants, hiring culturally responsive YPSSs, and working to ensure the integration of youth voice throughout not only the residential program but the local systems of care as well.

Implementing youth-guided/driven care is an essential step toward creating and sustaining a trauma-informed environment, which includes eliminating coercion. One of the Six Core Strategies™—to reduce seclusion and the use of restraints—involves the full and formal inclusion of youth, families, and external advocates in various roles at all levels of the program (Huckshorn, CAP, & Director, 2005). The approach further promotes the intentional integration of youth and advocates in event oversight, monitoring, debriefing interviews, and peer support services and mandates significant roles in key program committees. Moving beyond the basics of engagement to this full integration throughout the organization helps a residential intervention move from youth-guided to youth-driven.

Conclusion

Becoming youth-guided or, better still, youth-driven, is a journey that involves: Establishing and maintaining a growth mindset; providing training and skill building for youth, families, staff, and others involved with the youth; committed system partners; and significant structural and cultural change. As one youth who has become a statewide youth advocate advised: "Don't wait until the timing, resources, staffing are 'perfect'; find good examples to get started and start somewhere" (Dani).

> *"There will be thousands of interventions you may choose from yet changing your approach to making a way for youth voice and choice will be the easiest to implement if everyone buys into it. In my perspective this change you make can have long-term effects on the sustainability of relationships and impact on the individual to believe in themselves."*
>
> (Casa Pacifica staff person)

A youth-driven approach allows an effective means for residential interventions to do a better job of creating the services, opportunities, and supports that young people need to develop in healthy ways. Young people have the right to participate in decisions that affect them, particularly in their services and supports. When afforded this opportunity by residential interventions that are youth-guided/driven and supported by YPSSs, transformational change occurs and positive sustained outcomes benefit the youth, the families, and the community.

Resources

The following resources are excellent tools for building understanding amongst families, advocates, leadership, and staff regarding the benefits of advancing youth voice and involvement.

- **Building Bridges Initiative**: www.buildingbridges4youth.org/products/tools
- **Effectively Employing Young Adult Peer Providers:** www.umassmed.edu/globalassets/transitionsrtc/publications/effectivleyemploying youngadultpeerproviders_a_toolkit.pdf
- **Inventory of Adult Attitudes and Behavior**: https://northwoods coalition.org/wp-content/uploads/2016/10/Chapter-5-Inventory-of-Adult-Attitudes-and-Behavior.pdf (Lofquist, 1989)
- **Person-centered planning:** www.ncdhhs.gov/document/person-centered-planning.
- **Promoting Youth Engagement in Residential Settings:** www.buildingbridges4youth.org/sites/default/files/Promoting%20Youth%20Engagement%20in%20Residential%20Settings%20-%20%20Suggestions%20from%20Youth.pdf
- **Using Youth and Family Advocates/Partners Effectively with Residential Interventions:** https://togetherthevoice.org/bbitraining/

conference_session/workshops_ii_session_b2_using_youth_and_family_advocatespartners_effectively

- **Youth Involvement in Systems of Care: A Guide to Empowerment:** https://nwi.pdx.edu/NWI-book/Chapters/App-6e.3-Youth-Involvement-In-Systems-Of-Care.pdf
- **Youth Advocate 2 Advocate for Youth**: The Next Transition: www.pathwaysrtc.pdx.edu/pdf/pb-Youth-Advocacy-Guide.pdf

References

ACT for Youth Center for Community Action. (2019). *What is youth engagement really?* [Webpage]. Retrieved from http://actforyouth.net/youth_development/engagement/

Adolescent Health Initiative. (2013). *Developing and sustaining a thriving youth advisory council.* Retrieved from www.umhs-adolescenthealth.org/wp-content/uploads/2017/02/manual-for-website.pdf

Anderson, K. (2019). Personal communication.

Blau, G. M., Caldwell, B., & Lieberman, R. E. (Eds.). (2014). *Residential interventions for children, adolescents, and families: A best practice guide.* New York, NY: Routledge.

Brach, T. (2015). Healing traumatic fear: The wings of mindfulness and love. In V. M. Follette, J. Briere, D. Rozelle, J. W. Hopper, & D. I. Rome (Eds.), *Mindfulness-oriented interventions for trauma: Integrating contemplative practices* (pp. 31–42). New York, NY: The Guilford Press. Retrieved from https://search-ebscohost-com.libezp.lib.lsu.edu/login.aspx?direct=true&db=psyh&AN=2015-10559-002&site=eds-live&scope=site

Browne, C. H., Notkin, S., Schneider-Munoz, A., & Zimmerman, F. (2015). Youth thrive: A framework to help adolescents overcome trauma and thrive. *Journal of Child and Youth Care Work, 25,* 33–52. Retrieved from https://cssp.org/wp-content/uploads/2018/09/Youth-Thrive-A-Framework-to-Help-Adolescents-Overcome-Trauma-and-Thrive.pdf

The Carter Center. (2009, November 17–18). *Pillars of peer support: Transforming mental health systems of care through peer support services.* Atlanta, GA: The Pillars of Peer Support Services Summit.

Chopra, K. (2018). *Why your millennials are leaving and how to keep them* [Blogpost]. Forbes. Retrieved from www.forbes.com/sites/theyec/2018/03/23/why-your-millennials-are-leaving-and-how-to-keep-them/#58f3c4a71e87

Coates, D. (2013). Integrated leadership development programmes: Are they effective and what role does coaching play? *International Journal of Evidence Based Coaching and Mentoring, (S7),* 39. Retrieved from https://search-ebscohost-com.libezp.lib.lsu.edu/login.aspx?direct=true&db=edsdoj&AN=edsdoj.860a92f0ba254d4ea3c500be07c7d129&site=eds-live&scope=site

Committee on the Rights of the Child. (1992). Resolution 44/25 of 20 November 1989, entry into force 2, September 1990, in accordance with article 49. United Nations.

Davidson, L., Chinman, M., Kloos, B., Weingarten, R., Stayner, D., & Tebes, J. K. (1999). Peer support among individuals with severe mental Illness: A review of the evidence. *Clinical Psychology: Science and Practice, 6*(2), 165–187.

Delman, J., & Klodnick, V. V. (2017). Factors supporting the employment of young adult peer providers: Perspectives of peers and supervisors. *Community Mental Health Journal, 53*(7), 811–822.

Donnelly, T., Baker, D., & Gargan, L. (n.d.). *The benefits of family peer support services: Let's examine the evidence* [PowerPoint slides]. Retrieved from www.nasmhpd. org/sites/default/files/Benefits%20of%20Family%20Peer%20Support%20FIC%20 SAMSHA%20Updated.pdf

Ecke, L., Stenslie, M., Alibert, M., Broderick, S. J., Cross, A., Freeman, J., & Robe, A. (n.d.). *FLUX*. Foster Care Alumni of America. Retrieved from https://fostercare alumni.org/flux/

Family and Youth Services Bureau. (2012). *5 C's that promote positive youth development and youth engagement.* Retrieved from www.acf.hhs.gov/sites/default/files/ fysb/whatispyd20120829.pdf

Fry, R. (2018, April 11). *Millennials are the largest generation in the U.S. labor force.* Retrieved January 13, 2018, from www.pewresearch.org/fact-tank/2018/04/11/ millennials-largest-generation-us-labor-force/

Gaskill, R. L., & Perry, B. D. (2017). A neurosequential therapeutics approach to guided play, play therapy, and activities for children who won't talk. In C. A. Malchiodi & D. A. Crenshaw (Eds.), *What to do when children clam up in psychotherapy: Interventions to facilitate communication* (pp. 38–66). New York, NY: Guilford Press.

Hamilton, E. (2019). Life story approaches and relationships within residential child care: A practice reflection. *Scottish Journal of Residential Child Care, 18*(2), 57–67. Retrieved from https://search-ebscohost-com.libezp.lib.lsu.edu/login.aspx?direct= true&db=sih&AN=137283718&site=eds-live&scope=site

Huckshorn, K. A., CAP, I., & Director, N. T. A. C. (2005). *Six core strategies to reduce the use of seclusion and restraint planning tool.* Washington, DC: National Association of State Mental Health Program Directors.

Kendrick Burk, L. (2019, March). *Developing 21st Century skills for the young adult lived expertise workforce: A gap analysis and approach for implementation.* 31st Annual Children's Mental Health Policy and Research Conference, University of South Florida, Tampa, FL.

Kendrick Burk, L., Bergan, J., Long, J., Noelle, R., Soto, R., Richardson, R., & Waetzig, E. (2013). *Youth advocate to advocate for youth: The next transition.* Portland, OR: Research and Training Center for Pathways to Positive Futures.

Kendrick Burk, L., & Sikes, S. (2018, March). *Elevating lived experience through coaching.* 30th Annual Children's Mental Health Policy and Research Conference, University of South Florida, Tampa, FL.

Li, J., & Julian, M. (2012). Developmental relationships as the active ingredient: A unifying working hypothesis of 'what works' across intervention settings. *American Journal of Orthopsychiatry, 82*(2), 157–166.

Lofquist, W. (1989). *Inventory of adult attitudes and behavior.* Tucson, AZ: Associates for Youth Development Publications. Retrieved from https://northwoodscoali tion.org/wp-content/uploads/2016/10/Chapter-5-Inventory-of-Adult-Attitudes-and-Behavior.pdf

Lulow, E., Harrington, K., Alexander, M., & Kendrick Burk, L. (2014). Becoming a youth-guided residential organization. In *Residential interventions for children, adolescents, and families: A best practice guide* (pp. 46–60). Washington, DC: SAMHSA.

Masten, A. S. (2001). Ordinary magic: Resilience processes in development. *American Psychologist, 56*(3), 227–238.

Mezirow, J. (2003, January). Transformative learning as discourse. *Journal of Transformative Education, 1*(1), 58–63. doi:10.1177/1541344603252172

NC Dept. of Health and Human Services. (2013). *Person-centered planning* [Webpage]. Retrieved from www.ncdhhs.gov/document/person-centered-planning

Oliveras, C., Cluver, L., Bernays, S., & Armstrong, A. (2018). Nothing about Us without RIGHTS-meaningful engagement of children and youth: From research prioritization to clinical trials, implementation science, and policy. *Journal of Acquired Immune Deficiency Syndromes (1999), 78*(1) (Suppl 1), S27–S31. doi:10.1097/QAI.0000000000001746

Ontario Trillium Foundation. (2007). *Meeting the needs of Ontario's youth* [Report]. Retrieved from https://web.archive.org/web/20110716064254/http:/www.trilliumfoundation.org/cms/en/publications/cms/html/knowledge_sharing/knowledge.aspx?menuid=258

Perry, B. D. (2019). *Trauma-informed care: The impact of trauma on brain development and what to do about it.* 63rd Annual Conference of the Association of Children's Residential Centers, New Orleans, LA.

Pittman, K. (2017). Positive youth development as a strategy for addressing readiness and equity: A commentary. *Child Development, 88*(4), 1172–1174.

Rossiter, L., & Socho, A. (2018). Workplace bullying and burnout: The moderating effects of social support. *Journal of Aggression, Maltreatment, & Trauma, 27*(4), 386–408.

Strangler, G. J., & Shirk, M. (2004). *On their own: What happens to kids when they age out of the foster care system.* Nashville, TN: Westview Press.

Substance Abuse and Mental Health Services Administration. (2014). *SAMHSA's working definition of recovery: 10 guiding principles of recovery.* Retrieved from https://store.samhsa.gov/system/files/pep12-recdef.pdf

Substance Abuse and Mental Health Services Administration. (2017). *Value of peers.* Retrieved from www.samhsa.gov/sites/default/files/programs_campaigns/brss_tacs/value-of-peers-2017.pdf

Warren, L. J., & Moses, K. (n.d.). *Understanding the stages of grief* [Website]. Retrieved from www.google.com/url?q=www.parentcompanion.org/article/understanding-the-stages-of-grief&sa=D&ust=1563394200162000&usg=AFQjCNFhvSTNw3muth_FslafLA35xp4-vQ

The Young Adult Peer Mentor Practice Profile Workgroup. (2017, June). *Young adult peer mentor practice profile.* Boston, MA: Department of Mental Health, Commonwealth of Massachusetts.

Zarrett, N., & Lerner, R. M. (2008). Ways to promote the positive development of children and youth. *Child Trends, 11*(1), 1–5. Retrieved from www.childtrends.org/wp-content/uploads/01/Youth-Positive-Devlopment.pdf

4

ADVANCING EQUITY, DIVERSITY, AND INCLUSION IN RESIDENTIAL INTERVENTIONS

Tanvi Ajmera, Julie Collins,
Linda Henderson-Smith,
Chandler Coggins, and Gary M. Blau

Since the publication of the previous book *"Residential Interventions for Children, Adolescents, and Families: A Best Practice Guide"* in 2014 (Blau, Caldwell, & Lieberman, 2014), there have been significant advances in the field's understanding of cultural and linguistic competence. Changing demographics and a heightened awareness about discrimination and disparities warrants greater attention to culture and creates a new focus on equity, diversity, and inclusion. For example, in the past five years, there has been a significant rise in and attention to immigration to the United States from Central and South America, and the largest number of new immigrants are now coming from Asia. These trends are likely to continue in the coming decades (Cohn & Caumont, 2016).

The number of diverse youth is increasing—48 percent of youth under the age of 18 are youth of color. This number is projected to rise to 64.4 percent by 2060 (U.S. Census Bureau, 2015). It is estimated that 737,000 adolescents (around 1.3 percent of 12–17-year-olds in the US) received residential services (Center for Behavioral Health Statistics and Quality [CBHSQ], 2017). Approximately 360,000 (49 percent) of these youth were youth of color (CBHSQ, 2017), which means that residential providers (and their community-based partners) must address, adjust, and adapt to the needs of increasingly diverse populations.

This chapter aims to advance cultural and linguistic competence (CLC) by focusing on how organizations and systems can further Equity, Diversity and Inclusion (EDI) to ensure appropriate access to treatment and improve outcomes for diverse populations. The chapter will: 1) Define the concepts of CLC and EDI and how they relate to one another; 2) explore the impact of historical trauma and structural racism; and 3) provide EDI strategies on how systems and residential programs can serve youth with trauma histories, and/or behavioral, and/or emotional challenges, including their families.

Defining Equity, Diversity, Inclusion, and Cultural Competence

"*Equity* is the fair access, opportunity, and advancement for all people, while at the same time striving to identify and eliminate barriers that have prevented the full participation of some groups" (Kapila, Hines, & Searby, 2016, Independent Sector, para. 4).

Diversity "includes all the ways in which people differ, encompassing the different characteristics that make one individual or group different from another (e.g. race, ethnicity, gender, age, disability, religion, sexual orientation, nationality, socioeconomic status, marital status, language, physical appearance etc.)" (http://racialequitytools.org).

Inclusion is "authentically bringing traditionally excluded individuals and/or groups into processes, activities, and decision/policy making in a way that shares power" (http://racialequitytools.org). Strategies to implement the principles and values of equity, diversity, and inclusion in organizational practice are provided throughout this chapter.

"*Cultural competence* is a process of learning that leads to an ability to effectively respond to the challenges and opportunities posed by the presence of cultural diversity in a defined social system" (National Health Care for the Homeless Council, 2016, Slide 12). When the culture of an individual/individuals is ignored, the individual/s being served will be at higher risk of not receiving the support they need; this can also lead to the individual/s receiving services that may be more harmful than helpful (Cabral-Johnson & Pumphrey, 2015). Essential elements of cultural competence include awareness of one's own culture, understanding the dynamics of difference, awareness and acceptance of difference, development and application of cultural knowledge, and the celebration of diversity (Prevent Child Abuse Iowa, 2017).

How Does Cultural Competence Relate to Equity, Diversity, and Inclusion?

Goodman (2014) discusses how "cultural competence for equity and inclusion is the ability to live and work effectively in culturally diverse environments and enact a commitment to fairness and to the full participation of all members" (p. 1). In environments that are deemed to be inclusive and equitable there is a fair distribution of resources and opportunities and therefore people feel valued and feel mentally, emotionally, and physically safe, thereby leading to people reaching their full potential. How can one integrate cultural competence and equity, diversity, and inclusion? Goodman (2014) emphasizes that this requires the following range of skills, knowledge, and awareness: 1) Self-awareness, 2) understanding and valuing others, 3) knowledge of societal inequities, 4) skills to interact effectively with a diversity of people in different contexts, and 5) skills to foster equity and inclusion.

Understanding the previous nuances and differences between CLC and EDI and how these concepts can be integrated to create responsive programs, is important to take CLC to the next level. Strategies organizations can use to begin this process involve understanding and addressing racism, structural racism, and historical trauma and embracing the concepts of cultural humility and culturally sensitive trauma-informed care.

Racism and Structural Racism

Racism and structural racism must be considered when understanding how to address and promote diversity, equity, and inclusion. The Anti-Defamation League (2019) defines racism as

> *The belief that a particular race is superior or inferior to another, that a person's social and moral traits are predetermined by his or her inborn biological characteristics. Racial separatism is the belief, most of the time based on racism, that different races should remain segregated and apart from one another.*

(www.adl.org/racism)

The Aspen Institute Roundtable on Community Change, 2004 (URL in reference section) defines structural racism as

> *A system in which public policies, institutional practices, cultural representations, and other norms work in various, often reinforcing ways to perpetuate racial group inequity. The Roundtable identified dimensions of our history and culture that have allowed privileges associated with "whiteness" and disadvantages associated with "color" to endure and adapt over time.*

Among other factors, Gee and Ford (2011) indicate that structural racism results in significant disparities in poverty outcomes, access to home ownership, and credit—in other words—many of the social determinants of health. The effects of structural racism continue to cause disparities in the form of worsened health outcomes overall among people of color and can continue to impact organizations and systems across the country (Gee & Ford, 2011).

Program staff and leadership are encouraged to self-assess the history of the organization with respect to cultural competence, racism, and structural racism in order to create a plan that embraces the importance of EDI.

Trauma and Historical Trauma

According to the National Child Traumatic Stress Network (NCTSN)

> *When a child feels intensely threatened by an event he or she is involved in or witnesses, we call that event a trauma. There is a range of traumatic events or trauma types to which children and adolescents can be exposed, including but not limited to bullying, violence, physical and sexual abuse etc.*
>
> (*NCTSN*, URL in resource section)

Trauma is impacted by a wide variety of cultural indices (NCTSN, n.d.b):

- social and cultural realities strongly influence children's risk for and experience of trauma;
- children with minority backgrounds are at increased risk for trauma exposure and subsequent development of PTSD; and
- adolescents who identify as lesbian, gay, bisexual, transgender, or questioning (LGBTQ) often have to contend with violence directed at them in response to their LGBTQ status.

Mental health and trauma expert Maria Yellow Horse Brave Heart, a Lakota social worker and current Research Associate Professor and Director of Disparities Research at the University of New Mexico, developed the first model of historical trauma for her people that is now used broadly for indigenous populations. She defines historical trauma as "a constellation of characteristics associated with massive cumulative group trauma across generations" (Brave Heart, 1999, p. 2). For African American communities, the historical experience of life in the United States is fundamentally linked with the reality of slavery, the traumatic effects of which continue to exert their influence on the descendants of African Americans who originally experienced the trauma of slavery.

The effects of forced relocation of some populations has also led to historical trauma experiences. Over 120,000 Japanese Americans were placed in United States internment camps during World War II, an event whose traumatic effects persist to this day (Frail, 2017). Genocide is another cause of historical trauma; the terror of the Holocaust has had measurable effects on health outcomes and levels of distress on descendants of survivors (Bowers & Yehuda, 2016).

58 Tanvi Ajmera et al.

Immigrant and refugee families often face additional traumas and stressors and this will have harmful effects on the mental well-being of children and families. "Public representations of refugees in North America and Europe have progressively shifted from vulnerable individuals deserving protection to potential criminals and fraudsters seeking to abuse host country resources, in particular, the health care system" (Rousseau, Oulhote, Ruiz-Casares, Cleveland, & Greenaway, 2017, p. 2). This quote is from a study that speaks to the negative attitudes of healthcare personnel toward refugees, which can further affect their health outcomes.

In the Native American community, child removal is another form of trauma that is being transmitted across generations. In 1819, the United States government established the Civilization Fund, which had the goal of "civilizing" Native Americans by destroying their traditional practices and ways of life. By the 1860s, government-sponsored missionaries were separating Native American children from their tribes; Native American parents were deemed "unfit," and their children were forcibly sent to geographically distant boarding schools. Tragically, this is something that has been happening around the world for hundreds of years.

The impacts of historical trauma are far-reaching. The response includes a range of psychological, emotional, and spiritual symptoms, including mental health conditions such as substance use disorders, anxiety, depression, and post-traumatic stress disorder (PTSD), as well as physical illness and "erosion in family and community structures," exemplified by high rates of suicide, homicide, and domestic violence (Michaels, Rousseau, & Yang, 2010). It is important to note that even members of an affected cultural group who have not experienced trauma first-hand can exhibit symptoms of historical trauma, since it is passed down from one generation to the next (University of Minnesota Extension Children, Youth and Families, 2015).

Strategies to Address Historical Trauma and Structural Racism

Historical trauma can have intergenerational effects on children and families that can impact engagement and treatment with residential programs. As with other traumatic events, historical and intergenerational traumas can affect the development of children and families in multiple ways: Brain chemistry, the immune and human stress response systems, behavior, self-concept, and a person's worldview (JBS International Inc. and Georgetown University National Technical Assistance Center for Children's Mental Health, 2014).

How does one address the needs and varying stressors highlighted previously? Culturally sensitive trauma-informed care is one such way—it is "the capacity for healthcare professionals to effectually provide trauma-informed assessment and intervention that acknowledges, respects and integrates children's and families' cultural values, beliefs and practices" (Children's Hospital of Philadelphia [CHOP], 2014, URL in references). A culturally sensitive, trauma-informed care provider can help children and families who have been traumatized by: Helping to restore a sense of safety for the child and family through trust-building, attending to the distress of the child or family in the way that they define it, and working within and through the family structure to promote emotional and social support and utilization of coping resources (CHOP, 2014).

When considering the implementation of culturally sensitive, trauma-informed approaches, residential providers should pay special attention to building relationships with the youth and family and ensuring that the assessments and interventions are viewed through a culturally sensitive, trauma-informed lens. One concrete strategy to implement culturally sensitive trauma-informed care is the D-E-F (Distress, Emotional Support, and Family Needs) protocol—a practical tool to guide providers in implementing this approach. The Distress in this protocol focuses on asking about fear or anxiety, the Emotional Support focuses on the who and what the individual needs at that moment, and the Family focuses on understanding potential family-related stressors and providing available resources. While this protocol is created for the health care industry, it can be used by any human service professional, whether they provide health care or not (CHOP, 2014).

Cultural Humility

Cultural humility is a practice of being self-reflective, other-oriented, and practicing power-attenuating openness to clients as multicultural beings (Hook, Davis, Owen, Worthington, & Utsey, 2013). This means that organizations and their staff place a high value on the client as the expert in their lives and the staff as collaborators in the family's journey: Show respect, openness, "egolessness" (the ability to put others needs and perspectives first), and consideration of the client's cultural background. In doing so, staff can develop true partnerships with youth and families, address power imbalances, and create an "other-oriented" approach to cultural needs and perspectives.

Cultural humility is the counterbalance to cultural competence by attending to the client's cultural background in the moment with critical reflection of one's biases and privileges. Cultural humility works toward building a real relationship (being genuine, viewing the client as a fellow person) with strong emotional bonds, agreement on goals and tasks, and a collaborative experiential process (Mosher et al., 2017). Cultural humility allows those who work directly with youth and families to not have to be "perfectly culturally competent," (i.e., to be okay to not know about every culture or be aware of the specific culture of the individual being served) and creates opportunity for staff to invite the youth or family to teach them about their culture.

Because of the changing demographics in the United States, the implementation of cultural humility is of critical importance (Hook et al., 2013). According to the American Psychological Association (2018), there are strategies that can be implemented in daily work with youth and families that can help an organization become more culturally humble. Workforce development strategies that residential and community programs can implement are briefly described here and readers can find links to detailed strategies in the resource section at the end of the chapter:

1. Staff can consider youth through the lens of a social ecological framework, systems of bidirectional influence using such tools as:
   - Ecomaps—visual representation of relationships, social support, and cultural context (Crawford, Grant, & Crews, 2016);
   - culturagrams—tool to assess and empower by recording immigration, language, health beliefs, celebrated holidays and special events, impact of crisis events, values regarding family, education and work, and contact with cultural institutions (Congress, 2004).
2. Staff who work with residential or community programs can foster racially and ethnically diverse youth engagement through trainings in culturally sensitive methods such as:
   - Using Motivational Interviewing—listening on the same side vs. resistant;
   - repeated assessments of barriers to treatment over time;
   - fostering a strong therapeutic alliance by viewing the client as the expert, embodying strengths-based techniques, and focusing on positive body language.
   Some examples of culturally adapted and emergent clinical practices include, *Culturally-Modified Trauma-Focused Cognitive Behavioral Therapy* (de Arellano & Danielson, 2005), *Womanist and Mujerista Psychologies* (Bryant-Davis & Comas-Díaz, 2016), *Emotional Emancipation Circles* (Association of Black Psychologists, 2009) and *Culturally Modified Mindfulness Cognitive Therapy* (Erazo & Hazlett-Stevens, 2014).
3. Staff can learn how to view youth and families through the lens of racial equity through these resources: *Advancing the Mission: Tools for Equity, Diversity and Inclusion (Annie E. Casey Foundation, 2009)* and *Race Equity and Inclusion Action Guide (Annie E. Casey Foundation, 2014).*
4. Hire and sustain a diverse workforce that recognizes the importance of health equity and is culturally competent (see two examples to follow):

Uplift Family Services (formerly EQM Family First) created a Leadership Academy (BBI, 2011), and the focus of this academy was to develop managers' knowledge in cultural and linguistic competence. Regular trainings on CLC principles, diversity, equity, and inclusion are a part of their Leadership Academy. Uplift Family Services, in addition to the diversity training mentioned earlier, has been creating Cultural Brokers. These brokers are a group of key staff who work together on building their cultural and linguistic competence. One of the responsibilities of this group of brokers is to recognize when organization practices are not in line with cultural and linguistic competency principles and offer solutions and employee support.

The Jewish Board (the largest human service provider in New York City), began an agency-wide effort to focus on organizational racism approximately 20 years ago. They named the effort and their work: *Confronting Organizational Racism* (COR). COR is a multidisciplinary ethnically and racially diverse committee whose focus is to confront, discuss, address, and resolve all forms of organizational racism identified within the organization. The COR groups have focused on many issues, including: Providing healing spaces for those with vulnerable identities and those with privilege, partnering with agency leadership to initiate policy change, advocating for diverse representation at all levels of staffing, and educating and building staff competency around addressing these issues in client care.

Residential and community programs can embed many of the strategies highlighted previously in workforce development initiatives.

Serving Youth With Unique Needs

Language Barriers and Changing Linguistic Needs

As previously noted in this chapter, a disproportionate number of youth and families who receive residential interventions are of color. Though being culturally humble and infusing "universal" culturally sensitive trauma-informed approaches are important for all populations, there are some populations that require specific strategies to ensure that the youth and families benefit from relevant services and supports provided by an organization. For example, language barriers pose a significant challenge with increasing numbers of youth who communicate in languages other than English. The number of

62 Tanvi Ajmera et al.

English language learners in grades K-12 is approximately 4.6 million children representing 9.4 percent of the K-12 population (National Center for Education Statistics, 2017).

Linguistic Competence

Linguistic competence is defined as:

> *The ability of an organization and its employees to successfully communicate information in a manner that is uncomplicated and easily understood by diverse individuals and groups, including those with limited English proficiency, low literacy skills or who are illiterate, and those with disabilities.*

(Goode & Jones, 2004, p. 6)

Linguistic competence integration requires intentional staff development and formal supervision, coaching, mentoring of staff, supervisors, and volunteers (Building Bridges Initiative, 2011). Residential and community programs may consider the following practices and strategies:

1. Recruit staff who speak the languages spoken by youth and families that frequently are served by the residential or community program. Do this by advertising positions in local cultural publications, with culture specific professional and fraternal organizations, online job search engines, radio stations, online listservs, and newsletters and magazines.
2. Ensure access to appropriate translation for all screening, assessment, and interventions by: Using interpreters trained in working with youth and families and using technology programs or apps that allow for written communication and using language lines offered in some states.

Youth and/or Families Who Have Limited English-Speaking Proficiency

For residential and community providers that serve many young people and their families from the same country or region, it is recommended to hire and train staff who know the language and culture of the region. This can reduce misunderstandings between youth, families, and staff and help establish creditability and good will (Hannay, 2018). For residential and community providers who serve youth and families from a wide range of ethnic identities and regions, staff can be educated about typical communication issues for non-native English speakers such as speaking too quickly, not leaving enough time for a response, pronunciation, and asking, "Do you understand?"

Youth Who Are Deaf or Hard of Hearing

Importantly, the construct of equity, diversity, and inclusion goes beyond race and ethnicity and includes individuals with other challenges that separate them from the mainstream. For example, individuals who are deaf or hard of hearing have difficulty finding services that are culturally affirmative and linguistically accessible. Few residential programs in the nation focus on the needs of deaf or hard of hearing youth. Simply having one staff member who signs or hiring American Sign Language (ASL) interpreters will not make a program fully accessible or appropriate for many youth and families. Significant cultural understanding and ability to adapt treatment to meet individualized learning styles is often a critical missing component.

In order to provide the least restrictive environment for therapeutic healing, most Deaf Services providers would recommend a specialized program where all services are offered directly in ASL or the child's primary language. While accessible specialized services are severely limited, some places such as The Learning Center for the Deaf: Walden School-Therapeutic Program are able to provide those (URL in Resources).

There are many strategies related to the provision of linguistically accessible services. Examples include family engagement and empowerment, workforce development and advocacy, and financial support. Outlined in the following are strategies residential program leaders can consider (M. Niehaus, personal communication, January 25, 2019):

- Training families and staff around deaf culture, specifically the child's current and emerging identity(ies) and intersectionality as it relates to their needs;
- include line items in the budget for:
    - American Sign Language Interpreters, Certified Deaf Interpreters, and Communication Specialists. Many children will have experienced language deprivation and dysfluency. Traditional interpreting will not be enough (Glickman & Hall, 2019);
    - equipment such as Video Phones, dry erase boards, and visual alerting devices;
    - sending staff to specialized training on working with youth who are deaf;
    - consultation with experts on Deaf Mental Health;
- proactively seeking funding from sources such as state authorities, managed care organizations and/or child protection agencies at the state level is needed to develop or sustain such specialized services;
- note that, even with a skilled interpreter, group experiences will be different if the other youth and/or families are not also deaf or hard-of-hearing. Write treatment plans to include more 1:1 service and meet

with youth and their families often to ensure that there is understanding and comprehension of daily activities;

- include the interpreting team as a part of the core treatment team and consider pairing the youth and/or their family with mentors who are deaf or hard of hearing;
- as with all residential programs, begin discharge planning at or pre-admission. Recognize that community-based services and supports that include staff who sign and/or competent interpreters may be hard to find; put the extra time in working with the family, schools, and all community-based organizations, including places of worship and recreational programs, to identify deaf and hard-of-hearing competent staff and supports. Ensure that youth are engaged with other youth who have similar hearing differences.

Co-Occurring Developmental/Intellectual and Behavioral Health Disabilities

It is estimated that between 30–70 percent of youth with developmental or intellectual disabilities also experience co-occurring behavioral and/or emotional challenges. According to NCTSN (2015), service providers have faulty beliefs about youth with co-occurring intellectual and developmental disabilities (IDD) and behavioral disabilities. These "myths" include:

- Youth with IDD cannot engage in treatment;
- standard mental health treatment is ineffective with children with IDD;
- behavior modification is the only option; and
- IQ scores are static and cognitive improvement is not possible.

To address these common misperceptions, NCTSN (2015) identified several best practices when working with this population:

1) Conduct a battery of screening and assessments to identify the youths' cognitive and communication (linguistic) abilities. Examples include:
   i) Ages & Stages Questionnaires, Third Edition (ASQ-3)—a comprehensive screening tool that reliably measures development in five key domains (URL in Resources):
   ii) Adaptive Functioning Assessments, including but not limited to:
      - The Vineland Adaptive Behavior Scales—Third Edition (Vineland-3)—a measure of adaptive behavior from birth to adulthood (Sparrow, 2016) (URL in Resources);
      - The Adaptive Behavior Assessment System—Third Edition (ABAS-3)—a complete assessment of adaptive skills across the life span (URL in Resources).

Implement adaptations by all members of the treatment team in doing the following in their daily interactions:

- Slow down speech;
- use language that is comprehensible to the youth;
- present information one item at a time;
- take frequent pauses during any type of interaction or session to check comprehension;
- use multisensory input;
- allow time to practice new skills;
- do not assume that information will generalize to new situations

Additionally, ensure delivery of screening, assessments, and interventions takes into account the communication (linguistic) style of the youth, e.g., non-verbal by utilizing assistive communication devices including but not limited to picture systems or computer programs on tablets.

2) Consult with experts on the use of evidence-based or emerging best practices or adaptations and their feasibility with your program.

3) Enhance the family's well-being and resilience. Strengthen families and their protective factors by:

  i) Providing culturally sensitive and trauma-informed education, services, and supports to the families, recognizing that families may have trauma histories themselves or be experiencing secondary traumatic stress and may need appropriate support and intervention. Other ideas include: Ask and answer family's questions; address cultural and traumatic experiences of the families themselves; work hard throughout the entire residential intervention to promote secure attachments; and provide support to help families navigate systems of care, including addressing systems challenges.

Youth That Identify as Lesbian, Gay, Bisexual, Transgender, Questioning, Intersex, or Two-Spirit (LGBTQI2-S)

Residential interventions also serve cultural groups that may require focused and individualized attention, such as youth who identify as being Lesbian, Gay, Bisexual, Transgender, Questioning, Intersex, and Two-Spirit or LGBTQI2-S, from here on referred to as LGBT. Research has shown that youth who identify as LGBT have an increased likelihood of placement in a more restrictive setting (Woronoff, Estrada, & Sommer, 2006). Additionally, they are more likely to be moved between placements and far less likely to develop strong, enduring connections with adults, compared to youth who do not identify as being LGBT (Jacobs & Freundlich, 2006).

Many of these youth may face legal discrimination, bullying, less access to safe community spaces or recreational facilities (Office of Disease Prevention and Health Promotion, 2019), and disparate access to healthcare services (Ward, Dahlhamer, Galinsky, & Joestl, 2014). Furthermore, youth who identify as LGBT are more vulnerable to harassment and assault; either in school or in child welfare and/or juvenile justice settings (Kosciw et al., 2010). LGBT youth who try to report abuse may be blamed, adding to trauma and victimization (Estrada & Marksamer, 2006). The Coalition for Juvenile Justice (2013) created a resource: *The National Standards for the Care of Youth Charged With Status Offenses*. Within this, there are standards that speak to the challenges faced by LGBTQ youth who have been charged with status offenses. These standards and strategies can be helpful to professionals serving youth who identify as LGBT, even beyond juvenile justice settings (URL in Resources).

Standards of Care

Many systems have developed standards of care to address cultural and linguistic competence and to develop and implement services that include a focus on equity, diversity, and inclusion. This section will highlight several of these "standards" that can guide an organization's plans and actions.

Health and Behavioral Health

The US Department of Health and Human Services developed standards for culturally and linguistically appropriate services (CLAS) as part of its effort to address inequities in healthcare (U.S. Department of Health and Human Services, Office of Minority Health, 2016). These standards were updated in 2012, and the enhanced National Standards for Culturally and Linguistically Appropriate Services are now required to be used by providers in the health and behavioral health systems to promote equity, reduce disparities, and improve the quality of health services. These standards can be seen as a "blueprint" for culturally and linguistically competent health services. The text box to follow provides an example of a behavioral health system that implemented a policy of non-discrimination and cultural competency through the adoption of the CLAS standards.

Public Health

The public health sector has its own set of standards, the Public Health Accreditation Board (PHAB, 2013) Standards and Measures—this accreditation process advances the performance of state, local, territorial, and tribal public health agencies, and there are specific PHAB standards that address CLC (URL in reference section).

Child Welfare

The Child Welfare League of America (CWLA) has created national standards for child welfare related services. These national standards are not compliance driven, as with the CLAS and the PHAB Standards and Measures; rather, they are aspirational and to be used as goals for practice in the field of child welfare.

The CWLA Standards of Excellence for Residential Services (CWLA Residential Standards) (CWLA, 2004) contain cultural and linguistic competence standards at the residential, organizational, and worker levels, and address the issues of diversity, equity, and inclusion. The standards are consistent with the CLAS standards and provide more specificity across the various phases of residential intervention services as well as at the organizational level. These standards also reflect federal requirements related to the Indian Child Welfare Act and the Multi-Ethnic Placement Act (Idaho Department of Health and Welfare (n.d.)).

As with public health departments, public child welfare agencies have performance requirements that include CLC. For example, state-level performance on the Child and Family Services Reviews (CFSRs) has demonstrated the ongoing challenge that state child welfare agencies and their providers have with the overrepresentation of youth of color in the child welfare system and the ongoing concern with the poor outcomes for this population of children and families. The resulting Performance Improvement Plans (PIP) have necessitated that state agencies and their provider network work together to address issues such as structural racism, disproportionality, and disparity. The California Department of Social Services (DSS) is a good example of how a state has used the CFSR to improve practice. Specifically, DSS developed a Case Practice Model called the CORE Practice Model for the county level public child welfare agencies, which includes practicing cultural humility, and residential programs are using this model (California Dept. of Health Care Services & Dept. of Social Services, 2013).

Juvenile Justice

As referenced earlier in the chapter the Coalition for Juvenile Justice (2013) has created the National Standards for the Care of Youth Charged with Status Offenses that includes a section on cultural and linguistic competent services in residential interventions for youth placed there.

Other Accreditation Standards

There are three main national accrediting bodies for residential interventions services for children and families: The Joint Commission (2014), Commission on Accreditation of Rehabilitation Facilities (CARF), and Council on Accreditation (COA). The three entities have specific accreditation standards that address CLC, which are embedded across the various components of their accreditation standards from values and principles to client rights, leadership, assessment, planning, services delivery, data collection, quality improvement processes, and satisfaction surveys. The Joint Commission and COA have created crosswalks of their cultural and linguistic competence standards with the National CLAS Standards. The COA and CARF accreditation standards are also consistent with the CWLA Standards of Excellence and the CWLA National Blueprint.

Best Practices

The National Building Bridges Initiative Cultural and Linguistic Competence Workgroup has created numerous resources identifying CLC best practice strategies for residential interventions, like the *Cultural and Linguistic Competence Guidelines for Residential Programs 2014*, which identifies strategies at the organizational level that residential providers can use specific to cultural and linguistic competence.

Best Practices for Data Collection

The following are best practice strategies that programs can use to reduce bias in data collection:

- Ensure the data surveys collect information on—racial, ethnic, and tribal affiliation; primary language and literacy level; demographics such as age, sexual orientation, and gender identity; location/home base, and immigration and/or refugee status. These data can then be analyzed by the various demographics mentioned previously to track progress and provide quality reporting on disproportionality and disparities;
- use standardized data reports that track the previous information and regularly communicate the findings with organizations and programs that provide residential interventions. Assistance with the interpretation of the data (specifically the disproportionalities) is critical. These disparities can be seen in placement decisions, Baker Acts,[1] and juvenile justice arrests. Within these, length of stay, recidivism rates, quality of care, restrictions, and disciplinary actions, are important factors to address and understand;
- these data should be made easily readable and available to program leadership, clinical staff, and others involved with serving youth and families— such as crisis intervention professionals, the police force and law enforcement officers, school authorities, and child welfare workers.

These data can help influence and dictate policy change across child serving systems by detecting, responding to, and reducing implicit bias and stereotyping and focusing on overall quality improvement efforts through better diagnoses, healthcare decisions, and treatment (Fitzgerald & Hurst, 2017).

Best Practices for Funding CLC and EDI

Generally, fiscal resources are not provided for states and their providers to implement CLC strategies. Some state agencies offer additional funding to providers to deliver culturally responsive services, including the provision of bonus payments to bilingual staff.

The recent Family First Prevention Services Act H.R.253 of 2017–2018 has research requirements around culturally specific and location- or population-based adaptations related to the allowable prevention services. It also includes additional CLC requirements related to the new Qualified Residential Treatment Program (QRTP). This new Act includes a host of requirements that the strategies identified in this chapter will help residential and community providers meet (link to Family First Prevention Services Act in reference section).

Conclusion

In conclusion, services and supports that are responsive to an individual's culture, belief system, and diverse needs are key to reducing and closing the gap in service disparities across many of the youth- and family- serving systems mentioned throughout this chapter.

The need to understand diversity and the pursuit of equity must be at the forefront of intervention efforts for all residential and community programs and state, county, and managed care organizations/agencies that oversee them. "Dignity and quality of care are rights of all and not the privileges of a few" (www.thinkculturalhealth.hhs.gov/clas/what-is-clas). This chapter presented strategies tools and resources to better equip residential interventions to improve and enhance the focus on equity, diversity, and inclusion (EDI) and to ensure that EDI is the foundation for all services, supports, and interactions.

Resources

American Psychological Association. (2018). *Addressing racial and ethnic differences in youth mental health*. Retrieved from www.apa.org/pi/families/resources/disparities-mental-health.aspx

Annie E. Casey Foundation. (2016). *Tools for thought- using racial equity impact assessments for effective policymaking*. Retrieved from www.aecf.org/resources/tools-for-thought-a-race-for-results-case-study/

Data Related Decision Making- Database—CultureVision. Retrieved from www.crculturevision.com

Jewish Board. Retrieved from https://jewishboard.org/

Lopez, M., Hofer, K., Bumgarner, E., & Taylor, D. (2017, March). *Developing culturally responsive approaches to serving diverse populations: A resource guide for community-based organizations.* National Research Center on Hispanic Children and Families, Publication #2017–17. Retrieved from https://www.nsvrc.org/sites/default/files/2017-06/cultural-competence-guide.pdf

National Association for the Deaf. Retrieved from www.nad.org/about-us/position-statements/position-statement-on-mental-health-services/

National Child Traumatic Stress Network Treatments that Work. Retrieved from www.nctsn.org/resources/topics/treatments-that-work/promising-practices

The National Council for Behavioral Health 7 Domains of TIC Model. Retrieved from www.thenationalcouncil.org/areas-of-expertise/trauma-informed-behavioral-healthcare/

National Standards for Culturally and Linguistically Appropriate Services in Health and Health Care: A Blueprint for Advancing and Sustaining CLAS Policy and Practice. Retrieved from www.thinkculturalhealth.hhs.gov/assets/pdfs/EnhancedCLASStandardsBlueprint.pdf

A Practical Guide to Implementing the National CLAS Standards. Retrieved from www.cms.gov/About-CMS/Agency-Information/OMH/Downloads/CLAS-Toolkit-12-7-16.pdf

Uplift Family Services. Retrieved from https://upliftfs.org/

Warshaw, C., Tinnon, E., & Cave, C. (2018). Tools for transformation: Becoming accessible, culturally responsive, and trauma-informed organizations—An organizational reflection toolkit. Retrieved from www.nationalcenterdvtraumamh.org/wp-content/uploads/2018/04/NCDVTMH_2018_ToolsforTransformation_WarshawTinnonCave.pdf

Note

1. The Florida Mental Health Act of 1971, also called the "Baker Act," allows the involuntary institutionalization and examination of an individual (for up to 72 hours) in a mental health treatment facility). It can be initiated by judges, law enforcement officials, physicians, legal guardians, or mental health professionals—www.leg.state.fl.us/Statutes/index.cfm?App_mode=Display_Statute&URL=0300-0399/0394/0394.html

References

American Psychological Association. (2018). *Strategies to enhance cultural humility within clinical encounter.* Retrieved from www.apa.org/pi/families/resources/humility-inside-clinical.pdf

Annie E. Casey Foundation. (2009). *Advancing the mission: Tools for equity, diversity and inclusion*. Baltimore, MD. Retrieved from www.aecf.org/m/resourcedoc/aecf-AdvancingtheMissionRESPECT-2009.pdf

Annie E. Casey Foundation. (2014). *Embracing equity. Race equity and inclusion action guide*. Baltimore, MD. Retrieved from www.aecf.org/resources/race-equity-and-inclusion-action-guide/

Anti-Defamation League. (2019). *Racism definition*. Retrieved from www.adl.org/racism

The Aspen Institute. (n.d.). *Glossary for understanding the dismantling structural racism/promoting racial equity analysis*. Retrieved from https://assets.aspeninstitute.org/content/uploads/files/content/docs/rcc/RCC-Structural-Racism-Glossary.pdf

The Association of Black Psychologists. (2009). *Emotional emancipation initiative* [PDF file]. Retrieved from www.abpsi.org/pdf/EmotionalEmancipationInitiative2014.pdf

Blau, G. M., Caldwell, C., & Lieberman, R. E. (2014). *Residential interventions for children, youth and families: A best practice guide*. New York, NY: Routledge.

Bowers, M. E., & Yehuda, R. (2016). Intergenerational transmission of stress in humans. *Neuropsychopharmacology, 41*, 232–244.

Brave Heart, M. Y. (1999). Gender differences in the historical trauma response among the Lakota. *Journal of Health and Social Policy, 10*(4), 1–21.

Bryant-Davis, T., & Comas-Díaz, L. (Eds.). (2016). *Psychology of women book series. Womanist and mujerista psychologies: Voices of fire, acts of courage*. Washington, DC: American Psychological Association. Retrieved from http://dx.doi.org/10.1037/14937-000

Building Bridges Initiative. (2011). *Cultural and linguistic competence guidelines for residential programs*. Retrieved from www.buildingbridges4youth.org/sites/default/files/BBI_CLC_Guidelines_FINAL.pdf

Cabral-Johnson, B., & Pumphrey, N. (2015, October). *Improving outcomes through cultural competency* [PowerPoint slides]. Retrieved from www.nhchc.org/wp-content/uploads/2013/08/improving-outcomes-through-cultural-competency_cabral-johnson.pdf

Cal. Dept. of Health Care Services and Cal. Dept. of Social Services. (2013). *Core practice model guide 9*. Retrieved from www.countyofsb.org/behavioral-wellness/Asset.c/4382

Center for Behavioral Health Statistics and Quality. (2017). *2016 National survey on drug use and health: Detailed tables*. Rockville, MD: Substance Abuse and Mental Health Services Administration.

Child Welfare League of America. (2004). *CWLA standards of excellence for residential services* (pp. 10–11). Washington, DC: Author. Retrieved from www.cwla.org/our-work/cwla-standards-of-excellence/national-blueprint-for-excellence-in-child-welfare/

Children's Hospital of Philadelphia. (2014). *Healthcare toolbox*. Retrieved from www.healthcaretoolbox.org/for-parents-and-children/12-health-care-toolbox/cultural-considerations.html

Coalition for Juvenile Justice. (2013). *National standards for the care of youth charged with status offenses*. Washington, DC: Coalition for Juvenile Justice. Retrieved from www.juvjustice.org/sites/default/files/ckfinder/files/National%20Standards%20for%20the%20Care%20of%20Youth%20Charged%20with%20Status%20Offenses%20FINAL(1).pdf

Cohn, D., & Caumont, A. (2016, March 31). *10 demographic trends that are shaping the U.S. and the world*. Pew Research Center. Retrieved from www.pewresearch. org/fact-tank/2016/03/31/10-demographic-trends-that-are-shaping-the-u-s-and-the-world/

Congress, E. (2004). Cultural and ethnic issues in working with culturally diverse patients and their families: Use of the culturagram to promote cultural competency in health care settings. *Social Work in Health Care, 39*(3/4), 249–262. Retrieved from https://pdfs.semanticscholar.org/c21d/d384fa67e3deb4bfd8072ed8210bd 74cf5bd.pdf

Crawford, M. R., Grant, N. S., & Crews, D. A. (2016). Relationships and rap: Using ecomaps to explore the stories of youth who rap. *The British Journal of Social Work, 46*(1), 239–256. Retrieved from https://doi.org/10.1093/bjsw/bcu096

de Arellano, M. A., & Danielson, C. K. (2005). *Culturally modified trauma-focused therapy for treatment of Hispanic trauma victims*. Paper Presented at the Annual San Diego Conference on Child and Family Maltreatment, San Diego, CA.

Erazo, E., & Hazlett-Stevens, H. (2014). Cultural competency and mindfulness-based cognitive therapy for depression. In A. Masuda (Ed.), *Mindfulness and acceptance in multicultural competency* (pp. 93–108). Oakland, CA: New Harbinger Publications.

Estrada, R., & Marksamer, J. (2006). The legal rights of LGBT youth in state custody: What child welfare and juvenile justice professionals need to know. *Child Welfare, 85*(2), 171-194. Retrieved from www.questia.com/library/journal/1P3-1073693281/the-legal-rights-of-lgbt-youth-in-state-custody-what

FitzGerald, C., & Hurst, S. (2017). Implicit bias in healthcare professionals: A systematic review. *BMC Medical Ethics, 18*(1), 19. doi:10.1186/s12910-017-0179-8. Retrieved from https://bmcmedethics.biomedcentral.com/track/pdf/10.1186/ s12910-017-0179-8

Frail, A. (2017, January). *The injustice of Japanese American internment camps resonates strongly to this day*. Retrieved from www.smithsonianmag.com/history/ injustice-japanese-americans-internment-camps-resonates-strongly-180961422/

Gee, G. C., & Ford, C. L. (2011). Structural racism and health inequities: Old issues, new directions. *Du Bois Review, 8*(1), 115–132.

Glickman, N., & Hall, W. (Eds.). (2019). *Language deprivation and deaf mental health*. New York City: Routledge.

Goode, T., & Jones, W. (2004). *Definition of linguistic competence*. The National Center for Cultural Competence. Retrieved from www.nccccurricula.info/linguis ticcompetence.html

Goodman, D. (2014). *Cultural competence for equity and inclusion*. Retrieved from www.dianegoodman.com/documents/TheCulturalCompetenceforEquityandInclu sionl-2pages.pdf

H.R. 253 Family First Prevention Services Act of 2017. Retrieved from www.con gress.gov/bill/115th-congress/house-bill/253/text?q=%7B%22search%22%3A%5 B%22family+first+prevention+services+act%22%5D%7D&r=1

Hannay, C. (2018). *3 Essential tips for working with limited English proficiency youth*. Retrieved from https://centerforadolescentstudies.com/3-tips-for-working-with-limited-english-proficiency-youth/

Hook, J. N., Davis, D. E., Owen, J., Worthington, Jr., E. L., & Utsey, S. O. (2013, July). Cultural humility: Measuring openness to culturally diverse clients. *Journal of Counseling Psychology, 60*(3), 353–366. doi:10.1037/a0032595

Idaho Department of Health and Welfare. (n.d.). *Indian child welfare act: Historical perspective.* Retrieved from https://healthandwelfare.idaho.gov/Children/Indian ChildWelfareAct/HistoricalPerspective/tabid/1363/Default.aspx

Jacobs, J., & Freundlich, M. (2006). Achieving permanency for LGBTQ youth [Special issue]. *Child Welfare: Journal of Policy, Practice, and Program, 85*(2), 299–316.

JBS International Inc.; Georgetown University National Technical Assistance Center for Children's Mental Health. (2014). *Trauma informed care: Perspectives and resources,* (Issue Brief No. 1—Understanding the Impact of Trauma). Retrieved from https://gucchdtacenter.georgetown.edu/TraumaInformedCare/issueBrief1_ UnderstandingImpactTrauma.pdf

The Joint Commission. (2014, November). *A crosswalk of the national standards for culturally and linguistically appropriate services (CLAS) in health and heath care to the joint commission ambulatory health care accreditation standards.* Retrieved from www.jointcommission.org/assets/1/6/Crosswalk_CLAS_AHC_20141110.pdf

Kapila, M., Hines, E., & Searby, M. (2016, October 6). *Why diversity, equity and inclusion Matter.* Retrieved from https://independentsector.org/resource/why-diversity-equity-and-inclusion-matter/

Kosciw, J. G., Greytak, E. A., Diaz, E. M., & Bartkiewicz, M. J. (2010). *The 2009 national school climate survey: The experience of lesbian, gay, bisexual and transgender youth in our nation's schools.* New York, NY: GLSEN (the Gay, Lesbian, and Straight Education Network).

Michaels, C., Rousseau, R., & Yang, Y. (2010). Historical trauma and microaggressions: A framework for culturally-based practice. *Children's Mental Health eReview,* 1–9.

Mosher, D. K., Hook, J. N., Captari, L. E., Davis, D. E., DeBlaere, C., & Owen, J. (2017). Cultural humility: A therapeutic framework for engaging diverse clients. *Practice Innovations, 2*(4), 221–233. Retrieved from http://dx.doi.org/10.1037/pri0000055

National Center for Education Statistics. (2017). *The condition of education—English language learners in public schools.* Retrieved from https://nces.ed.gov/programs/coe/indicator_cgf.asp.

National Child Traumatic Stress Network. (n.d.a). *Essential elements of a trauma-informed child welfare system.* Retrieved from www.nctsn.org/trauma-informed-care/trauma-informed-systems/child-welfare/essential-elements, National Child Traumatic Stress Network. (n.d.b). *Populations at risk.* Retrieved from www.nctsn. org/what-is-child-trauma/populations-at-risk

National Child Traumatic Stress Network. (2015). *The road to recovery: Supporting children with intellectual and developmental disabilities who have experienced trauma.* Retrieved from http://nctsn.org/products/children-intellectual-and-developmental-disabilities-who-have experienced-trauma

National Health Care for the Homeless Council. (2016). *Improving outcomes through cultural humility.* Retrieved from www.nhchc.org/wp-content/uploads/2016/04/denverrt culturalcompetency.pdf

Office of Disease Prevention and Promotion, Lesbian, Gay, Bisexual, and Transgender Health. (2019). Retrieved from www.healthypeople.gov/2020/topics-objectives/topic/lesbian-gay-bisexual-and-transgender-health

Prevent Child Abuse Iowa Regional Meetings. (2017, September 6–13). *Five key elements of cultural competence* [PowerPoint Slides]. Retrieved from https://pcaiowa.org/downloads/library/eci-cultural-competence-slides.pdf

Public Health Accreditation Board. (2013, December). *Standards and measures, 1.5*, 112–113. Retrieved from www.phaboard.org/wp-content/uploads/PHABSM_WEB_LR1.pdf

Rousseau, C., Oulhote, Y., Ruiz-Casares, M., Cleveland, J., & Greenaway, C. (2017, February 14). Encouraging understanding or increasing prejudices: A cross-sectional survey of institutional influence on health personnel attitudes about refugee claimants' access to health care. *PLoS One, 12*(2), e0170910. doi:10.1371/journal.pone.0170910

Sparrow, S. S., Domenic, V., Cicchetti, D. V., & Saulnier, C. A. (2016). *The Vineland adaptive behavior scales* (3rd ed.) [Measurement Instrument]. Retrieved from www.pearsonclinical.com/psychology/products/100001622/vineland-adaptive-behavior-scales-third-edition-vineland-3.html

University of Minnesota Extension Children, Youth and Families. (2015, March 4). *What is Historical Trauma?* [Video File]. Retrieved from www.youtube.com/watch?v=AWmK314NVrs

U.S. Census Bureau. (2015). *Projections of the size and composition of the U.S. population: 2014 to 2060*. Retrieved from www.census.gov/content/dam/Census/library/publications/2015/demo/p25-1143.pdf

U.S. Department of Health and Human Services, Office of Minority Health. (2016). *National standards for culturally and linguistically appropriate services in health and health care: Compendium of state-sponsored national CLAS standards implementation activities*. Washington, DC: U.S. Department of Health and Human Services.

Ward, B., Dahlhamer, J. M., Galinsky, A. M., & Joestl, S. S. (2014, July 15). Sexual orientation and health among U.S. adults: National health interview survey, 2013. *National Health Statistics Reports*. Number 77.

Woronoff, R., Estrada, R., & Sommer, S. (2006). *Out of the margins: A report on regional listening forums highlighting the experiences of lesbian, gay, bisexual, transgender, and questioning youth in care*. Washington, DC: Child Welfare League of America & Lambda Legal.

5

RESIDENTIAL TRANSFORMATION

Successful Strategies and Examples

Janice LeBel, Martha J. Holden,
Deborah A. Fauntleroy, Leticia Galyean,
William R. Martin, and Carlene Casciano-McCann

Introduction & Background

"Timing isn't everything, but it's a big thing" (Cook, 2018). When the first wave of change comes, some people pause, observe, and hesitate while others adopt the change early on. Once the wave is established, a curious phenomenon occurs: *The fear of missing out.* This phenomenon generates urgency and compels those on the fence to jump in. More change then follows (Hindley & Vassy, 2016).

This type of change process is currently underway within the residential field serving youth and families. A wave of reform started more than a decade ago in response to an admonition to *"change or die!"* (American Association of Children's Residential Centers, 2001). The reform ushered in several change processes including the Building Bridges Initiative (BBI), which brought together a wide range of constituents to focus on fundamental residential change through partnership-focused, youth-guided, family-driven practice improvement. The goal of BBI was to improve and sustain positive residential outcomes for youth and their families served through this form of intervention (LeBel, Caldwell, Martone, Levison-Johnson, & Collins, 2017).

Early adopters of BBI and other like-minded leaders braved new ground with exciting innovations. Impressive results followed, such as: Reduced use of restraint and seclusion, improved functioning of youth and families, improved home/family connection, shorter lengths of stay, and concerted permanency focus. One bold leader, Dr. Jim Dalton, CEO of Damar in Indiana, was so inspired by BBI and confident in their transformative work, the organization decided to guarantee their outcomes, meaning "if a youth requires a return to care, Damar intervenes in the clinical and financial support and funds a return to their program" (LeBel et al., 2017, p. 25).

76 Janice LeBel et al.

The residential transformation is now being bolstered by the Family First Prevention Services Act (FFPSA). This new legislation, like BBI, is re-envisioning the child-serving system, focusing on strengthening families, and seeking to substantially improve outcomes for children and families. The FFPSA is also "shifting long-held mindsets and committing to a different way of working with communities" (Milner, 2018). The central mechanism for compelling this change is funding. The legislation shifts how federal IV-E dollars can be spent to prevent foster care placement, broaden the scope of applicable services, and focus on incorporating trauma-based knowledge and evidence-based interventions to achieve the positive outcomes. The net effect of FFPSA, BBI and similar change efforts is galvanizing residential transformation. Astute residential providers realize they must evolve to stay competitive in the industry and ride the wave of change.

Residential transformation is becoming the new norm, and leaders are making bold changes. Some leaders are redesigning their intervention models and working in the home. For example, the FACTS program in Minnesota developed a successful hybrid intervention that reduced lengths of stay, recidivism, and costs with a phased approach: a) 2–4 weeks of intensive skills-focused family treatment in the home, b) 30 days in the residential setting with the same treatment team and approach, and c) 4–6 months back in the home when the youth leaves the residence (FACTS, 2019). Other providers are shifting to smaller, homelike settings in the community. Some leaders are making permanency the primary goal of care (see Chapter 6: Residential Intervention Strategies to Accelerate Permanency). Many organizations are hiring families and peers. All of the innovators recognize out-of-home placement is not a destination but rather the locus of an *intervention*— underscoring the strategic, time-limited intent of the service to help youth and families stay connected to each other, their home, and their community (LeBel et al., 2017).

Premise and Methodology for Change

The essential reason for transformation reflects a deep commitment by residential leaders to continually improve the outcomes of their service. Most leaders recognize their interventions are not as effective as desired and want to capitalize on evidence that supports positive outcomes (James, Thompson, & Ringle, 2017). By implementing key components associated with improved intervention like: Meaningful youth, family and staff engagement, pragmatic skills development, time spent in the home/community, and effective integration with aftercare supports and the discharge environment, leaders are addressing the concerns raised about possible harmful effects of group living environments (family/social/educational disruption, adverse functional impact). Moreover, leaders are changing the trajectory of residential intervention by creating short-term models, developing more in-home supports, and finding new methods of integrating services in the community with families (LeBel et al., 2017).

The methods for residential transformation vary by provider. Each leader creates their own route to redesign their service. Some leaders start their change process because they are compelled by clinical reasons (e.g., operational efficiency, adverse events). Some leaders are compelled by an outside entity, such as an oversight authority, that has expressed concerns about the service and has mandated change. Some leaders are compelled by fiscal reasons and are either supported through enhanced funding or threatened with viability (James et al., 2017). Regardless of the impetus to change, transformation starts with a commitment to: Change current practice, identify obstacles to improved outcomes, work with all constituents, craft solutions, and take actionable steps to improve outcomes (Litré, Michels, Walter, & Burke, 2018).

The core elements of residential transformation are remarkably similar. Common to all change efforts are: a) Strong leadership with vision and a goal, b) focused workforce support and development, c) active youth and family engagement, and d) a clear commitment to relevant service revision that is trauma-informed, culturally and linguistically competent, data- and quality-driven, and fiscally flexible. Like the process and method, the implementation staging and focus on these elements varies by organization and circumstance (LeBel et al., 2017).

Successful Examples

Examples of residential transformation offer important guidance and pragmatic assistance for leaders contemplating significant change. Three organizations that are transforming their residential programs and improving their outcomes through a values-based commitment to meeting the needs of those they serve and their staff have written their "transformation stories." These providers represent large and small organizations from different parts of the country and their leaders are available to readers who want to learn more about their change process (see Author Contact Information).

Seneca Family of Agencies Leticia Galyean

Founded in 1985 by several individuals including founder and CEO, Ken Berrick, Seneca Family of Agencies (Seneca) is a large multi-service agency located in California that annually serves over 18,000 individuals in community-based, educational, and residential intervention services. For 33 years, Seneca has been expanding continuums of support for system-involved families and developing innovative systemic solutions to better serve impacted populations. The primary driver of this change process has been a fundamental and unwavering commitment to ensure success for each youth and family served by Seneca. Indeed, this commitment was in response to what was seen as a great injustice—foster youth with significant mental health and behavioral needs being moved between foster homes and residential treatment settings, compounding the trauma of disrupted attachments, inconsistent caregiving and severed social support networks. This led to Seneca's "Unconditional Care" treatment model and book, *Unconditional Care: Relationship-Based, Behavioral Intervention with Vulnerable Children and Families*, written by Ken Berrick and Clinical Director Dr. John Sprinson in 2010. The model is based on a commitment to do "whatever it takes" to support families dealing with profound trauma, complex stress, and systemic and sustained oppression.

However, the successes youth experienced with Seneca's Unconditional Care model did not always effectively transfer to their homes and communities, at times resulting in readmission to residential care. In response, Seneca's leadership brought the agency's skills and resources to community environments through home and school-based services and family-driven and team-based service planning, supported by a flexible service continuum. Seneca helped bring legislation to California that expanded Wraparound using blended mental health and Aid to Families with Dependent Children funding and Intensive Treatment Foster Care statewide.

Based on feedback from youth and families through Seneca's Youth Advisory Board, Caregiver Advisory Board, bi-annual satisfaction surveys, and other experts in the field, Seneca's residential programs became part of a broader continuum of care within the organization and across the broader community system, with youth transitioning from Seneca's residential programs to families supported by Wraparound or Intensive Treatment Foster Care services. Between 2000 and 2010, there was a 40 percent reduction in the number of youths placed in residential care (Danielson & Lee, 2010) through the collective efforts of Seneca and other providers and public social services and mental health partners across the state. With this change, the service needs of those remaining in group homes intensified, yet programming and funding models remained unchanged, so youth with the highest needs continued to experience poor outcomes.

Launch of Residentially-Based Services (RBS)

To address these poor outcomes, Seneca and providers from four counties in California agreed to participate in California's Residentially-Based Services (RBS) pilot program, which resulted from successful legislation by state leaders and advocates. The intent of RBS was to design program and funding models to improve permanency outcomes, while not increasing the significant cost to the state. Although program strategies differed by county (for county specifics see: www.rbsreform.org), a stakeholder group and subsequent efforts established universal practices of the RBS model including:

1. An early and intense engagement of families.
2. A focus on therapeutic enhancement of child well-being and, at the same time, immediately pursuing permanency planning and concurrent planning in case the intended adult cannot be the youth's permanent caregiver.
3. Family services to help parents improve their parenting knowledge and skills.
4. Post-permanency support that provides ongoing aftercare services to youth and families.

Seneca Family of Agencies, in collaboration with Edgewood Center and Catholic Charities/St. Vincent's School for Boys, partnered with San Francisco County to pilot RBS. Seneca served a total of 25 families (up to eight youth and their families at a time), for an average length of stay of 9.2 months (including residential placement and community-based step-down services), reflecting a significantly reduced length of stay as compared with Seneca's previous Community Treatment Facility, which served up to 18 youth at a time and had an average length of stay in the residential facility of 13.9 months.

This new RBS model maintained a central focus on family engagement and preparation for transition to a home setting from day one. RBS practitioners focused on providing behavioral and emotional stabilization for each child, getting them ready to heal at home and in the community, rather than in the residential milieu. A key goal was to intervene intensively with each youth and family, building upon their sense of hopefulness to help them achieve significant changes in their attitudes and behaviors. Supporting children and families when they were doing well provided momentum to increase the pace of reunification and motivation to utilize community supports. In many cases, the initial, intensive treatment focused on reducing the effects of trauma through evidence-based treatments, such as Trauma-Focused Cognitive Behavioral Therapy. At the same time, RBS staff supported family members, including them in designing their child's individualized program, inviting regular visits and participation in the milieu, and using individual and family therapy to provide reparative therapeutic experiences between the youth and their family.

Discharge planning and use of parallel community services (both by RBS family services staff and facility-based staff) began as soon as a child enrolled. As in Wraparound, teams comprised of the most significant stakeholders in the child and family's life met regularly, and decisions were driven by the youth and families as opposed to service providers and staff.

80 Janice LeBel et al.

The parallel, pre-discharge, and post-discharge community services closely followed wraparound philosophy (www.senecafoa.org/wraparound), with RBS family services staff intervening more frequently and intensively at the beginning of the process, followed by the increasing transition of each youth and family to supports provided by partner agencies and other formal and informal resources in the community.

With the RBS model development and other state efforts came core areas of transformation in both practice and philosophy (LeBel & Galyean, 2017).

Next Steps in the Ongoing Transformation for Seneca

While RBS represented an important shift in the approach to residential services, the challenges experienced helped to refine the next iteration of residential intervention in California. Some of the most notable lessons included the following: Ensure that all team members participate in permanency planning—including child welfare workers and milieu counselors alike, create funding structures that can flex to the individualized needs of each youth and family, and initiate permanency transitioning as soon as possible. Based on the lessons learned from RBS implementation and the ongoing leadership of public and private stakeholders, California's Continuum of Care Reform (CCR) was created, as well as the recent launch of Short-Term Residential Therapeutic Programs (STRTPs) and Therapeutic Foster Homes (TFCs). The first STRTPs are just now opening in the state, many evolving out of existing group home placements.

The initial outcomes of Seneca's STRTP programs show promising stabilization and permanency outcomes with recidivism to the STRTPs at 2% (one reentry of 46 total enrollments) since April 1, 2017. Seneca hopes to be a leader in eliminating the need for STRTP placements by focusing on the implementation of TFC Professional Parent homes—a professionally-trained family, ready to meet the emotional and behavioral needs of youth in their home, while preparing them for a permanent transition back to their family. With the focus to do whatever it takes to effectively serve youth and families with the highest needs—diversity, equity, and inclusion are a central focus of Seneca today. Ensuring that the workforce is culturally competent, responsive, and reflective of the families served is at the center of efforts. Utilizing assessment tools like 360 evaluations, IAT (Implicit-Bias Assessment Test), and comprehensive organizational health assessments (through the National Child Welfare Workforce Institute), Seneca understands how critical the cultural health of the youth, families, and communities is and what can be done to strengthen approaches of support. Incorporating the voices and lived wisdom of youth (current and former clients) through youth advisory boards, adopting service standard frameworks (i.e., The Joint Commission, CLAS (culturally and linguistically appropriate services) standards, creating employee affinity groups (Employee Resource Groups) to support employees in this complex work, establishing a full time Director of Diversity Equity and Inclusion, and creating an embedded graduate degree program for staff who otherwise couldn't afford graduate school, to name a few, have been some concrete strategies implemented in order to address this critical skill set for the effective delivery of complex family supports. Seneca believes that the work of cultural and linguistic competence and high engagement with families is never finished and remains committed to staying on the path of continuous quality improvement. Seneca believes people can change and grow—and that includes the organization itself!

Waterford Country School Bill Martin

Waterford Country School (WCS), serving children and families for nearly 100 years, began as a family business in Brooklyn, New York, in the 1920s. In the home of the Schacht family, both gifted and special-needs students were provided the education they could not get in public schools. This program grew into a 24-hour program and in the 1930s moved to a 700-acre farm in Connecticut, which now serves as WCS's main campus. Over the past 30 years, the program has diversified and now offers a variety of programs and services including three different types of residential interventions with between 30 and 46 beds at any point in time. WCS also operates a short-term (two-week) intensive family treatment program with between 20 and 28 beds. WCS also provides therapeutic foster care, adoption, and outpatient services, as well as school, afterschool, summer camp, and outdoor education programs.

A Sense of Urgency

During 2006–2007, there were three significant injuries to young people as a result of using restraints during crisis events. WCS leadership and staff as well as the Connecticut Department of Children and Families (state licensing body) were alarmed by these injuries and were determined to find a way to reduce the risk of future similar events.

Through the examination of policies, procedures, training records, and incident reports, it became clear that the key to better outcomes was to address the relationships between staff and the young people and focus on the needs of the young people. WCS also identified a need for a cultural change. In order to decrease aggressive behaviors and reduce restraints, staff, young people, and families would need to change the way they viewed and interacted with each other. WCS decided to implement CARE, Children and Residential Experiences: Creating Conditions for Change (Holden, 2009) and began a university/agency collaboration that was transformative. CARE, a principle-based program model, is designed to create the conditions for positive change by focusing on developmental relationships and developmentally appropriate practice. By incorporating the six evidence-informed principles (relationship-based, developmentally-focused, trauma-informed, family-involved, competency-centered, and ecologically oriented) and three key processes (reflective practice, data-informed decision making, and participatory management practices) throughout the organization and into daily practice, organizations can support staff members and families in providing normative experiences that help children achieve a healthier developmental pathway (Holden, 2009). The leadership at WCS made an unwavering commitment to implement the model—unconditionally. In effect, the agency went "all in."

The Transformation

With support from the Connecticut Department of Children and Families, in January of 2009 WCS began the journey of organizational transformation in a week-long training and planning session followed by three additional days of training trainers. This new way of thinking was not an "easy sell." Old paradigms such as "children will not learn unless they have consequences" that had guided WCS guide for years had to be surrendered. Staff learned to shift their thinking from

- enforcing rules to setting expectations;
- trying to control the children to establishing a sense of order;
- "treating families" to partnering with families;
- and consistency across children to consistency within children.

In addition, staff learned that much of the challenging behavior is pain-based from past trauma and negative experiences, and, by addressing the behavior with harsh consequences, staff are basically compounding their pain. Staff learned that traumatized children are often unable to meet expectations and how to identify those times and respond with flexibility.

Implementation

Implementation occurred at all levels: External organizations and community partners, leadership, supervisors and clinical staff, child and youth care/teachers/caregivers, and children and families. The first year of implementation, all 300 WCS staff, including full and part time-staff members, support workers such as food service, maintenance, and business office staff received the training. The decision to include all staff was an enormous investment and commitment, which was very well received by the non-program staff. This decision was critical to achieving a sense of organizational congruence.

Each program team evolved at their own pace. There were no administrative edicts—short of being faithful to the new concepts. Each individual staff member had to learn to think at a more complex level and develop a different mindset in order to change their practices and strategies while continuously doing the work. WCS leadership and supervisors worked intensely to help each staff evolve, even those who resisted the change process, by adopting the notion that staff want to do well in their work, and it was up to WCS to create continual opportunities for success. WCS invested heavily in training and supporting supervisors as they were the primary guides and support for direct-care staff. Supervisors did less direct care work and provided coaching, feedback, support, and guidance, allowing the direct care staff to develop relationships and skills. Supervisory sessions were focused on helping staff understand and apply the principles. Now regular supervision focuses on reflective practice, training, work groups, and forums for discussion and problem solving.

The Results

As relationship-based and trauma-informed practice increased, the use of restraint in the residential programs dropped immediately and remains at unprecedented low levels. It was a slower process of implementation in the education program. Using a data-informed approach to analyze and respond strategically, it was discovered that high use was coming from interactions with the younger students who had challenges with self-regulation. Using the framework of the six principles, a deeper focus on the ecological factors, the setting conditions, and increasing family involvement resulted in a decrease in the use of restraints. It required a year to fully realize the changes, but the use of restraints also significantly decreased and remains a rare event. Research conducted by WCS in partnership with Cornell University has demonstrated a positive impact on the reduction in the use of psychotropic medications and restraints (WCS does not utilize seclusion) (Nunno, Smith, Martin, & Butcher, 2017). Currently WCS is studying the impact on staff injuries and length of time staff chooses to stay employed at WCS. Table 5.1 shows the decrease in restraint rates over a 15-year period of time. At this time, there has been no data mining related to factors of culture, race, gender, or any related assessment of disproportionality.

Data-Informed, Youth and Family-Involved Decision Making

The agency/university partnership has provided the opportunity for extended data analysis to continually inform practice. The data-informed decision-making processes of the CARE model include staff practice surveys, which solicit staff knowledge, beliefs, and practice in relationship to the principles and a young people's perception survey of staff's interactions according to these principles. These surveys are used to guide implementation as well as help to sustain and maintain fidelity to the principles. The young people's voice in the survey process is particularly meaningful as they share how they experience staff's use of the model.

84 Janice LeBel et al.

Table 5.1

Traditional Residential Placement	Residentially-Based Services (RBS)
Purpose: Long-term placement intended to provide a stable, protective home for youth to grow up in.	Purpose: Short-term service that integrates milieu, school, and community-based interventions to stabilize and transition youth to community settings.
Interventions: Targeted at changing the youth's behaviors and needs	Interventions: Intended to support youth's improved safety coupled with equal focus on strengthening the family and community
Caregivers: Staff serve as fictive family and "protectors" of youth in placement	Caregivers: Wide net is cast to locate and engage all available family and build permanent relationships
Systems and Services: Work in isolation and youth "passed off" as they transition to new programs and service levels	Systems and Services: Integrated both across levels of intensity and across sectors
Permanency Plan: Potential placements and preparation occur when youth shows improved behaviors that indicate readiness for living in a community setting	Permanency Plan: Begins before/at intake including identification and engagement of lifelong connections, who remain engaged throughout the residential intervention
Decision-Making Approach: Professional-driven treatment plan	Decision-Making Approach: Child and Family Team-driven

Input from the young people is encouraged and integrated into the structure of WCS. The residential treatment program has a Youth Council and there is a Student Council in the school. Both Councils are actively involved in reviewing operations and planning activities. The Youth Council has also been working on developing the welcoming process for new residents including preparing baskets of materials (such as hygiene supplies) that new residents need and have been working with the staff to enhance the room design including colors, lighting, flooring, and furnishings. Their input has taken a lead in improvements in each of these areas.

After implementation of CARE, a panel of family members was convened so that they could share their perceptions of WCS and the new approach. Family members commented on feeling for the first time that their children were understood and feeling a sense of hope that things would get better. Not long after this forum, one of the parents was appointed to the Board of Trustees, joining a former residential service recipient who also sits on the Board. All parents in all of the programs are surveyed either at the point of their child's discharge or annually. The results of these surveys are published for all staff to see and used to inform the agency's annual planning process.

A New Organizational Culture

After three years of an intense and focused change process, the new way of thinking became more natural, the environment more peaceful, and the staff more comfortable. Over the last eight years, visitors from all over the world have come to observe the program, and they typically comment on the sense of calm, kindness, positive interactions, and congruence in thinking. Even when witnessing staff working with young people expressing challenging behaviors, visitors observe confident and positive staff working together to address the needs of the youth. They observe staff partnering with struggling youth and providing support during the struggle, which enables the young person to enter back into the program more quickly and successfully.

The more the children and families struggle, the more support they receive. For example, if time at home does not go well, instead of decreasing the time spent at home, additional time at home is arranged as quickly as possible with the supports in place to best ensure success. When a child has an unsuccessful experience during an activity in the community, staff quickly identify the supports necessary for a successful experience and schedule that opportunity with the supports in place as quickly as possible. The children and families are provided with whatever they need to get through their "moment" and then back into regular activities and into the community as soon as possible. Sometimes it is tangible things like food or gas cards to reduce the financial stress. (The food service staff prides themselves on the quality of food baskets made for children to take home to the families who would like them.) Other times it is a phone call to provide support to the family and child when at home. Children and families are not defined by their challenging moments. Everyone works to help them establish a pattern of successful experiences.

A new way of looking at their relationship with their child is introduced to families from the first interaction and through every contact thereafter as staff and families discuss how things work at WCS. Through these conversations, families begin to think differently about the relationship they have with WCS. Parents can call or come anytime to WCS, or their child can spend time at home whenever the family wants. Their child does not need to earn things and none of their child's things are ever taken away. Also, their child will never be punished or denied an activity, since all activities have a purpose. Family education strategies are personalized through the discussions about their child and through the constant staff and family interactions. For example, some family members are provided written materials and/or invited to attend training sessions specific to their individual needs and what works best for each individual family.

WCS is now seven years into this process, yet every day the staff are challenged to stay true to the principles and practices and stay congruent in thinking and practice. It is hard work to maintain strong relationships with the young people and families we serve and, equally important, with each other.

WCS participates in a community of practice with other agencies who have implemented this model. It is a phenomenal experience to interact with other agencies who share the same passion for quality care for youth and families and who are involved in the implementation practices that generate better outcomes for youth and families. The culture that has evolved out of the implementation of the principle-based model has created a very desirable work and treatment environment. WCS regularly mines its data to measure the effects of the work as well as to keep fidelity with the model. With the goal of building and maintaining positive and productive relationships at the forefront and guided by regular reflective practice, the vast majority of daily interactions have taken on a positive and supportive tone.

WCS has evolved to a higher level of thinking and therefore a more sophisticated and effective culture and set of responses to the issues and needs expressed by the young people and their families. Deeply embedded in all interactions are key concepts including:

- The critical importance of therapeutic relationships as the primary conduit to effective treatment;
- the understanding and appreciation of the effects of trauma on the young people and families;
- the importance of family involvement in any level of work with young people.

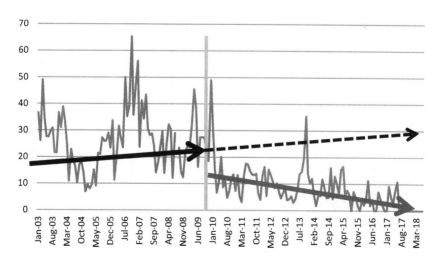

Figure 5.1 Waterford Country School Residential Treatment over the Last Fourteen Years Rate of Restraints per 1,000 Bed Days

St. Mary's Home for Children Carlene Casciano-McCann

Founded in 1877 as an orphanage in an Episcopal church, St. Mary's Home for Children has evolved into a multi-service human service agency located in North Providence, Rhode Island. St. Mary's provides residential interventions, special education services, office-based therapy, and a number of community-based programs to young people and families affected by trauma and mental illness. St. Mary's serves 450–500 clients a year.

St. Mary's change process began in 2006 when the agency transitioned from a behavioral approach that included point and level systems to a relational approach adapted from Holston United Methodist Home for Children. The decision to become a kinder, gentler residential provider was challenging because of the relatively drastic change in philosophy. At this time, St. Mary's also began to dismantle the seclusion rooms and focused on restraint reduction. Needless to say, the staff turnover during those first few years was high (approximately 35%), and the confusion about expectations created a culture of permissiveness that was just as ineffective as the strict point and level system that had been in place. It took a number of years and the addition of a strong focus on providing trauma-informed care before the agency had fully embraced the new "us."

St. Mary's leadership and staff understood that the transformational journey was not over because youth were still languishing in care, and young people continued to cycle back to St. Mary's multiple times, instead of finding permanency. This created questions about the effectiveness of the residential interventions. St. Mary's provided young people with a safe environment, free from abuse and neglect with strong clinical services, yet the end result was often a return back to residential services. Just as heartbreaking were the youth who had nowhere to go. The loss of hope was devastating, and a decline in functioning was all but guaranteed. Because of this, it was decided that the agency needed to do better and focus on supporting family connections and permanency.

In 2015, St. Mary's leadership looked at research regarding the effectiveness of residential treatment, and there were very few studies that supported long-term residential treatment. During the search, St. Mary's stumbled upon the Building Bridges Initiative (BBI) website (www.buildingbridges4 youth.org), which included the Joint Resolution (JR)—a consensus document that provided agreed upon foundational values and principles that should guide residential interventions. Reading the Joint Resolution led the agency to conduct a deeper dive into the site: White papers, tip sheets, and resources. This became the next step in the agency's evolution. Agency leadership and staff liked that the framework was not prescriptive and allowed for flexibility and creativity in carrying out BBI values and principles. Most important to the organization was ensuring that the BBI values permeated all aspects of agency functioning and that staff "bought in."

Transformation Process

To prepare for a January 2016 launch of the Building Bridges Initiative, St. Mary's leaders methodically and systematically created a plan for implementation that included: a) Learning from others, b) creating a program design and logic model, c) embedding implementation into the strategic plan, d) revising policies and procedures, e) re-writing job descriptions, f) partnering with others with specific expertise, and g) creating a team.

The first step was to educate staff. Dr. Jeremy Kohomban and his team at The Children's Village in Dobbs Ferry, NY, graciously agreed to host the St. Mary's team for a day to discuss their BBI journey. This energized the BBI champions as they saw what was possible for the youth and families St. Mary's serves. This was followed with additional training by Beth Caldwell, National Director of BBI, reinforcing the new direction and creating additional enthusiasm. The program's clinicians, supervisors, and direct care staff recognized the benefits of moving forward but had some understandable hesitancy, questioning if there were sufficient resources to implement all aspects of the Initiative. Leaders acknowledged the deficits and approached the next phase of development from a strength-based perspective, identifying areas of strength consistent with BBI values and principles. From here, it was a matter of putting the puzzle pieces together.

The St. Mary's team created a program design and logic model based on the BBI framework. This provided the roadmap for the agency's implementation effort. With the logic model, it was clear that St. Mary's brought strengths and resources to the Initiative. The logic model also identified some of the resources the organization would need for successful implementation of a residential best practice framework.

BBI implementation was built into the strategic plan, focusing on one major practice enhancement at a time to ensure success. The first year, the focus was on family engagement/family-driven care. Youth voice and choice was the focus of the second year. The strategic plan is organized around ongoing implementation in the same way.

Job descriptions were rewritten to include a commitment to BBI values and principles, so now when new employees receive their job description, they see the agency's commitment. When reviewing the program's policies and procedures, the word "family" was conspicuously absent from the policies that focused on treatment. The BBI values, language, and philosophy served as a guide for revising program policies. Wherever the St. Mary's team members looked, staff would understand the importance of living residential best practice values and principles. A mandatory BBI training for all new residential staff members was also developed. To ensure the agency's commitment to family-driven care, the first item on the agenda at every agency meeting is "family engagement." The expectation is for staff to share a story about the positive work and outcomes they see with the families they are working with. This constant repetition and the opportunity to share successes drives home the importance of partnership with families.

Hiring a Parent Support Partner, a person with lived experience, was key to transformation success, but St. Mary's did not have experience with this. Through a contract with the Parent Support Network of Rhode Island, a full time Parent Partner was hired. This person has an unmatched ability to engage parents, staff, and youth. She was kind, compassionate, and relentless in her pursuit of the underlying causes of parental "disengagement." The Parent Partner, in concert with other members of the team, removed barriers and helped the residential staff understand the parent's perspective. She supported families in obtaining resources, provided transportation, and helped to meet basic needs. Strong partnerships with families developed as a result of this relationship. The Parent Partner and the St. Mary's team lived the concept of "Residential without Walls," creating a fluidity of service between the family's home and the residential campus. Despite Rhode Island's small size, transportation can be an obstacle, so efforts were made to find and obtain grant funding to assist families with transportation.

St. Mary's also created a Family Liaison role. This is a person who works in the residential houses, community, and family's homes. The Family Liaison works with youth to determine their interests and enrolls them in activities in their communities. They may share transportation duties with the family. Family Liaisons spend time with youth and families in the community to reinforce open lines of communication and share interventions that help support the youth.

The Family Therapist rounds out the BBI team providing clinical treatment to the families. This takes place in the setting of the family's preference, typically in their homes.

All three members of the team provide aftercare services for at least six months post-discharge. Continuity of care coupled with the relationships developed during the residential intervention help maintain that successful partnership with the family through reunification. The aftercare team can also include the youth's individual clinician, natural supports, or other community providers. The team is tailored to fit each family's individual needs.

There are so many considerations in launching a new initiative. An often-overlooked part of the process is the initial meeting with the youth and family. Fortunately, St. Mary's Clinical Director understood that "You don't get a second chance to make a first impression." So, with help from the Parent Partner, the program worked to ensure that the intake and admissions process was welcoming and nonjudgmental. The families choose where the initial meetings take place. St. Mary's reinforces the commitment to partnering with families and, more importantly, offering hope. The family is also introduced to many members of the team who may interact with their child.

Families are also provided the BBI Tip Sheet for Families Considering a Residential Program (www.buildingbridges4youth.org). It is imperative that this initial meeting puts parents at ease and makes them feel welcome. The Parent Partner is instrumental in this endeavor. Their lived experience helps ease the parent's fears and reinforces that they are not alone.

St. Mary's encourages face to face contact with family at least three times a week—known as family time—and daily phone contact between youth and family. Parents had become accustomed to getting calls when their child had exhibited challenging behaviors. To provide a different experience, now staff report the "good stuff," which helps family members change old patterns of thinking and assumptions about their child.

Once concept of family-driven care was internalized and driven into practice, the strategic focus shifted to Youth Voice and Choice. Consistent with the Parent Partner role development, St. Mary's sought external assistance and expertise and found Foster Forward, an agency that helps youth in care develop their leadership skills, among many other things. St. Mary's partnered with Foster Forward to bring a Youth Engagement Specialist on board to push this initiative. The addition of a Youth Engagement Specialist added a much-needed dynamic to the existing Youth Council, assisting the Clinical Director by having youth trained in interviewing skills so that they participate in second interviews for residential staff. Youth served at St. Mary's have participated in twice yearly strategic plan presentations, reviewed and revised relevant policies and procedures, advocated for child welfare issues at the Rhode Island State House, assisted in staff training from a youth's perspective, and are preparing to run their own treatment team meetings.

During the second year, St. Mary's focused efforts on Family Search and Engagement due to the number of youth who still come through the agency's doors seemingly unattached to family. The Youth Engagement Specialist meets with every youth within the first few days of admission to complete The Youth Connection Scale (Jones & Laliberte, 2013). A thorough record review is also conducted to look for possible connections and work with the state agency to determine appropriateness of contact. The goal is to ensure that every young person has a connection in the community.

While St. Mary's is still a relative newcomer to residential best practices, program leaders recognized that some initial ideals and expectations were not being carried out consistently (e.g., daily calls from staff to family, expectation of family time occurring three times per week). The leadership team met to discuss this and recognized that turnover in house leadership led to misunderstanding and misinformation about expectations. The leadership team also discovered that, when the focus shifted to implementing youth voice and choice, family engagement was not being as closely monitored. This led to "drift." The agency needed a reset and called together program leadership, clinicians, Family Liaisons, a Parent Partner, a Youth Engagement

Specialist, and Administrators to reaffirm the commitment and clarify the expectations. If there is a lesson to be learned it is that the entire team should come together to assess the success of the initiative, clarify expectations, and celebrate the good work being done at least a twice a year. Since St. Mary's started its effort to implement BBI principles and practice, length of stay has been reduced from 7.1 months (2015) to 4.7 months (2017). The use of restraints has also decreased by 20 percent, which the residential supervisors attribute to youth enrollment in community activities and an increase in family time and/or time with other important adults in the youth's lives.

As St. Mary's continues its BBI implementation, there are three main areas for future focus: Permanency, cultural and linguistic competence, and supporting undocumented youth and families. Family search and engagement practices will be strengthened in addition to strengthening the working relationship with the state child welfare agency to ensure greater urgency when working on finding permanent connections for youth. Cultural and linguistic competence will also be key areas of additional focus and attention in order to be more responsive to the values, preferences, experiences, and languages of the families and children served. St. Mary's is committed to bringing greater awareness and education on privilege, internalized oppression, and institutional racism to help staff understand how the program may be contributing to oppressive practices as well as understand the negative impacts on those served. In addition, the agency will focus on outreach to allies in the community to help support undocumented youth and families.

St. Mary's does not believe that the work of implementing the BBI framework will ever be completely done because, as an organization and as individuals, learning is an evolving process. The BBI framework gives residential providers an excellent foundation for improving service delivery and approaching youth and families from a holistic perspective, which, in turn, supports better outcomes.

Conclusion

Residential transformation is happening. This change is being supported by industry imperatives, initiatives, and federal legislation, all of which is compelling those with fear of missing out to mobilize. But leading change successfully is complicated. Business leaders report that transformation efforts often produce mediocre results, and most organizations have learned how to avoid complete failure rather than learned how to succeed. Organizations that do succeed have endurance and "build a deep commitment at all levels of the organization from the outset and prepare for the difficult phase of sustaining change after the initial enthusiasm disappears" (Litré et al., 2018).

Each of the leaders who shared their transformation story in this chapter built a deep commitment to change throughout the organization. These leaders implemented change with a multi-faceted perspective: a) A sense of urgency that compelled them to action and b) recognition that transformative work requires a long-term commitment to the change process—because change is hard. Each leader also implemented change collaboratively with staff and constituents. Moreover, they imbedded a process of continual oversight, monitoring, and communication. In short, each of these leaders and organizations committed to a long-term effort to ensure success (Litré et al., 2018).

A theme that emerged from the literature as well as from the featured agencies is the need for "total buy-in," commitment, and leadership (James et al., 2017). Evident throughout each example is how the leadership not only led change but drove transformation. Total buy-in was described by WSC as going "all in," and St. Mary's similarly emphasized staff buy-in to ensure the values permeated everything. Commitment was also key. Seneca described the primary driver of their change process as a fundamental and unwavering commitment to do whatever it takes to support youth and families. Ultimately, what distinguishes these innovators and leaders is not the *fear of missing out* but the absence of fear and the courage and conviction to embrace change and strive to deliver the most effective, relevant service for youth and families.

References

American Association of Children's Residential Centers. (2001). *Contributions to residential treatment*. Washington, DC: Author.

Cook, G. (2018, January 9). Timing is everything. *Scientific American*. Retrieved from www.scientificamerican.com/article/timing-is-everything1/

Danielson, C., & Lee, H. (2010). *Foster care in California: Achievements and challenges*. Public Policy Institute of California. Retrieved from www.ppic.org/content/pubs/report/R_510CDR.pdf

FACTS. (2019). *Collaborative intensive bridging services*. Family and Children Therapy in Minnesota website. Retrieved from www.facts-mn.org/services/cibs/collaborative-bridging-cibs

Hindley, S., & Vassy, S. (2016). *FOMO: A new tool to drive organizational change*. Deloitte. Retrieved from https://www2.deloitte.com/content/dam/Deloitte/us/Documents/human-capital/us-cons-fomo.pdf

Holden, M. J. (2009). *Children and residential experiences: Creating conditions for change*. Arlington, VA: Child Welfare League of America.

James, S., Thompson, R., & Ringle, J. (2017). The implementation of evidence-based practices in residential care: Outcomes, processes, and barriers. *Journal of Emotional and Behavioral Disorders, 25*(1), 4–18.

Jones, A. S., & LaLiberte, T. (2013). Measuring youth connections: A component of relational permanence for foster youth. *Children and Youth Services Review, 35*(3), 509–517.

LeBel, J., Caldwell, B., Martone, W., Levison-Johnson, J., & Collins, J. (2017, July). *Implementing effective short-term residential interventions: A building bridges initiative guide.* Retrieved from http://buildingbridges4youth.org/sites/default/files/BBI%20Short%20Term%20Residential%20Intervention%20Guide.pdf

LeBel, J., & Galyean, L. (2017, December). *BBI case study: Leading innovation outside the comfort zone: The Seneca family of agencies journey.* Retrieved from www.buildingbridges4youth.org/products/tools

Litré, P., Michels, D., Walter, S., & Burke, M. (2018). *Soul searching: True transformations start within.* Bain & Company. Retrieved from www.bain.com/insights/soul-searching-true-transformations-start-within/

Milner, J. (2018, July 24). *Testimony to the United States house of representatives committee on ways and means subcommittee on human resources.* Retrieved on October 19, 2018, from www.acf.hhs.gov/olab/resource/testimony-of-jerry-milner-on-family-first-prevention-services-act

Nunno, M., Smith, E., Martin, W., & Butcher, S. (2017). Benefits of embedding research into practice: An agency-university collaboration. *Child Welfare, 94*(3), 113–133.

Author Contact Information

Carlene Casciano-McCann, LMHC/Executive Director
Patricia A. Olney-Murphy, LICSW, MPA/Clinical Director
St. Mary's Home for Children
420 Fruit Hill Avenue/North Providence, RI 02911
(401) 353-3900 ext. 218
cmccann@smhfc.org/polney@smhfc.org

Leticia Galyean, LCSW/Executive Director
Data, Evaluation, and Strategic Initiatives (DESI)
Seneca Family of Agencies
6925 Chabot Road/Oakland, CA 94618
Cell: 510.760.6858
leticia_galyean@senecacenter.org

William R. Martin, Executive Director
Waterford Country School
78 Hunts Brook Road/Quaker Hill, CT 06375
Tel: 860-442-9454
www.waterfordcountryschool.org/

6

RESIDENTIAL INTERVENTION STRATEGIES TO ACCELERATE PERMANENCY

Christopher Behan, James Lister,
Dianna Walters-Hartley, Lauren Frey,
Evette Jackson, and Marlony Calderon

Introduction

When children or adolescents (hereafter referred to as "youth") and their families find themselves struggling and in contact with behavioral health, juvenile justice, or child welfare systems, they may require help and support from short-term residential interventions to address acute health- and safety-related challenges. Given persuasive research connecting permanency to positive youth outcomes (Salazar et al., 2018), more and more residential interventions are reconsidering their practice models to focus squarely on permanency: Strengthening, building, and maintaining lifelong, supportive family relationships while also building the skills youth and families need for life in the community—even seeking family for young people when necessary. Success is measured by whether residential interventions help youth achieve permanency, defined as returning to and remaining with family. By centering residential interventions on permanency, providers are more likely to achieve safety and well-being for youth served by public child welfare, juvenile justice, and behavioral health systems—and improved short- and long-term outcomes for youth and their families (Lister, Frey, & Estella, 2018).

What Is Required to Focus an Organization on Permanency?

This chapter includes lessons learned from five organizations that have transformed their residential interventions: A community program, Catholic

Community Services (WA); plus nonprofit organizations with residential interventions, Hathaway-Sycamores (CA), Plummer Youth Promise (MA), Seneca Family of Agencies (CA), and Walker (MA). Examples and quotes from interviews with key leaders who have helped bring about the transformation of these organizations will be shared throughout this chapter.

These providers have found that successfully meeting youth's permanency needs requires significant, though manageable, adjustments to organizational leadership, practice, and culture. In implementation science, these are called "implementation drivers"—interactive processes that are "integrated to maximize their influence on staff behavior and organizational functioning" (National Implementation Research Network, 2016, p. 3). In other words, focusing on changes to organizational leadership and culture can support permanency practice change. What follows is background on these implementation drivers, including:

- Best permanency practice for residential interventions;
- organizational shifts that reinforce a focus on permanency;
- and thoughts from providers, families, and youth about the value of this shift.

Best Practice Is Permanency Practice

Parenting and caregiving relationships are the vehicles through which children and youth develop resilience, safety, and well-being, even in the face of significant adversity (Heineman, 2016). Youth require safe, stable, and continuous caregiving relationships, and they experience toxic stress when their critical relationship needs are not met (Lister et al., 2018; Lister, Lieberman, & Sisson, 2015). As a result, more residential interventions prioritize identifying and implementing best practices for strengthening family relationships, involving family in treatment and post-residential intervention, and finding family for youth who need those critical relationships. A key role of residential interventions is to ensure that each youth can be safely parented within supportive family relationships. In short, the work is to intervene to assure each youth can stay home, go home, or find a home. More concretely:

- For youth who are at risk of an out-of-home placement, all interventions and supports should focus on keeping them safely at home;
- for youth who require short-term residential intervention, all interventions and supports must prioritize timely and safe return home;
- for youth who are not able to return home, providers must help locate a home and identify safe, lifelong parenting and family relationships (Dozier et al., 2014).

Key Permanency Principles

Consensus in the field is growing around a set of permanency principles, approaches, and priorities for child and family services, including residential interventions.

- *Principles*: Available services should be comprehensive, family-driven, youth-guided, strengths-based, culturally and linguistically competent, individualized, evidence- and practice-informed, and consistent with research on sustaining positive outcomes for youth and families after discharge (Blau, Caldwell, & Lieberman, 2014);
- *approaches*: Involving and connecting families during and after residential interventions is a process to enact these principles and sustain treatment progress and is supported by decades of research (Frensch & Cameron, 2002; James, 2011; Leichtman, Leichtman, Barber, & Neese, 2001). Residential interventions should be short-term and treatment-focused. Meeting youth and family needs in the least restrictive setting possible is generally preferred (The Annie E. Casey Foundation, 2015; Chadwick Center & Chapin Hall, 2016);
- *priorities*: Because youth are separated from their families while they are in residential intervention, providers need to prioritize efforts to maintain attachments with family during and after the intervention. Permanency—safe, supportive, and lifelong families for youth—drives positive outcomes (such as behavioral change and school attendance) and is a desired outcome itself (Salazar et al., 2018).

It's About Outcomes, Not Tradition

While it is not easy to change intervention approaches, the evidence indicates that it is necessary (Okpych, Park, Feng, Torres-García, & Courtney, 2018). In the past, many residential providers viewed themselves as "a home away from home" and did not prioritize family and community connections. In addition, public agencies have come to value permanency and well-being in addition to safety and independence. As the field has evolved, knowledge has advanced, and more providers have assumed responsibility for permanency. It is clear that permanency is achievable—and a markedly better option for youth than leaving the system without family or community engagement.

Youth and Family Perspectives

When asked what they want from residential interventions, youth invariably request meaningful involvement in planning their lives and a thoughtful approach to family connections. Marlony, a co-author of this chapter and a young adult with lived experience in residential interventions, spent 1,461 days waiting for permanency. He describes how he would like to see providers work with young people. "They should help youth through this time. Because nobody wants to be alone and hurt. I feel like they should try to connect them to their families, or to new families or to someone they feel comfortable with" (personal communication, March 25, 2019).

Kevin, 15, spent 1,580 days waiting for permanency and has experienced more than one residential intervention. He discusses the advantages of an approach in which permanency is a key goal, saying,

> *"To be honest, this is the first group home that wants me to go with family. So, we've talked about reaching out to my grandparents—even family I don't even know. Just getting me to meet my family. And I thought that was awesome. At first, I thought, what—do you guys not want me here anymore? But I guess it's just what their main goal is—family."*
> (personal communication, October 16, 2018)

Parents and family members want residential providers to engage them and support them to remain a family. Among their messages to providers: Work harder to understand our perspectives. Don't withhold spending time together as punishment. And recognize that ambivalence and anxiety make sense in this challenging situation. Emily, mother of Isaac, who is involved in a residential intervention, often dreaded attending required family therapy, stating, "I don't want to go. I just always feel like I'm getting in trouble" (personal communication, August 21, 2018). This lack of trust led to frequent breakdowns in communication, with Emily afraid to report struggles that happened when Isaac was home as they might cause her to lose time with her son. Emily identified concrete, logistical interventions such as help with additional groceries and transportation when Isaac was spending time at home, as well as nonjudgmental attitudes from staff, as crucial to her engagement with permanency work.

Focusing on Permanency: The Transformation of Plummer Youth Promise

The transformation of Massachusetts-based Plummer Youth Promise in Salem, Massachusetts illustrates how one provider (which includes some of the co-authors of this chapter) used the implementation drivers of organizational leadership, practice, and culture to center residential intervention on permanency. Established in 1855 as reform school for juvenile offenders called Plummer Home for Boys, Plummer today is a permanency-focused organization that prioritizes family for all.

Prior to its recent transformation, Plummer sought to provide youth with the best possible trauma-informed residential intervention, with a focus on promoting youth's well-being, connection to community, and viable life skills. The agency ensured each youth received clinical intervention, customized treatment planning and enriching experiences such as yoga, music lessons and participation in sports teams. Despite pride in their organization, Plummer staff were discouraged by the outcomes they saw, as many youth were discharged from the program to a future without family—"couch-surfing," homelessness, or higher levels of care.

Plummer leaders and staff knew there had to be a way to ensure better outcomes for these young people, so in 2010 they formed an advisory committee to explore a new direction: Permanency.

As Plummer leaders began reflecting on the agency's vision and practice, they saw language that focused on preparing youth to live without family—exactly the result they were seeing among youth leaving their organization. To prioritize permanency outcomes, a new vision statement, theory of change, and intervention model were developed (North American Council on Adoptable Children, 2018). Each underscored that all youth need a family unconditionally committed to nurture, protect, and guide them to successful adulthood. Three nationally-recognized best permanency practices form the intervention model: Family search and engagement; a youth-guided, family-driven teaming approach; and permanency readiness for both youth and parents.

Figure 6.1 Plummer Youth Promise Intervention Model.

An evaluation model was developed in tandem with the intervention model through a process that included internal and external stakeholders, national experts, and staff experience.

Plummer leadership also invested in staff development and supports, including:

- Staff training provided in permanency best practices and supplemented by training in other approaches, such as Collaborative Problem Solving and Therapeutic Crisis Intervention;
- professional consultation to support professional development and implementation of new permanency skills and practices with youth and families;
- clinical supervision tied directly to the intervention model to focus on the three permanency best practices. This involved developing a list of key supervisory questions designed to standardize oversight and maintain fidelity to the intervention model;
- alliances between direct care and clinical staff. Because direct care staff play key roles in advancing youth permanency, they join monthly meetings with clinical staff to review youth permanency goals and progress. As Joshua Metcalfe, Plummer's group home director, frequently says, "The most critical incident that can happen on the floor on any given day is that a youth doesn't see or talk to family" (personal communication, May 30, 2018).

Plummer added permanency-related competencies to supervisory expectations, including:

- Ability to guide workers in engaging and building authentic relationships with families and skills in overseeing use of permanency practice tools in clarification and permanency readiness work with youth and their families in a manner that is culturally appropriate and responsive;
- strength in supporting permanency social workers in youth-guided team building, facilitating various team meetings, and collaborating with counterparts in state agencies;
- capacity to guide permanency social workers in building teams that continue to provide post-permanency supports, both formal and informal, after system discharge.

Leadership From All Levels Drives Improvement

As can be seen from the example just shared, permanency practice with youth and families in residential interventions needs a supportive context to succeed—and effective leadership is a prerequisite for lasting practice improvement (Fixsen et al., 2015). The Building Bridges Initiative found that "one of the most important elements in creating an effective short-term . . . residential intervention is bold, committed leadership that stays attuned to the needs of those they serve, their staff, and the evolving industry" (Building Bridges Initiative, 2017a, p. 14).

As leaders steer an organization toward change, they must shift how they, their board, their staff, families, and their community think about youth and what is possible for them. Frequently, adults believe youth don't want permanency or that families aren't willing to care for older youth with challenging behaviors. Others may believe that families are the source of the problem and that youth will benefit from being separated from them.

For permanency to become a practice priority, everyone involved must believe all youth have the right to safe, nurturing, and lifelong family relationships. They must believe youth can live with and belong to family and that being parented is not optional. Further, they must agree that public systems are not designed to raise children.

How can permanency-focused leadership be promoted within residential intervention? The following seven approaches have worked well for the providers highlighted in this chapter:

1. *Provide board training.* Share the latest research on child and family well-being, underscoring the connection between family relationships and positive outcomes. Help the board understand why adding new, best practice interventions must be accompanied by thoughtful implementation efforts that explicitly connect permanency to the agency's mission (James, Thompson, & Ringle, 2017). Convening the board on this topic may also lay the groundwork for strategic planning that centers agency transformation efforts on permanency (Fixsen, Naoom, Blasé, Friedman, & Wallace, 2005). Once the board understands the family-driven, youth-guided permanency focus, they are more likely to make and support decisions based on those values.

2. *Create champions for change.* Often the work of implementing a permanency focus begins as a top-down effort. But soon enough, leadership emerges from within and outside an organization as the practice resonates for staff, families, and youth. To spur members of the organization to examine beliefs, attitudes, and assumptions:
   - Bring all staff together early in the process. It is critical to get buy-in from those who will ultimately be responsible for implementing permanency practices. Some staff will be natural champions for permanency work, while others might carry some beliefs about youth and families that do not serve as a strong foundation for permanency practices;
   - use staff meetings and supervision focused on permanency to reinforce the necessary philosophical and attitudinal shifts and assess if they are occurring. Introduce and coach staff in new supervisory

approaches, provide strategic professional development opportunities, and share relevant data.

"Whenever we roll out an organizational change project or initiative, we are careful to identify and leverage support of early adopters and champions," says Walker's Shannon Lee. "It has been no different with permanency. You have to ask, who are the staff who deeply engage with parents, caregivers, family members? Who are the staff who understand that another day in the program may be an 8 to 12-hour work shift for them—but an eternity for the child?" (personal communication, November 14, 2018).

All levels of the organization must embrace permanence as a central mission. Lee emphasizes the effects of changing how work itself is described, saying:

> *One critical way that leadership—from the president to directors and supervisors—sparked change was to shift our language when talking about our responsibility to the children we work with. We moved away from saying things such as "going home for a visit." Children do not "visit" their homes. They are visiting the program. It needs to be clear for staff in all positions that we are a temporary placement for the child. We can care deeply about children and their well-being, but the program is not home and staff are not family.*
> (personal communication, November 14, 2018)

3. *Conduct an organizational permanency self-assessment.* To re-envision the role of residential intervention, begin by assessing internal readiness to enhance permanency practice. Several tools to assess organizational readiness exist and can be customized to meet an organization's needs. These include one from the National Center for Child Welfare Excellence (n.d.), www.nccwe.org/toolkits/youth-permanency/component-5.html, and another from Building Bridges Initiative (n.d.), www.buildingbridges4youth.org/sites/default/files/Building%20Bridges%20SAT%20for%20web_updated.pdf

    In addition, leaders of an organization can ask these self-study questions:
    - Is safe and timely exit to family the driving goal of the residential intervention—and is that reflected in the organization's mission, values, strategic plan, budget, development efforts, and human resources practices, and in the contract with the public agency?
    - Does the organization communicate to state agencies and custodial agents a commitment to partnering in this work and advancing timely permanency progress and outcomes?
    - Does the clinical approach address permanency at every step of the way—during pre-admission, intake, treatment planning, goal setting, assessment, discharge, and post-discharge?

- Do data collection systems and reporting tools assess and measure progress toward permanency in ways that align with a permanency-focused intervention model?
4. *Involve stakeholders in the assessment.* Consider engaging staff at all levels in responding to the self-assessment questions or in conducting a literature review on best permanency practice. Leaders should also solicit input from close-in stakeholders, such as public agency partners and other youth-serving organizations in their community, following up to share how their ideas shaped implementation plans.
5. *Develop a culture of learning and adaptive leadership.* Permanency values should be reflected in an organization's vision statement, theory of change, choice of interventions, and evaluation models (Morrill & Metcalfe, 2018). When Plummer reviewed their mission statement, they determined it needed a sharper focus on family. Their revised statement more accurately reflects the organization's mission—which is also highlighted in its new name.
6. *Be strategic in sequencing changes in practice and organizational mission.* While introducing a new vision seems like a logical first step for driving practice change, sometimes a formal new vision follows, rather than precedes, practice change. For example, Plummer started by making small practice shifts. Upon seeing small positive results for youth and families, staff began to understand the need for a larger change in vision and mission.

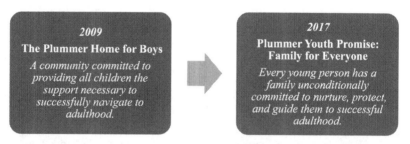

Figure 6.2 Notice it wasn't necessary to include the word "permanency" to convey youth's need for family. In fact, for some—family, staff, youth, young adults—the word permanency may have no meaning, while the concept is widely embraced. If modifications need to be made to the vision or theory of change, bring all levels of staff together to rebuild these together to help everyone see how their role contributes to the overarching vision and strategy for ensuring permanency for all youth participating in the residential intervention. This sets a solid foundation for building and operating an evaluation system to track and measure progress toward the vision.

Nicole McLaughlin, Plummer's director of strategy and advancement, says,

> I think it would have been really hard to get staff behind a permanency vision if they were still stuck in the old way of thinking. You have to show everyone what's possible. They get excited—then they start to push the work. Later, when you show them the old vision or mission statement, they'll be the first to tell you it has to change because it doesn't really reflect the organization. That way, the new vision grows from the bottom up—they own it.
>
> (personal communication, November 16, 2018)

7. *Assess the organization's residential intervention model with a permanency lens.* A sample organizational self-assessment can be found at: https://plummeryouthpromise.org/wp-content/uploads/2018/11/PlummerOrgPermanencyAssessment.pdf

    To deepen the permanency focus, review whether an organization has the following:

    - A strategic plan that focuses its programmatic, operational, training, and financial approaches on permanency;
    - leadership that advances a culture of permanency, advocating with partner organizations for each youth to have a primary and concurrent permanency goal and ensuring each youth is making timely progress toward safe and lasting family relationships and family living;
    - hiring practices that make explicit the organizational focus on permanency and are designed to recruit staff who share the organization's belief in permanency as possible, powerful, and a priority for all young people;
    - budgeting and financial reporting procedures that reflect a focus on permanency, such as providing flexible funds for advancing permanency, using algorithms that project costs and savings of permanency, etc.;
    - staff members who advocate and arrange for flexible spending (such as travel vouchers, Uber, hotel, meal vouchers, etc.) to provide "whatever it takes" to increase connections and time together for youth, parents, family, and/or caring adults to build relationships and parenting practice.];
    - measurable goals and outcomes that align with the permanency intervention model are identified and tracked over time for individuals and across programs;
    - policies reflecting the central importance of permanency and procedures describing the steps required by staff and supervisors to operationalize permanency;

- peer-to-peer permanency learning and training through required activities such as internal permanency consultations and other activities designed to deepen permanency practice among clinical and residential staff and supervisors.

The self-assessment may yield a long list of needed changes. Undoubtedly, reorganizing residential intervention with permanency as the fundamental goal is a true adaptive challenge for leaders. Simply put, an adaptive challenge is when there is a gap between the shared values that people hold and the reality in their lives or a conflict among people in a community over values and strategy (Heifetz, 1998). Taking on these key leadership tasks requires significant effort, determination, time, and persistence.

Shifting Practice to Build Permanency With Youth and Families

Organizations that have successfully shifted toward short-term, permanency-focused residential interventions recommend taking the five following steps to boost an organization's practice strategies (National Center for Child Welfare Excellence, n.d.):

Conduct Youth and Family Permanency Assessments

To design permanency-focused treatment goals, organizations need permanency-related information not available in standard bio-psycho-social summaries, clinical assessments, and public agency referrals. As a result, they'll need to design permanency assessments for youth and their families that capture:

- The state's/court's primary and concurrent permanency goals, including the name of a primary or potential parent;
- the reasons a youth is involved with the system, has not been returned home, and is placed in the residential intervention;
- a rating of progress toward permanency and steps taken in the past to return the youth home or achieve permanency through other family relationships;
- the youth's permanency strengths (e.g., is motivated to go home or join a family, is not exhibiting behaviors that preclude living in a family-based setting, participates in permanency planning) and permanency challenges (e.g., has lived in non-family settings for multiple years, has had few opportunities to build relationships other than with paid staff);
- family permanency strengths (e.g., is actively taking steps to demonstrate safe and supportive parenting of this youth, motivated to have this youth home or join their family) and permanency challenges (e.g., youth

cannot reunify safely and no alternate family has been identified, several unsuccessful attempts have been made to develop a parenting relationship for the youth);

- youth and family readiness (e.g., identifying specific clinical next steps for youth, parents, and family members—not just the youth—that will build family communication, strengthen family relationships, increase family time together, and implement a timeline for youth's transition to family);
- and program-related barriers (e.g., staff do not view the youth as "ready for family," program does not adequately resource opportunities for youth to spend time with family or building family-like relationships) or system-related barriers (e.g., delays in processing a criminal record check or lack of clarification by the courts of the permanency goal).

An assessment is critical for designing goals for permanency-focused treatment plans. An assessment can also re-conceptualize the intervention as stretching beyond the walls of the building to find and engage family, meet with families in their homes, maximize time spent by youth at home and in their community, and actively assist families in building relationships with local aftercare service providers. A good assessment demonstrates that it is the role of staff to cross back and forth across those boundaries to best focus on permanency.

Search for and Engage Families

Family search and engagement is a set of strategies, skills, and tools to identify and locate family members, community members, and other adults who are significant to system-involved youth and to establish or re-establish relationships between a youth and significant adults who can play a variety of roles in the youth's life (Winokur, Crawford, Longobardi, & Valentine, 2008). These adults can clarify and explain the circumstances that have shaped the youth's history. They can also provide family history and information, participate in team planning for permanency, build relationships with a youth and increase the youth's feelings of connection, and explore placement of the youth or becoming the youth's permanent parent (Building Bridges Initiative, 2015).

Family search is initiated by talking with a youth and asking questions about who they love, who loves them, who they would call in an emergency, who took care of them when their parents could not, etc. The search continues with a comprehensive case record review, talking to any known relatives or adults, plus using internet searches and social media tools. The next phase involves expanding the inquiry to the youth's close network, which often yields promising connections. For example, by asking a youth named Craig who he cared about, he named Celia, the mom of his best friend. When staff reached out to Celia, she said, "It's kind of ironic that, wow, finally, you came to talk to me since you are the people who are supposed to be helping Craig get to another family and for years he's been dropped off and picked up here many, many times" (personal communication, August 21, 2018). One staff member reflected, "It seems silly now, but of course Craig's best friend has parents. We just never thought to ask about them or think they could be part of the solution" (personal communication, August 21, 2018).

Residential interventions use several models to find and connect youth with family. One such model, Family Finding, is built on two assumptions: 1) Everyone has between 100 to 300 living relatives; and 2) what troubles kids in residential interventions are isolation and loneliness. Guided by these premises, Family Finding follows six steps: Discovery, Engagement, Planning, Decision-Making, Evaluation, and Follow-Up Support (Campbell, 2017; "What is Family Finding and Permanency," n.d.).

Mark Nickell, who heads Seneca's residential interventions in Santa Clara and San Francisco counties, says that, upon adopting Family Finding, the organization asked staff, "Who is your loneliest kid?" It was a simple question, but it led to a fundamental shift in role. "We used to think we were saving kids from their families. Now we know we need to reconnect them to their families and support," he says (personal communication, October 19, 2018).

Family Finding includes a number of search strategies, from mining case files to interviewing a youth and family members to internet searches. Internet searches can be as simple as exploring Facebook or Google or using subscription services such as LexisNexis/Accurint and LocatePlus. While different models offer various avenues for the detective work of locating family members, all emphasize building connections once family members are found.

Mary Stone-Smith of Catholic Community Services, a pioneer of this approach, comments,

> Search has become the easiest part of the process. Because of social media, 99 percent of the time one can find at least one connection for a youth to begin with. Once you find one family member, it is easy to find other family members. But first and foremost, before that first search, it is essential to engage the youth.
>
> (personal communication, October 28, 2018)

Indeed, active youth engagement in permanency planning and decision making is essential. Planning must genuinely be guided by each youth's wishes, hopes, and dreams and respectfully honor their feelings about past and current relationships. For that reason, active youth engagement is a core component of youth permanency practice.

Implementing family search and engagement practice includes the following:

- Develop a search and engagement mindset, ruling everyone in as permanency options from the start by beginning background checks immediately, ensuring timely transitions to permanency;
- begin immediately to identify significant adults and persist with family finding and engagement throughout work with a youth, using the first contacts with parents as opportunities to glean information about extended family and other significant adults in a youth's life;
- mine case records for potential permanency resources, conduct formal internet searches, and become a permanency detective while maintaining a belief that the best information is going to come directly from parents and youth;
- use outreach strategies that locate and reach out to anyone who is important or could become important to the youth, broadly defining family to include as many supportive adults as possible;
- send introductory letters and follow-up with personal contacts or phone calls, since permanency workers often have greater success with this approach than with cold calls;
- recognize the importance of apologies when reaching out to reconnect family and restore relationships;
- allow time for adults to become child-centered, honoring the relational process that must unfold to build trust with relatives who may have negative past experiences with system professionals;
- and explore multiple roles for relatives and caring adults to be included in permanency solutions (Building Bridges Initiative, 2015; Campbell, 2017; Catholic Community Services of Western Washington, & EMQ Children & Family Services, 2008; Vandivere & Malm, 2015).

Mary Stone-Smith says, "Nearly every time we reach a family member, they are very happy to assist. They want to know how the youth is doing." She adds,

> The engagement phase begins with the philosophy of 'reaching out for a date, not a marriage proposal.' Our initial contact involves inquiring whether a family member is interested in writing a letter to the child or sharing a picture. We focus on a family member's strengths until we determine if the family member can really be involved in the child's life. As the work progresses, we know we need to spend a lot of time helping to heal relationships broken in the past and assisting adults to make realistic decisions about how they can be involved in a youth's life.
>
> (personal communication, October 28, 2018)

Implement Youth-Guided and Family-Driven Teaming

Plummer, where Marlony currently resides, uses a youth-guided, family-driven teaming model that allows a youth's voice to guide the permanency planning process. He says, "They always talked to me before they did stuff. Like they sit down and talk to me. We have real life conversations. They ask me 'how can I help you with this?'" Marlony describes the contrasting experience of being excluded from planning about his life in the past and how it impacted his engagement in the process, saying "I didn't like that I was sent to a foster home without my consent. I said I wasn't comfortable going there and they still sent me there. That was it for me for a long time" (personal communication, March 25, 2019).

A customized permanency team can be built for every youth, including the youth, family members and other caring adults, oversight agency partners, and key professionals. Regardless of a child or youth's age or circumstances, they should always be involved in planning and have a voice in determining who should participate on the team working to identify who is or will be family for them now and in the future. This team is responsible for creating a realistic, individualized, timely plan for permanency that includes at least one back-up plan and person.

There are four types of facilitated conversations or meetings in an effective youth-guided, family-driven teaming process:

- *Safety parameters discussions* with or within the custodial agency. This is an opportunity and an imperative for public agency professionals and providers to reach an understanding about the direction of permanency planning and prioritize next steps before bringing youth and family into meetings. This discussion may also be important to address legal issues and to provide courts with information about permanency plans;
- *individual conversations* with youth, family, and team members to gain their perspectives, listen to their voices, and understand their wishes and worries about what is best for this youth in terms of permanency;
- *joint meetings* between one or more family or team members to facilitate relationships between key adults, resolve conflicts, develop alliances, and build consensus;
- *and large team meetings* to bring together youth, family, caring adults, and key professionals to advance efforts leading to safety, permanency and well-being, and discharge from the child welfare system to family.

The large team meeting is only as productive as the three kinds of conversations that precede it. Safety parameter, individual, joint, and large team meetings continue in a progressive fashion until a youth has safe, stable, and lifelong family relationships and exits the system.

Build Permanency Readiness

Building readiness for permanency is a critical element of any residential clinical intervention for youth, parents, and family members. Readiness work includes defining the steps and actions needed to help the youth get ready to live with family and prepare identified adults to effectively parent the youth (Pollastri, Epstein, Heath, & Ablon, 2013). Building readiness facilitates a youth's return to family and reduces the likelihood of difficulty in the transition. For youth and young adults whose plan is living on their own in the community, permanency preparation is about assuring supportive and committed family relationships to protect and guide them.

Permanency readiness must be a purposeful clinical pursuit and includes the need to:

- Train staff in specific permanency topics, such as adoption competency, readiness expertise and resources (including activities, books, videos, and therapeutic techniques, such as the 3–5–7 Model), cultural competence, and race/ethnic/class biases;
- prevent system re-entry—and recognize that permanency readiness may develop over time. Youth may not be ready to make best use of family relationships. Parents may not be sufficiently prepared to be successful. Family relationships may need ongoing attention to safety and security, strengthened commitment, or additional support to endure;
- prioritize time for family contact, communication, and time spent together, whether at home or in family or community settings. This allows youth and families to strengthen relationships and practice being a family, with parents practicing parenting approaches, skills, and techniques—often with the support of staff;
- create opportunities for "do-overs." As in all families under stress, youth and parents will make mistakes, require adjustments, need practice, and benefit from opportunities for second chances. Residential interventions provide an atmosphere of support with the understanding that perseverance and progress are the goals, not perfection;
- develop a realistic assessment of a youth's past, present, and future. This requires a careful review of placement history, family relationships, critical events, and experiences in family. A residential intervention approach must facilitate honest conversations about what it will take for a family relationship or living situation to be successful and identify existing challenges and potential supports to sustain successful family relationships;
- take steps to blend a youth's multiple family relationships and attachment figures (birth, relative, foster, adoptive, etc.). This helps prevent family loyalty conflicts and joins adults in working together in a youth's best interests;

- prioritize a youth's time with permanency social workers or clinicians to ensure progress toward identifying unique permanency-related goals, needs, skills, and next steps;
- facilitate peer group discussions that encourage youth to share their experiences with others in similar circumstances, brainstorming strategies for handling challenges and applauding peer successes with family.

As Kevin, a youth in residential intervention quoted earlier, points out, staff and family members must be prepared to have conversations with youth about their understandable reluctance to be with or search for family.

> *To be honest, I haven't really worked with stuff like that because I've told them I don't want to leave here. Like, I'm done with moving. But I've seen like other people do it. Some of my friends here, they go see their family all the time and I think it's really good. I'm happy for my friends. . . . Also, I'll see them when they're down because they're not doing what they want to do, like going to see their families. Here they see them a lot. Yes, makes them happy and keeps the house happy.*
>
> (personal communication, October 16, 2018)

Prioritize Post-Permanency Supports

A successful permanency outcome is best sustained by developing a plan for youth and family support during the transition to family and beyond. The final phase of the youth-guided, family-driven teaming process should include identifying, locating, and engaging both the informal supports and formal services a youth and family defines as most helpful to them. Professionals tend to identify formal services, such as referrals to individual or family counseling or home-based interventions. However, when youth and families are involved in planning, they generally say informal supports are the most effective and helpful. Informal supports often comprise people in their network who understand their family situation and are willing to stand by them through ups and downs—key family members, a teacher, mentor, neighbor, or other member of their permanency planning team.

It's All About Culture Change

Driving culture change may seem like a difficult challenge, but its rewards are significant for sustaining practice change. Here are suggested steps to embed permanency.

1. *Build partnerships to create a culture of permanency.* Develop coalitions with critical external stakeholders, since collaboration is key to

creating a culture of permanency (Building Bridges Initiative, 2015). Organizations can build partnerships by scanning their local community to identify the most critical partners in advancing permanency for youth in residential interventions. Who are the champions for family involvement and permanency among public child welfare, juvenile justice, and mental health agencies; community partners; and other relevant stakeholders? While it is often best for leadership to reach out to potential partners, staff at various levels of organizations may also have valuable connections and relationships. Messages developed in the self-assessment, vision, and theory of change stages will demonstrate the organization's intentions to potential partners. Use workgroups, advisory committees, and other vehicles to build and expand relationships and shape the agenda for permanency-driven residential interventions.

Likeminded providers can form coalitions to support each other's improvement efforts. For example, the Massachusetts Permanency Practice Alliance is exploring outcome measurement. Staff from The Home for Little Wanderers, Justice Resource Institute, Plummer Youth Promise, and Youth Villages MA, as well as a research partner from the Boston University School of Education, are evaluating the effectiveness of the permanency intervention model and assessing the short-term, intermediate, and long-term outcomes of youth and family receiving permanency services.

Building relationships with oversight organizations can also influence the larger system culture. When providers continue to ask oversight agencies, "How can we make your job easier?" it can break down the "us versus them" dynamic that is sometimes present between private agency and public system leaders. Walker formed a Permanency Advisory Council in 2017 to "champion cross-systems partnerships" and "identify opportunities to strategically impact barriers to . . . advance permanency for youth in their care." The Council is made up of private providers; a parent representative; an advocate; the Commissioners of the child welfare, juvenile justice, and behavioral health agencies; the Chief Justice of the Juvenile Court; and policy leaders and experts in related fields. For more information see www.walkercares.org/walker-trieschman-institute/walker-permanency-center.asp

2. *Promote a safe environment for learning.* Shifting to a learning culture requires dedicated resources, adequate time, and a trusting environment in which staff are supported in a nonjudgmental way to learn new skills. Supervisors are vital to ensuring a positive environment that demonstrates how staff can reexamine their values or change their own behaviors for the sake of better outcomes for youth. Supervision and evaluation should not be about "catching" staff performing poorly but

should highlight and reinforce examples of what is being done well. A safe learning environment includes:

- Training. Provide ongoing opportunities for training in best permanency practices and ensure supervision reinforces those practices. Staff need to understand child and adolescent development, the impact of trauma, and the importance of safe, secure, supportive, and lasting relationships with parents, family, and caring adults. They must also be equipped with best practice skills and tools to contribute to permanency outcomes—such as how to approach a first-time conversation with a relative that is identified by the youth or to deepen the conversation to explore the multiple roles that the relative might play in the youth's life.
- Internal permanency case consultation. This approach has proven to be a valuable management and professional development tool at many residential interventions. Strategically facilitated consultations can help move clinical practice to deeper levels by advancing permanency progress for individual youth and fine-tuning permanency practice skills. The format of these consultations involves 1) a staff member sharing a brief summary of a youth's family situation and providing an organizing question to guide group discussion of the youth's permanency strengths and challenges and 2) the facilitator assisting group brainstorming on next steps to advance permanency using strategies or tools that reflect three permanency best practice components (family search and engagement, youth-driven family-driven teaming, and permanency readiness). The Plummer Permanency Consultation Outline may be helpful. Find it at: https://plummeryouthpromise.org/wp-content/uploads/2019/02/Plummer-Permanency-Case-Consult.pdf

3. Recognizing and addressing bias, especially about race and class. African American and Latino youth are overrepresented in group placements compared to white youth (The Annie E. Casey Foundation, 2015). Inevitably, permanency work with youth and families brings up issues for staff around implicit bias, especially about race and class. "As an organization we have had to look at bias at both the personal and institutional level. In hiring and in supervision, we now realize we are looking for people who are willing to look at their own biases," says Nickell (personal communication, October 19, 2018). For example, staff may need to question their assumptions about middle class values, parenting styles, or family structures.

4. Building a robust evaluation system. The system should measure whether an intervention's permanency practice is making progress toward desired outcomes. Evaluation data should also assist residential staff in connecting

their everyday work to the broader permanency goals for a particular youth. To that end:

- Design data systems to link clinical and direct care staff notes to specific permanency and treatment goals and tasks. This creates more buy-in from staff, who can begin to see how making time to enter data benefits everyone;
- simplify forms and ensure various electronic documentation systems are integrated and uniform so both clinical and direct care staff can access needed information. For example, documenting a phone call between a child and parent/caregiver/family member before bedtime serves the double purpose of assisting overnight staff and the clinician in real time and ensuring proper data collection;
- seek input from staff when revising or creating an evaluation system to ensure that it makes sense to them. Often, staff experience can help efforts to examine and revise the existing evaluation system. Or find external partners with expertise in program evaluation, if necessary;
- disaggregate data, whenever possible, by race, ethnicity, gender, and age to examine where disparate permanency outcomes may be occurring;
- seek post-release information when possible. Gathering information about a youth once they have returned to the community is a challenging; however, as Weiner et al. (2018) found, it is definitely feasible to collect post-discharge outcome data.

To be specific, organizations that are successfully focusing their efforts on permanency suggest that evaluation systems be capable of identifying and tracking outcomes. Design outcome measurement and performance management systems to capture treatment goals—both during the residential intervention and after the youth returns home.

Domains to consider for measuring outcomes include:

- Family/home: A safe, emotionally supportive relationship with parents or parent figures, siblings, and extended family and a safe, stable, supportive living environment;
- purpose: Meaningful daily activities, such as a job, school, volunteerism;
- community: Relationships and social networks that provide support, friendship, love;
- health: Sustained behavioral and physical health, overcoming or managing health challenges (Building Bridges Initiative, n.d.);
- experiences and risk factors: Arrest and police custody, alcohol and drug use or engaging in risky behavior in exchange for drugs, food, shelter, protection, money, or other basic life needs (Weiner et al., 2018).

Also, the new BBI post-residential discharge outcome survey provides a quickly administered tool that can gauge how the youth is doing in these areas and that can be used to correlate with practice indicators to identify quality improvement opportunities (BBI, 2017b).

5. Aligning financial and staffing resources to support permanency. It is not necessary to have extensive new resources to support improved permanency practice. The most important strategy is to shift existing resources to achieve greater efficiency and free up funds for permanency practice. Likewise, major shifts in staffing might not be necessary—but it's important to look closely at changes that will improve outcomes. For example:

- Revise job descriptions, roles, and titles. Include a family finding or permanency core component and remove any outdated responsibilities to make room for new tasks. Mark Nickell of the Seneca Family of Agencies advises,

  > You don't want this to be an 'unfunded mandate.' We are not asking our team to do something more, we are asking them to do something different. We are asking our staff to change the activity. The good news is that it will feel like dancing instead of wrestling;
  >
  > (personal communication, October 19, 2018)

- reconsider how staff are deployed. For example, Shannon Lee points out, "We decided to staff up on weekends when there are adoption parties and we need additional staff to accompany children to the parties. We have had several children matched through adoption parties, so it is more than worth it" (personal communication, November 14, 2018);

- feature the organization's shift toward permanency in fundraising. Joe Ford of Hathaway-Sycamores recommends, "You need to change your fundraising stories to help the community and donors understand your belief that all children should be connected to loving and caring adults" (personal communication, October 19, 2018);

- prioritize funds for permanency practices and building a robust system to measure permanency outcomes. Seek new funding from public agencies, philanthropic sources, and private donors to bolster residential intervention transformation efforts—or even underwrite a certain youth and family's unique needs or goal toward permanency.

6. Providing staff with tools and resources needed to advance permanency. Shifting toward permanency practice requires nurturing the development of committed staff throughout an organization, from the hiring process to supervision and performance evaluation. Negative attitudes or culture among staff regarding youths' families of origin or the

Strategies to Accelerate Permanency **115**

importance of permanency can hinder implementation of family finding efforts (Vandivere & Malm, 2015).

7. Building a staff that is focused on permanency is critical to getting the outcomes the organization seeks. The organization—supervisors, in particular—must support and challenge staff to stay engaged with youth and family even when they are frustrated or lapsing into blame. Mark Nickell of Seneca Family of Agencies notes that supervisors must constantly ask, "How do you bring a level of compassion and curiosity to the family work? How can we safely expose kids to their own family instead of protecting from their families?" (personal communication, October 19, 2018). Leaders also note that retaining a team with shared values and goals may mean separating from some long-time employees who are not on board with the shift toward permanency.

Conclusion

Implementing permanency practice in residential interventions involves more than changing practice; it requires a renewed focus on organizational leadership and culture. Together, these implementation drivers create champions of change among staff and stakeholders and ensure the necessary momentum to create positive, measurable improvements for youth and families. Youth and their families need to be actively engaged in treatment and post-residential intervention to achieve permanency. Residential intervention providers must fully partner with families to build skills and strengthen family relationships. Residential interventions' success is measured by their ability to help youth achieve the goal of permanency: Returning to and remaining with family or creating family for youth when necessary.

Contact Information

The Annie E. Casey Foundation, Child Welfare Strategy Group—Christopher Behan, Senior Associate cbehan@aecf.org (The findings and conclusions presented in this report are those of the authors alone, and do not necessarily reflect the opinions of the Foundation.)

Catholic Community Services Western Washington Mary Stone-Smith, Vice-President, Family Behavioral Health System, MarySS@ccsww.org

Hathaway-Sycamores—Debbie Manners, CEO DebbieManners@hathaway-sycamores.org

Plummer Youth Promise—James Lister, Executive Director jlister@plummeryouthpromise.org

Seneca Family of Agencies—Mark Nickell, Executive Director mark_nickell@senecacenter.org

Walker—Shannon Lee, Director of Business Development & Strategic Initiatives slee@walkercares.org

Resources

- A Building Bridges Initiative Guide: Finding and Engaging Families for Youth Receiving Residential Interventions: Key Issues, Tips, and Strategies for Providers www.buildingbridges4youth. org/sites/default/files/Finding%20and%20Engaging%20Families%20 Main%20%20Document%20Final%20July%206%202015(2).pdf
- Building Bridges Initiative. Implementing effective short-term residential interventions: A Building Bridges Initiative guide. 2017. www.buildingbridges4youth.org/sites/default/files/BBI%20Short %20Term%20Residential%20Intervention%20Guide.pdf
- Building Bridges Initiative Informational Document: Permanency Practices Collaboration Strategies for Child Welfare and Residential Programs www.buildingbridges4youth.org/sites/default/files/ BBI%20Informational%20Permanency%20Document.pdf
- Lister, James, Lieberman, Robert E., Kari Sisson. *Redefining Residential: Strategic Interventions to Advance Youth Permanency.* AACRC. April 2015. http://aacrc-dc.org/sites/default/files/paper 13final.pdf
- NACAC. *The Plummer Youth Promise: Infusing Permanency in Residential Care.* Adoptalk. 2018: Issue 1, pages 10–13.
- *Youth Permanency Toolkit.* National Center for Child Welfare Excellence. www.nccwe.org/toolkits/youth-permanency/index.html

References

The Annie E. Casey Foundation. (2015). *Every kid needs a family: Giving children in the child welfare system the best chance for success* [PDF file]. Retrieved from www. aecf.org/m/resourcedoc/aecf-EveryKidNeedsAFamily-2015.pdf

Blau, G. M., Caldwell, B., & Lieberman, R. E. (Eds.). (2014). *Residential interventions for children, adolescents, and families: A best practice guide.* New York, NY: Routledge.

Building Bridges Initiative. (n.d.). *A building bridges initiative tip sheet: Evaluating and improving outcomes for youth* [PDF file]. Retrieved from www.buildingbrid ges4youth.org/sites/default/files/Outcomes%20Tipsheet%20Exec%20Sum mary%20-%20Final.pdf

Building Bridges Initiative. (2015). *Finding and engaging families for youth receiving residential interventions: Key issues, tips and strategies for residential leaders* [PDF file]. Retrieved from www.buildingbridges4youth.org/sites/default/files/Find ing%20and%20Engaging%20Families%20Main%20%20Document%20Final%20 July%206%202015(2).pdf

Building Bridges Initiative. (2017a). *Implementing effective short-term residential interventions: A Building Bridges Initiative guide* [PDF file]. Retrieved from www.

Strategies to Accelerate Permanency **117**

buildingbridges4youth.org/sites/default/files/BBI%20Short%20Term%20Resi dential%20Intervention%20Guide.pdf

Building Bridges Initiative. (2017b). *Post-residential outcomes pilot survey* [PDF file]. Retrieved from www.buildingbridges4youth.org/sites/default/files/BBI%20Post-Discharge%20Survey%20-%20report%20version%203.23.17_0.pdf

Campbell, K. A. (2017). *Family finding revision one: Implementation and practice manual.* Cambridge, Canada: Family & Children's Services of Waterloo Region.

Catholic Community Services of Western Washington, & EMQ Children & Family Services. (2008). *Family search and engagement: A comprehensive practice guide* [PDF file]. Retrieved from https://ccsww.org/wp-content/uploads/2017/04/Fam ily_Search_and_Engagement_Guide_CCS-EMQ.pdf

Chadwick Center and Chapin Hall. (2016). *Using evidence to accelerate the safe and effective reduction of congregate care for youth involved with child welfare.* San Diego, CA and Chicago, IL: Collaborating at the Intersection of Research and Policy.

Dozier, M., Kaufman, J., Kobak, R., O'Connor, T. G., Sagi-Schwartz, A., Scott, S., . . Zeanah, C. H. (2014). Consensus statement on group care for children and adolescents: A statement of policy of the American Orthospsychiatric Association. *American Journal of Orthopsychiatry, 84*(3), 219–225. http://dx.doi.org/10.1037/ ort0000005

Fixsen, D. L., Blase, K., Naoom, S., Metz, A., Louison, L., & Ward, C. (2015). *Implementation drivers: Assessing best practices.* Chapel Hill, NC: National Implementation Research Network, University of North Carolina at Chapel Hill.

Fixsen, D. L., Naoom, S. F., Blasé, K. A., Friedmen, R. M., & Wallace, F. (2005). *Implementation research: A synthesis of the literature* [PDF file]. Tampa, FL: University of South Florida, Louis de la Parte Florida Mental Health Institute, The National Implementation Research Network (FMHI Publication #231). Retrieved from https://nirn.fpg.unc.edu/sites/nirn.fpg.unc.edu/files/resources/NIRN-Mon ographFull-01-2005.pdf

Frensch, K. M., & Cameron, G. (2002). Treatment of choice or a last resort? A review of residential mental health placements for children and youth. *Child and Youth Care Forum, 31*(5), 307–399.

Heifetz, R. A. (1998). *Leadership without easy answers.* Cambridge, MA: Harvard University Press.

Heineman, T. (2016). *Relational treatment of trauma: Stories of loss and hope.* New York, NY: Routledge.

James, S. (2011). What works in group care? A structured review of treatment models for group homes and residential care. *Child Youth Services Review, 33*(2), 308–321.

James, S., Thompson, R. W., & Ringle, J. L. (2017). The implementation of evidence-based practices in residential care: Outcomes, processes, and barriers. *Journal of Emotional and Behavioral Disorders, 25*(1), 4–18.

Leichtman, M., Leichtman, M. L., Barber, C. C., & Neese, D. T. (2001). Effectiveness of intensive short-term residential treatment with severely disturbed adolescents. *American Journal of Orthopsychiatry, 71*(2), 227–235. http://dx.doi. org/10.1037/0002-9432.71.2.227

Lister, J., Frey, L., & Estella, D. (2018). *Building bridges initiative webinar: Residential and child welfare partnerships towards ensuring permanent connections.* Texas System of Care Initiative. Retrieved from https://utexas.box.com/s/h89ed6m307fl4oqq9wlbnlugxe3eugw9

Lister, J., Lieberman, R., & Sisson, K. (2015). *Redefining residential: Strategic interventions to advance youth permanency* [PDF file]. Retrieved from https://plummeryouthpromise.org/wp-content/uploads/2017/04/AACRC-Paper-13.pdf

Morrill, S., & Metcalfe, J. (Producer). (2018). *Outcomes design to promote a permanency-focused culture* [Video Webinar]. Retrieved from the Association of Children's Residential Centers, 648 N. Plankinton Ave, Suite 425 Milwaukee, WI 53203.

National Center for Child Welfare Excellence. (n.d.). *Youth permanency toolkit*. Retrieved from www.nccwe.org/toolkits/youth-permanency/index.html

National Implementation Research Network. (2016). *Active implementation practice and science* [PDF file]. Retrieved from https://nirn.fpg.unc.edu/sites/nirn.fpg.unc.edu/files/resources/NIRN-Briefs-1-ActiveImplementationPracticeAndScience-10-05-2016.pdf

National Institute for Permanent Family Connectedness. (n.d.). *What is family finding and permanency*. Retrieved from www.familyfinding.org/

North American Council on Adoptable Children. (2018). The plummer youth promise: Infusing permanency in residential care. *Adoptalk*, 1, 10–13.

Okpych, N. J., Park, K., Feng, H., Torres-García, A., & Courtney, M. E. (2018). *Memo from CalYOUTH: Differences in social support at age 19 by extended foster care status and placement type*. Chicago, IL: Chapin Hall at the University of Chicago.

Plummer Youth Promise. (2018). *Are we permanency focused? An organizational self-assessment tool* [PDF file]. Retrieved from https://plummeryouthpromise.org/wp-content/uploads/2018/11/PlummerOrgPermanencyAssessment.pdf

Pollastri, A., Epstein, L., Heath, G., & Ablon, J. (2013). The collaborative problem solving approach: Outcomes across settings. *Harvard Review of Psychiatry*, *21*, 188–195.

Salazar, A., Jones, K., Amemiya, J., Cherry, A., Brown, E., Catalano, R., & Monahan, K. (2018). Defining and achieving permanency among older youth in foster care. *Children and Youth Services Review*, *87*, 9–16. Retrieved from www.sciencedirect.com/science/article/pii/S0190740917308204

Vandivere, S., & Malm, K. (2015). *Family finding: A summary of recent findings* [PDF]. Retrieved from www.childtrends.org/wp-content/uploads/2015/01/2015-01Family_Finding_Eval_Summary.pdf

Weiner, D., Lieberman, R. E., Huefner, J. C., Thompson, R., McCrae, J., & Blau, G. (2018). Feasibility of long-term outcomes measurement by residential providers. *Residential Treatment for Children & Youth*, *35*(3), 175–191. doi:10.1080/0886571X.2018.1455563

Winokur, M. A., Crawford, C. A., Longobardi, R. C., & Valentine, D. P. (2008). Matched comparisons of children in kinship care and foster care on child welfare outcomes. *Family in Society*, *89*(3), 338–346.

7

RESIDENTIAL OVERSIGHT AGENCIES

Successful Strategies and Examples for Residential Transformation

Elizabeth Manley, Janice LeBel, and Kamilah Jackson

Introduction

Residential oversight agencies (hereafter referred to as oversight agencies) are organizations that purchase/fund, license/regulate, and/or set standards for residential interventions for youth and families served. These agencies are integral to the viability and operation of residential services. As such, oversight agencies have an important leadership role in residential intervention transformation efforts. With leadership comes great power. Great power, in turn, confers great responsibility and capacity for good (Haynes, 1879, p. 12).

A fundamental responsibility of oversight agency leadership is to ensure that children and adolescents (hereafter referred to as youth) with behavioral and/or emotional challenges and their families receive effective services that are free from harm (Brown, 2008), clinically indicated, and designed to maximize the positive outcomes associated with this intervention. In short, oversight agencies exercise their power, responsibility, and "capacity for good" (Haynes, 1879) by creating the conditions for residential intervention success.

As articulated in the Building Bridges Initiative (BBI) Joint Resolution, residential intervention should only be used when a youth is unable to live safely in his/her home or community and must temporarily reside in a group living environment while the youth and family receive intensive services and supports to support their successful reunification. By definition and function, residential intervention is intensive and expensive. The service exacts a substantial social, emotional, and financial cost. Noted child welfare researchers underscore the imperative for the judicious use of residential intervention, the compelling demand for operational effectiveness, and sum up the essence of industry survival:

> *The fundamental question for any human services system is whether clients—children and families in this case—are better off for having received services. Mission-critical outcomes are the sine qua non of any investment strategy. Investments of tax dollars may yield a variety of secondary benefits, but without a strong, unambiguous link to mission critical outcomes, it will be hard to build a strong case for future investments.*
> (Wulczyn, Orlebeke, & Haight, 2009, p. 2)

This is why oversight agencies must use their statutory and standard-setting authority to establish clear operational parameters in regulations, standards, policies, and licensing requirements that govern the use of these interventions. If the oversight function is compromised or insufficient, resources may be used inefficiently, and ultimately youth and families could be harmed (Brown, 2008). This chapter will outline several strategies through which oversight agencies can use their power effectively to meet their responsibilities to the youth and families served and to continue to improve the good outcomes associated with residential intervention.

Roles and Responsibilities

Regardless of the oversight agency population or purview—all child-serving entities (e.g., behavioral health, child welfare, juvenile justice, education, intellectual and developmental disabilities, Medicaid, managed care, or private payer system) must ensure that residential intervention practices align with current research on sustained positive outcomes post-residential intervention for youth and families. "Oversight agencies and systems (including federal agencies, states, counties, cities, and funding/insurers) have key roles in facilitating the changing role of residential invention into short-term services with sustained outcomes for youth and their families" (LeBel et al., 2018, p. 230). With this unique position in service delivery, oversight agencies and residential providers must continually work to assure that youth are safe from physical and emotional harm (Brown, 2008) and ensure that youth and families receive a range of strength-based, trauma-informed, culturally and linguistically competent, family-driven, and youth-guided practices and supports that are consistent with their individual needs.

Establishing a Culture of Evidence

Fulfilling the oversight agency mandate requires the organization to assure that interventions are high quality, efficient, and a worthy investment of fiscal resources. In order for oversight agencies to purchase high quality interventions, they must know what the best and promising practices for residential intervention include—particularly specific to engaging and supporting families and trauma-informed and nonviolent, non-coercive practices. They must have clear knowledge of the strengths and limitations of current research. Fundamentally, oversight agencies must establish a culture of evidence and make decisions informed by data (Stroul & Blau, 2008). A culture of evidence values objective and subjective data, understands and uses data to inform practice improvement, and supports rigorous debriefing of all untoward events, including readmissions to out-of-home care post-residential discharge (Huckshorn, LeBel, & Caldwell, 2019). A culture of evidence also explicitly values and incorporates the experience of the youth and families during the residential intervention as well as the impact of the intervention one to three years post-discharge (BBI, 2017).

The enormity of the responsibility of the oversight agency to foster cultures of evidence cannot be underestimated. The most productive oversight agencies have a sense of urgency to find, implement, and monitor best practices. These agencies also use measurement tools to understand the outcomes for the youth and families they serve. Magellan Health Service (MHS), for example, created a task force and authored a white paper: *Perspectives on Residential and Community-Based Treatment for Youth and Families* (2008). Magellan's analysis identified concerns about the over-reliance on residential treatment for children and the underuse of evidenced-based alternative treatments. Magellan concluded that residential treatment is an important component of a system of care, but for most youth community-based interventions are more appropriate and a less costly alternative to residential placement (MHS, 2008). Magellan has used this evidence to develop its service system.

Establishing Expectations

Oversight agencies can assist residential providers and referral sources by developing and implementing a method to determine when a residential intervention is necessary, adopting the concepts of: a) First do no harm, b) clinical/medical necessity, c) ensuring permanent connections, d) successfully engaging families, e) listening to youth/family voice, and f) trauma-informed care. Once it is clear that residential intervention is indicated, oversight agencies must establish service expectations, facilitate intentional partnerships, coordinate funding, and provide rigorous monitoring to ensure safety, well-being, and high-quality service is delivered (Blau, Caldwell, & Lieberman, 2014). If there are multiple oversight agencies involved in the delivery of service, it is important that expectations are not redundant, burdensome, or inefficient for the residential provider. For this reason, oversight agencies should collectively develop a collaborative approach to oversight

122 Elizabeth Manley et al.

methods and requirements. This could include sharing relevant data, adopting synchronous reporting criteria/methods (e.g., incidents, acuity) and collaborating in monitoring activities (e.g., on-site visits and reviews).

Strategies and Tools

System of Care and System Collaboration

In 2010, the Center for Health Care Strategies (CHCS) reported that residential intervention settings would benefit from using a system of care approach (Allen, Pires, & Brown, 2010). A system of care is defined as:

> *A spectrum of effective, community based services and supports for children and youth with or at risk for mental health or other challenges and their families, that is organized into a coordinated network, builds meaningful partnerships with families and youth, and addresses their cultural and linguistic needs, in order to help them to function better at home, in school and in the community and throughout life,*
>
> (Stroul, Blau, & Friedman, 2010, p. 6)

Key strategies of a system of care or a system collaboration approach can facilitate implementation of residential transformation and help sustain oversight agency responsibilities and efforts (Stroul, Dodge, Goldman, Rider, & Friedman, 2015):

I. **Implement Policy, Regulatory, and Partnership Changes**—System changes directed at infusing and "institutionalizing" the system of care approach into the larger service system include revisions to existing policy and licensing regulations and/or creating additional requirements to improve practice.

II. **Develop or Expand Services and Supports**—System changes to implement and sustain a broad array of home and community-based services and supports that are individualized, coordinated, family-driven, youth-guided, and culturally and linguistically competent could include adoption of practices like Intensive Care Coordination as part of a utilization management structure (CHCS, 2013) or a Mobile Response and Stabilization (MRSS) to prevent emergent behavioral crises (Manley, Schober, Simons, & Zabel, 2018).

III. **Create or Improve Financing Strategies**—System changes to create or improve financing mechanisms and use funding sources more strategically to support system of care infrastructure and services are discussed in the New Jersey example provided in this chapter and in the fiscal strategies chapter of this book.

IV. **Provide Training, Technical Assistance, and Workforce Development—**
System changes to develop a skilled workforce to provide services and
supports within a system of care framework, for example: Developing
a workforce with lived-experience, creating on-line training capacities, implementing effective on the job supervision, and mentoring
of staff.

V. **Generate Support through Strategic Communications—**Strategies
to generate support from high-level policy makers, key constituencies,
and stakeholders include ensuring relevant data to demonstrate residential intervention effectiveness, timely reporting and dissemination
of positive outcomes and systemic changes, and reporting on the benefits of system of care practice.

The system of care or system collaboration approach can help guide oversight agencies in their residential reform efforts and connect/integrate the
work being done with other related systemic reform efforts underway. More
specifically, oversight agencies can ensure that all residential intervention
purchasers (child welfare, mental health, juvenile justice, developmental disabilities, education, and substance use) are invited into the discussion and
process for initiating and advancing transformative change and look to create systemic consensus and alignment regarding the rationale for change, the
intended direction, new expectations, and the goals/desired outcomes for
the transformation effort.

Creating the Culture, Vision, and Values

Oversight agencies and residential agency leaders have many tools in their
toolbox to deliver a successful service. Chief among their tools are those
related to creating a positive, productive organizational culture. According
to Anthony and Huckshorn (2008), leaders have an essential role in creating
an organizational culture and living by key values.

Leaders, whether from oversight agencies or residential agencies, can
develop their organizational culture by creating a vision and setting expectations for their residential interventions (BBI, 2017). By establishing the
vision, leaders identify the intent and goal of the service and signal contract expectations at the outset. When Massachusetts (MA) Departments
of Mental Health (DMH) and Department of Children and Families (DCF)
re-procured their residential services with BBI principles and values, the
agencies imbedded their shared vision in the beginning of the Request for
Responses, which stated, in part:

> *The primary goal in this service procurement is to achieve better and more*
> *sustainable positive outcomes for children and families who come to the*

attention of either DCF or DMH. This requires full family engagement during the course of the residential service in all aspects of a child's care and treatment unless there are safety concerns that require alternative planning. The objective is to prepare families, including foster, kinship or adoptive families, to manage their children successfully at home and promote their capacity to sustain their child's and the family's well-being.

(Commonwealth of Massachusetts Executive Office of Health and Human Services [COMEOHHS], 2012, pp. 21–22)

Achieving the vision requires more than expectations—it requires leaders to use their budgets, make changes to policies and procedures that impede youth-guided/family-driven practice, and/or develop new training for staff to develop competencies in: Customer service, relationship building, dispute resolution/negotiation, and problem-solving (Stroul & Blau, 2008).

Implementing Policy, Regulatory, and Partnership Changes

Implementing relevant policy and regulatory change are additional important tools that oversight agencies can use. Policy development is the process of deciding what services to fund and how and by whom services will be delivered (Greenhalgh, 2018). Oversight agencies can establish policies that support the use of practices aligned with research and science, (e.g., promoting family-driven, youth-guided, culturally and linguistic competent, trauma-informed, and effective aftercare practices), limiting the use of coercive interventions (e.g., decreasing police calls and seclusion/restraint [S/R] use), and creating standards for effective clinical practice (e.g., judicious use of psychotropic medication) during the residential intervention. For example, the New Jersey Department of Children and Families (NJ DCF) Office of Child Health Unit implemented a new statewide policy to improve psychotropic medication prescribing practices for youth in residential interventions, which focused on addressing target symptoms, enhancing oversight, and improving outcomes (NJ DCF, 2011).

Similarly, oversight agencies can advance their regulations in a synchronous or complementary fashion to promote effective practices and improved residential intervention outcomes. In MA, the DMH and DCF convened an Interagency Initiative with seven child-serving state agencies to develop a common framework for trauma-informed practice and S/R prevention and adopt the Six Core Strategies© (Huckshorn, LeBel, & Caldwell, 2019). This collaborative effort resulted in individual oversight agencies advancing their specific S/R regulatory requirements with core strategy elements that were consistent across the service sectors and designed to improve outcomes and services delivered to MA youth and families. Participation in this interagency effort was subsequently required for all residential providers who were funded by DMH and DCF through the Caring Together procurement described later in this chapter (COMEOHHS, 2014).

Families and youth are essential partners for oversight agencies and residential providers. Creating opportunities for family and youth voice at the policy and practice level is a powerful tool that can influence policy, quality, and outcomes. Supporting the role of family and youth voice in the intervention requires fiscal support for participation, training, and supervision and establishing clearly defined expectations (National Federation of Families for Children's Mental Health, 2008).

Contracting and Using the Request for Proposal Process

A powerful tool for oversight agencies is the Request for Proposal (RFP) and/or Request for Qualification (RFQ) process and contracting for services. The RFP/RFQ creates and identifies a set of expectations as part of an overall scope of work for a contract (Diamond, 2015). Within the RFP/RFQ process, the oversight agency has an opportunity to: Provide relevant data, trend analysis (local and national), and research; set performance expectations; and outline the level of support that oversight agencies will offer around anticipated interventions.

Oversight agencies can also set the standards of care through contracting, by identifying the staffing configuration, necessary licenses, and required accreditation standards that are indicated to achieve the anticipated outcomes. Standard-setting is achieved by clearly communicating and articulating expectations and measurable goals for critical residential practices, such as achieving permanency, family and youth engagement, skill-building and supports, cultural and linguistic competence, residential staff working in the homes and home communities of youth and families, transition planning beginning pre-admission, and aftercare outreach, as outlined in the BBI publication, Implementing Effective Short Term Residential Interventions (2017). By requiring these standard setting elements, oversight agencies establish the foundation for residential intervention transformation (Lieberman & Bellonci, 2007).

Oversight agencies can ensure that residential intervention transformation is achieved by ensuring youth-guided/family-driven practice is prioritized, requiring consumer roles (e.g., peer mentors, family advocates, etc.), and including these roles in the residential staffing pattern. Similarly, oversight agencies can ensure providers are focused on elements that promote positive long-term outcomes for youth and families by:

- Requiring permanency as a primary intervention focus, ensuring tools and methods to prevent permanency/discharge disruption (family finding practices, working with families in the home/community, and teaching families the skills that staff have to manage day-to-day challenges);

- prioritizing crisis/conflict prevention/reduction (e.g., police calls, seclusion/restraint [S/R], and coercive practices like points and level systems);
- implementing recovery-promoting, self-comforting strategies (e.g., soothing planning, de-escalation techniques, sensory integration/modulation, educating youth and families in dispute resolution) within a larger framework such as the Six Core Strategies© (Huckshorn et al., 2019).

Oversight agencies can also include contract language that specifies practice expectations, including measurable goals and clear deliverables. Contract deliverables set clear expectations for the residential provider and give the funding agency the authority to address deficiencies. Contract deliverables allow the oversight agencies to work with the provider to achieve the intended goals of the service. Alternatively, when problems exist, a contract can help funders, providers, and oversight agencies work collaboratively to revise goals or modify the scope of the service and/or the population served (especially if a funder or oversight agency determines that the provider is better suited to work with a different population or deliver a different type of service).

The BBI is working with several state child welfare and behavioral health oversight agencies on Quality Improvement Collaboratives (QICs) to help residential programs improve practices, enhance staff skills, and successfully engage families. In addition to the Rhode Island QIC mentioned in **Chapter 11** (Measuring the Impact of Residential Outcomes), teams representing different residential providers in Kentucky, Louisiana, and Colorado are working to improve practices. State oversight agency and provider leaders have identified measures to assess progress. One state oversight agency working on family engagement practices required these metrics:

- 100% of the implementation sites will complete the family component of the BBI Self-Assessment Tool;
- 100% of the implementation sites will develop an action plan to implement a range of family-driven care practices and strategies to improve family engagement;
- 50% of families will have clinical staff work in family's homes or communities at least once weekly by month nine of the QIC.

Another state oversight agency, with programs just beginning their family engagement journey, is tracking percentages over time and using this data to inform practice improvement. They chose the following metrics:

- % of families receiving a minimum of three staff communications weekly;
- % of staff who received a training module or formal supervision/mentoring/coaching on successfully engaging families;

Residential Oversight Agencies **127**

- and % of meetings that plan for the treatment, supports, discharge, and/or aftercare for a family that include the physical/telephonic/video presence of a family member (specifying % of each—i.e., in person or by phone/video).

Focusing on Transitions and Aftercare

Transitions are an important and vulnerable time in the residential intervention process for youth, families, and staff. Oversight agencies can support the process by focusing on and paying for effective transition/planning as part of the intervention. A transition process and plan that are not well conceptualized, viable, or inclusive of youth, families, and next level service providers are unlikely to be effective. When the process works, skills are reinforced, relationships are strengthened, and gains made during the residential intervention remain. A well-managed transition enhances treatment, maximizes resources, and helps youth/families navigate life challenges more effectively together. To effect a seamless transition oversight agencies can:

- Embed transition expectations in contracts (e.g., planning for transition pre-admission and identify home/community supports likely needed; extending on-site/in-home and telephonic outreach/support until the transition is solidified);
- implement pragmatic policies/practice standards (e.g., creating multiple viable plans [plan a, plan b, plan c] to prevent youth from "getting stuck" in the event a next step service is not available;
- establish functional goals for the residential intervention and know the functional expectations for the next service/intervention;
- identify objective measures of goal achievement;
- and ensure permanency is a primary goal of the intervention particularly when family/kin are not involved/engaged at the time of referral.

The oversight agencies can also monitor these expectations to ensure systemic barriers are addressed and outcomes of the transition effort and residential intervention are reported, measured, tracked, and responded to once the data is produced.

Using a Continuous Quality Improvement Approach and Data to Drive Change

To facilitate residential transformation, oversight agencies must assure that a system of continuous quality improvement (CQI) is in place at both the oversight level and the residential intervention level. Having a thorough quality improvement plan is essential. The CQI plan is developed by identifying current concerns and challenges that are driving change and identifying what it looks like when changes occur. A thorough CQI plan includes ongoing feedback from youth, families, and residential and community providers and assists the oversight agencies to identify strategies to understand needs and address challenges.

An essential tool to help residential providers with their CQI efforts and transformation process is the BBI Self-Assessment Tool, which provides a useful assessment of key youth-guided, family-driven, and other residential intervention practices. The tool is available on the BBI website: www.build ingbridges4youth.org/products/tools

The ability to track real time data at the macro (oversight agency) and micro (residential intervention) levels is necessary for oversight agencies to make decisions and meet their responsibilities. Data helps oversight agencies adjust programs, services, and supports as necessary to meet the needs youth and families (Stroul & Blau, 2008). Helpful questions to ask include: What are the gender/racial/ethnic/linguistic demographics of the population served? How many youth and families received a residential intervention? Were youth/family goals achieved? Has the youth remained at home/in the community without hospitalization/arrest/return to placement? Has the youth stayed in school? Is the youth engaged in the community (e.g., activities, friends, job)? Is the family actively engaged with the youth? What data are available regarding the youth/family experience, and how do these data align with the intended outcome of the treatment intervention?

Youth and family functioning post-discharge is of particular importance (LeBel et al., 2018). Data elements to consider tracking include:

- Number of youth and families served by the residential program;
- average length of stay;
- number of youth entering a residential intervention without a permanent connection and still not having one at one month post admission;
- number of youth who are not spending time with their families in their homes and communities at least once per week;
- acuity indicators (e.g., episodes of seclusion/restraint, police calls, elopements);
- number of youth and families who meet and do not meet the youth- and family-identified transition goals;
- number of youth who are readmitted to a residential one-year and two-years post-residential intervention

These data indicators must be evaluated as part of a process to understand trends and opportunities for service improvement. The use of a data dashboard is a very important component of an oversight agency's continuous quality improvement activities. However, Stroul and Blau (2008) underscore that use of a dashboard is not the full scope of the CQI activities and recommend adopting: Clearly conceptualized theories of change, reliable measures, feedback systems to review progress and determine goals, and select relevant measurement strategies.

Creating or Improving Financing Strategies—Payment Mechanisms

There are multiple funding mechanisms that states and communities use for residential interventions. For example, some states are using a Non-Categorical Approach to residential oversight by developing a single contracting, reporting, and payment structure. This approach, along with regular reviews of anticipated outcomes, is a tenet of the system of care approach (Pires, 2010). A "non-categorical approach" focuses reforms on improving outcomes for children and families and not a specific system. Non-categorical approaches support the use of the same tools for the child welfare, juvenile justice, Medicaid and behavioral health systems, such as the use of the same assessment tools, rates, regulations, and accreditation standards for all residential providers within a particular community or state. Building the capacity to set consistent practice standards, rates, and outcome measures for all public purchasers of residential interventions is the first step in moving toward a non-categorical approach to systems reform. For more information, please see Massachusetts Experience section of this chapter. Also, many other payment mechanisms are identified in **Chapter 12** (Developing Fiscal and Financing Strategies for Residential Interventions) in this book.

Providing Training, Technical Assistance, and Workforce Development

In 2007, the Government Accountability Office (GAO) issued a report citing incidents of youth maltreatment and death that occurred in publicly-funded and private residential facilities across the country. The report focused attention on staff who did not receive adequate training to meet the needs of the youth within the residential intervention. Training is a key tool for supporting and transforming the workforce.

Implementation research emphasizes that it is critical for direct care staff to receive training, practice the training, and receive coaching and mentoring related to the training (Fixen, Naoom, Blasé, Friedman, & Wallace, 2005). Reducing the time between when a skill is learned and then applied is a challenge for any organization (Moldoveanu & Narayandas, 2019). Building workforce competency tools (training, supervision, and coaching) into the service design is important for both the oversight agency and the residential provider and serves as "important 'drivers' to develop or enhance practitioners' competence to implement evidence-based practices as intended" (Snyder, Hemmeter, & Fox, 2015, p. 133). Oversight agencies can work with residential providers and support their workforce development efforts. Moreover, oversight agencies can define acceptable credentials/experience, outline required trainings, provide technical assistance, and track adherence to contract/service requirements.

Building Partnerships Through Effective Communication

Communication is an essential component of the work of the oversight agencies. The communication in formal and informal settings should be consistent with numerous opportunities for oversight agencies and residential providers to raise questions, identify challenges, offer solutions, and continually provide mutual feedback to enhance the quality of implementation. The stage for this communication is set at both the oversight agency and provider level. As a provider example:

David and Trish Cocoros, Co-Executive Directors of Youth Development Institute (YDI) in Arizona believe that oversight agencies are important partners and help enhance the knowledge and skills of staff working with youth and families (T. Cocoros, personal communication, November 12, 2018). The YDI team follows a pragmatic approach in their partnership and interactions with their oversight agencies:

- Know the rules;
- recognize oversight as free consulting that will make you better;
- be transparent;
- tell on yourself;
- always tell the truth.

Oversight Agency Communication Strategy: Kentucky

The work in Kentucky (KY), as reported by a leader from the KY Cabinet for Health and Family Services (CHFS), provides an example of how child welfare and behavioral health oversight agencies can use strategic communication to support and work with residential and community providers, family and youth partners, and other residential stakeholder partners, such as Managed Care Companies. To begin, the Child Welfare Commissioner sent a contingent of public and private providers to the three-day Building Bridges Initiative (BBI) Training Event in 2015. Following the BBI event, a workgroup group, named the KY Statewide BBI Team, was established that expanded over time and continues to meet at least every other month. Members of this partnership group began looking for ways to improve residential practice in KY, with different programs, organizations, and even the oversight agencies addressing challenges and/or implementing different BBI best practices. Through ongoing communication with the oversight agencies, hope began to grow among the workgroup partners that together they could address issues quickly and fix many problems in the system of care while practice changes occurred over time. Some of the top strategies used were open, clear, proactive, and regular communication; holding consistently scheduled meetings; identifying and supporting the early adopters; being pragmatic and solution focused; having a passionate leader of the group; assuring there was an educational component to the meetings; and building trust among participants over time. The workgroup leaders also worked closely with BBI leadership to bring training and technical assistance opportunities to KY and to support stakeholders in attending different BBI training events across the country between 2016 and 2019.

Oversight Agency Transformation Strategies: Examples and Experiences

The Massachusetts Experience

In 2012, The Massachusetts (MA) DCF and the DMH redesigned and re-contracted all their residential services together through a re-procurement framework called Caring Together, which adopted the BBI principles and practices to provide a common foundation for all residential interventions provided by these two state agencies. The intent of this multi-year effort was to infuse all residential services purchased by the agencies with youth-guided, family-driven practice by: Creating integrated oversight, developing new service criteria, establishing new standards of care applicable to all contracted services, creating new youth/family roles, and addressing provider payment inequities that resulted in a new state law (Chapter 257) and new reimbursement methodology and rates (Commonwealth of Massachusetts Executive Office of Health and Human Services [COMEOHHS], 2014).

This procurement represented approximately $250M worth of annual purchased service and included 22 models of residential intervention (COMEOHHS, 2014). The size and complexity of the procurement resulted in six different state agencies becoming involved in the process, and the response to the RFP generated more than 350 proposals requiring the development of more than 82 review teams.

DCF and DMH designed Caring Together based on shared core values and principles consistent with a system of care approach and BBI. The focus was on a vision that would allow for mutual oversight and utilization and quality management activities (BBI, 2018). All residential interventions were required to use a trauma-informed approach and positive behavioral supports (COMEOHHS, 2014). In addition, all providers were required to adopt the Six Core Strategies© (Huckshorn et al., 2019) to prevent S/R use and fade point and level systems. Several residential interventions included new positions (e.g., family and youth roles, Occupational Therapy) and new transition/post-discharge outreach services to promote and sustain positive outcomes (COMEOHHS, 2014).

The procurement process was lengthy and complex. Important first steps included meeting with youth and families across the state, holding dedicated provider forums, and having youth-graduates from residential interventions survey peers currently in programs for their recommendations on needed changes to residential models. The collective feedback was incorporated into: Residential intervention design, standards applicable to all services, and the procurement methodology. Moreover, every procurement team included youth and family participants in the review process. Youth and families were paid for their time and travel.

Caring Together was/is supported by a central team and regional teams of staff representing both state agencies. Regional teams included clinical social workers, network specialists, and coordinators of family-driven practice (individuals with lived-experience of raising a child with behavioral health needs) to share oversight functions such as: Monitoring vacancies, reviewing barriers to admissions, assessing programmatic operations/acuity, and meeting individually with providers and program staff (COMEOHHS, 2014).

One of the first tasks of Caring Together was to develop a standardized process for service access and create a level of service decision support tool. Caring Together staff also developed a standardized process for conducting joint service utilization reviews, treatment plan reviews, case consultation, and transition and discharge planning. The goal of monitoring transitions closely was to prevent discharge resulting from crisis, promote seamless movement within the residential system, and ensure positive outcomes/behavioral stability post intervention.

The Caring Together team also standardized the process for performance management, which includes semiannual regional meetings with providers, family engagement forums, and Continuum Community of Practice service development to bring community providers together and share emerging promising practices and Continuum performance management meetings to resolve challenges in implementation (MA DCF & DMH, 2016). In addition, Caring Together provided and continues to provide ongoing training for all partners, which includes problem solving and support from the oversight agencies.

Caring Together was formally evaluated on an annual basis. Findings of an early evaluation resulted in additional training and quality improvement activities to support providers' practice consistent with Caring Together desired outcomes and BBI principles. Some examples of those activities include: A pilot project to assess the effectiveness of integrating family partners in Caring Together services, hosting webinars and an annual symposium on the subject of effectively integrating psychiatric services in child and adolescent residential and group home treatment settings, offering supervision and family therapy training for clinicians and supervisors in provider organizations, supporting a permanency initiative for provider organizations, and providing consultation and training regarding family-driven practice to agency and provider staff (DMA Health Strategies, 2018).

The most extensive QI effort was the development and implementation of a Practice Profile for the Continuum service. Continuum is a wraparound service with a residential intervention component (as needed) for youth and families in their home and community. Families have a core team that works with them whether the youth is in or out of the home. The main goal of the service is to keep youth successfully at home. A practice profile is a tool that breaks down large concepts such as "engagement" into discreet skills and activities that can be taught, learned, and observed. The Caring Together Continuum Practice Profile is a co-created product that was produced by the Children's Behavioral Health Knowledge Center at DMH in partnership with the Caring Together staff, family members, state agency staff members, and experienced Continuum practitioners from across the Commonwealth, and it now provides a standard for practice across the state.

In addition, two advisory committees were formed: An implementation advisory group that included providers, trade organizations, and parent representatives and a family advisory committee comprised of family members of youth receiving Caring Together services. Both groups helped to provide real-time problem solving and implement course-correction. The integration of providers and families and agencies in the process aided the work of residential providers and provided consistency in oversight expectations, outcomes, and subsequent rate refinement.

Both state agencies, residential intervention providers, and parents/families found the addition of family partners/roles and youth peer mentors as well as Occupational Therapists in the high intensity and Continuum services and the inclusion of families in an advisory capacity to be essential additions to the services. Other examples of innovations supported by this effort include a standardized process for service access (focused on child and family needs), supported local decision making through child and family teams, and the development of practice profiles for Peer Mentor roles (DMA Health Strategies, 2018).

Despite innovations and transformation intent, Caring Together encountered a range of challenges that impeded the framework from being fully implemented as designed. A significant challenge was the difficulty of joint governance and management. The goal of aligning two agencies with different missions and operational approaches was both ambitious and never fully realized. Several key executive leaders who designed Caring Together retired from their positions and took with them their skill in implementing systemic change. In addition, highly publicized deaths of youth in the community, the opioid crisis, an increase in commercially sexually exploited youth, and concurrent juvenile justice reform diverting youth from the juvenile justice system to the child welfare system increased the number of youth referred for residential intervention. At the provider level, concerns were raised about integrating youth with different needs in shared programming as previously specialized DMH or DCF specific services became blended. Some providers and some staff from each agency viewed the regional teams as an added bureaucratic layer that compromised efficiency and local decision making. In short, implementing systemic transformation did not/does not occur in a vacuum, and the combination of challenges impeded full implementation.

Even though initial goals of Caring Together were adversely impacted by unanticipated circumstances beyond either agencies' control, the transformative impact of both DCF and DMH coming together to create a new foundation and adopting the BBI framework for residential intervention statewide was significant. By addressing challenges, Caring Together minimized service disruptions, prioritized transitions from residential interventions to community supports, created new community-based models, established new youth and family focus and roles, actively engaged all stakeholders, and streamlined the processes that providers experience when working with multiple oversight agencies. Moreover, the development of common standards created uniform expectations across the range of residential interventions and joint oversight allowed quality assurance/management and performance management to be uniformly adopted. Ultimately, the collective partnership of oversight agencies, residential providers, families, and youth created a solid foundation for future transformative work to occur.

The New Jersey Experience

The New Jersey (NJ) Children's System of Care (CSOC) is the division within the Department of Children and Families tasked with providing services and supports for youth with moderate and complex behavioral, substance use, intellectual/developmental disabilities, and child welfare involvement. The Children's Initiative Concept Paper (New Jersey Department of Children & Families [NJ DCF], 2000) set the vision for the reforms and identified the CSOC as responsible for managing the service array and setting policy. Using a public health approach, CSOC allows all NJ families to access interventions through a single point of access called the contracted systems administrator (CSA). The CSA is a call center with responsibilities that include developing and maintaining the electronic record, utilization management, determining intensity of service, and care coordination.

CSOC has worked to increase access to a full-service array that includes 24-hour access to Mobile Response and Stabilization, Care Management (grounded in Wraparound with a child family team model of care), peer support and a wide variety of home and community-based services and support, and, when necessary, residential intervention. Statewide implementation of CSOC occurred in January 2006 for youth with complex behavioral health needs, and as the rollout was completed the state began to implement strategies to improve access and quality of care for all youth engaged in CSOC. Once the core components of the system of care were in place the state moved to improve the experience of youth connected to residential interventions. ValueOptions (VO) was the first organization to contract as the systems administrator. NJ with VO participated in the Center for Health-Care Strategies (CHCS) Best Clinical and Administrative Practices workgroup. According to Angelo McClain, VO Executive Director:

> *New Jersey has about 2,000 children in out-of-home treatment facilities. There is a cultural mindset among some providers that certain children need to be in a program until they complete high school. However, best practice indicates that these children need to be treated for their specific issues and returned home as soon as possible. Through projects like this we are beginning to see a bit of a cultural change.*
>
> (VO NJ, 2006)

The goal of this quality initiative was to identify and reduce the number of youth who were waiting to be discharged by working with partners to return the youth to their community with identified supports and services. As a result of the project, McClain reported that 85 percent of the children returned to their communities (CHCS, 2006).

To improve the quality of care for youth CSOC worked to connect all youth receiving a residential intervention with a care management organization (CMO) and have a care manager and a child and family team (CFT). The CFT determines the interventions that are necessary to meet the child and family needs, which includes when a residential intervention is necessary.

CSOC uses an electronic record for all professional partners to document their work and submit requests for changes in services. CSOC developed and implemented clinical criteria and utilization management processes to ensure equal access to residential intervention for all youth needing this service. CSOC ended all out of state referrals and implemented an oversight review team that provided consultation for all out of state youth and developed a plan to bring them back to their communities. CSOC also built capacity in the system that included home and community-based services and supports and residential interventions to meet the needs of the youth who returned to NJ. Eventually, all children placed out of state returned to NJ.

CSOC also implemented changes for providers including implementing a "no eject, no reject" policy. The policy required a residential provider to document why they were unable to meet the needs a particular youth. The policy, developed in coordination with the Provider Information Form (PIF), reflects a process in which the provider identifies the youth that they are able to serve and then admissions are limited to the identified population. This matching process allows for a better fit of the youth and residential provider. The residential providers are able, with consultation of CSOC, to change their PIF as they change their expertise.

Since implementation, CSOC has also moved to a five-bed model for all residential interventions (NJ DCF, 2013), although several programs continue to have contracts "grandfathered" in that are larger than five beds. CSOC developed an RFP for specialty residential interventions to meet the needs of youth presenting with sexually reactive behaviors, fire-setting, animal cruelty, and aggression resulting in injury. Rigorous review of the process through which youth were connected to a residential intervention and the data resulted in the creation of a process redesign to bring additional resources for youth who were identified to have substantial barriers to transition from the intervention.

The CSA is responsible for completing quality reviews of specific populations and reviewing their findings with the leadership of CSOC, working on solutions to challenges presented and implementing strategies as identified with leadership.

As capacity and access to home and community-based services increased, residential interventions were used more effectively and efficiently and the percentage of youth who engaged in residential intervention decreased (Lyons, Woltman, Martinovich, & Hancock, 2009).

CSOC also focused attention on the needs of the workforce. CSOC partnered with Rutgers (RU) University to provide ongoing training on system of care values and principles and provide tools and skills that are essential for the workforce. RU coordinates training and coaching to system partners and has developed and implemented multiple certification processes for different parts of the workforce. CSOC has a specific focus on language as a part of the transformation (Manley, 2016).

In 2015, CSOC successfully applied for a SAMHSA System of Care Expansion Grant, Promising Path to Success (PPS). PPS provides training, coaching, and structural changes to the CSOC to ensure the long-term sustainability. The PPS grant has three areas of effort. The first area was to increase the capacity of all parents/caregivers, providers, and communities to understand the impact of trauma and move toward a trauma-informed system. The second area was to reduce the use of S/R and coercion in all residential interventions by implementing the Six Core Strategies©, an evidence-based practice that focuses on preventing violence, trauma, and the use of S/R in behavioral health settings (Huckshorn et al., 2019). The third area was to implement the Nurtured Heart Approach© (NHA) (Glasser, 2018) statewide for all partners within the CSOC. The NHA is a method for adults to intervene with youth who demonstrate intense, challenging behaviors.

A NJ Residential Provider's Experience: Bonnie Brae

Bonnie Brae is a residential provider within the CSOC network. The organization specializes in providing residential and aftercare services for boys and young men with complex behavioral health and substance use challenges. Bonnie Brae was one of the organizations engaged in the first round of PPS in NJ. Paul Rieger, the CEO of Bonnie Brae and Principal Investigator for PPS agreed to share responsibility through a Partnership Agreement Memorandum of Understanding. The memorandum required CSOC to provide training, coaching, and support around implementation of both the Six Core Strategies© (Huckshorn et al., 2019) and the NHA (Glasser, 2018). Bonnie Brae in turn agreed to implement these two interventions, participate in the coaching, and work to enhance the culture of the organization with goal of reducing restraint, seclusion, and coercion within the residential intervention. The connection to community supports was a focus of attention with a specific connection to local planning and governance known as the Children's Interagency Coordinating Council.

Bonnie Brae embraced the vision of the CSOC and worked to implement the interventions within the organization. As part of their work, Bonnie Brae staff and managers increased training and support, enhanced their clinical interventions by adding structural family work, and viewed the goals as a cultural change within the organization. Because of the organizational changes, Bonnie Brae data reflects decreased use of restraints, decreased staff "call-outs," and substantially decreased lengths of stay. The organization is now working to enhance their ability to provide aftercare for youth who are transitioning so they can continue to provide support during this important and challenging time.

Philadelphia's Recent Experience

Community Behavioral Health (CBH) is a not-for-profit 501I3 organization contracted by the City of Philadelphia to provide coverage for mental health and substance use services for Philadelphia County Medicaid recipients. CBH works closely with the larger Department of Behavioral Health and Intellectual Disability Services (DBHIDS) to administer the Medicaid Behavioral Health Program. Because of the focus and commitment to a system of care and BBI principles, there has been a decrease in the number of children placed in Psychiatric Residential Treatment Facilities (PRTF) by 72%; from its peak in calendar year 2006 (2,723 youth) to calendar year 2016 (760 youth).

In 2017, CBH implemented a more intensive care management and monitoring strategy for PRTF programs. The agency had previously partnered with the BBI to promote a shift in the philosophy of care at PRTFs from an orientation toward campus-based care to more intensive, time-limited treatment and support for young people and their families oriented toward integration back to the home environment and community from the beginning of treatment. Through the support of BBI, workshops were held with system stakeholders (for example, child welfare partners), and internal agency staff and providers engaged in care management and quality assurance activities for PRTFs. The agency was also part of the DBHIDS System of Care Expansion grant which is focusing on: Addressing disparities in PRTF placements, reducing PRTF length of stays, and promoting High Fidelity Wraparound through a CBH-led high fidelity team for youth in PRTFs who have distant family/kinship relationships. The system of care effort also supported the development of family and youth peer leadership throughout the system, which includes the development of a new workforce of family and youth peers including in PRTFs.

In the Fall of 2018, the organization committed to partnering with providers to reduce and strive to eliminate the use of restraints in PRTFs through training in and implementation of the Six Core Strategies© (Huckshorn et al., 2019). Following the training, contracted providers were required to develop an action plan to reduce restraint use, which is continually monitored and evaluated.

To date, one PRTF procurement for an in-county, community based residential program with core components of BBI has been developed and is in early stages of implementation. There are current efforts through collaboration with PRTF provider agencies to develop performance standards for all existing contracted PRTFs, adoption of which will allow for greater alignment of quality monitoring and fiscal strategies to support transformation.

Conclusion

This chapter reviewed the powerful role that oversight agencies can play if the agency's authority and responsibility are exercised properly and the focus on achieving positive outcomes is clear. With current knowledge of service gaps, trends, best practices, and outmoded practices, oversight agencies can lead transformation by: a) establishing the vision and values of a transformed service system; b) setting and upholding advanced standards of practice; c) contracting for residential intervention services that are designed to promote positive outcomes with particular emphasis on effective system partnership and collaboration, youth/family inclusion, and pragmatic workforce development; d) creating a culture of evidence by identifying objective deliverables and outcome measures, and e) adequately funding the intervention to assure sustained quality service delivery.

This chapter also illustrated with examples that residential transformation is not fast or easy. Transformation also does not occur in a vacuum. Active, consistent oversight and leadership is necessary to achieve the desired outcomes. Fundamentally, transforming residential intervention is the work of creating change. But, "If nothing changes, nothing changes" (Dalton, 2014, p. 171). Oversight agency and residential provider leaders must embrace the risk; accept the shared responsibility; mutually prioritize the needs of the youth, families, and staff; and intentionally work to make transformation happen.

Contact Information

David and Trish Cocoros
Co-Founders and Co-Executive Directors
Youth Development Institute
david.cocoros@ydi.org
trish.cocoros@ydi.org

Kamilah Jackson
Deputy Chief Medical Officer for Child and Adolescent Services
CBH/Department of Behavioral Health and Intellectual Disability Services
Philadelphia, PA
Kamilah.Jackson@phila.gov

Janice LeBel
Director of Systems Transformation
MA Department of Mental Health
Janice.Lebel@state.ma.us

Elizabeth Manley
Clinical Instructor for Health and Behavioral Health Policy
Institute for Innovation and Implementation, University of Maryland School
  of Social Work
elizabeth.manley@ssw.umaryland.edu

Carol Murphy
Caring Together Director
MA Department of Mental Health
Carol.Murphy@state.ma.us

Paul Rieger
Chief Executive Officer
Bonnie Brae
PRieger@bonnie-brae.org

Jane Walker
Executive Director
Family Run Executive Director Leadership Association (FREDLA)
jwalker@fredla.org

References

Allen, K., Pires, S., & Brown, J. (2010). *System of care approaches in residential treatment facilities serving children with serious behavioral health needs*. Center for Health Care Strategies Issue Brief. Retrieved from www.chcs.org/media/System_of_Care_Approaches_in_RTFs.pdf

Anthony, W. A., & Huckshorn, K. A. (2008). *Principled leadership in mental health systems and programs*. Boston, MA: Boston University Center for Psychiatric Rehabilitation.

Blau, G. M., Caldwell, B., & Lieberman, R. E. (Eds.). (2014). *Residential interventions for children, adolescents, and families: A best practice guide*. New York, NY: Routledge.

Brown, K. E. (2008, April 24). Testimony before the committee on education and labor, house of representatives. *Residential facilities: State and federal oversight gaps may increase risk to youth well-being*. Retrieved from www.gao.gov/new.items/d08696t.pdf

Building Bridges Initiative. (2017, July). *Implementing effective short-term residential interventions: A building bridges initiative guide*. Retrieved from www.building bridges4youth.org/sites/default/files/BBI%20Short%20Term%20Residential%20Intervention%20Guide(1).pdf

Building Bridges Initiative. (2018, March 27). *Overview of the national building bridges initiative*. PowerPoint presentation at the Association of Children's Residential Centers 2018 Conference. Retrieved from https://togetherthevoice.org/sites/default/files/bbitraining/streamed_building_bridges_initiative_-caldwell.pdf

Center for Health Care Strategies. (2006, February). *ValueOptions New Jersey: Shortening residential care stays for teens*. Retrieved from www.chcs.org/resource/valueoptions-new-jersey-shortening-residential-care-stays-for-teens/

Center for Health Care Strategies. (2013, June). *Technical assistance brief: Utilization management considerations for care management entities*. Retrieved from www.chcs.org/media/Utilization_Management_Considerations.pdf

Commonwealth of Massachusetts Executive Office of Health and Human Services. (2012, August). *Request for responses for caring together: RFRFinal081412*. Retrieved from www.commbuys.com/bso/external/bidDetail.sdo?docId=S141757-vCurrent

Commonwealth of Massachusetts Executive Office of Health and Human Services. (2014, July). *PowerPoint presentation: Caring together overview: CBHI level of care meetings*. Retrieved from www.masspartnership.com/pdf/Caring%20Together%20Overview%207.2014.pdf

Dalton, J. L. (2014). Creating organizational culture change. In G. M. Blau, B. Caldwell, & R. E. Lieberman (Eds.), *Residential interventions for children, adolescents, and families: A best practice guide* (pp. 170–181). New York, NY: Routledge.

Diamond, E. B. (2015). *How to write an RFP and manage an RFP project*. Retrieved from www.amazon.com/How-Write-RFP-Manage-Project-ebook/dp/B00TQBLM3I

DMA Health Strategies. (2018, May 25). *PowerPoint presentation: DCF title iv-e evaluation: Findings from year 4—performance measures and surveys of DCF and DMH staff, providers, families, & youth*. Boston, MA: Department of Mental Health.

Fixen, D. L., Naoom, S. F., Blasé, K. A., Friedman, R. M., & Wallace, F. (2005). *Implementation research: A synthesis of the literature*. Tampa, FL: University of South Florida, Louis de la Parte Florida Mental Health Institute, The National

Implementation Research Network (FMHI Publication #231). Retrieved from http://ctndisseminationlibrary.org/PDF/nirnmonograph.pdf

Glasser, H. (2018). *The nurtured heart approach.* Retrieved from https://childrens successfoundation.com/

Government Accountability Office. (2007, October 10). *Residential treatment programs: Concerns regarding abuse and death in certain programs for troubled youth.* GAO-08-246T. Retrieved from www.gao.gov/products/GAO-08-146T

Greenhalgh, T. (2018). *How to implement evidenced-based healthcare.* Hoboken, NJ: Wiley- Blackwell.

Haynes, H. W. (1879). *Twenty-seventh annual report of the trustees of the public library* (Vol. 78, p. 12). Boston, MA: City of Boston Document. Retrieved from https://books.google.com/books?id=mjsAQAAMAAJ&q=%22great+powers%22 #v=snippet&q=%22great%20powers%22&f=false

Huckshorn, K. A., LeBel, J., & Caldwell, B. (Eds.) (2019). *Six Core Strategies©: Preventing violence, conflict and the use of seclusion and restraint in inpatient behavioral health settings. An evidence-based practice curriculum training manual.* Originally developed with the National Association of State Mental Health Program Directors (2002–2009), Alexandria, VA.

LeBel, J. L., Galyean, L., Nickell, M., Caldwell, B., Johnson, K. A., Rushlo, K., & Blau, G. M. (2018). The changing role of residential intervention. *Residential Treatment for Children & Youth, 35*(3), 225–241. doi:10.1080/0886571X.2018.1437376

Lieberman, R. E., & Bellonci, C. (2007). Ensuring the preconditions for transformation through licensing, regulation, accreditation and standards. *American Journal of Orthopsychiatry, 77*(3), 346–347.

Lyons, J. S., Woltman, H., Martinovich, Z., & Hancock, B. (2009). An outcomes perspective on the role residential treatment in the system of care. *Residential Treatment for Children & Youth, 26*, 71–91. doi:10.1080/08865710902872960

Magellan Health Services. (2008). *Perspectives on residential and community based treatment for youth and families.* Magellan Health Services Children's Services Task Force. Retrieved from https://alphacarecms.magellanhealth.com/media/445489/innovativeapproach2.pdf

Manley, E. (2016, October). *Children's system of care 15-year anniversary.* PowerPoint presentation to New Jersey Department of Children & Families. Retrieved from www.nj.gov/dcf/about/divisions/dcsc/CSOC_15.Year.Conference.Presentation.pdf

Manley, E., Schober, M., Simons, D., & Zabel, M. (2018, August). *Making the case for a comprehensive children's crisis continuum of care.* Alexandria, VA: National Association of State Mental Health Program Directors. Retrieved from www.nasmhpd. org/sites/default/files/TACPaper8_ChildrensCrisisContinuumofCare_508C.pdf

Massachusetts Department of Children & Families and Department of Mental Health. (2016, March/May 1). *Quarterly caring together implementation update.* Retrieved from https://docs.digital.mass.gov/dataset/caring-together-quarterly-implementa tion-update-march-1-may-31-2016-2

Moldoveanu, M., & Narayandas, D. (2019, March–April). The future of leadership development: Gaps in executive education are creating room for approaches that are more tailored and democratic. *Harvard Business Review, 97*(2), 40. Retrieved from https://www.scribd.com/document/405279029/Vol-97-No-2-Harvard-Busi ness-Review-Harvard-Business-Review-March-April-2019-2019-Harvard-Business-Review-pdf

National Federation of Families for Children's Mental Health. (2008). *Family peer-to-peer support programs in children's mental health: A critical issues guide.* Retrieved from www.ipfcc.org/bestpractices/Family-Peer-to-Peer-Critical-Issues.pdf

New Jersey Department of Children & Families. (2000). *Children's initiative concept paper.* Retrieved from www.nj.gov/dcf/about/divisions/dcsc/Childrens.Initiative.Concept.Paper.pdf

New Jersey Department of Children & Families. (2011, May). *Psychotropic medication policy.* Retrieved from www.nj.gov/dcf/policy_manuals/Psychotropic%20Medication%20Policy.pdf

New Jersey Department of Children & Families. (2013, October 2). *Request for proposals for residential treatment center beds.* Retrieved from www.state.nj.us/dcf/providers/notices/RFP_NewBeds6RTC.pdf

Pires, S. A. (2010). *Building systems of care: A primer.* Washington, DC: National Technical Assistance Center for Children's Mental Health, Georgetown University Center for Child and Human Development. Retrieved from https://gucchd.georgetown.edu/products/PRIMER_CompleteBook.pdf

Snyder, P. A., Hemmeter, M. L., & Fox, L. (2015). Supporting implementation of evidence-based practices through practice-based coaching. *Topics in Early Childhood Special Education,35*(3), 133–143. doi.org/10.1177/0271121415594925

Stroul, B. A., & Blau, G. M. (Eds.). (2008). *The system of care handbook: Transforming mental health services for children, youth and families.* Baltimore, MD: Paul H. Brookes Publishing Co.

Stroul, B. A., Blau, G. M., & Friedman, R. M. (2010). *Issue brief: Updating the system of care concept and philosophy.* Washington, DC: Georgetown University Center for Child and Human Development, National Technical Assistance Center for Children's Mental Health. Retrieved from https://gucchdtacenter.georgetown.edu/resources/Call%20Docs/2010Calls/SOC_Brief2010.pdf

Stroul, B. A., Dodge, J., Goldman, S. K., Rider, F., & Friedman, R. M. (2015, May). *Toolkit for expanding the system of care approach.* Washington, DC: Georgetown University for Child and Human Development, National Technical Assistance Center for Children's Mental Health. Retrieved from https://gucchd.georgetown.edu/products/Toolkit_SOC.pdf

ValueOptions New Jersey. (2006, February). *Shortening residential care stays for teens.* Retrieved from www.chcs.org/resource/valueoptions-new-jersey-shortening-residential-care-stays-for-teens/

Wulczyn, F. H., Orlebeke, B., & Haight, J. (2009). *Finding the return on investment: A framework for monitoring local child welfare agencies.* Chicago: Chapin Hall at the University of Chicago.

8

ESTABLISHING PARTNERSHIPS TO IMPROVE AFTERCARE AND LONG-TERM OUTCOMES FOR YOUTH AND FAMILIES SERVED THROUGH RESIDENTIAL INTERVENTIONS

*Joe Ford, Debra Manners, Wendy Wang,
Robert E. Lieberman, JuRon McMillan,
and Beth Caldwell*

Within the child and adolescent (hereafter called "youth") and family-serving systems, residential interventions are becoming more community-based and family-focused. Residential providers are collaborating across sectors of community-based nonprofits, businesses, government, donors, and families to achieve positive outcomes for youth and families who can benefit from short-term, high-quality residential intervention. Community partnerships have been found to be critical to achieving sustained positive outcomes post-residential discharge for youth and families and are recognized as an essential component of key residential transformation best practice elements in the Building Bridges Initiative's (BBI) Guide, "Implementing Effective Short-Term Residential Interventions" (2017). In addition, considerable research illustrates that continuity of experience between residential and community services is a key mediator of positive outcomes (Lieberman & DenDunnen, 2014). The compelling evidence of family and youth experience with integrated residential and community/aftercare services and the outcomes of key state reform initiatives addressing long lengths of stay and repeat placements underscore the importance and power of effective external partnerships (Pecora & Blackwell, 2015).

The new Families First Prevention Services Act (Family First) legislation requires the integral involvement of, at a minimum, families, the courts, the permanency team, and accreditation bodies for youth and families referred to Qualified Residential Treatment Programs. Families First also requires six months of family-based aftercare and supports. To adhere to these expectations will require providers and the child welfare agency to collaboratively design service reform initiatives and payment models (The Family First Prevention Services Act, 2018).

This important systemic change underscores the necessity of effective partnerships, defined broadly as

> *Connections between and among people and groups to share interests, concerns and create visions for the future. . . . Partnerships are created when:*
> - There appears to be no one person or group responsible for the entirety of the issue;
> - it doesn't seem possible to solve the problem or address the situation by just one group—due to magnitude, lack of knowledge, or complexity of the issue;
> - the cost of solving the problem or addressing the issue is too costly for one group to address;
> - and/or it is important to have a large number of people involved to educate and have good buy-in to the process.
>
> (ALA Special Presidential Committee, retrieved from library.austincc.edu/presentations/Community Partnerships/communitypartnerships1.htm)

This chapter intends to support readers in increasing their understanding about the importance of partnerships and learning about strategies to strengthen their own partnerships. While the chapter will not delve into all of the different types and levels of partnerships, it will review some of the most important partnerships for residential transformation. The chapter will offer examples of partnerships that have generated positive change at the system, organization, and practice levels and highlight successful residential aftercare practices that have been established, in part, through effective partnerships.

Primary Partnership Considerations

At the practice level, partnerships that align the purpose and goals of the residential intervention with the youth, family, advocates, and every community partner and service organization that families will be connected to in their home communities are critical. To achieve this type of alignment and subsequent integrated efforts requires leaders to ensure that their programs put concerted focus on key partnerships that most directly impact youth and families. Examples of these essential partnerships include those between the residential providers and the youth and families, schools, medical and clinical services, advocates, formal and informal community services and supports, and oversight/payer/legal agencies.

One of the important strategies identified by residential providers that have improved family and youth partnerships is hiring and/or partnering with family and youth advocates (often referred to as peer partners). More information about incorporating family and youth peer partners into the workforce, examples of successful youth engagement strategies, and examples of how different residential leaders have focused on effective partnerships as a strategy for successful family engagement are described in Chapters 2 and 3.

A particularly important partnership for residential programs to develop and maintain is with educational systems. Courtney (2007) found that education is the strongest predictor of post out-of-home care success and recommends using community schools during residential interventions. Youth and families who received residential interventions and participated in focus groups and/or training program panels for BBI training events also strongly recommend that residential programs establish close partnerships with the community schools the youth attend during and after the residential intervention and the school district administrations where the schools are located (Nickell & Tate, 2018). An example of this shift is highlighted in the experience from Washington State later in this chapter.

Partnerships with oversight agencies and managed care companies that residential providers work with, at the state and local level, are also vital. These partnerships can address multiple issues that impact positive outcomes for youth and families, e.g., decreasing the geographical distances between residential programs and the family's home, establishing collaborative permanency practice expectations, developing creative funding strategies, and supporting the needs of both families and youth with complex challenges that prevent the youth from living at home successfully.

Residential leaders who have successfully transformed their residential programs to short-term interventions have indicated that if they had to begin the transformation process over again, they would have put more emphasis on partnering with local child welfare workers, probation officers, and judges (Martone, 2016). Other leaders have found it important to develop partnerships with foster family organizations, mental health and substance use clinics, respite and crisis services, mentoring organizations, and housing authorities. (See Chapter 2.) Many residential programs have started partnering with local religious organizations, community centers, recreational programs, and other local programs offering activities that match the strengths, needs, interests, and talents of individual youth (Nickell & Tate, 2018). These programs work to keep youth involved in their home community activities with pro-social peers throughout the residential intervention. To repeat what was shared earlier, partnerships with virtually every local program and support service that the family and youth will connect with during the residential intervention and post-discharge, including services and supports needed

146 Joe Ford et al.

by the family to successfully parent their youth, are essential for achieving sustained positive post-residential discharge outcomes. It is ideal for these partnerships to begin prior to admission, certainly by admission.

Partnership Examples at the Organizational and Systemic Levels

This section provides examples of organizations that took a partnership-oriented approach to either address specific challenges their organization and/or their youth and families were facing and/or to transform their residential programs by implementing practices that align with the research on increasing long-term positive outcomes post-residential discharge.

Hathaway-Sycamores Child and Family Services (CA): Joe Ford, Senior Vice President; Debra Manners, Chief Executive Officer, Family Member

Over the past 20 plus years, an important shift in residential interventions has occurred in California and other areas of the country through intentional and meaningful external partnerships that are resulting in best practices and positive outcomes. In California, an important catalyst for this shift happened in 2017 with the Continuum of Care Reform (CCR), which requires system-wide changes toward family-driven, youth-guided, permanency-focused residential interventions that produce positive, sustained change (CA. Stat. AB 403. Ch. 773. 2015–2016). The stage for this reform was set in part by Hathaway-Sycamores Child and Family Services, a leader since the 1990's in establishing partnerships with families, youth, the legal system, oversight agencies, and the overall provider system. The agency identified four guidelines that they have used in several iterative partnership-oriented efforts that helped in the system transformation process.

- *Be at the table*—Be at the table with policy makers, partners, family members, youth, and advocates; share and learn in professional arenas (e.g., conferences, trade associations); come to the table with real data and ideas. Consult with all relevant participants to establish a clear need for the partnership that is aligned with the goals of the senior management of all partner organizations;
- *common understanding*—Utilize meeting facilitation processes that foster understanding between partners of each other's perspectives, experiences, cultures, and values. Ensure that all stakeholders' vision, mandates, and goals are aligned, with a clear understanding of each individual agency's role and mechanisms for maintaining and monitoring the partnership as it progresses;

- *sit on the same side of the table*—Establish a shared vision and purpose that builds trust and recognizes the value and contribution of all parties. Devote the necessary time and thoughtful leadership to achieving goals that each partner can understand the importance of and agree to. Shared and transparent decision-making processes are also essential as partners work toward their common purpose. Although the win-win outcomes are best, collaboration will be needed to find solutions for those situations in which a complete win-win is not apparent. The return on these investments includes greater voice and buy-in for all involved, better coordination of policies and programs, improved processes and outcomes, and less frustration for youth, families, and the system;
- *advancement of the Community and the Field*—Partnership with oversight agencies can be challenging for some residential providers due to the tensions inherent in the regulatory relationship. There may also be tensions between providers due to the implicit competition for contracts and funding, and similarly there may be tensions with some family members and/or youth due to the traditional and historic power imbalance in the professional-client relationship. Focusing on long-term advancement for the community and the field, as well as the more immediate needs of the youth and families, helps generate immediate short-term solutions, while envisioning systemic improvements both locally and more broadly. Creating partnerships with a big-picture focus has proven to be an effective strategy for testing immediate interventions and for gathering, analyzing, and using data to improve outcomes.

Employing these guidelines Hathaway-Sycamores began partnering with the California child welfare system to shorten the timeframes to achieve permanency for children receiving residential intervention. At the time, a push to move youth out of residential placements came up against a lack of community supports or services to support family reunification efforts or achieve permanency for youth. To address this issue, Hathaway-Sycamores began to intentionally incorporate partnerships with families into its model. The agency hired parent partners and invited parents into the residential program right at intake in order to help prepare families to care for their youth at home.

Hathaway-Sycamore used a number of strategies in their beginning stages of partnering with families to engage families, including: Requesting parents to attend trainings with staff, building a family cottage for parents to spend the night in close proximity to their child, and having families engaged alongside staff in the milieu so that the staff could learn and understand each individual family's preferences in caring for their child. The agency continued to advance their partnership strategies with families, including working with oversight agencies to create policy changes that would allow for daily phone calls and for transitioning from primary work in the program to work in the home and community, with regular time at home regardless of youth behavior in the program.

The expected skepticism from oversight agencies as well as residential provider community partners diminished as youth safely returned home in shorter timeframes and did not return to a residential intervention (Ford, 2019). The family partnership model was steered by salient principles guiding the agency's work that were developed by the California Department of Social Service, Department of Health Care Services:

- All youth deserve to live with a committed, nurturing, and permanent family that prepares youth for a successful transition into adulthood;
- the experiences, perspectives, and viewpoints of youth and families are important and should be incorporated into assessment, placement, and service planning;
- youth should not have to change living situations to get the services and supports they need. For home-based placements to be successful, services should be available at home;
- all partner agencies serving youth, including child welfare, juvenile probation, mental health, education, and other community service providers, must collaborate effectively to engage and surround the youth and family with needed services, resources, and supports, rather than requiring the youth and family to navigate multiple service providers;
- the goal for all youth in foster care is normalcy in development while establishing permanent, lifelong, familial relationships. Therefore, youth should not remain in a group living environment for long periods of time (California Department of Social Services, 2018).

Hathaway-Sycamores' development of family partnerships and family-driven care eventually came into conflict with state licensing requirements in a specific situation in which a youth and family were conjointly served in a house owned by the agency. As a result, a class action lawsuit followed which became transformative litigation known as Katie A. This legislation created a mandate for the state to ensure that children in child welfare receive mental health services. In the process, the litigation brought together opposing parties along with other interested stakeholders into the negotiations and forged strong external partnerships, despite initial reluctance by the involved parties.

The systemic paradigm shift resulting from the Katie A. litigation meant that counties and non-profit residential providers serving foster youth and their families needed to re-fashion the way they did business. The external partnerships became forums for developing manuals and guides to assist in implementing a Core Practice Model (CPM) developed by Hathaway-Sycamores and shared within its partnerships and for documenting the *Katie A.*-related services appropriately.

Hathaway-Sycamores was further instrumental in developing external partnerships leading to system-wide positive outcomes. The Hathaway-Sycamores Homeward Bound program infused wraparound into a residential intervention at intake and then followed the youth and family into the community with the same staff to sustain permanency. The data from its internal Research and Evaluation Department showed that the youth in both wraparound and residential had the same identified needs; wraparound simply had the supports to safely maintain permanency at home. Hathaway-Sycamores presented this data to the Los Angeles County Director of the Department of Children and Family Services (DCFS) and proposed a pilot that would eventually become known as "Res-Wrap." It included an external partnership with child welfare and private agency providers to do family search and engagement for youth who were disconnected from their family. The pilot led to an increased presence of families at service delivery and in decision making, greater trust and alignment with oversight partners and substantive results that included decreased length of stay, improved well-being, and an increased willingness for oversight agencies to trust private agencies to safely provide services to youth at home who would otherwise be in out-of-home care. Services and interventions were portable across settings. Access to a residential intervention was not tied to admission, discharge was not a reward based on behavior, and support was provided to the family in their communities while treatment continued. Between 2004 and 2008 Hathaway-Sycamores witnessed a dramatic drop in average length of stay, from 70 months to six months, after implementation of Res-Wrap/Homeward Bound (Ford, July 30, 2019).

The Hathaway-Sycamores' Homeward Bound pilot was influential in the development of the CA Residentially Based Services-Open Doors model, which involved high-level leaders (e.g., agency Directors, CEO) from oversight agencies, residential providers, stakeholder groups, and the community who were committed to figuring out how to fund and implement the full continuum of care across all settings, addressing key practices, including: residential treatment without walls, permanency, aftercare, and crisis stabilization to prevent recidivism (California Residentially Based Services, 2014; Johnson, 2018). All of this work was supported by partnerships—between provider agencies, child welfare, juvenile justice (at the local and state level), advocates, families and youth, trade associations (such as the California Alliance of Children and Family Services and the Association of Children's Residential Centers), legislators, and consultants (including Casey Family Programs)—and eventually matriculated into the Continuum of Care Reform and implementation of the statewide Short Term Residential

150 Joe Ford et al.

Therapeutic Program system implemented throughout the state in November, 2017 (CA. Stat. AB 403. Ch. 773. 2015–2016).

KVC Health Systems (KS): Chad Anderson, Chief Clinical Officer

Another noteworthy example of utilizing effective partnerships to transform a system of care was the work of KVC Health Systems to build community capacity for youth who would otherwise be served with a residential intervention, which over time resulted in a huge reduction in group home beds and an increase in foster and relative caregiver homes. KVC Health Systems, which started in 1970, has used relationship-based techniques to establish effective external partnerships and was selected as one of the first lead contractors for the privatization of child welfare reform in Kansas. KVC's guiding philosophies include:

- "What would you want for your own child who needed a residential intervention?"
- "Children grow best in families."
- "Excellence is not an act; it's a habit."

Specific to establishing external partnerships, KVC's managerial beliefs are "Collaboration fuels our improvement" and "Diverse perspectives are key to our progress." As a true believer in residential interventions done in the right way, at the right time, with the right service model, KVC was instrumental in the successful reform of residential services in Kansas by optimizing residential interventions through effective external partnerships. Its outcomes speak to this. From 1996 KVC Kansas went from 30% of their youth in congregate care (Kansas Department of Social and Rehabilitation Services Commission of Children and Family Services, 1996) to 7% in 2019 (KVC's Performance Management Data Daily Report, July 23, 2019).

The method KVC used to achieve this significant transformation, i.e., increase in foster families and decrease in residential beds is the ABC model (coined by KVC executives): A) Assessing all youth; B) Be Brave; C) Community Outreach.

A. In Assessing All Youth, KVC discovered by talking to the youth that the paper record did not match the youth's true narrative of what they were capable of or their perspective of what the treatment goals and objectives should be.

B. Being Brave entailed calling all the previous assessors, updating the assessments, and ensuring a strengths-/needs-based assessment. What KVC discovered was that the diagnosis that described the youth's behaviors was more about billing than a genuine assessment of needs. Changing this

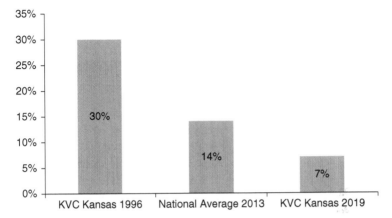

Figure 8.1 The majority of KVC services, pre-privatization (1997), became different types of residential programs five years later. KVC had reduced its beds by half and begun the shift to providing only Psychiatric Hospitalization (only 12 beds at that time) and Psychiatric Residential Treatment (PRTF) services, serving youth with complex challenges and their families whom others generally would not accept. Key to this change was that KVC significantly grew its foster family care and In-Home Therapy services while inspiring its network of providers to do the same. KVC uses a Performance Management Data Daily Report for tracking data. In 1997, KVC had 200 residential beds and 200 foster families; in 2002 it had 100 residential beds and 600 foster families, and 15 years later only 48 residential beds and 800 foster families. The post reform average residential length of stay went from 365 days in 1996 to 61 days in 2017.

perspective led to KVC using residential as a more effective intervention, achieving better permanency outcomes, and shortening the length of stay.

C. Community Outreach entailed collaborating with community partners such as the judicial system, law enforcement, and public/private agencies and focused on building trust. One of the key barriers was that there was no common assessment tool, particularly for youths' severe behaviors such as sexual acting out. There was hesitation from judges about placing youth in the community who might pose a safety risk. This concern caused an unwillingness to send a youth from a locked program to a short-term residential intervention, much less sending a youth home to live with a family or foster family. Through their focus on learning the genuine details of a youth's strengths and needs, KVC was able to tell a youth's accurate story in a strengths-based way. Success in this effort tended to reduce reluctance among systems partners and oversight agencies. A successful strategy for building trust and managing risk with oversight agencies has been to view the intervention as treating the whole family. In doing so, viable safety plans can be created to minimize and share the risks across public and private agencies. A community outreach approach that gained the confidence of the judges and child welfare professionals was to implement program safety enhancements such as door alarms, monitors, and emergency intervention plans in the foster homes.

In general, the community needed support in effectively working with youth who have extremely high needs and their families, so KVC provided supervision in the field, transferring the KVC skillset to the community providers and system professionals. This effort also reduced the reluctance that oversight agencies had about reducing residential interventions, as youth and families now had increased community services and supports, particularly interventions that could be delivered in the family's home or a foster home. Even while adding 800 foster homes, KVC remained focused on permanency and family reunification as the overarching goal.

Through all the lessons learned KVC now sees that foster care might become a thing of the past and views the Families First Prevention Services Act as a way to engage the community before a youth even needs to receive an out-of-home intervention. When asked what advice KVC had for residential leaders who want to optimize residential interventions though external partnerships, KVC executives highlighted the importance of starting with family-focused assessment and treatment and the need to be relentless in collaboration with community partners. KVC recommends educating the community by sharing expertise while using a common language across settings and focusing on how to mitigate the risks through monitoring and supervision. KVC leaders share that the three most important components for good partnerships are relationship, relationship, relationship. Chad Anderson, KVC's Chief Clinical Officer recommends "reduce silos and be kind to system partners, and trust will increase. If they don't trust you as a provider, assessor, etc. you will not establish effective external partnerships."

According to KVC, perhaps the most complex change is to reduce fragmentation between the residential, community-based care and external partners. KVC's change process involves communicating more thoroughly and frequently. For example, they discuss discharge at residential admission; they expand contact with family (rather than restrict), because more contact creates opportunity to work on emotions and behavior; they have treatment reviews weekly or at least every other week; they have "community contact" expectations, which charge staff with getting youth ten or more community contacts per week.

All of this has really redefined the focus of residential interventions and pushed the field to do the same. Residential is no longer this "place" a youth has to go to because of negative behavior. Rather KVC has had to become a safe place where youth can engage in treatment to get home as soon as possible with as few barriers as possible. As the private child welfare contractor responsible for case management, KVC focuses on youth living with a family in a community as soon as possible, which has led to fewer youth in residential and an increase in permanency for youth and families in the state of Kansas.

Judicially sensitive partnerships (MA): Judge Jay D. Blitzman

A judge in Massachusetts (Jay D. Blitzman) used his experiences as a public defender to help create the Roxbury Youth Advocacy Project (Dohan & Duffy, n.d.), which became "the template for the creation of a statewide juvenile defender system." The community-based interdisciplinary public defender's unit project "focused on due process and giving youth voice and was designed to consider the larger frames and systems that affect them" (Blitzman, 2019). Representing a youth early in his career, Judge Blitzman discovered that the case being heard in juvenile court required help from multiple systems. The youth's background and complex needs required "contextual understanding," which he defined as an understanding of the totality of the youth's background and experiences (Blitzman, 2018). The project integrated attorneys into a multi-disciplinary team that included a community liaison, social workers, and a clinical psychologist.

Judge Blitzman sees judicially driven partnerships as "part of the larger conversation entailing consideration of the systemic issues that affect youth and families outside of the courtroom. Honoring due process and fundamental fairness in the courtroom does not preclude, nor should it, taking advantage of opportunities to engage in collaborative conversations outside of the courtroom." (Blitzman, 2019) For example:

- School court meetings in Lowell, MA led to the creation of a pretrial diversionary restorative justice program;
- work in Middlesex, MA has included participation in efforts to deconstruct the school-to-prison pipeline through the National Council of Juvenile Court Judges School Pathways to Juvenile Justice Initiative and the nationally sponsored Annie E. Casey Juvenile Detention Alternative Initiative (JDAI) (www.aecf.org/work/juvenile-justice/jdai/), which with the judge's assistance has convened "school court meetings" that bring together law enforcement, public defenders, Probation Department, and school campus representatives to discuss candidly different ways of doing business.

The school-court meetings have resulted in developing relationships and promoting a greater understanding of systemic positions and perspectives as

154 Joe Ford et al.

well as more strength-based models for interacting with youth, which have included community and school-based restorative justice initiatives.

The lessons learned from these partnerships have been mutually beneficial as systems engaged with youth and their families have greater understanding of each other's perspectives. They are similar to those noted throughout this chapter and this book:

- Maintain strong partnerships with the youth's families, schools of origins, and other natural supports in communities;
- it is important to be attentive to what stakeholders have in common. "As regards out of court collaborative conversations it is counterproductive to demonize each other in lieu of focusing on the reality that we all like children. BUT, when we are in court hearing cases, due process requires vigorous adversarial advocacy" (Blitzman, 2019).

Secret Harbor (WA): Jenn Ryan, Chief Program Officer

Secret Harbor is a residential program that moved from a location on an island in the Puget Sound to the mainland in 2008 for a variety of reasons, including the opportunity to better connect youth with family and community resources. In a major transformation it shifted from a traditional residential treatment center located on an island with a school on-campus to community-based residential group homes, with education provided in public school districts. In a proactive measure, agency leadership embraced this challenge by meeting with the impacted school districts to discuss the plan for the move into the community, identify opportunities for collaboration, and answer any questions the districts had, in an attempt to promote transparency. While this was an effective strategy to begin, it was complicated in that education was being provided by public schools in three districts and the regional Educational Service District's alternative schools in three counties. Like any new venture, there were other issues that cropped up over time, which seemed to be rooted in misunderstanding of the program's role in the youths' care, how the youth came to be in the group homes, and what the long-term educational plan would be with respect to the districts' roles.

Roughly two years after the transition into the community, another local agency had a significant situation occur regarding one of their youth and the services the school district was expected to provide. This situation was the catalyst for the creation of a work group called the Multi Agency Collaboration for Youth (MACY). MACY's intent was to provide a framework for the collaboration between all agencies to provide quality care and education to the children of our community. MACY was comprised of members of

Children's Administration, Division of Development Disabilities, three local school districts, Secret Harbor, another local child placing agency, Treehouse Educational Advocates, and Ombudsman. Through this work group emerged a shared understanding of each organization's role in family and youths' care, the impact each organization can have on the other entities, and agreed upon priorities around relationship building, communication, problem solving, and keeping the shared agreement of understanding active.

Secret Harbor also implemented strategies to support the success of the partnership.

- The program director reached out to develop positive working relationships with the special service directors of the School Districts and the Northwest ESD Administration;
- the program director ensured that Special Service Directors are notified as soon as possible when a youth requiring special education services will be placed in one of the residential group homes;
- Care Managers and House Managers are easily accessible by phone for the school staff to contact on a daily basis;
- group home staff members build positive relationships with families, teachers, and administrators of the youths' individualized schools/school programs and are available for support at the school if needed and deemed appropriate.

These strategies, along with the Shared Agreements of Understanding with the school administration in the different public elementary, middle, high, and alternative schools, as well as with Treehouse Educational Advocates, have been effective at addressing educational needs for youth in the residential intervention as soon as they enter the program. The partners work together to develop the initial education plan and throughout the school year. The positive relationships with families, advocates, and school staff enable communication and problem solving of issues that may arise in both the group home and school settings. Over the years, the partnerships with school districts have become stronger, more effective, and ultimately more beneficial to the youth and families

Examples of Aftercare Practices Built Upon Partnerships

Aftercare is important for achieving positive outcomes for youth and families post-residential discharge (Walters & Petr, 2007). State and county oversight agencies have required or are beginning to require aftercare as a component of residential interventions, as is the federal government through the Families First Prevention Services Act, as noted earlier in the chapter. Many providers across the country focused on positive sustained outcomes post-residential discharge have made aftercare practices a critical strategy of their program services. This section will highlight practices used by five providers who have been recognized for their successful aftercare practices—three residential programs who partner with multiple community partners, one community program partnering with a residential program, and one between residential and a university. The five programs are at different stages of implementing their aftercare practices. It must be noted that each of these providers built strong partnerships with families that began pre- or at admission and were built on throughout the residential intervention. Each found that building and sustaining successful partnerships is vital for effective aftercare practices.

Youth Development Institute (AZ): Trish Cocoros, Co-Executive Director; Luis Lopez, Therapist and First Coordinator of YDI's Building Bridges Project

Youth Development Institute's (YDI) Building Bridges Project is based on the guiding principles of the Building Bridges Initiative (Building Bridges Joint Resolution, 2006). YDI's Building Bridges Project provides family-driven, youth-guided services to bridge a youth's transition from residential services to services provided in the community by community providers. In-home services, begun shortly after admission to residential, support and bolster the youth's connection to family and community while in residential, transitioning services provided during residential to services provided in the home and community. These services are all provided by YDI residential staff, including therapists and direct care staff, who work with the youth in residential, in the home during residential, and then in aftercare services, so that there is no disconnect at discharge from residential.

Pre-admission or as soon as possible after admission, services such as family therapy, Child and Family Team meetings, and behavior coaching and psycho-educational sessions for both parents and youth begin in the home with the residential therapist and direct care workers who also work with the youth within the residential program. After residential discharge, the same team continues to work in the home and community, providing wraparound type services and supports until the youth and the family are ready to fully transition to community-based providers and supports.

The service goals of YDI are simple and highly individualized: Stabilize the youth, stabilize the home, stabilize the youth in the home and community. Several aftercare practices YDI has found important to achieve these goals include:

- Conduct thorough and accurate discharge planning beginning with the *initial* Biopsychosocial Assessments;

- provide continuity of staff with residential staff also providing services in the home and community;
- use the resources and staffing of the residential program to allow for true 24/7/365 crisis response by staff in the home who know the youth and family;
- ensure continuing medication services and direct doctor to doctor hand off communication of the medication history and rationale for the regimen;
- establish strong relationships with schools, including direct principal to principal communications, to ensure smooth transition back into the home school;
- ensure that the Child and Family Team and project funding sources understand and support the family's participation in the project (i.e., YDI's Building Bridges Project);
- truly do "whatever it takes" to stabilize the home. This can include anything such as providing home maintenance and cleaning, providing furnishings, utility payments, food boxes, transportation, whatever is needed by the family to provide a safe and stable home environment;
- conduct ongoing data collection and aftercare surveys continuing a minimum of two years after discharge from residential.

When the Building Bridges Project first began, YDI was satisfied with providing in-home services for a couple of hours a day, a couple of times a week. There were initial failures with this approach which taught YDI leaders and staff the importance of a thorough Biopsychosocial assessment which required significantly longer time in the home (6–8 hours a day, several days a week). YDI staff becoming more like "one of the family" facilitated engagement and involvement and also improved the assessment of a family's strengths and needs.

YDI's top recommendations for programs wishing to create an effective aftercare component for their residential program include:

- As shared previously, allow the time to complete thorough Biopsychosocial assessments; ensure that environmental strengths and barriers are identified pre- or during admission;
- provide education and/or access to programs and information for families to address their needs as soon as possible after admission;
- be prepared to use the agency's own in-house resources and materials for families in their homes;
- actively address family trauma and relationship challenges to mitigate the distance and disruption created by separation of the family and a youth's admission into residential, always seeking to strengthen resources and resiliency, to stabilize the home and family relationships and to mitigate risk;

- have a strong focus on permanency: Consider utilizing the Family Search and Engage practice model, starting at admission (Catholic Community Services of Western Washington, & EMQ Children & Family Services, 2008). This allows for the support network of children to be expanded, providing back-up if needed for fragile home situations. It also ensures finding family for all children, with time to work with the family both during residential and post-discharge.

Methodist Children's Home Society (MI): Kevin Roach, Chief Executive Officer

The Methodist Children's Home Society (MCHS) aftercare program began in early 2018, though much of the previous year was spent on planning and preparation. While MCHS understood the importance of providing strong aftercare programming to improve family engagement and residential intervention outcomes, there was not much research MCHS could find that highlighted effective aftercare practice models.

The driving force for implementing the aftercare program was not the Families First Prevention Services Act but rather fatigue and frustration of the revolving door of the residential system, seeing young person after young person return to the system after being discharged to a family setting. As a result, MCHS began to transform much of their treatment model, which included expanding aftercare services to families. Previously, the child's therapist provided aftercare support, following the contractual obligations set forth by the Michigan Department of Health and Human Services (MDHHS), which were minimal. Yet, it was clear that this was not enough. To become serious about extending meaningful aftercare services as opposed to "checking in," MCHS decide to dedicate professional staff to solely provide these services. MCHS started with a program director and two aftercare case workers, with caseloads being capped at 20 families.

Two other driving principles central to the MCHS aftercare program was purposeful and intensive family engagement and working with community partners, such as schools and other nonprofit agencies offering services and support in other capacities. Whether that was afterschool programs such as a Boys and Girls Club or mentoring or behavioral health services, MCHS leaders understood that they could not take on every need of every family. Rather, MCHS needed to develop partnerships with community providers to offer more options to the family. Additionally, whichever partnerships were important to the family, which often included extended family, MCHS worked on enhancing support for each family served.

During the first year of implementation, MCHS strived to begin offering aftercare services three months prior to discharge. Those aftercare services would be free to the family and ongoing for 12 months post-discharge.

In addition, services would be completely voluntary as MCHS pledged to never pressure families or try to sell them the services. Yet, MCHS found that if they continued to empower families and build trust with them, many families would be interested in additional support. Still, MCHS leaders and staff were quite surprised that over 90 percent of families who were eligible for services enrolled in the MCHS aftercare program and stayed in the program.

Currently, three months prior to anticipated discharge, the aftercare case worker meets with all the stakeholders in case conferences and Family Team Meetings. Upon the discharge of the young person to his/her family, face to face contract is made weekly in the first three months and then in alternating weeks the next six months. The other weeks include phone contact with the family. For the final three months, there are weekly phone conversations and monthly in-person contact. Services are coordinated with the family, which have predominantly been regarding behavioral health and education support to the family. Families are free to increase contact with the aftercare case worker, which happens frequently during times when the parent(s) feel their child is in crisis. Working with the families during those times enhances the bond between MCHS staff and the family.

One of the challenges identified early on was the number of services offered to the young person and family unit during the first month following discharge would suddenly drop off. The families were initially inundated but then left on their own. As a result, MCHS changed their program structure to better accommodate the family. MCHS was also worried about stepping on the toes of DHHS but found that they welcomed the additional engagement with the families.

With every young person, MCHS completed a couple of different assessments, including CAFAS and, if appropriate, the Ansell Casey Life Skills assessment. Once again, MCHS leaders were quite surprised at the steady improvement seen in assessment scores as nearly 80 percent saw improvement three months post-discharge and 90 percent saw improvement six months post-discharge. Combined with the numerous anecdotal stories of children and families experiencing success, MCHS leaders believed their residential interventions had greatly improved. During the first year, aftercare services were provided to 38 families. In three of those cases, the young person returned back into the system, which gave MCHS opportunities to continue learning about ways to improve services. The remaining families remained intact with placement not disrupted.

For agencies who provide residential interventions, MCHS believes it's critical that aftercare services be an essential element of the program. The top two MCHS recommendations for others wanting to implement effective aftercare include:

- Partner with families early on. MCHS's goal for the second year of their aftercare project is to have the aftercare case worker begin working with the young person and family in the first month of the residential intervention, along with the other members of the residential treatment team;

- engage a wide diversity of community partners, in collaboration with the family and the young person.

The Children's Village (NY): Kristina Coleman, Program Manager; Warren Kent, Vice President; Vincent Madera, Program Director for Permanency Supports; Tina Schleicher, MST Clinical Coordinator; Daphne Torres, Director of Evidence-based Initiatives

The Children's Village (CV) began providing long-term aftercare (Shirk & Stangler, 2004) over 35 years ago. Over the years, CV developed and adapted several aftercare strategies, all of which are founded on a nonnegotiable understanding that Children's Village operates on: "Children who are connected to family do dramatically better" and "children want to be with their families." When biological family is not an option, children still need someone to belong to, not to institutions, charity, or government services (Kohomban & Schwartz, 2016). The Children's Village defines family broadly: One appropriate, willing adult capable of providing a child unconditional belonging.

Children's Village leadership recognizes that collaborative relationships, a focus on family and belonging, flex funds to support the family, and data collection are the critical components to successful aftercare. Children's Village also believes that four post-discharge variables provide adequate information to predict long-term prognosis: (1) Belonging and stability at home; (2) progress at school; (3) work—for those 17 and older; and (4) recidivism.

The preparation for aftercare begins as intake. Aftercare counselors support and help youth get established in an appropriate school quickly, work on educational goals and school attendance, and help the family deal with the transition. Youth are provided at least four years of support, most of which is privately funded. Over the course of these four years, counselors focus on education and employment, finding and maintaining a job, and developing pro-social peers and interests. Being available, being responsive 24 hours a day and seven days a week, and building relationships is the defining approach of aftercare at The Children's Village. If additional clinical interventions are needed, and sometimes they are required, the aftercare counselor can draw down services and supports from any program at The Children's Village or use flex-funds to purchase what is needed.

Children's Village sets specific annual goals on a large number of desired outcomes for youth and families involved in aftercare and tracks actual results to inform practice improvement. Examples of goals and results for their WAY Home aftercare program include:

- 90% of youth leaving CV who are still in school will have an appropriate school placement within a month of discharge (100% achieved for the past three years);
- 90% of seniors will graduate with a regents or local diploma (not IEP) (100% achieved for the past three years);
- 80% of graduates will enter college or trade school or be employed (100% achieved for the past two years);
- and 90% of youth in the community will be in stable living situations (100% achieved for the past three years).

Children's Village adapted their WAY Home aftercare program in 2012, with addition of the evidence-based MST-FIT (Multi Systemic Treatment—Family Integrated Treatment) program for youth involved in juvenile justice and cross-over youth who are currently in placement, in need of complex treatment, and who are at the highest risk of recidivism. This model adaptation combines interventions delivered while in the residential program, an approach called the Integrated Treatment Model (ITM), with MST-based in-home aftercare that begins three months prior to discharge from residential.

With MST-FIT, the youth and family get advance help on making the transition from residential to home. The goal is to lower recidivism by connecting the family with community supports, mitigating a youth's dependence on drugs and alcohol, promoting pro-social behavior, and effectively managing any mental health challenges. As with WAY Home, MST-FIT coaches are available to families 24/7. The coach uses teaching and reinforcing skills drawn from Motivational Interviewing and Dialectical Behavior Therapy to help the youth and family gain more control over their emotional responses to stressful situations and triggers. Because youth have been involved in egregious behavior that resulted in criminal activity, aftercare planning takes into consideration these strained and often volatile relationships and helps youth rebuild relationships and transition into family, school, and community.

The MST-FIT coach visits the family two to three times weekly to collaborate and partner with the family in developing treatment goals and to ensure that the youth is adjusting in the ecology: Attending and doing well in school, adjusting to family life and following rules set by parents, not using substances, and involved in pro-social programs and working, if able. In addition, flex funds are used to help youth enroll in programs that develop a vocational skill and/or allow pro-social opportunities for youth. Also, there is a priority to have families engage in activities that help to build their bond.

Program data shows that youth treated with MST-FIT are 30% less likely to commit crimes than other youth offenders (mstservices.com, n.d.). Positive outcomes are gained through intensive treatment guided by intensive supervision and consultation in the model to ensure adherence. Children's Village sets annual targets and tracks outcomes on over 30 metrics for this program, including "ultimate" outcomes of percent of youth living at home (75% for 2018), percent of youth with no new arrests (83.33% for 2018), and percent of youth in school/working (66.67% for 2018). Instrumental outcome examples for 2018 include:

- Parenting skills necessary to handle future problems—91.67%;
- improved family relations—83.33%;
- improved network of supports—91.67%;
- youth involved with prosocial peers/activities—75%.

These outcomes are also compared to youth and families with similar challenges who do not receive MST-FIT.

Lessons learned by CV with aftercare implementation include that aftercare is an essential requirement for all residential interventions, good aftercare begins at intake, and it is imperative that aftercare staff are included in treatment planning. Additionally, school placements must be secured prior to a youth's discharge so that the youth can begin school upon discharge, instead of waiting for a school placement. And perhaps most importantly, formalized opportunities for parents and other caregivers to be included throughout the residential intervention are critical; parents and caregivers must learn skills early and collaborate in achieving treatment goals.

Collaborative Intensive Bridging Services (MN): Luke Spiegelhoff, Clinical Director

Collaborative Intensive Bridging Services (CIBS) is a community-based intervention that pairs intensive in-home therapy services with a brief (30 to 45 day) residential intervention. The same therapist provides the assessment of the family system, therapy to the child and family while the child is in the residential intervention, and the intensive in-home therapy aftercare. This provides a seamless continuum of intervention for the child/family while avoiding having to change providers when the child transitions home from the residential program.

The intensive in-home therapy occurring after the residential intervention continues the work and skills practiced during the brief residential intervention. Therapy services occur multiple times a week. The work can include individual therapy (for both parent and child), family therapy, and couples counseling. Therapeutic interventions occur in the environments the child may be struggling in (home, school, and community).

CIBS is paid for by a combination of third-party insurance billing and county contract. Children's Mental Health Case Managers play an integral role in transitioning the child back into the home with appropriate services or school placement. 84% of youth who participate in CIBS remain in their home without a further out-of-home placement at 2 years post closure.

There are four primary partners in this process: The child and family, the Children's Mental Health Case Manager, the residential program providing the residential intervention, and the intensive in-home therapist. All these entities must be willing to partner within the specific expectations of the model. There are frequent staffings within this model to ensure there is alignment in the overall treatment and case direction. Considerable planning goes into the actual rollout and implementation of the service. The benefit of this process is that counties have had to think through how this service fits in their continuum of care and what resources need to be implemented to ensure fidelity. This seems to increase the buy-in to the model of care contained in CIBS.

The ongoing use of CIBS consultants in the model helps problem solve systems issues that impact program implementation or specific case difficulties. CIBS consultants are experts in the model who help provide model fidelity oversight with treatment teams through weekly or bi-weekly clinical feedback on cases.

A major challenge in implementing aftercare services was that children with school related difficulties were not adequately being assessed and treated for their school difficulties as part of the residential intervention. The solution that the team came up with is that school functioning was prioritized as part of assessment/treatment services during the residential intervention. Specific desired school treatment outcomes were identified at intake and tracked during the brief residential intervention. This involved working with the school on site at the residential program to more effectively communicate with the child's home school district regarding any transition or IEP related changes as part of the child's return home. The community-based therapist helps to ensure follow-through with the child's home district on any recommendations made from the residential intervention.

CIBS' top recommendations for aftercare services include:

- Services must be long enough (4 to 6 months post-discharge) for the child and family to practice new ways of interacting so they feel more confident in their ability to manage previously problematic situations and interactions. This also provides therapeutic support during one of the most high-risk times for children to return to residential placement;
- specific skills are identified for the child, parent(s), and other family members to work on during the residential intervention that they are expected to continue working on as part of the child's return home. Members of the family's natural support system are utilized to help support any changes made;

164 Joe Ford et al.

- having the same therapist who worked with the child and family during the residential intervention do the follow-up aftercare makes a significant difference in ongoing family engagement in post-residential intervention services.

Boys Town and University of Nebraska-Lincoln (NE): Ronald Thompson, PhD, Managing Member, RT Consulting, LLC., and retired Vice President and Director, National Research institute for Child and Family Studies, Boys Town; Alexandra Trout, Research Professor, and Matthew C. Lambert, Associate Professor, University of Nebraska-Lincoln

For over a decade, Boys Town and the University of Nebraska-Lincoln have worked to develop, implement, and evaluate On the Way Home (OTWH), a manualized evidence-based program designed to improve the education and placement stability outcomes of youth returning to home and community school settings following a residential intervention (Trout, Tyler, Stewart, & Epstein, 2012). Intervention components include evidence-based parent training and school dropout prevention programs along with a practical homework intervention. Aftercare services begin during the residential intervention by engaging families and inviting them to participate in discharge planning and individualized, home-based parenting sessions. Services including individualized family and school consultation and support continue to be provided for 12 months after reunification by a family consultant for two hours on average each week. Developed and tested for efficacy through two Department of Education grants (CFDA #R324B070034 2007–2012 and #R324A1202602012–2018), OTWH is listed as having promising research evidence on the California Evidence-based Clearinghouse for Child Welfare (www.cebc4cw.org).

In the initial randomized controlled trial (RCT) evaluation of OTWH ($N = 88$; 53 schools/22 districts), at 12-months post-reunification the odds of remaining at home and staying in school were five and three times greater, respectively, for OTWH youth than for youth in the control condition (Trout et al., 2013). In the larger efficacy and replication RCT ($N = 187$; 136 schools/47 districts), findings continued to demonstrate promising effects of OTWH and extended outcomes to 21-months after residential discharge. Specifically, while the immediate gains were similar between groups, long-term follow-up outcomes indicated the odds of youth staying in school and remaining at home were approximately 2.5 and 2.3 times greater, respectively, for youth in OTWH compared to those in the control condition. Finally, although the primary goals of OTWH are to promote school and placement stability, significant differences were also found between treatment and control conditions on family/caregiver self-efficacy ($d = 0.67$) and indicators of family ($d = 0.48$) and community ($d = 0.64$) empowerment. These outcomes provide evidence that when schools, youth, and family/caregivers are engaged and supported to navigate school and home environments during the residential intervention and after reunification, long-term educational and placement stability outcomes improve.

Conclusion

The examples provided throughout this chapter highlight the importance of partnerships involving the many key individuals and entities involved in residential interventions to generate improved practice and outcomes. While there are some differences in how each of the programs approached and evaluated achievement of this challenge, there are important cross-cutting themes: Early and ongoing engagement and partnership with family, active coordination with oversight agencies, identification of and engagement with relevant community partners including schools, and data driven decision making. Establishing partnerships through these practices also provides a foundation for successful aftercare services and supports and positive long-term outcomes.

Contact Information

Judge Jay Blitzman, JD, First Justice Massachusetts Juvenile Court, Middlesex Division (MA): jay.blitzman@jud.state.ma.us

Boys Town Project Reporters and University of Nebraska-Lincoln (NE): Ronald Thompson, PhD, Managing Member, RT Consulting, LLC., and retired Vice President and Director, National Research institute for Child and Family Studies, Boys Town: ronandcol3@gmail.com; Alexandra Trout, PhD, Research Professor, University of Nebraska—Lincoln: Alex.trout@unl.edu; Matthew C. Lambert, PhD, Associate Professor, University of Nebraska—Lincoln: matthew.lambert@unl.edu

Family, Adolescents, and Children Therapy Services, Inc./Collaborative Intensive Bridging Services (MN): www.facts-mn.org
Luke Spiegelhoff, MSW, LICSW, Clinical Director: luke@facts-mn.org

Hathaway-Sycamores Child and Family Services (CA): www.hathaway-sycamores.org
Debra Manners, LCSW, Chief Executive Officer, Family Member: Dmanners@hscfs.org;
Joe Ford, MA, Senior Vice President: jford@hscfs.org

KVC Health Systems (KS): www.kvc.org/kansas
Chad E. Anderson, LSCSW, Chief Clinical Officer: ceanderson@kvc.org

Methodist Children's Home Society (MI): www.mchsmi.org
Kevin Roach, MSW, Chief Executive Officer: kroach@mchsmi.org

Secret Harbor (WA): www.secretharbor.org
Brian Carroll, MSW, LICSW, President and Chief Executive Officer: brian.carroll@secretharbor.org
The Children's Village (NY): www.childrensvillage.org
Kristina Coleman, MSW, MPA, Program Manager; Warren Kent, MSW, Vice President for Community Based Services; Vincent Madera, MSW, Program Director for Permanency Supports; Tina M. Schleicher—Iannotti, MA, Director of Evidence-based Services; Daphne Torres, LCSW-R, Director of Evidence-based Initiatives
All contact info through: vmadera@childrensvillage.org
Youth Development Institute (AZ): www.ydi.org
David Cocoros, MS, Co-Executive Director and Co-Founder: David. Cocoros@ydi.org;
Trish Cocoros, BS, Co-Executive Director and Co-Founder: Trish. Cocoros@ydi.org;
Luis Lopez, MSW, Therapist and first coordinator of YDI's Building Bridges Project: Luis.Lopez@ydi.org

References

ALA Special Presidential Committee Community Partnerships Initiative. (n.d.). Retrieved July 23, 2019, from library.austincc.edu/presentations/Community Partnerships/communitypartnerships1.html
Blitzman, J. (2018, October 26). Personal communication.
Blitzman, J. (2019, July 8). E-mail communication.
Building Bridges. (n.d.). Retrieved July 24, 2019, from www.buildingbridges4youth.org/
Building Bridges Between Residential and Community Based Service Delivery Providers, Families and Youth Joint Resolution to Advance a Statement of Shared Core Principles. (2006). Retrieved July 24, 2019, from www.buildingbridges4youth.org/sites/default/files/BB-Joint-Resolution.pdf
Building Bridges Initiative. (2017). *Implementing effective short-term residential interventions: A building bridges initiative guide.* Retrieved from www.building bridges4youth.org/sites/default/files/BBI%20Short%20Term%20Residential%20 Intervention%20Guide.pdf
California Department of Social Service. (2018). Retrieved July 24, 2019, from www. cdss.ca.gov/
California Legislation. (2015–2016). AB 403. Ch. 773. [Statute].
California Residentially Based Services (RBS). (2014). *Reform project: Final evaluation report*, p. 8.
Catholic Community Services of Western Washington, & EMQ Children & Family Services. (2008). *Family search and engagement: A comprehensive practice guide* [PDF file]. Retrieved July 24, 2019, from https://ccsww.org/wp-content/uploads/2017/04/Family_Search_and_Engagement_Guide_CCS-EMQ.pdf
Courtney, M. (2007, August 17). Personal communication.
Department of Health Care Services. (2018). Retrieved July 24, 2019, from www. dhcs.ca.gov/

Director Dohan, J. M., & Assistant Director Duffy, P. (n.d.). Retrieved August 1, 2019, from www.publiccounsel.net/ya/

The Family First Prevention Services Act, Division E, Title VII of the Bipartisan Budget Act of 2018, Public Law 115–123. February 9, 2018.

Ford, J. (2019, July 17). E-mail communication.

Ford, J. (2019, July 30). E-mail communication.

Kohomban, J. C., & Schwartz, L. T. (2016, May 5). *Survival is not enough: Help children thrive, not just survive.* Retrieved July 16, 2019, from www.huffingtonpost.com/jeremy-christopher-kohomban-phd/survival-is-not-enough-he_b_6496650.html

Johnson, D. (2018, October). Personal communication.

Juvenile Detention Alternatives Initiative®. (n.d.). Retrieved July 24, 2019, from www.aecf.org/work/juvenile-justice/jdai/

Kansas Department of Social and Rehabilitation Services Commission of Children and Family Services. (1996). Community Forum: Privatizing child welfare. *Foster/group care*, 16. SRS Office of Design.

KVC Performance Management Data. (2019, July 23). *Daily Status Report.*

Lieberman, R. E., & DenDunnen, W. (2014). Residential interventions: A historical perspective. In G. Blau, B. Caldwell, & R. E. Lieberman (Eds.), *Residential interventions for children, adolescents, and families: A best practice guide.* New York, NY: Routledge.

Martone, W. (2016, October 3). Personal communication.

Navarro, L. A. (n.d.). Retrieved July 24, 2019, from http://library.austincc.edu/presentations/CommunityPartnerships/communitypartnerships1.html

Nickell, M., & Tate, L. (2018, July 24). *Seneca family of agencies* [PowerPoint Presentation: Residential Provider Transformation: Best Practices and Positive Outcomes]. Presented at the University of Maryland, Baltimore, Building Bridges Initiative Pre-Training Institutes, Washington, DC.

Pecora, P. J., & Blackwell, D. (2015). *Implementing group care in California: The RBS case study.* Seattle: Casey Family Programs. Retrieved from http://www.casey.org/media/rbs-full-report.pdf.

Services, M. (n.d.). *MST services: Multisystemic therapy for juveniles.* Retrieved July 24, 2019, from www.mstservices.com/

Shirk, M., & Stangler, G. J. (2004). *On their own: What happens to kids when they age out of the foster care system?* Boulder, CO. Retrieved July 24, 2019, from Westview Press.

Trout, A. L., Lambert, M. C., Epstein, M. H., Tyler, P., Thompson, R. W., & Daly, D. L. (2013). Comparison of on the way home aftercare supports to traditional care following discharge from a residential setting: A pilot randomized controlled trial. *Child Welfare, 92*(3), 27–45.

Trout, A. L., Tyler, P. M., Stewart, M. C., & Epstein, M. H. (2012). On the way home: Program description and preliminary findings. *Children and Youth Services Review, 34*, 115–1120.

Walter, U. M., & Petr, C. (2007). *Residential treatment: A review of the national literature.* Lawrence, KS: University of Kansas. Retrieved September 10, 2016, from http://childrenandfamilies.ku.edu/sites/childrenandfamilies.drupal.ku.edu/files/docs/residential%20treatment.pdf

9

EVIDENCE-INFORMED RESIDENTIAL PROGRAMS AND PRACTICES FOR YOUTH AND FAMILIES

Sigrid James with Lacy Kendrick Burk[1]

Hardly anyone would dispute that a foremost concern of interventions directed at the psychosocial well-being of children should be their effectiveness in achieving desired outcomes. As such, determining the effectiveness of residential programs and practices has been a pressing goal for the field. The urgency is in part explained by the current service delivery climate, which emphasizes accountability, quality assurance, cost effectiveness, and data-driven decision making and increasingly mandates the delivery of evidence-based practice. For residential programs, demonstrating quality of care as well as the effectiveness of their treatments and practices is of particular importance given the negative repute of this form of intervention as well as concerns about their cost, restrictiveness, potential for abuse and iatrogenic effects (e.g., Barth, 2005; Behar, Friedman, Pinto, Katz-Leavy, & Jones, 2007; Pavkov, Negash, Lourie, & Hug, 2010).

This chapter was included to provide an overview of evidence-informed and promising residential programs and practices for youth and families. This task is not as straightforward as it may appear. A simple presentation of programs and practices that may be evidence-informed is not possible because evidence-informed care implies a flexible and context-specific definition of evidence that draws on a range of sources, both tacit and formal (e.g., Arnd-Caddigan, 2011; Woodbury & Kuhnke, 2014). As such, this chapter will wrestle with the stated objective by first providing a brief overview of developments in *residential care* outcome research. It will further delve into a conceptual discussion about the distinction between evidence-based versus evidence-informed practice and what it means for our current understanding of evidence for residential programs. Finally, it will attempt to approach two of the core principles of the *Building Bridges Initiative (BBI)*—family-driven care and youth-guided care through an evidence-informed lens and conclude with a critical discussion of the implications for residential programs and their practices.

A Brief Overview of Developments in *Residential Care* Outcome Research

During the past decades, *residential care*[2] outcome research has gone through several iterations. There are a number of studies, which have primarily examined whether *residential care* as a whole can be effective in achieving certain outcomes. Such studies generally do not specify a particular type of residential program but treat *residential care* as an umbrella term encompassing a range of programs and practices. Many single outcome studies (e.g., Asarnow, Aoki, & Elson, 1996; Frankfort-Howard & Room, 2002; Landsman, Groza, Tyler, & Malone, 2001; Lyons, Terry, Martinovich, Peterson, & Bouska, 2001) followed by several reviews (e.g., Bettmann & Jasperson, 2009; Boel-Studt & Tobia, 2015; De Swart et al., 2012; Grietens & Hellinckx, 2004; Hair, 2005; Knorth, Harder, Zandberg, & Kendrick, 2008) have provided evidence that *residential care* can be effective in decreasing externalizing behaviors, depression, and other health-risking behaviors while improving prosocial behaviors and family functioning. Beyond generally establishing positive effects for *residential care*, a key finding of this line of research has been the salience of factors that moderate or mediate outcomes. Youths' initial characteristics, their family environment, their length of stay in *residential care*, and other program features, such as the quality of therapeutic relationships, are important contributing factors to positive outcomes (e.g., Duppong Hurley, Lambert, Gross, Thompson, & Farmer, 2017; Lee, Bright, Svoboda, Fakunmoju, & Barth, 2011). More rigorous studies have included comparison or even control groups and have compared the effectiveness of *residential care* with alternative interventions (e.g., Baker, Kurland, Curtis, Alexander, & Papa-Letini, 2007; Erker, Searight, Amanat, & White, 1993; Robst, Armstrong, & Dollard, 2011; Wilmshurst, 2002). This research has produced mixed findings, indicating in some studies that community-based interventions outperform generic *residential care* models (Briggs et al., 2012; Chamberlain & Reid, 1998). Yet, there has also been empirical evidence that when accounting for initial differences, children in *residential care* do not fare worse than children who have not experienced *residential care* episodes (e.g., Barth et al., 2007; James, Roesch, & Zhang, 2012; McCrae, Lee, Barth, & Rauktis, 2010).

Recognizing the considerable heterogeneity of residential programs, the question of interest has since shifted to what particular forms of programs or models work for what types of presenting problems and for which youth (Holden et al., 2010; James, 2011; Lee & Barth, 2011; Pecora & English, 2016;

Whittaker, del Valle, & Holmes, 2015) and, more recently, to what evidence-based practices and treatments can be effectively implemented by residential programs (James, Alemi, & Zepeda, 2013; James et al., 2015; James, Thompson, & Ringle, 2017; Thompson, Duppong Hurley, Trout, Huefner, & Daly, 2017). A growing field of inquiry concerns the complex process of the dissemination and implementation of evidence-based practices, from planning stage to sustainability, within specific organizational contexts such as residential programs (e.g., Albers, Mildon, Lyon, & Shlonsky, 2017; Bryson et al., 2017; Hodgdon, Kinniburgh, Gabowitz, Blaustein, & Spinazzola, 2013; Hummer, Dollard, Robst, & Armstrong, 2010; James et al., 2017). The process of identifying evidence-based practices and implementing them with fidelity has been referred to as a "top-down" approach (e.g., Okpych & Yu, 2014). Critics of this approach, which is judged by some as too constricting and unsuitable for clinical decision making in complex practice settings such as residential programs, have offered alternative conceptualizations for evidence as well as for practice and evaluation frameworks that seem to be more fitting for these realities (e.g., Barth, 2008; Barth, Kolivoski, Lindsey, Lee, & Collins, 2014; Lee & McMillen, 2017; Smith, 2017). Within this context, the term *evidence-informed* has emerged to explicitly embrace a more flexible and inclusive approach to determine evidence and guide clinical decision making (Shlonsky, Noonan, Littell, & Montgomery, 2011).

The *BBI* has deliberately chosen the evidence-informed terminology. Based on decades of practice experience with diverse residential programs, the testimony of youths and families, as well as supporting research, the argument is made that the field knows how to improve outcomes of residential programs (Harrington, Williams-Washington, Caldwell, Lieberman, & Blau, 2014). Building on six core principles (Blau, Caldwell, & Lieberman, 2014), the emphasis is placed on providing guidance and guidelines on how to implement these principles by different residential programs, thereby improving outcomes. Naturally, this perspective impacts how the evidence for residential programs and practices is gathered and appraised. To understand the implications, the next section will delve more deeply into the conceptual distinctions between evidence-based and evidence-informed practice.

What's in a Word?—On Evidence-Based, Evidence-Informed, Promising, and Other Terms

As service systems at all levels have increasingly embraced and solidified evidence-based practice through policy and funding mandates, questions remain about what constitutes evidence-based practice. Many of the current debates about what practices, treatments, or interventions should be adopted and implemented and which ones deserve the coveted evidence-based label, stem from definitional confusions, disagreements, and imprecisions about the concept of evidence-based practice. Over the years, multiple alternative terms to evidence-based practice have been introduced into the academic literature and the professional dialogue to presumably clarify or broaden its meaning, distinguish between degrees of evidence, or offer more nuanced conceptualizations (DiGennaro Reed & Reed, 2008; Epstein, 2011; Parrish, 2018; Woodbury & Kuhnke, 2014). Terms and concepts that can be found include the plural form "evidence-based practices" (or alternatively, evidence-based treatments or interventions) as well as empirically validated or supported interventions or treatments, evidence-informed practice, research-based practice, best practice, promising practice, as well as practice-based research or evidence and community-based evidence. Changes in semantics are frequently accompanied by their requisite acronyms (e.g., EBP, EST, EBI, EIP, EBT, PBE), creating an utterly confusing landscape for researchers, practitioners, and policymakers and contributing to fundamental misunderstandings about evidence and the methods to derive it (Gambrill, 2015, 2016).

Lacking a collective definition and understanding has been very problematic for the field (Parrish, 2018), often pitting practitioners against researchers. Practitioners lament that evidence-based practice implies a narrow view of evidence as well as process of implementation and frequently claim that researchers lack an understanding for the complexities of practice in real-world service systems. They also criticize that the evidence-based approach discriminates against indigenous or culturally embedded approaches that have found acceptance by families, youth, and consumers (e.g., Aisenberg, 2008; Conner & Grote, 2008). In addition, ethical concerns about conducting randomized trials with real-world clients are cited (e.g., Sullivan, 2011). Researchers, on the other hand, complain that practitioners offer up "watered-down" versions of evidence that reflect a lack of understanding of research and the scientific methods required to conclude that an intervention "works." Agreements or disagreements on this issue can have a direct impact on investment and funding decisions. Not meeting established criteria can mean a loss of contract or funding for established programs and the termination of programs that lack the required evidence (Walker, Lyon, Aos, & Trupin, 2017). Given limited funding for both program development and evaluation and the resultant competitive environment, being able to claim that a program delivers evidence-based practice can be a matter of program survival.

To understand the evolution and the "distortions" of the term *evidence-based practice* (Gambrill, 2007, p. 447), it is helpful to go back to its original conceptualization. As put forth by Sackett and his colleagues, evidence-based practice implies "the conscientious, explicit and judicious use of current best evidence in making decisions about the care of individual patients" (Sackett,

Rosenberg, Gray, Haynes, & Richardson, 1996, p. 71). Evidence emerges out of an integrative case-based process, which draws on three different sources of knowledge and evidence—clinical expertise, external evidence, and client values—with neither source being in and of itself sufficient to guide decisions about practice or treatment (Straus, Glasziou, Richardson, & Haynes, 2011). In their 1996 article published in the British Medical Journal, Sackett et al. actually stated that "without clinical expertise, practice risks becoming tyrannized by evidence, for even excellent external evidence may be inapplicable to or inappropriate for an individual patient" (p. 72). The authors further wrote that evidence should not be restricted to randomized trials and meta-analyses.

> Some questions about therapy do not require randomized trials . . . or cannot wait for the trials to be conducted. And if no randomized trial has been carried out for our patient's predicament, we must follow the trail to the next best external evidence and work from here.
>
> (p. 72)

Returning to the original understanding of evidence-based practice seems all the more important as in the policy arena and for funding purposes the top-down conception dominates. Here evidence-based practice refers to "interventions, programs, or policies that certain entities have deemed to have a desired level of research support regarding effectiveness" (Parrish, 2018, p. 407).[3] Evidence-based has thus become equated with "effective" according to established scientific standards. However, what is regarded as sufficiently persuasive research evidence may vary somewhat across organizations, which have created their own sets of criteria to attach a label to an intervention's evidence base. As an example, the well-regarded California Evidence-based Clearinghouse for Child Welfare (CEBC) uses six ratings to evaluate and rate the effectiveness of an intervention or treatment (1 = well supported, 2 = supported, 3 = promising, 4 = evidence fails to demonstrate effect, 5 = concerning practice, NR= not able to be rated). To be "well supported by research evidence," at least two rigorous randomized trials have to have been conducted in different settings and shown to produce positive outcomes, with one trial demonstrating sustained effects beyond one-year post-treatment. Another requirement concerns publication in the peer-reviewed literature.

There is a long list of resources and clearinghouses, all with their own rating and labeling schemes. These may vary with regard to the number of randomized trials or follow-up periods that are needed to be considered "effective" or "promising." The recent suspension of the National Registry of Evidence-Based Programs and Practices further highlights the consequences of disagreements about evidence and the methods to derive it (Green-Hanessy, 2018). And although discussions about the suitability of randomized controlled trials (RCT) for fields outside of medicine are ongoing (e.g., Sullivan, 2011), there is consensus in the scientific community about the need to deliver the science behind practice in the most rigorous way possible or agreed upon, and in the determination for empirical evidence and funding, the RCT continues to occupy a gold standard role (Harriton & Locascio, 2018). How this evidence is then used at the individual person or program level constitutes the integrative process of evidence-based practice.

Residential Care and the Evidence-Based Practice Dilemma

Using the RCT as a gold standard along with other criteria of scientific rigor, i.e., two independent investigators, use of treatment manuals, treatment fidelity, and long-term outcomes, it can be concluded that much of the outcome research on residential programs and practices falls short of meeting scientific criteria for effectiveness (and thus evidence-based practice as defined top-down). A number of residential program models have been identified in the literature (James, 2011; Pecora & English, 2016), but only the Positive Peer Culture model developed by Vorrath and Brendtro has had a requisite RCT (Leeman, Gibbs, & Fuller, 1993), which warrants a "supported by research evidence" rating by the CEBC. All other models (e.g., Teaching Family Model, Sanctuary Model, Children and Residential Experiences, etc.) have so far relied on less rigorous study designs (quasi-experimental and pre-post designs) and are either considered "promising" or not yet sufficiently supported by research evidence (see California Evidence-Based Clearinghouse for Child Welfare, n.d.; James, 2011; Pecora & English, 2016).[4]

The lack of persuasive scientific evidence, combined with the growing number of alternative community-based interventions for children and youth with problems similar to those encountered in youth served by residential programs, has put *residential care* as a type of program and form of intervention under considerable pressure to provide proof of its quality and effectiveness (Farmer, Murray, Ballentine, Rauktis, & Burns, 2017; Huefner, 2018). Whittaker and colleagues discuss this dilemma and its repercussions in their 2016 Consensus Statement of the International Work Group on Therapeutic Residential Care (Whittaker et al., 2016). In the US and other Anglo-American countries, placement in residential programs has primarily become a stop-gap option and an intervention of last resort, and in many child welfare systems it is in fact regarded as an adverse outcome rather than a viable, albeit temporary, alternative in a continuum of services for youth and their families. And even in countries that have long relied on *residential care* as a primary form of care and intervention for abandoned and abused children, a shift toward smaller programs or family-based care is occurring (e.g., Mackenzie et al., 2012; Nakatomi, Ichikawa, Wakabayashi, &

Takemura, 2018). Furthermore, the mandate to deliver evidence-based practice has led to the closure of some residential programs and a fundamental stance "against all things residential" (e.g., Dozier et al., 2014).

These developments have spurred the curious trend of delivering or implementing treatments and interventions within residential programs, which were not designed for them or, in most cases, have not been evaluated within the context of these settings (e.g., Bright, Raghavan, Kliethermes, Juedemann, & Dunn, 2010; James et al., 2013, 2015). Thus, treatments such as Dialectical Behavior Therapy, Trauma-Focused CBT, or Eye Movement Desensitization and Reprocessing are increasingly adopted by residential programs, thus allowing providers to report that evidence-based practices are indeed being used. While this practice has some appealing features (e.g., client-specific evidence-based interventions are meant to augment an overall residential program model and therefore do not require the reorganization of an entire residential program concept; they can be delivered and implemented in multiple ways, etc.), there are drawbacks. For instance, it remains unknown for many of these interventions whether they produce similar results with residential programs as within the settings that they were originally designed and evaluated for. Furthermore, adaptations may be necessary given the residential program context, and, most of all, it remains unclear whether or how a chosen treatment or intervention fits with an overall program concept (James et al., 2017). As Whittaker et al. (2016) point out, *residential care* is "something more than simply a platform for collecting evidence-based interventions or promising techniques or strategies" (p. 97). It should be understood as a transformational environment where "learning through living and . . . a series of deeply personal, human relationships" occurs (p. 97).

Toward Evidence-Informed Practice

While some experts argue for more rigorous outcome studies of residential programs and practices (along with the requisite funding to conduct them), others push back against the presumably narrow definition of evidence-based practice, which has placed primary weight on available external evidence derived through randomized controlled trials or quantitative research more generally. They suggest that information used to make decisions in clinical practice should include evidence from a variety of sources—including qualitative studies, practice wisdom, case reports, and expert opinion—and be inclusive of the perspectives of youth and families to address a wider range of goals besides reducing bias in intervention research (e.g., Arnd-Caddigan, 2011; Estabrooks, 1998; Miles & Loughlin, 2011; Tickle-Degnen & Bedell, 2003).[5] In this context the term *evidence-informed* was introduced.

While the term *evidence-informed* is increasingly being used—including by the World Health Organization (WHO, 2013)—it is not without its problems. The term is often introduced without providing a clear definition or is used interchangeably with evidence-based practice. The greater flexibility and unclear standards also mean that it is more difficult to specify or recognize evidence-informed practice and determine what evidence may be lacking or which of the many acceptable sources hold more evidentiary weight (Gambrill, 2018). Lacking standards opens the potential for an exaggerated reliance on anecdotal data and claims of evidence by almost anybody without being able to challenge it. This dilemma has been recognized and addressed, for instance, in the context of a prior discussion on practice-based research (ORCF, 2011). Here efforts were made to delineate criteria by which practice-based evidence could be judged, including being "(a) community valued, (b) culturally and socially embedded," and addressing "(c) heretofore unaddressed community/population conditions, and (d) emergent issues" (p. 4).

Whether there is a difference between the original integrative and process-oriented conceptualization of evidence-based practice and the concept of evidence-informed care remains unclear. Evidence-based practice appears to be clearer in its embracing of established scientific standards to determine effectiveness. However, as part of the evidence-based process, the best available evidence from research would still have to be balanced with consumer preferences and the clinical impressions of the practitioners. Thus, it could be argued that the many different terms—including the term "evidence-informed"—would not have been necessary if the original integrative conceptualization of evidence-based practice had been understood and applied in the first place. The introduction of so many different and at times diffuse terms has not served the field well.

Yet—and this is where the opportunities lie—the context-based and integrative approach, which is inherent to evidence-informed practice as well as the original understanding of evidence-based practice, would require a return to the individual person or program level, at which considerations about the integration of various evidentiary sources need to occur. Research on this integrative process is sorely missing (Gomersall, 2006; Shlonsky & Gibbs, 2004) and would require research methodologies that capture context and actively engage youth and families.

Guiding Principles for Residential Programs and Their Impact on Outcomes

By now it should be apparent why it is not possible to simply supply a list of evidence-informed practices. Instead, in the remainder of the chapter the attempt is made to take an evidence-informed stance and capture the evidence about practices and interventions related to two central principles of the *BBI*—family-driven care and youth-guided practices. Both are part and parcel of "good practice" in community-based mental health services for children and youth, and there is considerable consensus within the residential provider community as well as among child welfare researchers that *residential care* has the greatest potential for positive outcomes when youth and families are actively engaged (Walter & Petr, 2008). However, whether and how residential programs operationalize family-driven and youth-guided practices and to what extent they implement elements of these guiding principles remains largely unexamined.

Family-Driven Care

In his concise critique of *residential care*, Rick Barth (2005) argued that greater family involvement is "almost certainly the most important adaptation that residential care must make to bridge the evidentiary and philosophical concerns that cloud its future" (p. 159). Family-driven care as conceptualized by Hust and Kuppinger in the first edition of this book (2014) is reflected in a range of guiding principles—i.e., embracing of the concept by families, youth, providers, and administrators; fully informing families and youth about goals and involving them in all decision-making processes; allocating resources toward family-driven practice; etc. (p. 16)—all aimed at engaging and strengthening families, keeping the organization focused on the needs and contributions of families, and delivering services that involve them. The extent to which residential programs have adopted principles of family-driven care and operationalized them into deliverable treatment elements remains unknown but there is evidence of a lack of family-driven practices in residential programs as well as considerable variability when in fact it is implemented (Brown, Allen, Pires, & Blau, 2010).

Family-driven care is not an intervention or a program model but, first of all, a principled approach that can be realized in a diverse set of practices. To date, its impact on outcomes when family-driven principles—partially or in their entirety—are implemented has not been systematically examined. Instead, contributions in the professional and academic literature have focused on delineating recommendations for the implementation of family-driven care and the removal of structural barriers (e.g., American Association of Children's Residential Centers, 2009a, 2009b; Herman et al., 2011; Nickerson, Salamone, Brooks, & Colby, 2004; Sharrock, Dollard, Armstrong, & Rohrer, 2013). Lacking rigorous evaluative studies, family-driven care would not be counted as an evidence-based practice to be implemented. However, this does not mean that it is not informed by evidence. The following section draws on multiple sources that support the need and value of a family-driven approach.

The Foundation of Family-Driven Care

Family-driven care reflects professional values that are central to social work and other behavioral health professions (Friesen, Koroloff, Walker, & Briggs, 2011). The central role of the family to the healthy upbringing of the child is also enshrined in the United Nations Children's Rights Conventions

(Committee on the Rights of the Child, 1992), and, thus, a child's access to his or her family as well as his or her treatment while in out-of-home care can be argued as a matter of human rights (e.g., Ashton, 2014). In addition, the constitutions of many countries recognize the fundamental rights of children and families, thus providing a legal basis for practices that are family-driven (Habashi, Wright, & Hathcoat, 2012). While the US remains the only nation that has not ratified the Children's Rights Convention, US child welfare policy reflects the central role of the family, mandating the preservation and well-being of the family once the safety of the child has been ensured (U.S. Department of Health and Human Services, n.d.). Over the course of the last 50 years, child welfare policy has increasingly embraced a family-focused orientation, supported by conceptual shifts and empirical findings that substantiated the importance of the family. The Family First Prevention Services Act of 2018 is the latest federal law that promotes the rights of the family, allocating funding for in-home services to prevent children from entering out-of-home care (First Focus Campaign for Children, 2018). The law further limits and redefines the function and role of residential programs, which are not seen as congruent with a family-driven perspective. Over the last several decades, multiple initiatives at the federal, state, and local level have aimed to strengthen families, thereby reducing the need for out-of-home care and improving outcomes for children (U.S. Department of Health and Human Services, 2009). While current policy significantly limits the role of *residential care*, the need for residential programs to adapt to the service environment by being inclusive of family is all the more urgent.

Family-driven care also constitutes practice that is theoretically sound. A number of theories, from family and ecological systems theories, developmental theory, and resilience theory to attachment theory, emphasize the saliency of the family to the healthy development of the child and youth.[6] These theories have been tested in multiple epidemiological as well as clinical studies, validating the important role of the parents and/or family for healthy developmental outcomes (e.g., Hawkins, Amato, & King, 2006; Hoskins, 2014; Russell, Beckmeyer, & Su-Russell, 2018). Thus, it can be concluded that family-driven care is grounded in important professional, ethical, legal, and theoretical considerations about the central role of the family and is, in principle, supported by numerous empirical findings.

Parents and Families as Part of Evidence-Based Interventions for Children and Youth With Serious Emotional and Behavioral Problems

The theoretical and empirical basis for greater family involvement has spurred the development of numerous interventions and treatment elements aimed at engaging, involving, and strengthening parents and/or the entire family. In fact, a central element of many evidence-based interventions for children and youth with backgrounds of abuse and/or serious emotional and behavioral problems is the explicit involvement of their parents and, in some cases, the family more generally. For instance, of the most effective interventions for disruptive behaviors listed by the CEBC,[7] all involve parent components to various degrees, and some (e.g., Triple P) are primarily focused on intervening directly with the parents. In fact, working directly or primarily with parents has been shown to be an effective way of reducing child behavior problems (e.g., Barth et al., 2005). In 2016, Merritts reviewed effective family therapy models that are promising for complex settings such as *residential care*. These included multiple-family group intervention, family-directed structural therapy, narrative family therapy, brief strategic family therapy, multisystemic therapy, and functional family therapy. In addition, Casey Family Programs (2018) published a comprehensive list of family interventions that have empirical support. Many of these interventions were not developed for *residential care*; instead, they were designed as family- and community-based alternatives to *residential care*. However, it has been argued that these interventions may "be adapted within the framework of a family-centered, short-term residential placement" (Nickerson et al., 2004, p. 7) to optimally engage, strengthen, and treat families. Working with parents and/or families may encompass elements and techniques such as parenting skills training, parental support groups, family therapy, psychoeducation, active teaching and modeling, role play, and a range of engagement and family systems techniques.

While it is safe to state that the effectiveness of parent- or family-mediated interventions is supported by empirical evidence with regard to multiple outcomes, how central parent or family components as part of multi-component interventions are to the success of a treatment is less clear. Disentangling effects in multi-component interventions is methodologically difficult, yet this is an important empirical question for residential programs where it may be particularly difficult to engage parents and families in treatment. For instance, when implementing Dialectical Behavioral Therapy for Adolescents, a treatment that is increasingly being implemented by residential programs and by design involves explicit parent components, is it possible to obtain the full effects of the treatment when parents are not able or not yet willing to be involved? The contribution of parent or family involvement in multi-component interventions to treatment success thus remains an area in need of inquiry.

Parent and Family Involvement in the Context of Residential Programs

There have been a number of studies that have found that outcomes for youth in residential programs can be improved or moderated if families are involved (e.g., Affronti & Levison-Johnson, 2009; Knorth et al., 2008;

Lee, Hwang, Socha, Pau, & Shaw, 2013; Robst et al., 2013; Robst, Rohrer, Dollard, & Armstrong, 2014; Sunseri, 2004). Family involvement in these studies has been operationalized in a variety of ways, such as counting family visitations and participation in meetings, classifying reasons for visits, examining parental motivation, and evaluating relational quality and family functioning (see Affronti & Levison-Johnson's comprehensive review of "family engagement in residential care settings").

An examination of residential program models rated as having some empirical support by the CEBC (e.g., Positive Peer Culture, Children and Residential Experiences, Teaching Family Model, etc.) indicates that almost all have explicit parent or family components aimed at involving, educating, and strengthening families (California Evidence-Based Clearinghouse for Child Welfare, n.d.). However, compared to other treatment elements these appear to be less central, and, similar to the multi-component interventions already mentioned previously, it remains unclear to what degree these elements contribute to treatment success.

The Evidence of Family-Driven Care

As shown, family-driven care is based on solid professional, ethical, legal, and theoretical considerations. There is also overwhelming empirical evidence of the benefits of involving families in services both with residential programs as well as in the community. Yet family-driven care is not simply an intervention model but involves a set of principles meant to guide organizations. As laid out by the *BBI* these principles remain largely unexamined. An important step in the scientific process is to operationalize constructs and then to measure them in the real world. This has been accomplished by the *BBI* through their Self-Assessment Tool, which could serve as a fidelity measure against which residential programs assess to what degree they engage in family-driven care. However, to definitively establish the empirical evidence of family-driven care, these indicators would then have to be examined in relationship to target outcomes and compared to outcomes of programs that vary in the degree of implementation of family-driven care principles. This work has begun but needs to be further developed to meet expected scientific standards.

Youth-Guided Care

Similar to family-driven care, respect for the views of the child is steeped in human rights and legal and ethical considerations (e.g., Committee on the Rights of the Child, 1992). Not surprisingly, youth "voice" and participation are primary themes in the context of out-of-home care in many countries (e.g., Berejena Mhongera, 2017; Glynn & Mayock, 2019). They reflect the belief that children are "competent and deserving of participation" (Habashi et al., 2012, p. 65) and that residential programs have the responsibility to create opportunities for youth involvement. And finally, they are an acknowledgment that children and, by extension, societies, fare better when children and youth are actively engaged and have opportunities for participation.

Like family-driven care, youth-guided care is to date foremost a principled approach that has yet to be fully tested, particularly in the context of residential programs. There are, as noted previously, a number of treatments and clinical interventions that are utilized with residential programs and have been evaluated with regard to the perspectives/involvement of families and youth. However, the youth-guided care principle is particular in its focus on encouraging youth voice in their treatment planning, the program design in which they participate, the administrative/governance level of residential programs, and in the policies that govern residential program settings.[8]

While youth-guided care has not been measured or evaluated in its entirety or its effects disentangled from other intervention elements, there are many practices across multiple child-serving systems, which operationalize a youth-guided approach and have in part been evaluated. Further research is necessary to examine the direct application of these youth-guided practices specific to *residential care*. This section outlines the evidence of some of the practices, which can enhance the implementation of youth-guided care in residential programs.

Positive Youth Development and Resilience-Based Approaches

The conceptual shift toward a resilience-based approach likely began with Emmy Werner's longitudinal Kauai study, conducted in the 1950s (Werner & Smith, 1977), and was furthered by developments and research findings from several disciplines. Beginning in the early 1990s, researchers, practitioners, and policymakers worked in earnest toward the development of programs and structures that no longer reflected the deficit-based, problem-centered approach that had previously characterized interventive efforts but instead considered what optimal and ideal development for adolescents looked like. Pittman and others (1991, 2017) laid the foundation from which positive youth development (PYD) emerged as an innovative practice, and youth-serving programs began to adapt this model. Commissioned by several federal agencies, Catalano and colleagues (2002) conducted a systematic review of experimental and quasi-experimental evaluations of non-treatment PYD programs and in their findings offered a comprehensive overview of 25 rigorously evaluated programs, which studied positive behavior outcomes across community, school, and family settings (Catalano, Berglund, Ryan, Lonczak, & Hawkins, 2002).

> The study concluded that a wide range of positive youth development approaches can result in positive youth behavior outcomes and the

Evidence-Informed Residential Programs **181**

prevention of youth problem behaviors. . . . Promotion and prevention programs that address positive youth development constructs are definitely making a difference in well-evaluated studies.

(p. 82)

Since then there have been many more studies in multiple child-serving contexts and across countries, substantiating the positive effect of PYD. For instance, in a multi-year, community-based research project, Iwasaki (2016) found that the inclusion of youth engagement approaches resulted in positive gains in PYD and Social Justice Youth Development and offered the following specific PYD approaches:

(1) strengths-based empowering approach to youth engagement, (2) capacity building and positive outcomes for youth and youth-serving agencies and (3) youth-oriented, collaborative research processes that enable the promotion of these positive outcomes (e.g. honoring youth voice: "bottom-up process for youth by youth").

(p. 267)

As approaches to youth participation evolved beyond the positive development of youth, practitioners and researchers began to consider a more holistic, strengths-based approach to help youth reach maximum potential and thrive despite extreme trauma, adversity, and behavioral health diagnoses. The Center for the Study of Social Policy developed a concept of "Youth Thrive," which shifts the focus from a limited treatment approach to a holistic, strengths-based and healing-centered approach. From this research, five promotive and protective factors emerged: Youth resilience, social connections, knowledge of adolescent development, concrete support in times of need, and cognitive and social-emotional competence (Browne, Notkin, Schneider-Munoz, & Zimmerman, 2015).

In recent years, a few studies evaluating PYD have been conducted within residential programs. In a longitudinal randomized trial of a residential PYD program in Jamaica, Hull, Saxon, Fagan, Williams, and Verdisco (2018) found that PYD approaches in youth programming resulted in improved skillsets for problem-solving (rather than problem-creating) and increased self-efficacy for "unattached" youth (those who are not employed or involved with education systems). Quisenberry and Foltz (2013) also suggested that the utilization of PYD and resilience approaches can actually lead to more effective treatment interventions. In a correlational study, they observed that youth who exhibited characteristics of resilience had better PYD outcomes.

Given the cumulative evidence on youth-guided care, residential program administrators and workers would do well to carefully examine and consider the extent to which their residential practices are promoting resilience and

182 Sigrid James with Lacy Kendrick Burk

PYD approaches throughout the residential program. In this context, a study by Collins, Hill, and Miranda (2008) may be helpful. They reported on evaluative results of a training program for group home supervisors to facilitate the implementation of PYD principles and identified barriers to training and implementation.

Youth Leadership and Youth Advisory Boards

The positive outcomes from leadership development have been demonstrated for decades across corporate settings and to a lesser extent in human services. Positive outcomes also transfer to youth involved in leadership development programs, including significant increases in social self-efficacy, sense of connection to the community, and self-regulatory efficacy (self-control), which can be a common challenge for youth, particularly for those who enter residential programs (Anderson, Sabatelli, & Trachtenberg, 2006–07). Anderson et al. (2006–07) also found that higher gains were made for youth who entered the leadership training program as "less socially and emotionally skilled" (p. 14) than their peer counterparts, leading to an inference of possible significant implications for youth in residential program settings.

Youth advisory boards (YAB) are a key mechanism to pursue solutions that are mutually beneficial: Youth can develop leadership and advocacy skills (i.e., teamwork, communication, and problem solving), and residential programs can gain much needed input from their key constituents while implementing the youth-guided-care principle. There is no shortage of evidence of the use of YABs and youths as decision makers. As early as 1999, approximately one-half of non-profit agencies utilized youth advisors as key decision makers (Zeldin, 2000). Every state child welfare system utilizes a YAB in their child welfare agency, which serves the purpose of addressing youth advocacy issues and advises state agency directors (e.g., Forenza & Happonen, 2016; Havlicek, Lin, & Villalpando, 2016). Many systems of care initiatives utilize YABs as a means to implement youth-guided principles (e.g., Friesen et al., 2011). Havlicek and colleagues (2018) developed a YAB interview measure to assess their impact. YABs impact youth members in several positive ways: Positive increases in identity affiliation, identity affirmation, civic activism, self-efficacy, community supports, supports and opportunities, socio-emotional and identity well-being, sense of leadership, mentorship, and advocacy were found as a result of participation in YABs (Forenza & Happonen, 2016; Havlicek & Samuels, 2018; Naccarato & Knipe, 2015). As an example, Youth Development Institute in Arizona, a 120-bed residential program, credits its YAB as a significant contributor to culture and practice change that has reportedly resulted in having no restraints in over 600 days (Caldwell, Tate, Cocoros, & Cocoros, 2018).

Despite the success and positive outcomes of many YAB initiatives, use of YABs with residential programs is extremely limited. They are part of a few evidence-based program models such as the Teaching Family Model and Positive Peer Culture. Again, the effect of this part of the model vis-à-vis other program elements has not been determined. More attention is necessary to utilize YABs with residential programs in order to realize the positive effects on youth members and on the organizational setting. Such efforts should be accompanied by the requisite evaluation research.

Youth Peer Support

Peer support approaches to services have been in existence for decades across service systems and experiences, beginning with the 12-step community in the late 1930s. Peer support services in the mental health field specifically have also developed, including the later emergence of family and youth peer support (e.g., Burke, Pyle, Morrison, & Machin, 2018). Research on the outcomes of peer support practice is prevalent. Well documented outcomes of peer support include:

> *Reduced inpatient service use, improved relationship with providers, better engagement with care, higher levels of empowerment, higher levels of patient activation, and higher levels of hopefulness for recovery . . . help people attain other goals, such as employment, education, housing, and social relations . . . reduce the cost of care . . . increase the use of primary care over emergency services, reduce psychiatric rehospitalizations, make patients more active in treatment . . . [and] may be a cost-effective and cost-saving strategy for providing services for a chronic health condition.*
> (Gagne, Finch, Myrick, & Davis, 2018, p. S262)

While evidence for peer support practices continues to grow, YPS evidence is only starting to be gathered. Findings to date include increased trust, improved service delivery, and increased credibility (Cherna, 2012) as well as a higher rate of engagement, improved navigation of the transition from the children's mental health system to the adult serving system (Gopalan, Lee, Harris, Acri, & Munson, 2017), validation, and reciprocity (Delman & Klodnick, 2017). Though it remains to be seen if all the benefits of peer support and YPS are transferable to residential programs, the argument can be made that similar outcomes are possible when one considers the numerous encouraging outcomes from the peer support literature.

Youth have a right to participate in their own lives. Moreover, when youth are actively and meaningfully engaged in decisions that affect their lives and the world around them, positive outcomes occur as a result. Residential programs have an enormous opportunity to bolster youth-guided practices through implementing positive youth development approaches, establishing and supporting youth leadership activities, and in developing and offering youth peer support services. The positive benefits youth receive from participation with youth-guided programming serve to support the goal of residential programs and practices: To improve the lives of youth and their families. From a research perspective, however, there is still much room for systematic inquiry in all areas of youth-guided care to really understand what added contribution youth-guided elements make to program effectiveness and to determine whether they have a direct, moderating, or mediating effect on outcomes.

Conclusion

This chapter has shown that evidence-based practice can be a minefield. Developments in the concept, definitional imprecisions, and differing standards for evidence along with policy mandates for the implementation of evidence-based practice, i.e., empirically supported interventions, have contributed to a challenging landscape for service providers. This is particularly true for residential programs, which are often regarded as the comparison group against which the effectiveness of community-based programs is assessed. Given the very real consequences when not being considered evidence-based, there is a vested interest programs have in obtaining this label. Against this backdrop, it is entirely conceivable why many residential programs have begun to adopt interventions that are already considered to be evidence-based. It seems to be the surest and fastest way of being able to claim to deliver evidence-based practice. However, as was shown earlier, there are multiple concerns with this approach, not the least the need to determine whether imported evidence-based treatments are indeed effective as part of residential programs and what they contribute in the context of the totality of a program model.

As such, the approach chosen by the *BBI* appropriately refocuses residential programs to the core mechanisms or principles that are likely at work in effective programs. The term evidence-informed practice that is used in this context acknowledges the need to be inclusive of all relevant perspectives and voices when describing evidence and building evidence from the ground-up with flexible methods. This integrative approach that at least partially mirrors the original conception of evidence-based practice clashes in fundamental ways with the top-down approach, primarily concerned with identifying empirically supported interventions and implementing them with fidelity. And it has its own set of challenges! Most consequentially, the more diffuse and contextually-based evidence translates into difficulties of being recognized as an intervention "supported by research evidence." In addition, however, a lack of clarity about the standards for evidence-informed practice and a context-based conceptualization of evidence imply that recommendations for "best practices" should be dispensed and considered very cautiously. This chapter has shown how evidence can be drawn from ethical, policy, practice, and research considerations, but more work needs to be done to develop standards as well as help providers appraise the weight of different sources of evidence and draw inferences about its significance for their particular program. This integrative, program-level, and emergent way of generating evidence is what evidence-based practice was all about to begin with, and it is exciting to think how programs could contribute to the advancement of knowledge by demonstrating and documenting in transparent and systematic ways how they engage in this process.

However, a broadened understanding of evidence does not absolve one of the responsibility to deliver the necessary science in the most rigorous way possible. Thus, research that might begin "from within" would ultimately need to progress beyond qualitative studies, client or staff satisfaction surveys, and simple (pre-)post design studies. Such studies should be lauded for being a starting-point, but they do not suffice to build the science of a field. In their critical discussion of "pathways forward for embracing evidence-based practice in group care settings" (p. 19), Lee and McMillen (2017) propose how residential program models and interventions that are "home-grown" can gradually build the required empirical evidence and "nurture it into an EBP" (p. 21). This could begin with exploiting available data and systematically gathering pre-post outcome data. Implicit in this discussion is the recognition that rigorous evaluations and outcome research are necessary to claim empirical evidence.

Research approaches such as Participatory Action Research, which actively involve all stakeholders in the design and execution of a study, are particularly promising for capturing diverse perspectives and context while being reflective of the core principles of family-driven and youth-guided care itself. Findings from careful foundational research could then shape continued outcome research, perhaps redefining outcome targets to reflect stakeholder interests and drawing attention to important moderating or mediating processes. Yet in the end, the careful development and execution of randomized or at least quasi-experimental trials[9] will likely be necessary to demonstrate effectiveness empirically and attract funding. Federal agencies, such as the National Institute of Mental Health, have recognized the developmental nature of outcome research and provide funding for all its phases from developmental pilot work involving qualitative work and pre-experimental designs to large-scale implementation studies. However, the unfortunate reality is that at the present time such funding is almost impossible to obtain for research on *residential care* in the US given the strong ideological bent against this form of intervention. Whittaker et al. (2016) acknowledged the difficult road ahead for (therapeutic) *residential care* given the dearth of research funding for this type of programming and time-limited service contracts that may prevent launching rigorous research in a *residential care* context. As such, residential programs interested in knowledge development will have to proceed strategically, identifying research questions that reflect shared interests and perhaps partnering with other residential programs as well as academic institutions in research endeavors (Thompson et al., 2017).

What should not be done is using the terms *evidence-informed* and *evidence-based* interchangeably as a way of circumventing accepted scientific standards for effectiveness. It is entirely permissible for an agency to state that the evidence it has gathered (from multiple sources) is convincing enough to the program and its stakeholders to continue delivering a certain model or intervention. But it is troublesome for programs to present themselves as delivering empirically supported treatments when the necessary research has not been done.

The *BBI* has made an important contribution by addressing definitional issues on *residential care* and redefining it as a program and practice to be used in targeted and effective ways. It has drawn attention to the multiple perspectives that should shape current understanding of outcomes and processes and developed a measure that promises to link *BBI* principles and practices to measurable outcomes. It has also shown how problematic the "top-down" approach of evidence-based practice can be for complex settings such as residential programs. Finally, it has initiated efforts at systematic data-gathering in residential programs that could be built upon and contribute to a strengthening of the empirical knowledge base of residential programs. Going forward, continuing work to accumulate evidence about family-driven, youth-guided, and other BBI practices is needed and will undoubtedly further advance efforts to transform the use of residential interventions.

Notes

1. Lacy Kendrick Burk contributed the section on youth-guided care and was instrumental in linking the *Building Bridges Initiative* principles of family-driven and youth guided care to international children's rights. I want to thank her and Bob Lieberman for their critical and valuable feedback on the chapter.
2. The use of terminology has been a critical issue for residential programs (e.g., Lee & Barth, 2011). Various terms have been used in the professional and academic literature to describe congregate care settings, including residential care, residential group care, group care, group homes, residential treatment, residential programs, institutional care, etc. The *Building Bridges Initiative* has opted for the term residential interventions, provided by residential programs, to emphasize that *residential care* is not simply a setting but a form of intervention that can be used in targeted and effective ways. While this conveys an important conceptual point, it does not allow for an accurate review and capturing of the literature, which often does not make this distinction. To be consistent with the approach of this book, the term "residential program" will be used to connote the setting of *residential care*. The term "residential practices" will be used to refer to specific

interventions and treatments delivered by residential programs. However, to reflect the language in the literature and at times for linguistic reasons, the generic term *residential care* in italicized form will be used.

3. The reasons for the shift from a bottom-up or case-based integrative process toward the top-down implementation of empirically supported treatments are multifold and include the explosive growth of outcome research on psychosocial interventions since the mid-1990s and the impossibility for individual practitioners to comprehensively review and weigh the research evidence for individual cases. Furthermore, the complexity and cost of many psychosocial interventions necessitates a collective decision by an agency for a particular intervention, thus limiting which and how many empirically supported treatments and interventions can be offered.

4. The rating for the Positive Peer Culture model is deceptive in that its RCT was conducted more than 25 years ago and much more research is currently being conducted with regard to other models. Current research continues to be conducted particularly on the Boys Town Teaching Family Model, Cornell's Children and Residential Experiences (CARE) Model, and Multifunctional Treatment in Residential and Community Settings in Norway.

5. From a scientific perspective, these sources of evidence rank very low on the hierarchy of evidentiary sources (e.g., Greenhalgh, 1997). However, these hierarchies have also been the subject of critique (e.g., Hansen & Rieper, 2009).

6. In this context, the significant influence of psychoanalytic/-dynamic theory on *residential care* needs to be noted (e.g., Cohler & Friedman, 2004). This frequently implied a de-emphasis on the family as well as efforts to keep children from their families of origin and a perspective that viewed *residential care* as a corrective experience.

7. Coping Power Program, Generation PMTO, Incredible Years, Multidimensional Family Therapy, Multisystemic Therapy, Parent-Child Interaction Therapy, Problem Solving Skills Training, Promoting Alternative Thinking Strategies, Treatment Foster Care Oregon-Adolescents, Triple P—Positive Parenting Program®—Level 4.

8. As an example, youth were included in testifying during the development of the Family First Prevention Services Act.

9. Statistical methods such as propensity score matching offer viable and rigorous alternatives to experimental studies and may in many cases be the only option to approximate the rigor of experiments.

References

Affronti, M. L., & Levison-Johnson, J. (2009). The future of family engagement in residential care settings. *Residential Treatment for Children & Youth, 26*, 257–304. doi:10.1080/08865710903382571

Aisenberg, E. (2008). Evidence-based practice in mental health care to ethnic minority communities: Has its practice fallen short of its evidence? *Social Work, 53*(4), 297–306. doi:10.1093/sw/53.4.297

Albers, B., Mildon, R., Lyon, A. R., & Shlonsky, A. (2017). Implementation frameworks in child, youth and family services: Results from a scoping review. *Children & Youth Services Review, 81*, 101–116. doi:10.1016/j.childyouth.2017.07.003

American Association of Children's Residential Centers. (2009a). Redefining residential: Becoming family-driven. *Residential Treatment for Children & Youth, 26,* 230–235. doi:10.1080/08865710903256239

American Association of Children's Residential Centers. (2009b). Redefining residential: Becoming family-driven—Family members speak. *Residential Treatment for Children & Youth, 26,* 252–256. doi:10.1080/08865710903459221

Anderson, S. A., Sabatelli, R. M., & Trachtenberg, J. (2006–07). Evaluation of youth leadership programs. *Journal of Youth Development, 1*(3), 1–17.

Arnd-Caddigan, M. (2011). Toward a broader definition of evidence-informed practice: Inter-subjective evidence. *Families in Society, 92*(4), 372–376. doi:10.1606/1044-3894.4160

Asarnow, J. R., Aoki, W., & Elson, S. (1996). Children in residential treatment: A follow-up study. *Journal of Clinical Child Psychology, 25,* 209–214. doi:10.1207/s15374424jccp 2502_10

Ashton, S. (2014). The rights of children and young people in state care. *Educational Philosophy and Theory, 46*(9), 1082–1088. doi:10.1080/00131857.2014.931432

Baker, A. J. L., Kurland, D., Curtis, P., Alexander, G., & Papa-Letini, C. (2007). Mental health and behavioral problems of youth in the child welfare system: Residential centers compared to therapeutic foster care in the Odyssey project population. *Child Welfare, 86,* 363–386.

Barth, R. P. (2005). Residential care: From here to eternity. *International Journal of Social Welfare, 14,* 158–162. doi:10.1111/j.1468-2397.2005.00355.x

Barth, R. P. (2008). The move to evidence-based practice: How well does it fit child welfare services? *Journal of Public Child Welfare, 2,* 145–171. doi:10.1080/15548 730802312537

Barth, R. P., Greeson, J. K. P., Guo, S., Green, R. I., Hurley, S., & Sisson, J. (2007). Outcome for youth receiving intensive in-home therapy or residential care: A comparison using propensity scores. *American Journal of Orthopsychiatry, 76,* 358–366. doi:10.1037/0002-9432.77.4.497

Barth, R. P., Kolivoski, K. M., Lindsey, M. A., Lee, B. R., & Collins, K. C. (2014). Translating the common elements approach: Social work's experiences in education, practice, and research. *Journal of Clinical Child & Adolescent Psychology, 43*(2), 301–311. doi:0.1080/15374416.2013.848771

Barth, R. P., Landsverk, J., Chamberlain, P., Reid, J. B., Rolls, J. A., Hurlburt, M. S., . . . Kohl, P. L. (2005). Parent-training programs in child welfare services: Planning for a more evidence-based approach to serving biological parents. *Research on Social Work Practice, 15*(5), 353–371. doi:10.1177/1049731505276321

Behar, L., Friedman, R., Pinto, A., Katz-Leavy, J., & Jones, W. G. (2007). Protecting youth placed in unlicensed, unregulated residential "treatment" facilities. *Family Court Review, 45,* 399–413. doi:10.1111/j.1744-1617.2007.00155.x

Berejena Mhongera, P. (2017). Preparing for successful transitions beyond institutional care in Zimbabwe: Adolescent girls' perspectives and programme needs. *Child Care in Practice, 23*(4), 372–388. doi:10.1080/13575279.2016.1215291

Bettmann, J. E., & Jasperson, R. A. (2009). Adolescents in residential and inpatient treatment: A review of the outcomes literature. *Child & Youth Care Forum, 38,* 161–183. doi:10.1007/s10566-009-9073-y

Blau, G. M., Caldwell, B., & Liebermann, R. E. (Eds.). (2014). *Residential interventions for children, adolescents, and families. A best practice guide.* New York, NY and London: Routledge and Taylor & Francis.

Boel-Studt, S. M., & Tobia, L. (2015). A review of trends, research, and recommendations for strengthening the evidence-base and quality of residential group care. *Residential Treatment for Children & Youth, 35,* 13–35. doi:10.1080/0886 571X.2016.1175995

Briggs, E. C., Greeson, J. K. P., Layne, C. M., Fairbank, J. A., Knoverek, A. M., & Pynoos, R. S. (2012). Trauma exposure, psychosocial functioning, and treatment needs of youth in residential care: Preliminary findings from the NCTSN core data set. *Journal of Child & Adolescent Trauma, 5*(1), 1–15. doi:10.1080/19361521. 2012.646413

Bright, C. L., Raghavan, R., Kliethermes, M. D., Juedemann, D., & Dunn, J. (2010). Collaborative implementation of a sequenced trauma-focused intervention for youth in residential care. *Residential Treatment for Children & Youth, 27*(2), 69–79. doi:10.1080/08865711003712485

Brown, J. D., Allen, K., Pires, S. A., & Blau, G. (2010). Family-driven youth-guided practices in residential treatment: Findings from a national survey of residential treatment facilities. *Residential Treatment for Children & Youth, 27,* 149–159. doi: 10.1080/0886571X.2010.500137

Browne, C. H., Notkin, S., Schneider-Munoz, A., & Zimmerman, F. (2015). Youth thrive: A framework to help adolescents overcome trauma and thrive. *Journal of Child and Youth Care Work,* 33–52. Retrieved from https://cssp.org/wp-content/uploads/2018/09/Youth-Thrive-A-Framework-to-Help-Adolescents-Overcome-Trauma-and-Thrive.pdf

Bryson, S. A., Gauvin, E., Jamieson, A., Rathgeber, M., Faulkner-Gibson, L., Bell, S., . . . Burke, S. (2017). What are effective strategies for implementing trauma-informed care in youth inpatient psychiatric and residential treatment settings? A realist systematic review. *International Journal of Mental Health Systems, 11*(1), 36–52. doi:10.1186/s13033-017-0137-3.

Burke, E. M., Pyle, M., Morrison, A. P., & Machin, K. (2018). Providing mental health peer support 2: Relationships with empowerment, hope, recovery, quality of life and internalized stigma. *International Journal of Social Psychiatry, 64*(8), 745–755. doi:10.1177/0020764018810299

Caldwell, B., Tate, L., Cocoros, D., & Cocoros, T. (2018, July). *Youth-guided residential practices that support positive outcomes—from basic to advanced.* Washington, DC: Building Bridges Pre-Institute Presentation at the University of Maryland Baltimore Training Institutes.

California Evidence-Based Clearinghouse for Child Welfare. (n.d.). Retrieved from www.cebc4cw.org

Casey Family Programs. (2018). *Executive summary: Interventions with special relevance for the family first prevention services act (FFPSA)* (2nd ed.). Retrieved from https://familyfirstact.org/sites/default/files/Family%20First%20Interventions%20 Catalog_from%20Casey%20Family%20Programs_11-10-18%20%281%29_1.pdf

Catalano, R. F., Berglund, L., Ryan, J. A. M., Lonczak, H. S., & Hawkins, J. D. (2002). Positive youth development in the United States: Research findings on evaluations of positive youth development programs. *Prevention & Treatment, 5*(15), 1–111. doi:10.1037/1522-3736.5.1.515a

Chamberlain, P., & Reid, J. B. (1998). Comparison of two community alternatives to incarceration for chronic juvenile offenders. *Journal of Consulting and Clinical Psychology, 66*, 624–633. doi:10.1037/0022-006X.66.4.624

Cherna, M. (2012). Youth support partners: Building trust and improving service delivery for youth. *Policy and Practice*, 28–29.

Cohler, B. J., & Friedman, D. H. (2004). Psychoanalysis and the early beginnings of residential treatment for trouble youth. *Child and Adolescent Psychiatric Clinics of North America, 13*(2), 237–254. doi:10.1016/S1056-4993(03)00115-9

Collins, M. E., Hill, N., & Miranda, C. (2008). Establishing positive youth development approaches in group home settings: Training implementation and evaluation. *Child and Adolescent Social Work Journal, 25*, 43–54. doi:10.1007/s10560-008-0111-7

Committee on the Rights of the Child. (1992). Resolution 44/25 of 20 November 1989, entry into force 2, September 1990, in accordance with article 49. United Nations.

Conner, K. O., & Grote, N. K. (2008). Enhancing the cultural relevance of empirically-supported mental health interventions. *Families in Society, 89*(4), 587–505. doi: 10.1606/1044-3894.3821

De Swart, J. J. W., van Den Broek, J., Stams, G. J. J. M., van der Lann, P. H., Holsbrink-Engels, G. A., & van der Helm, G. H. P. (2012). The effectiveness of institutional youth care over the past three decades: A meta-analysis. *Children & Youth Services Review, 34*, 1818–1824. doi:10.1016/j.childyouth.2012.05.015

Delman, J., & Klodnick, V. V. (2017). Factors supporting the employment of young adult peer providers: Perspectives of peers and supervisors. *Community Mental Health Journal, 53*, 811–822. doi:10.1007/s10597-016-0059-6

DiGennaro Reed, F. D., & Reed, D. D. (2008). Towards an understanding of evidence-based practice. *Journal of Early and Intensive Behavior Intervention, 5*(2), 20–29. doi:10.1037/h0100416.

Dozier, M., Kaufman, J., Kobak, R., O'Connor, T. G., Sagi-Schwartz, A., Scott, S., . . . Zeanah, C. H. (2014). Consensus statement on group care for children and adolescents: A statement of policy of the American orthopsychiatric association. *American Journal of Orthopsychiatry, 84*(3), 219–225. doi:10.1037/ort0000005

Duppong Hurley, K., Lambert, M. C., Gross, T. J., Thompson, R. W., & Farmer, E. M. Z. (2017). The role of therapeutic alliance and fidelity in predicting youth outcomes during therapeutic residential care. *Journal of Emotional and Behavioral Disorders, 25*(1), 37–45. doi:10.1177/1063426616686756

Epstein, I. (2011). Reconciling evidence-based practice, evidence-informed practice, and practice-based research: The role of clinical data-mining. *Social Work, 56*(3), 284–288. doi:10.1093/sw/56.3.284

Erker, G. J., Searight, R. H., Amanat, E., & White, P. D. (1993). Residential versus day treatment for children: A long-term follow-up study. *Child Psychiatry and Human Development, 24*(1), 31–39. doi:10.1007/BF02353716

Estabrooks, C. A. (1998). Will evidence-based nursing practice make practice perfect? *Canadian Journal of Nursing Research, 30*(1), 15–36.

Farmer, E. M., Murray, M. L., Ballentine, K., Rauktis, M. E., & Burns, B. J. (2017). Would we know it if we saw it? Assessing quality of care in group homes for youth. *Journal of Emotional and Behavioral Disorders, 25*(1), 28–36. doi:10.1177/1063426616687363

First Focus Campaign for Children. (2018). *Family fist prevention services act: Bill summary.* Retrieved from https://campaignforchildren.org/wp-content/uploads/sites/2/2016/06/FFCC-Short-Summary-FFPSA.pdf

Forenza, B., & Happonen, R. G. (2016). A critical analysis of foster youth advisory boards in the United States. *Child Youth Care Forum, 45,* 107–112. doi:10.1007/s10566-015-9321-2

Frankfort-Howard, R., & Room, S. (2002). Outcomes of residential treatment of antisocial youth: Development of our cessation from adult antisocial behavior. *Residential Treatment for Children & Youth, 19,* 53–70. doi:10.1300/J007v19n03_04

Friesen, B. J., Koroloff, N. M., Walker, J. S., & Briggs, H. E. (2011). Family and youth voice in systems of care. *Best Practices in Mental Health, 7*(1), 1–25.

Gagne, C. A., Finch, W. L., Myrick, K. J., & Davis, L. M. (2018). Peer workers in the behavioral and integrated health workforce: Opportunities and future directions. *American Journal of Preventive Medicine, 54*(6S3), 258–266. doi:10.1016/j.amepre.2018.03.010

Gambrill, E. (2007). Special section: Promoting and sustaining evidence-based practice. View of evidence-based practice. Social workers' code of ethics and accreditation standards as guides for choice. *Journal of Social Work Education, 43*(3), 447–462. doi:10.5175/JSWE.2007.200600639

Gambrill, E. (2015). Integrating research and practice: Distractions, controversies, and options for moving forward. *Research on Social Work Practice, 25*(4), 510–522. doi:10.1177/1049731514544327

Gambrill, E. (2016). Is social work evidence-based? Does saying so make it so? Ongoing challenges in integrating research, practice and policy. *Journal of Social Work Education, 52*(S1), 5110–5125. doi:10.1080/10437797.2016.1174642

Gambrill, E. (2018). Evidence-based practice: An alternative to authority-based practice (revisiting our heritage). *Families in Society, 99*(3), 283–294. doi:10.1177/1044389418786699

Glynn, N., & Mayock, P. (2019). "I've changed so much within a year": Care leavers' perspectives on the aftercare planning process. *Child Care in Practice, 25*(1), 79–98. doi:10.1080/13575279.2018.1521378

Gomersall, A. (2006). I've found it: What do I do now? *Evidence & Policy, 2*(1), 127–143. doi:10.1332/174426406775249651

Gopalan, G., Lee, S. J., Harris, R., Acri, M. C., & Munson, M. R. (2017). Utilization of peers in services for youth with emotional and behavioral challenges: A scoping review. *Journal of Adolescence, 55,* 88–115. doi:10.1332/174426406775249651

Greenhalgh, T. (1997). How to read a paper: Getting your bearings (deciding what your paper is about). *British Medical Journal, 315*(7102), 243–246. doi:10.1136/bmj.315.7102.243

Green-Hanessy, S. (2018). Suspension of the national registry of evidence-based programs and practices: The importance of adhering to the evidence. *Substance Abuse Treatment, Prevention, and Policy, 13,* 26–29. https://doi.org/10.1186/s13011-018-0162-5

Grietens, H., & Hellinckx, W. (2004). Evaluating effects of residential treatment for juvenile offenders by statistical meta-analysis: A review. *Aggression and Violent Behavior, 9,* 401–415. doi:10.1016/S1359-1789(03)00043-0

Habashi, J., Wright, L., & Hathcoat, J. D. (2012). Patterns of human development indicators across constitutional analysis of children's rights to protection, provision, and participation. *Social Indicators Research, 105*, 63–73. doi:10.1007/s11205-010-9763-8

Hair, H. J. (2005). Outcomes for children and adolescents after residential treatment: A review of research from 1993 to 2003. *Journal of Child and Family Studies, 14*, 551–575. doi:10.1007/s10826-005-7188-9

Hansen, H. F., & Rieper, O. (2009). The evidence movement: The development and consequences of methodologies in review practices. *Evaluation, 15*(2), 141–163. doi:10.1177/1356389008101968

Harrington, K., Williams-Washington, K., Caldwell, B., Lieberman, R. E., & Blau, G. M. (2014). Improving outcomes in residential. In G. M. Blau, B. Caldwell, & R. E. Liebermann (Eds.), *Residential interventions for children, adolescents, and families. A best practice guide.* New York, NY and London: Routledge and Taylor & Francis.

Harriton, E., & Locascio, J. J. (2018). Randomised controlled trials: The gold standard for effectiveness research. *BJOG, 125*(13), 1716. doi:10.1111/1471-0528.15199

Havlicek, J., Curry, A., & Villalpando, F. (2018). *Youth advisory boards interview measure.* Retrieved from PsycTESTS. http://dx.doi.org/10.1037/t67012-000

Havlicek, J., Lin, C. H., & Villalpando, F. (2016). Web survey of foster youth advisory boards in the United States. *Children & Youth Services Review, 60*, 109–118. doi:10.1016/j.childyouth.2015.11.023

Havlicek, J., & Samuels, G. M. (2018). The Illinois state foster youth advisory board as a counterspace for well-being through identity work: Perspectives of current and former members. *Social Service Review, 92*(2), 241–289. doi:10.1086/697694

Hawkins, D. N., Amato, P. R., & King, V. (2006). Parent-adolescent involvement: The relative influence of parent gender and residence. *Journal of Marriage and Family, 68*, 125–136. doi:10.1111/j.1741-3737.2006.00238.x

Herman, K. C., Borden, L. A., Hsu, C., Schultz, T. R., Carney, M. C., Brooks, C. M., & Reinke, W. M. (2011). Enhancing family-driven engagement in interventions for mental health problems in youth. *Residential Treatment for Children & Youth, 28*, 102–119. doi:10.1080/0886571X.2011.569434

Hodgdon, H. B., Kinniburgh, K., Gabowitz, D., Blaustein, M. E., & Spinazzola, J. (2013). Development and implementation of trauma-informed programming in youth residential treatment centers using the ARC framework. *Journal of Family Violence, 28*(7), 679–692. doi:10.1007/s10896-013-9531-z

Holden, M. J., Izzo, C., Nunno, M., Smith, E. G., Endres, T., Holden, J. C., & Kuhn, F. (2010). Children and residential experiences: A comprehensive strategy for implementing a research-informed program model for residential care. *Child Welfare, 89*, 131–149.

Hoskins, D. H. (2014). Consequences of parenting on adolescent outcomes. *Societies, 4*(3), 506–531. https://doi.org/10.3390/soc4030506

Huefner, J. C. (2018). Crosswalk of published quality standards for residential care for children and adolescents. *Children & Youth Services Review, 88*, 267–273. doi:10.1016/j.childyouth.2018.03.022

Hull, D. M., Saxon, T. F., Fagan, M. A., Williams, L. O., & Verdisco, A. E. (2018). Positive youth development: An experimental trial with unattached adolescents. *Journal of Adolescence, 67*, 85–97. doi:10.1016/j.adolescence.2018.06.006

Hummer, V. L., Dollard, N., Robst, J., & Armstrong, M. I. (2010). Innovations in implementation of trauma-informed care practices in youth residential treatment: A curriculum for organizational change. *Child Welfare, 89*(2), 79–95.

Hust, J. A., & Kuppinger, A. (2014). Moving toward family-driven care in residential. In G. M. Blau, B. Caldwell, & R. E. Liebermann (Eds.), *Residential interventions for children, adolescents, and families. A best practice guide.* New York, NY and London: Routledge and Taylor & Francis.

Iwasaki, Y. (2016). The role of youth engagement in positive youth development and social justice youth development for high-risk, marginalised youth. *International Journal of Adolescence and Youth, 21*(3), 267–278. doi:10.1080/02673843.2015.1067893

James, S. (2011). What works in group care? A structured review of treatment models for group homes and residential care. *Children & Youth Services Review, 33,* 308–321. doi:10.1016/j.childyouth.2010.09.014

James, S., Alemi, Q., & Zepeda, V. (2013). Effectiveness and implementation of evidence-based practices in residential care settings. *Children & Youth Services Review, 35,* 642–656. doi:10.1016/j.childyouth.2013.01.007

James, S., Roesch, S., & Zhang, J. (2012). Characteristics and behavioral outcomes for youth in group care and family-based care: A propensity score matching approach using national data. *Journal of Emotional and Behavioral Disorders, 20,* 144–156. doi:10.1177/1063426611409041

James, S., Thompson, R. W., & Ringle, J. L. (2017). The implementation of evidence-based practices in residential care: Outcomes, processes, and barriers. *Journal of Emotional and Behavioral Disorders, 25*(1), 4–18. doi:10.1177/1063426616687083

James, S., Thompson, R. W., Sternberg, N., Schnur, E., Ross, J., Butler, L,. . . . Muirhead, J. (2015). Attitudes, perceptions, and utilization of evidence-based practices in residential care. *Residential Treatment for Children & Youth, 32,* 144–166. doi:10.1080/0886571X.2015.1046275

Knorth, E. J., Harder, A. T., Zandberg, T., & Kendrick, A. J. (2008). Under one roof: A review and selective meta-analysis on the outcomes of residential child and youth care. *Children & Youth Services Review, 30,* 123–140. doi:10.1016/j.childyouth.2007.09.001

Landsman, M. J., Groza, V., Tyler, M., & Malone, K. (2001). Outcomes of family-centered residential treatment. *Child Welfare, 80,* 351–379.

Lee, B. R., & Barth, R. P. (2011). Defining group care programs: An index of reporting standards. *Child & Youth Care Forum, 40,* 253–266. doi:10.1007/s10566-011-9143-9

Lee, B. R., Bright, C. L., Svoboda, D. V., Fakunmoju, S., & Barth, R. P. (2011). Outcomes of group care for youth: A review of comparative studies. *Research on Social Work Practice, 21,* 177–189. doi:10.1177/1049731510386243

Lee, B. R., Hwang, J., Socha, K., Pau, T., & Shaw, T. V. (2013). Going home again: Transitioning youth to families after group care placement. *Journal of Child and Family Studies, 22*(4), 447–459. doi:10.1007/s10826-012-9596-y

Lee, B. R., & McMillen, J. C. (2017). Pathways forward for embracing evidence-based group care settings. *Journal of Emotional and Behavioral Disorders, 25*(1), 19–27. doi:10.1177/1063426616688210

Leeman, L. W., Gibbs, J. C., & Fuller, D. (1993). Evaluation of a multi-component group treatment program for juvenile delinquents. *Aggressive Behavior, 19*(49), 281–292. doi:10.1002/1098-2337(1993)19:4<281::AID-AB2480190404>3.0.CO;2-W

Lyons, J. S., Terry, P., Martinovich, Z., Peterson, J., & Bouska, B. (2001). Outcome trajectories for adolescents in residential treatment: A statewide evaluation. *Journal of Child and Family Studies, 10*(3), 333–345. doi:10.1023/A:1012576826136

MacKenzie, M. J., Brewer, L. B., Schwalbe, C. S. J., Gearing, R. E., Ibrahim, R. W., Batayneh, J., . . . Al-Zu'bi, M. H. (2012). Foster care as a viable alternative to institutional care in the Middle East: Community acceptance and stigma across type of placement in Jordan. *Journal of Developmental & Behavioral Pediatrics, 33*(6), 517–521. doi:10.1097/DBP.0b013e31825c4881

McCrae, J. S., Lee, B. R., Barth, R. P., & Rauktis, M. E. (2010). Comparing three years of well-being outcomes for youth in group care and nonkinship foster care. *Child Welfare, 89*(2), 229–249.

Merritts, A. (2016). A review of family therapy in residential settings. *Contemporary Family Therapy, 38*, 75–85. doi:10.1007/s10591-016-9378-6

Miles, A., & Loughlin, M. (2011). Models in the balance: Evidence-based medicine versus evidence-informed individualized care. *Journal of Evaluation in Clinical Practice, 17*, 531–536. doi:10.1111/j.1365-2753.2011.01713.x

Naccarato, T., & Knipe, J. (2015). *Impact of advocacy study: Preliminary results of a multi-year, multi-state evaluation of mental health, wellbeing and positive youth development impacts of trainings in leadership and policy advocacy for current and former foster youth*. San Francisco: Foster Youth in Action.

Nakatomi, T., Ichikawa, S., Wakabayashi, H., & Takemura, Y. C. (2018). Children and adolescents in institutional care versus traditional families: A quality of life comparison in Japan. *Health & Quality of Life Outcomes, 16*, 1–8. https://doi.org/10.1186/s12955-018-0980-1

Nickerson, A. B., Salamone, F. J., Brooks, J. L., & Colby, S. A. (2004). Promising approaches to engaging families and building strengths in residential treatment. *Residential Treatment for Children & Youth, 22*(1), 1–18. doi:10.1300/J007v22n01_01

Okpych, N. J., & Yu, J. L. (2014). A historical analysis of evidence-based practice in social work: The unfinished journey toward an empirically grounded profession. *Social Service Review, 88*(1), 3–58. doi:10.1086/674969

Outcomes Roundtable for Children and Families (ORCF). (2011). *Issue brief: Using practice-based evidence to complement evidence-based practice in children's mental health*. Retrieved from http://cfs.cbcs.usf.edu/_docs/publications/Outcomes RoundtableBrief.pdf

Parrish, D. E. (2018). Evidence-based practice: A common definition matters. *Journal of Social Work Education, 54*(3), 407–411. doi:10.1080/10437797.2018.1498691

Pavkov, T. W., Negash, S., Lourie, I. S., & Hug, R. W. (2010). Critical failures in a regional network of residential treatment facilities. *American Journal of Orthopsychiatry, 80*, 151–159. doi:10.1111/j.1939-0025.2010.01018.x

Pecora, P. J., & English, D. J. (2016). *Elements of practice for children and youth served by therapeutic residential care (Research Brief)*. Casey Family Programs. Retrieved from https://caseyfamilypro-wpengine.netdna-ssl.com/media/Group-Care-complete.pdf

Pittman, K. J. (2017). Positive youth development as a strategy for addressing readiness and equity: A commentary. *Child Development, 88*(4), 1172–1174. doi:10.1111/cdev.12872

Pittman, K. J., & Wright, M. (1991). *Bridging the gap: A rationale for enhancing the role of community organizations promoting youth development.* Report prepared for The Task Force on Youth Development and Community Programs at the Carnegie Council on Adolescent Development. Washington, DC: Center for Youth Development and Policy Research.

Quisenberry, C. M., & Foltz, R. (2013). Resilient youth in residential care. *Residential Treatment for Children & Youth, 30*, 280–293. doi:10.1080/0886571X.2013.852448

Robst, J., Armstrong, M., & Dollard, N. J. (2011). Comparing outcomes for youth served in treatment foster care and treatment group care. *Journal of Child and Family Studies, 20*(5), 696–705. doi:10.1007/s10826-011-9447-2

Robst, J., Rohrer, L., Armstrong, M., Dollard, N., Sharrock, P., Batsche, C., & Reader, S. (2013). Family involvement and changes in child behavior during residential mental health treatment. *Child Youth Care Forum, 42*(3), 225–238. doi:10.1007/s10566-013-9201-6

Robst, J., Rohrer, L., Dollard, N., & Armstrong, M. (2014). Family involvement in treatment among youth in residential facilities. Association with discharge to family-like setting and follow-up treatment. *Journal of Emotional and Behavioral Disorders, 22*(3), 190–196. doi:10.1177/1063426614523651

Russell, L. T., Beckmeyer, J. J., & Su-Russell, C. (2018). Family-centered care and positive developmental outcomes for youth with special health care needs: Variations across family structures. *Journal of Family Nursing, 24*(1), 29–59. doi:10.1177/1074840717745520

Sackett, D. I., Rosenberg, W. M. C., Gray, J. A. M., Haynes, R. B., & Richardson, W. S. (1996). Evidence-based medicine: What it is and what it isn't. *British Medical Journal, 312*, 71–72. doi:10.1136/bmj.312.7023.71

Sharrock, P. J., Dollard, N., Armstrong, M. I., & Rohrer, L. (2013). Provider perspectives on involving families in children's residential psychiatric care. *Residential Treatment for Children & Youth, 30*, 40–54. doi:10.1080/0886571X.2013.751807

Shlonsky, A., & Gibbs, L. (2004). Will the real evidence-based practice please stand up? Teaching the process of evidence-based practice to the helping professions. *Brief Treatment and Crisis Intervention, 4*(2), 137–153. doi:10.1093/brief-treatment/mhh011

Shlonsky, A., Noonan, E., Littell, J. H., & Montgomery, P. (2011). The role of systematic reviews and the Campbell collaboration in the realization of evidence-informed practice. *Clinical Social Work, 39*, 362–368. doi:10.1007/s10615-010-0307-0

Smith, Y. (2017). "Sense" and sensitivity: Informal apprenticeship among youth care workers in a residential treatment center for children. *Child & Family Social Work, 22*(3), 1330–1337. doi:10.1111/cfs.12350

Straus, S. E., Glasziou, P., Richardson, W. S., & Haynes, R. B. (2011). *Evidence-based medicine: How to practice and teach it* (4th ed.). Toronto, Ontario: Churchill Livingston Elsevier.

Sullivan, G. M. (2011). Getting off the "gold standard": Randomized controlled trials and education research. *Journal of Graduate Medical Education*, 285–289. doi:10.4300/JGME-D-11-00147.1

Sunseri, P. A. (2004). Family functioning and residential treatment outcomes. *Residential Treatment for Children & Youth, 22*(1), 33–53. doi:10.1300/J007v22n01_03

Thompson, R. W., Duppong Hurley, K., Trout, A. L., Huefner, J. C., & Daly, D. L. (2017). Closing the research to practice gap in therapeutic residential care: Service provider-university partnerships focused on evidence-based practice. *Journal of Emotional and Behavioral Disorders, 25*(19), 46–56. doi:10.1177/1063426616686757

Tickle-Degnen, L., & Bedell, G. (2003). Heterarchy and hierarchy: A critical appraisal of the 'levels of evidence' as a tool for clinical decision making. *The American Journal of Occupational Therapy, 75*(2), 234–237. doi:10.5014/ajot.57.2.234

U.S. Department of Health and Human Services. (n.d.). *Child welfare goals, legislation and monitoring*. Retrieved from https://training.cfsrportal.acf.hhs.gov/book/export/html/2987

U.S. Department of Health and Human Services. (2009). *Strengthening families and communities*. Retrieved from www.childwelfare.gov/pubpdfs/2009guide.pdf

Walker, S. C., Lyon, A. R., Aos, S., & Trupin, E. W. (2017). The consistencies and vagaries of the Washington state inventory of evidence-based practice: The definition of "evidence-based" in a policy context. *Administration and Policy in Mental Health and Mental Health Services Research, 44*(1), 42–54. doi:10.1007/s10488-015-0652-y

Walter, U. M., & Petr, C. G. (2008). Family-centered residential treatment: Knowledge, research, and values converge. *Residential Treatment for Children & Youth, 25*(1), 1–16. doi:10.1080/08865710802209594

Werner, E. E., & Smith, R. S. (1977). *Kauai's children come of age*. Honolulu, HI: University of Hawaii Press.

Whittaker, J. K., del Valle, J. F., & Holmes, L. (2015). *The current landscape of therapeutic residential care. Therapeutic residential care for children and youth: Developing evidence-based international practice*. Philadelphia: Jessica Kingsley Publishers.

Whittaker, J. K., Holmes, L., del Valle, J. F., Ainsworth, F., Andreasson, T., Anglin, J., . . . Zeira, A. (2016). Therapeutic residential care for children and youth: A consensus statement of the international work group on therapeutic residential care. *Residential Treatment for Children and Youth, 33*(2), 89–106. doi:10.1080/0886571X.2016.1215755

Wilmshurst, L. A. (2002). Treatment programs for youth with emotional and behavioral disorders: An outcome study of two alternate approaches. *Mental Health Services Research, 4*(2), 85–96. doi:10.1023/A:1015200200316

Woodbury, M. G., & Kuhnke, J. L. (2014). Evidence-based practice vs. evidence-informed practice: What's the difference? *Wound Care Canada, 12*(1), 18–21.

World Health Organization [WHO]. (2013). *Evidence-informed policy making*. Geneva: WHO. Retrieved from www.who.int/evidence/en/

Zeldin, S. (2000). Integrating research and practice to understand and strengthen communities for adolescent development: An introduction to the special issue and current issues. *Applied Developmental Science, 4*(1), 2–11. doi:10.1207/S1532480XADS04Suppl_1

10

UNDERSTANDING AND APPLYING A NEURODEVELOPMENTAL APPROACH IN RESIDENTIAL INTERVENTIONS

Robert E. Lieberman, Tina Champagne, Emily Y. Wang, and Katie Rushlo

Introduction

When youth and families are referred for residential interventions, youth often are identified as having high levels of clinical acuity and a number of emotions and behaviors that they and others find challenging. Unfortunately, when identifying these challenges, there is often a lack of awareness and understanding about the contributing factors. Recognizing the impact of adverse experiences, particularly those that give rise to overwhelming stress and trauma, are important to shift the dialogue from "problem behaviors" and "what is wrong with you" (Bloom, 2005), to a focus on skills and strengths and "what has happened to you" (Bloom, 2005). While traditional residential interventions can yield stabilization during the residential intervention, the approaches used are sometimes ineffective at generating enduring change, especially if the intervention does not also include a strong focus on permanency, family skills, and supports in the community. As a result, if symptoms return, youth and families may feel helpless and hopeless, leading to a cycle of further challenges and potential recidivism into other treatment programs or other public systems (e.g., juvenile justice and child welfare).

The Building Bridges Initiative (BBI) offers transformational strategies and approaches described throughout this book that begin to break these cycles. Additionally, advancements in neuroscience and research on childhood adversity over the past two decades offer increased clarity and insight into how to understand and address the neurodevelopmental challenges and skill deficits of youth and families who have difficulty living together successfully. The scientific literature is expanding rapidly, and there are many trauma-informed approaches that have become available, including approaches used with residential interventions.

This chapter utilizes some of the core concepts from Dr. Bruce Perry's Neurosequential Model of Therapeutics (NMT) along with other models and approaches aligned with the research, seeking to connect the guiding principles and neuroscience with interactive approaches and strategies that can be implemented by youth, families, and staff at home, in the community, and in the residential program (LeBel & Champagne, 2010; MA DMH, 2013; Hambrick et al., 2018; NASMHPD, 2003, 2018; Warner, Koomar, Lary, & Cook, 2013). In some examples, readers will be able to learn new ways of thinking and responding, in others they will recognize approaches they already use and become able to continue to do so with greater intentionality. The chapter will introduce relevant science, review key principles related to the impact of stress and adversity on neurobiology and development, provide interpersonal and sensory-focused strategies, and discuss how these neuroscientific concepts are integrated with the BBI framework and foster residential transformation. Comments from a young person with lived experience are interspersed throughout the chapter.

Relevant Science

Over the last 20 years, the impact of childhood adversity on long-term health outcomes and well-being has become a significant national focus due to the Adverse Childhood Experiences (ACEs) Study (Felitti et al., 1998). The largest public health study of its kind in the United States, this ground-breaking epidemiological research conducted by the Centers for Disease Control and Kaiser Permanente found that ACEs are the leading determinant of negative physical and behavioral health outcomes, with follow-up research expanding the impact to social outcomes and even early death (Anda et al., 2006; Felitti et al., 1998). The ACEs study highlights the magnitude of the problems faced by young people and families and redefines the pervasive impact of trauma. The results of the ACEs study underscore the necessity of preventing adversity in childhood and guide greater focus on understanding its epidemiological findings.

Since the initial ACEs study, there has been a growing body of neuroscientific research examining the impact of adversity, toxic stress, and trauma on brain development that has established that any experience that overwhelms the ability to cope, not just the original ten ACEs,[1] can also have detrimental impacts on neurobiological and neurophysiological development (brain and body) (Luxenberg et al., 2001; Kelly et al., 2013; Perry, 2001, 2002; Perry, Pollard, Blakely, Baker, & Vigilante, 1995; Perry & Pollard, 1998; McDonnell & Valentino, 2016; Miller, Chen, & Parker, 2011). Research findings also suggest that racism, poverty, bullying, and other significant stressors yield similar effects (Public Health Management Corporation, 2013; Teicher et al., 2010). Subsequently, the impact of stress has become recognized as a neurobiological phenomenon that affects everyone differently, whether or not they develop Post Traumatic Stress Disorder (PTSD) (Engel-Yeger, Palgy-Levin, & Lev-Wiesel, 2013; Murrough et al., 2011; Perry & Pate, 1994; Perry et al., 1995; Perry & Pollard, 1998; van der Kolk, 2005).

Research has clarified what is necessary to influence and change brain development and function (Boyd, Lanius, & McKinnon, 2018; Hebb, 1949; Perry, 2006, 2009, 2013; Stein & Kendall, 2014). For example, it has shown that strong personal capabilities, relationships, and social connectedness are essential for healthy cognitive, emotional, and social function (Ludy-Dobson & Perry, 2010; Masten, 2001). Key findings from neuroscience offer a universal baseline of principles that can be applied across situations and settings—in the program, at home, and in the community—to support young people and families who find themselves in need of a residential intervention (Zelechoski et al., 2013).

The emergence of this research coincides with increasing expectations for residential programs. The federal Families First Prevention Services Act, a law passed by Congress (Bipartisan Budget Agreement Act of 2018) and statutes being passed at state levels require organizations to implement *trauma-informed care* (TIC), i.e., services and supports that are based on an understanding of the science and applying it in practice (SAMHSA, 2014a, 2014b; Zelechoski et al., 2013). The TIC lens helps staff and family members become less focused on behavior and more focused on understanding the source and function of behaviors (Jackson, Frederico, Cox, & Black, 2019) Being trauma-informed allows staff, family members, and youth to better comprehend how what is perceived as stressful or traumatic by one person may not be perceived in the same way by another and why dysregulation may ensue in the absence of a known stressor. Thinking of TIC through a neurodevelopmental (ND) lens generates a greater possibility of implementing existing trauma-informed approaches, strategies, and practices that can be used each day to support the development of youth and their families (Champagne, 2011).

Residential interventions provide a unique opportunity for moment-in-time focused strategies. The very nature of a residential intervention offers significant access to the youth and family throughout the day regardless of whether the young person is participating in the program, home, or in the community at any given time. This degree of intervention intensity enhances the ability to leverage the science and evidence; in order to learn new skills, the neural circuits responsible for the development of those skills must be repeatedly activated in real life situations over time (Hebb, 1949; Perry, 2006, 2009).

The framework for residential intervention developed by BBI, together with the strategies and practices provided in this book, creates such opportunities for leveraging transformational change. The integrated BBI approach advances practices that—when implemented thoughtfully and intentionally—support neurodevelopmental capacities and skills necessary for the improvement of safety, coping, relationships, functional performance, and behavior.[2] Implementing this framework can help transform what has traditionally been referred to as "residential treatment" away from a social and cultural quarantine (Campbell, 2018; Hambrick et al., 2018) to an effective and robust intervention that affords relational engagement, predictability, learning, and growth for youth and their families. In the BBI framework, this skill development occurs not only for the youth and family but, through the process, also for all members of their therapeutic support system (e.g., teachers, staff, and community). In this way, the youth and family's capacity for connectedness and healing increases, the impact of adversity is counteracted, and future adversities are prevented (Ludy-Dobson & Perry, 2010).

Neurophysiology: Impact of Stress and Trauma on Development

Stress can have both positive and negative effects on the brains and bodies of developing children and adolescents (CTA, 2013a). Stress supports development when it is moderate, predictable, and controlled (CTA, 2013a; Perry, 2006, 2009, 2013). Some of the positive effects of stress include the increased burst of energy when getting ready for the day, playing sports, or meeting deadlines, etc. When stress is prolonged, chronic, intense, or traumatic, however, it can cause *distress* and changes in the size, structure, and function of the brain (CTA, 2013a; Perry, 2006, 2009). Differences in genetic predisposition, life experiences, and socioeconomic factors influence how each person's neurophysiology develops, perceives, and responds to stressors and ongoing traumatic exposure(s) (Anda et al., 2006; Ayres, 2005; Felitti et al., 1998; Perry, 2004b; Perry et al., 1995; Perry & Pollard, 1998). Providing neurodevelopmentally targeted interventions—attuned to the stress response systems of the youth and families who receive residential interventions—requires a basic understanding of the brain, body, neurodevelopment, and the impacts of trauma (Champagne, 2011; Perry, 2006, 2009, 2013; van der Kolk, 2005, 2014).

The Brain, Body, and the Stress Response: An Overview of the Neuroscience

The brain is a highly complex organ that requires years of study to even begin to comprehend (CTA, 2103b). Nonetheless, there are some core neuroscientific principles that are helpful to understand when trying to develop a stronger working knowledge of neurodevelopmental approaches (Perry, 2004b, 2006, 2009). While each of these principles is supported by significant research and technical explanation, some of the most relevant neuroscientific

A Neurodevelopmental Approach **201**

concepts and seven corresponding key principles (drawn significantly from NMT) are reviewed in this section (Perry, 2006, 2009, 2013; Perry & Dobson, 2013). In the sections that follow, each key principle is explained and followed by an example of its practical application in the context of a residential intervention.

1. **The brain is organized hierarchically.** The nervous system includes the brain, the spinal cord, and all of the sensory and motor systems of the body. These complex brain and body structures are highly interconnected and work together to help us functionally navigate the demands of day-to-day life. The brain develops and is organized hierarchically and sequentially. The hierarchical organization and structure of the brain is often referred to as brain levels, each containing specialized areas with associated functions. Fundamental regulatory functions are mediated by the lower parts of the brain (brainstem), which are directly associated with survival mechanisms (e.g., heart rate, breathing) that develop first—starting in utero. More complex functions (abstract thought, language, planning) develop more fully in adolescence and early adulthood. As the brain develops, its neural networks become more capable of mediating the more complex functions. Due to the sequential nature of neurodevelopment, the optimal development of the higher levels of the brain is dependent on a strong and organized foundation of the lower levels (Ayres, 2005).

    The neural networks contain a variety of neurotransmitters (e.g., dopamine, serotonin, and norepinephrine) that are located in target areas and influence development. In utero and early childhood, exposure to toxins, ACEs, and trauma impact the pattern, frequency, and quantity of the developing neurotransmitters and neural networks, generating a measurable difference in the way the system develops and functions from the lower levels to the higher more complex areas of the brain. Thus, interventions that support regulation and organization at the lower (brainstem) level such as body-based, sensory, and motor strategies (often referred to as bottom-up) are often used to support the development and organization of the higher (cortical) levels (Ayres, 2005; Perry, 2006).

    Practical Application: Match the intervention with the developmental level of brain function, such as when a youth may be age 15 chronologically but functioning more like a six-year-old in terms of social and emotional development. This is critical to understand because higher (cortical) levels of response, e.g., ability to process and respond to verbal interactions, may not be readily available, and expectations for how a 15-year-old "should" function must be rethought. For example, rather than cognitive approaches, it may be more developmentally appropriate to use calming, body-based strategies (discussed further later) to support both emotional regulation and higher-level function.

2. **The brain processes information sequentially; the sequence of engagement.** Sensory input is initially received by way of the brainstem before signals travel up to the midbrain (often referred to as the limbic system or the "emotion center" of the brain). Both of these areas of the brain operate at a pre-cognitive level of awareness, meaning that the cortex, where the brain has capacity for reasoning and understanding, is not immediately engaged (Ayres, 2005; Perry, 2001). Thus, external and internal stimuli influence an initial response to what is experienced before cognitive awareness occurs. "We feel, then we think" (Blodgett, 2015); this is referred to as the "sequence of engagement" (Perry, 2006, 2009; Perry & Ablon, 2019).

    Practical Application: The timing of engagement is important. Engage with the youth and/or family members through the use of a regulating activity first, which will allow the youth and/or family member to feel safe, more organized, and better able to relate and subsequently reason. For example, following a day of school for a youth that has been fraught with emotion and conflict may not be the best time to engage in emotionally laden questions or corrective conversations. The optimal immediate response from staff or adults would be to support the youth using body-based and/or relational regulating activities. These may include using the prosody of one's voice, supportive body language, empathy, and/or regulating strategies that have been identified by the young person and parent. Any attempts to discuss issues or problem solve will be most effective after the youth is regulated and positive relational interaction has been established. Table 10.1 provides an example from Cutchins Programs for Children and Families of a youth's preferred strategies and regulation scale (self-created). These activities are in-the-moment tools for regulation and help support connection with parents, peers, and staff.

3. **Experience shapes the brain.** Brains are use-dependent. (Doidge, 2007; Hebb, 1949; Perry et al., 1995; Perry, 2006). Repetition of experience builds neural pathways, whether health supporting or health damaging. This neurodevelopmental process is analogous to going to the gym and working out only certain areas of the body but not others. Those areas used become larger (more developed) and stronger, and those not used as much do not develop in the same way or may even become weak depending on the degree of disuse.

    Eight sensory systems (see Table 10.2) enable each person to notice and respond to what they experience and perceive whether they are safe or in danger—a process that is occurring at every moment across the lifespan (Champagne, 2017). In this way, experiences influence neurodevelopment and function and how we perceive and interact in the world. Different areas of the brain support different capacities, such as

Table 10.1 Youth's Preferred Strategies and Regulation Scale

Angry	Annoyed	Scared	Happy	Calm	Sad
Sensory space	Transition to a quieter setting	Quieter setting	Being in Nature	Being in Nature	Being in Nature
Swinging	Sensory space	Ball toss	Building/Crafts	Building/Crafts	Sensory space
Biking	Biking	Biking	Gardening	Gardening	Building things
Music	Music	Music	Biking	Biking	Gardening
Oral motor:	Swinging	Rocking chair	Ball toss	Ping-pong	Biking
• Frozen fruit	Oral motor:	Soft blanket	Ping-pong	Playing with puppets	Swing/Rocker
• Gum	• Tea	Stuffed animals	Playing with puppets	Coloring	Ball toss
• Mints	• Frozen fruit	Make Tea	Cooking (smoothies)	Cooking	Stuffed animals
	• Gum				Music

those involved in learning, memory, impulse control, attention, concentration, motor skills, and the ability to self-regulate (CTA, 2013b).

Practical Application: Every interaction and intervention matters. It is incumbent upon us to be attuned to and mindful of what we might be activating at any given moment with a youth and family members, in our tone, language, and actions and to create experiences that build relationships and skills.

4. **The stress response system drives immediate response.** The brain is equipped with what is known as the stress response system (Cannon, 1932; Perry & Pate, 1994; Perry, 2001, 2004a, 2006, 2009, 2013), which is activated by novel stimuli. Information from both the environment and bodily sensations are detected by this system and are interpreted based on past experience. For example, a past association that was stressful could activate a fear response. A person's perception of the stressor, based primarily on past associations, bodily sensations, and safety concerns, modulates the degree of activation.

Additionally a person's internal state at any given moment can be characterized on an arousal continuum, which includes states of calm, alert, alarm, fear, and terror (Cannon, 1932; Perry et al., 1995; Perry, 2004a, 2006, 2009; Porges, 2001, 2003, 2007). At higher levels of arousal, individuals' ability to use their cortex to respond will be compromised or unavailable. Therefore, one's state at any moment will be driven by both the individual's primary adaptive response to stress and the situation at hand.

It is important to note, as previously explained, that stress in itself is not negative. Stress is required for any growth or change to occur in the brain and, by definition, learning requires some activation of the stress response system. When stress is severe, unpredictable, and uncontrolled, it often leads to the vulnerabilities described throughout this chapter. Predictable, moderate, and controlled stress, on the other hand, creates an environment for people to learn and build resilience (CTA, 2013a). When working with youth and families, the challenge is to help caregivers learn how to detect and attune to the level of stress the youth and/or family member is experiencing at any given time.

Practical Applications: Youth and family member responses reflect their history and the way they have learned to adapt to life stressors, and, as such, their behaviors should not be taken personally. For example, youth who seem to "go from 0 to 100" in situations that others may not consider stressful are often reflecting a sensitized stress response (refer to #5). We typically assume the person with whom we're interacting is able to understand what is being verbally communicated, but in situations in which the person is experiencing fear, strong emotions, or significant stress, whether in response to external reality or an internal trigger, this is often not the case.

Table 10.2 Sensory Systems (adapted and reprinted with permission from **Champagne, 2017**)

Sensory Systems and Receptors	Primary Function(s)	Contributions	Strategies
Proprioception Receptors are located in the muscles, joints, ligaments, tendons, connective tissue, and fascia Receptors are stimulated by movements causing muscles to stretch, contract, or co-contract (particularly when movement is against resistance)	The proprioceptive system supports: Body awareness; the ability to assume and maintain body positions; and the grading, timing, and efficiency of movements The proprioceptive system works with the tactile system to support body awareness (body-based felt sense) and the vestibular system to support efficient and fluid movements and postural control (body in space)	Contributes to the awareness of: • Where the body and body parts are located in space and time • Body movement • Body position • Body boundaries • Body image • Proprioceptive information from the environment providing safety-related cues	• Climbing (playground, rock wall) • Push/pull activities • Stretching (yoga, exercise) • Kneading dough • Clay work • Squeezing a stress ball • Gardening and yard work (digging, planting, raking leaves, shoveling snow) • Weight lifting
Vestibular The vestibular system receptors are tiny hair cells within the otoliths and semicircular canals. These structures are within each inner ear. Receptors (hair cells) are activated during acceleration, deceleration,	The vestibular system supports the ability to be aware of the spatial orientation of the body (including equilibrium, speed, timing, and rhythmicity of positioning and movement) The vestibular system works with the proprioceptive system to support efficient movements and postural control. It works with	Contributes to the awareness of: • Spatial awareness of where the body is in space and time (your own personal GPS) • Balance • Body coordination • Muscle tone • Gravity detection • Awareness of the speed and direction of movements	• Activities requiring balance (biking, skateboarding, skiing, surfing) • Swinging • Rocking chair or glider rocker • Jumping activities (trampoline, pogo stick) • Acrobats/gymnastics • Walking • Hiking • Riding/driving in a car

(Continued)

Table 10.2 (Continued)

Sensory Systems and Receptors	Primary Function(s)	Contributions	Strategies
spinning, linear, angular movements, and any other movements involving the head, body, and the pull of gravity	the visual system to support the ability to maintain a stable visual field, balance, and equilibrium. The vestibular and auditory systems are also interconnected	• Awareness of whether things around us are moving or stationary • Spatial information from the environment providing safety-related cues	• Swimming • Playing movement-based video games (Wii) • Amusement park rides • Playing volleyball • Use of yoga/therapy balls
Tactile Receptors are located in the skin and there are different types that pick up sensations related to what you touch, of being touched, temperature, vibration, and pain related to input to the skin Receptors are activated during any type of skin contact (e.g., when touching something, showering, tooth brushing, eating, drinking, dressing)	The tactile system supports the ability to detect safety concerns, comfort, discomfort/pain sensations (protective function), and to discrimination and localize stimulation detected by the tactile receptors The tactile system works with the proprioceptive system to support body awareness	Contributes to the awareness of: • Tactile sensations and tactile discrimination • Pressure sensations (light/deep) • Pain coming from the pain receptors of the skin • Temperature • Vibration • Body boundaries • Tactile information from the environment providing safety-related cues	• Petting animals (cat, dog, horse) • Warm, soft blanket • Cool compress, ice pack • Skin and self-care supplies (lotions, brushes) • Stuffed animals • Manipulatives of different textures: Play dough, slime, putties, kinetic sand, stress balls • Compression garments • Weighted lap pad • Pillow with vibration • Knitting/crocheting • Cooking/baking • Breeze from a fan • Art/craft supplies

👁 Visual Receptors are located in the retina of the eye (rods and cones) and stimulated by visual input (light, colors, contours, shades, etc.)	The visual system supports the ability to discriminate visual stimuli in order to see, identify, and locate objects, symbols, boundaries, people, map spatial relationships, etc. The visual system also works with the vestibular system to support a stable visual field, balance, and equilibrium	Contributes to the awareness of: • Gradations of colors, light, darkness • Shapes, symbols, contours • Movement detection • Visual information from the environment providing safety-related cues.	• Looking at: Pictures of animals, nature scenes, mobile, wall art, murals, projected images • Looking at a fish tank, lava lamp, bubble lamp • Playing matching and other types of games • Reading books/magazines • Different colors and brightness of lighting and dimmer switches • Where's Waldo books, optical illusion books • Zentangle activities • Puzzles
👂 Auditory The auditory receptors are the hair cells of the cochlea located within the inner ear and stimulated by sound waves and vibrations	The auditory system supports the ability to detect the distance, directionality, and qualities of sounds The auditory system is interconnected with the vestibular system	Contributes to the awareness of: • Volume of sound(s) • Tone of sound(s) • Directionality/location of sound(s)	• Listen to music • Use of musical instruments • Engaging in sing-a-longs • Listening games (musical chairs, name that tune) • Listening to nature sounds • Engaging in conversation • Use of meditation bowl • Listening to stories/books

(Continued)

Table 10.2 (Continued)

Sensory Systems and Receptors	Primary Function(s)	Contributions	Strategies

Olfaction
The tissue inside the nasal cavity contains the chemical receptors of the nose and also osmoreceptors (detect osmotic pressure changes)
 	
The olfactory sense is primarily stimulated by different scents and the air through breathing
	The olfactory system supports the ability to detect and localize odors/scents, has a protective function and a direct connection to the limbic system (emotion center of the brain)
	
	The olfactory and gustatory systems work together to enhance the sense of taste
		Contributes to the awareness of:
		• The nature of odors: (pleasant, familiar, unpleasant)
		• How strong an odor is perceived to be
		• Provides emotional and safety-related cues
		• Supports the ability to taste
			• Scents that are familiar and provide positive associations:
			  ○ Flowers
			  ○ Essential oils
			  ○ Lotions and soaps
			  ○ Chocolate
			  ○ Citrus
			  ○ Pine
			  ○ Potpourri
			  ○ Variety of foods

Gustatory
Taste buds contain the chemical receptors of the tongue and are stimulated when tasting or manipulating things in the mouth (drinking, tasting, chewing)
	The gustatory system assists in the ability to discriminate between different tastes and helps to gather information about stimuli entering the mouth
	
	The gustatory and olfactory systems work together to enhance the sense of taste. Works with the tactile system to notice textures and temperatures of anything put into the mouth
		Contributes to the awareness of:
		• The nature of taste sensations: (pleasant, familiar, unpleasant)
		• How strong the taste stimuli is perceived to be
		• Provides safety-related cues
			• Tasting activities or guessing games:
			  ○ Different types of tea, flowers, fruits
			  ○ Blowing activities: Bubbles, windmill
			  ○ Chew or crunch (includes proprioception): Popcorn, granola bar, sugar free gum
			  ○ Sucking: Popsicle, thick liquids through straw (milkshake)

Interoception

Sensory nerve endings contained within the muscles, organs, and viscera across different systems within the body.

Interoception supports the ability to be aware of internal states, corresponding feelings, urges, and emotions

Contributes to the awareness of varying degrees of the following internal states/sensations:
- Pain
- Hunger
- Muscle tension
- Sleepiness/Alertness
- Heart rate
- Respiration rate
- Digestion and bowel/bladder functions
- Illness/wellness
- Nervousness
- Temperature

- Self-awareness and self-monitoring strategies:
  - Activities supporting increasing self-awareness (taste testing, drawing a picture of yourself, body tracings, books and puppets about parts and functions of the body)
  - Creation and use of self-rating and self-monitoring tools
  - Biofeedback measures: Heartmath, Biodots, heart rate monitor, Neurofeedback

We want to work with youth and families to collaboratively identify their most helpful, regulating strategies and to support the ability to create patterns of activation that are controllable and moderate. For instance: Reflective listening and appreciative inquiry help reduce the felt sense of fear or danger; music may provide regulating rhythms, which may improve the capacity for regulation and self-expression.

5. **Experiences impact an individual's sensitization and stress tolerance.** The more a person experiences stress and trauma in uncontrollable doses, with no opportunities to return to a baseline level of arousal, the more the entire nervous system becomes sensitized (CTA, 2013a; Perry & Pate, 1994; Perry, 2004a; Perry et al., 1995)—in other words, the brain develops in a way that keeps it directed toward survival, ultimately shaping the individual's perception of the world, others, and one's self as unsafe. The stress response system of such an individual becomes overly active at baseline and overly reactive when challenged (e.g., questioned, confronted, corrected), ultimately leading to a shift in baseline level of arousal. This is why every person's perception of what is stressful or traumatic is unique. On the other hand, when the "dose" of stress is small and controlled the individual can increase their tolerance to novel situations and reduce the risk of developing a sensitized stress response system (CTA, 2013a; Perry, 2001, 2004a, 2004b).

   Practical Application: Environments in which there is structure, predictability, and some controllability on the part of the youth and family members will provide support to a sensitized stress response system, allowing the youth and family to feel safe enough to try new things. For example:

   - Establish consistency in expectations at home and in the program to increase predictability;
   - Consistently use empathy to facilitate co-regulation, reduce the stress response, and increase the possibility of relatedness and reasoning;
   - Provide "dosing" through graded adaptive challenges so as to not unintentionally overwhelm;
   - Help families and staff learn to be guided by the neurophysiological signals that help indicate whether we are going to fast or too slow with interventions over time;
   - Avoid operant (point and level) systems, which can add stress to already stressful situations.

6. **Brains change with experience.** Neuroplasticity is the process through which human beings remain sensitive to new or novel experiences across their lifespan, and it supports functional, emotional, and relational capacities (Ayres, 2005; Hebb, 1949; Perry, 2006). New neural pathways develop through experience, and the more frequently and the more intensely these experiences occur, the stronger the pathways. This means that

interventions that are tailored to each individual's preferences, strengths, developmental needs and personal goals also influence changes in the brain, thus supporting hope, development, health, and healing.

Practical Application: The science offers hope. Understanding that brains are constantly evolving and adapting can help all involved work to create environments and interventions that have been shown to improve brain functioning. Collaboratively working with youth and families to design experiences that support self-regulation and relational skills helps to achieve mutually shared goals and increase resilience. For example, using family-driven and youth-guided practices on a regular basis throughout treatment provides recurring experiences that have the capacity to change neural pathways.

7. **Brains are designed to benefit from rich and supportive social relationships**. A relationally rich environment is essential to brain development (Bowlby, 1988; Carter et al., 2005; Jaffee et al., 2013; Kuypers & Sautter, 2012; Ludy-Dobson & Perry, 2010; Merrick, Leeb, & Lee, 2013; Miller, Coll, & Schoen, 2007; Perry, 2002, 2013; Siegel, 2012). The ability to form relationships exists even at the level of our genes. However, in order to express these capabilities, we require significant "doses" of safe, responsive, nurturing relational interactions throughout infancy, early childhood, and beyond (Ayres, 2005; Wang, 2018). Consistent doses of supportive relational interactions allow children to form positive attachments and develop relational and regulatory skills. As an individual becomes more distressed, the individual moves up the arousal continuum, becoming dysregulated. If early attachment experiences proved that caregivers are supportive, youth will turn to caregivers in times of distress, finding neurobiological reward in the interaction. If, on the other hand, early attachment experiences were somewhat chaotic and unsafe, the youth's tendency is to feel safer outside the context of relationships, resulting in a reduced capacity to regulate themselves in the context of relationships. Since the brain changes with experience and the neurobiological reward of social relationships is significant (Ludy-Dobson & Perry, 2010), the goal then is to work with youth and family members in building the capacity to experience positive relational interactions and relationships that are safe and rewarding. The concept of "dosing," i.e., providing intentional relational interactions and opportunities, may be helpful in this process, as it often takes time to build the capacity necessary to engage in a way that youth and families begin to experience relational reward; doing so incrementally increases regulatory capacity through the interconnectedness of relationships and interpersonal reward (Supin, 2016).

Practical Application: Focus on the interconnectedness of relationships, regulation, and the neurobiological reward system by providing a relationally rich environment within the residential, school, and home environments with the focus on building capacity for the youth and family members to regulate themselves in the context of their family and community relationships. Family members, including siblings, also need support in understanding these basic principles and developing new skills and will benefit from more time with their child/siblings with the supports necessary to ensure successful interactions and relationship affirming and building.

VOICE OF LIVED EXPERIENCE

These practical applications are all important, but the one that may be most important is about relationship. Being in our home community with our family/friends from "before" wasn't something we had access to or were even allowed to have. I had some amazing staff, caseworkers, and even a great foster mother who offered so much love and guidance. These relationships were greatly helpful, still follow me now, and still have a positive impact on my adult life. However, losing contact with other family members and friends, being ashamed of having to tell everyone "where I was," not being a part of my home community, and most importantly losing time with my siblings left big holes in my relationship life. Overall, the social relationships I lost, as well as those I had and built, still do have an effect in my "recovery" journey.

Application of the Science: Sensory and Body-based Strategies

The growing body of knowledge of how the brain and body develop in the face of stress and traumatic experience has led to an increased emphasis on body-based approaches as part of TIC (Champagne, 2011; Champagne & Stromberg, 2004; LeBel & Champagne, 2010; LeBel, Champagne, Stromberg, & Coyle, 2010; NASMHPD, 2003; Perry, 2009; Porges, 2007; van der Kolk, 2014). With more severely traumatized individuals, interventions focusing solely on talk therapy approaches—without regard to the sequence of engagement or the influence of trauma on the body (Perry & Ablon, 2019; van der Kolk, 2014)—often prove to be ineffective and sometimes re-traumatizing (Porges, 2009; Perry, 2006; van der Kolk, 2014). Verbal teaching strategies and talk therapies are commonly referred to as top-down interventions, because they require the cortical ability to pay attention, reason, problem-solve, and control impulses. This ability is reliant upon the capacity to self-regulate and verbally communicate in the face of a sensitized

A Neurodevelopmental Approach **213**

stress response system. Sensory rich, bodily-oriented experiences (often referred to as bottom-up interventions) provide alternatives that specifically foster self-regulation and relational capacities. Over time, as neurodevelopmental capacities increase, interventions then shift to some combination of bottom-up and top-down.

As discussed previously, when a person moves up the arousal continuum, it becomes less probable that they will be able to take in information verbally, because the nervous system hijacks that capacity in the face of perceived stress or danger (Porges, 2001, 2009). Thus, the types of bottom-up strategies that are most helpful at the different phases of alarm activation are significantly important to help youth and family identify for prevention and crisis de-escalation purposes (LeBel & Champagne, 2010). Since what is sensory-supportive to one person may or may not be helpful to another, sensory and body-based strategies must be youth- and family-directed and therefore *individualized*. The intentional use of supportive nonverbal body language and access to preferred sensory supports help youth and families feel safe, increasing their capacity to communicate and engage in activities and routines (Champagne, 2011; Porges, 2001, 2003, 2007).

Becoming youth-guided and family-driven involves helping youth and families identify what is calming (improving regulation capacity as one becomes more hyper aroused), alerting (uplifting or more intense when one begins to lose attention), or bothersome (overwhelming, not helpful or safe, leading to dysregulation)—and when to use each strategy, often referred to as sensory modulation (Ayres, 2005; Champagne, 2011; MA DMH, 2013). Some youth and families are able to verbally discuss and try different alternatives while others may prefer primarily exploratory options. Some examples of sensory supportive strategies that may be more calming and/or alerting follow (Champagne, 2011).

It is important to note that once the stress response system is activated, depending on the degree, frequency, and type of activation, it will likely take time for the youth and/or family member to become fully regulated again (Perry & Pollard, 1998). It is critical to work with youth and families to make a plan for ways to best support the youth and family through this process in a way that prioritizes family and youth voice and choice. Remembering that the stress response system is a significant driver of concerning and unsafe behavior removes some stigma and perception of intentionality on the part of the youth and family members and can result in the reduction of reactive responses, power struggles, and unintentional re-traumatization. The emphasis then becomes more about how to best support feelings of safety and the development of neurodevelopmental capacities and skills over time by using the strategies that have been identified by and for the individual youth and family.

214 Robert E. Lieberman et al.

Table 10.3 Calming and Alerting Sensory Strategies (Champagne, 2011)

Calming Strategies	Alerting Strategies
• Warm/hot drink	• Cool/cold drink
• Swinging on a swing	• Spinning on a swing
• Rocking slowly in a rocker	• Rocking vigorously in a rocking chair
• Humming or singing softly	• Clapping or bouncing to music
• Blowing bubbles	• Riding a horse
• Deep pressure touch/massage	• Singing intensely or loudly
• Using a weighted vest or blanket	• Light touch
• Soothing scents	• Intense scents (eucalyptus)
• Chewing gum	• Jogging, bouncing, or running
• Soft/low lighting	• Playing ball toss
• Coloring or drawing	• Eating spicy foods
• Playing with Legos	• Bright/colorful lighting
• Listening to music	• Aerobic exercise
• Being in a calm and quiet place/ space	• Differing food textures
• Having a consistent routine	• Being in a busy, loud, or chaotic environment
• Gardening	• Inconsistent routines
• Petting or taking care of a cat, dog, or horse (pet)	• Playing sports
	• Doing/focusing on chores, school work, or working

Vignette: Kyle

When Kyle and his parents were welcomed to the residential program at Cutchins Programs for Children and Families, Kyle was experiencing significant dysregulation and his behaviors were frequently identified as "aggressive." He struggled significantly with the ability to verbally communicate. His therapist noted that any words other than "safe or unsafe" when referring to either his arousal level, behavior, or strategies seemed to move him up the arousal continuum. Staff worked closely with Kyle, his parents, and his therapist during the first days of admission to put together a plan (safety tool, MA DMH, 2013) that outlined some of his triggers, warning signs, and helpful strategies. This list was communicated to all who worked with Kyle, and staff were also educated by Kyle and his parents on his strengths and interests, as well as potential scenarios that may be difficult for him—how to and how not to interact, how to make helpful strategies accessible, and how/when to communicate with Kyle at different levels of escalation. Table 10.4 demonstrates this early sensory supportive safety tool that was used as an initial plan and modified over time.

Due to the severity of the early childhood trauma Kyle experienced and resulting impact on his brain functioning, it took a great deal of repetition

A Neurodevelopmental Approach **215**

Table 10.4 Kyle's Safety Tool Strategies When Upset I feel: "Unsafe"

When Upset I feel: "Unsafe"

- **Body:** I get hot, feels like I will explode, I feel "unsafe"
- **Mind:** I can't think, mind goes blank
- **Triggers:** Certain words: "no" or telling me I am getting a consequence (time out), when things feel too hard or when I feel frustrated
- **Warning signs:** I don't talk, I stop doing what I am supposed to, I pace, stop moving, or start to stare

Things that help me: "safe" strategies	Things other people can do that might help me "feel safe":
<ul><li>Cold cloth or my soft gel/ice pack</li><li>Squeeze or fidget with something (stress ball, my stuffed animal)</li><li>Jump and crash into a big bean bag</li><li>Swing</li><li>Playground use</li><li>Ride my bike around the yard</li><li>Jump on mini-trampoline or pogo stick</li><li>Play basketball</li><li>Swim at the YMCA</li><li>Go on a walk or hike</li><li>Watch the Boston Red Sox</li><li>Watch funny shows/movies</li><li>Go fishing</li></ul>	<ul><li>Use words safe/unsafe when asking about or talking about how I feel with me or to others</li><li>Give me space but stay nearby</li><li>Stay calm</li><li>Help distract me by offering a "safe" strategy from my list</li><li>Offer hugs, back rubs, massage, or joint compressions</li><li>If I get even more upset get other people away from me</li></ul>

Please do NOT:

- Leave me alone
- Use any of these words: Time out, consequence
- Put me in places with lots of loud noise
- Give me warnings or reminders that are upsetting to me
- Use too much deep touch pressure
- Tickle me
- Bring me to a room with breakable stuff

and support to impact the neurophysiological changes necessary to develop his capacities for stabilization. While for some individuals the stabilization process can occur relatively quickly with such an approach, for those with more severe childhood trauma, it may require both staff and family to work more sensitively and intensely with the child. Prior to coming to this program, Kyle's behaviors were viewed as intentional and, as a result, led to ongoing power struggles, the use of restraints, client and staff injuries, and re-traumatization for Kyle, his parents, and staff. Over time, Kyle's tolerance for changes in his routine and for relationship building expanded as his staff and parents used both a predictable and structured environment as well as sensory supportive approaches, being very mindful of his responses to help determine when the timing, frequency, and intensity of the "dosing" was optimal. By using these interventions and the key words that Kyle chose to help support him, he experienced smoother transitions, restraints were not necessary, and he was able to more successfully engage in his daily routine at the program at home, school, and in the community.

Sensory Approaches and Daily Routines

When designing sensory supportive approaches as part of a residential intervention, it is critical to work with youth and families to build these strategies into the daily routine and physical environment for prevention and crisis de-escalation purposes (Champagne, 2011; Lee et al., 2010). The collaborative creation of a menu of sensory supportive choices as part of a daily routine is sometimes referred to as a *sensory diet (SD)* (Champagne, 2011; Wilbarger, 1984; MA DMH, 2013). A sensory diet is a routine that is strategically created and used to help consistently offer the sensory input (a menu or range of options) needed to support neurodevelopment, self-regulation (prevention), and de-escalation. The youth and families' voice, preferences, and a variety of choices, along with an emphasis on both day and evening rituals and routines, are critical to creating a sensory diet. Attention to the entire routine is important since many struggle not only during waking hours but also with falling and staying sleep. Environments providing structure, comfort, reassurance, and predictability create more of a sense of safety and support, thereby improving their sleep. Knowing the significance of self-regulation through sensory supports such as providing comfortable pajamas, calming sounds/music, consistent temperature, supportive lighting, and other strategies emerging through the processes previously identified provide the individualized supports needed, whether in the residential program or at home. In this way, a preventive routine and strategies are outlined, accessible, and understood by those involved (family members, residential staff, teachers). The following presents a portion of Jenny's sensory diet (evening routine) used while she and her foster family received a residential intervention at Cutchins.

Jenny's Sensory Diet: Bedtime Routine

Bedtime Routine: Start to prepare for bed two—three hours before bedtime

1. Makes Tea—Mint "Magic" tea and honey—she makes the tea; she likes staff to put in the honey; she stirs

A Neurodevelopmental Approach **217**

2. Has a phone call with her foster mom while drinking her tea
3. Bedtime preparation activities

NOTE: When feeling calm/happy, Jenny does much of the following with her roommate and staff support (except activities requiring privacy). When Jenny is not calm/happy staff support her individually.

- Read a book with staff
- Picks out clothes for the next day and staff helps her get her backpack ready for school
- Arranging stuffed animals and puppets (gets them ready for bed, tucks them in)
- "Safety check" with aromatherapy spray (lavender): 1–2 sprays under bed, in closet, and on a cotton ball she puts under her pillow (process helps her to feel safe)
- Music—Jenny likes to listen to Frozen/Disney soundtracks while getting ready for bed
    - Brushes teeth with vibrating toothbrush and gel toothpaste (self-preferred)
    - Washes/dries face with soft face cloth
    - Puts on soft pajamas (no seams or tags)
    - Lowers dimmer switch on light in room
    - Gets tucked in by staff
    - Staff provide reassurance that they check on her throughout the night

Capitalizing on the Physical Environment

The physical environment is another area that benefits from using a sensory lens (Champagne, 2011; MA DMH, 2013). Keeping the physical environment in good repair, clean, organized, and non-chaotic helps to decrease incidences of stress and anxiety. The creation and use of sensory enhanced corners, rooms, sensory carts, sensory gardens, and access to playground and gym equipment promote the use of sensory and movement-based interventions at home, school, in the community, and in residential programs (Champagne, 2011; Champagne & Stromberg, 2004; MA DMH, 2013; Martin & Suane, 2012). Having comfortable furnishings (rocking chair, bean bags), wall art, murals, and different lighting options that support neurodevelopmental and therapeutic goals are examples of ways to enhance the physical environment (Bobler, 2015; Champagne, 2011; Champagne & Stromberg, 2004; LeBel & Champagne, 2010; Novak, Scanlan, McCaul, MacDonald, & Clarke, 2012; West, Melvin, McNamara, & Gordon, 2017). Youth and families can be supported in brainstorming sensory supportive enhancements for their home environments, a practice done routinely in Massachusetts residential interventions.

218 Robert E. Lieberman et al.

VOICE OF LIVED EXPERIENCE

Key points in this section stand out. Just like all areas of the "treatment plan", parents/family need to be actively involved so that they can be familiar with these strategies while the child is at home and when the residential intervention is finished, and the youth returns back home. The individualization of the plan is critical- the same book does not apply to every young person; this was one of my biggest complaints- we weren't able to really identify our own supports.

Application of the Science: Residential Intervention Design

Skillfully designed interventions have the capacity to positively "change the brain." The more frequently individualized neurodevelopmentally-oriented activities are structured throughout the day in the program, home, and community, the higher the probability for longer-term success. Hull Services in Alberta, Canada and Cutchins Programs in Massachusetts are organizations that have been using the brain science and research to design their residential interventions. At Hull Services, professionals and family members use a structured planning approach (Mobius Care Model) to capture what the youth experiences throughout the course of a week, by way of hour-long blocks. The information is then used to assess the programming and also used in the context of working with family members to better understand whether enough neurodevelopmental opportunities are available for the youth and if not, what is needed to fill the gap. Discussions with family address: Capacity to deliver such interventions, skill development necessary to provide more effective support, and the need for external resources to assist the family. Such discussions generate decisions about how to provide more growth opportunities. This in turn leads to the recognition that providing routine, predictability, and structure is key, in all aspects of the residential intervention, including supporting the family in ensuring these circumstances in home and community environments (Champagne, 2011; Perry, 2013).

Hull and Cutchins Programs recognize the complexity of trauma and development; this means that meeting the needs of the youth and families requires that multiple domains of functioning need to be addressed, rather than focusing on one specific form of treatment that may or may not capture all the domains. Determining which areas need most attention helps determine the dosing (intensity and frequency) of specific strategies. Therefore, at both programs, residential intervention is seen as uniquely positioned for high intensity, multidimensional treatment with the youth and family.

Cutchins Programs staff completes a comprehensive, collaborative assessment process emphasizing strengths, neurodevelopment, and relational capacities with the youth, family, clinical, occupational therapy, psychiatry, nursing, and other staff participating. This assessment process includes obtaining information related to strengths and supports, attachment, and trauma history and a thorough neurodevelopmental assessment (including sensory and motor processing) that includes the evaluation of the youth's ability to participate in life roles, routines, and activities. Staff are trained in evidence-based attachment and trauma models and interventions, trauma-informed care and BBI, in addition to the Sensory Modulation Program (SMP) (Champagne, 2011). This integrative, interdisciplinary approach is used to collaboratively assess and co-design individualized, youth-guided, and family-driven therapeutic goals and interventions. Additionally, therapeutic modalities such as neurofeedback, heartmath, sound therapies, pet therapy, weighted modalities, clinical aromatherapy, movement, and expressive arts are some of the therapeutic options available as part of the residential intervention. Recently, significant renovations were made to gym and playground spaces to support the ability to offer more sensory and motor neurodevelopmental (bottom-up) interventions with positive effects (reductions in restraint use, increased experiences of joy, and family participation).

Hull implements a thorough assessment using the Neurosequential Model of Therapeutics [NMT] Metric, providing a holistic perspective. This involves gathering the history of the child's developmental adversity and relational buffers and using that information to clinically reconstruct the history to better understand how the child's history impacts current brain functioning (Perry, 2009). Developmentally sensitive treatment recommendations are then provided to front line staff, family members, and other individuals involved in the child's therapeutic web. Interventions are provided in a sequential manner, which, for youth who have experienced developmental trauma, often means spending a significant amount of time on bottom-up strategies and relational regulation. All staff at Hull Services are trained in the core concepts of the NMT (Perry, 2006). With a better understanding of neurodevelopment, the staff members are more likely to be curious (about the child's history and how that has impacted their current functioning) rather than punitive and more likely to understand that a child's challenging behaviors may be a result of "what happened to them," rather than a result of being oppositional, manipulative, or defiant.

To translate knowledge of neuroscience and brain development into practice with staff and families, Hull applies Dr. Bruce Perry's "6 R's," which are biologically respectful core elements of positive developmental, educational, and therapeutic experiences. The "6 R's," described below, have been a strong framework for many agencies as they begin to operationally define the work and practice of being trauma-informed. The principles allow for an understanding of neurodevelopment and align with three very important components of the BBI, namely emphasizing family-driven, youth-guided, and culturally respectful (diversity, equity, and inclusion) practices. They provide impetus for healing and skill development and can be used as a lens through which to assess structures, routines, practices, and interventions being used or considered.

> **Relational** (safe): A trauma-informed approach requires creating a safe environment in the context of relationships. The focus is on the relational needs of the youth and families, rather than on the modification or management of behaviors. If, in a typical family relationship, interactions have the capacity to be a source of comfort, then, in situations with youth and families receiving residential interventions, the goal is to affirm or help create a positive relational template. Relationships are the key to creating a safe and predictable environment, and youth and families need to be provided with as many opportunities as possible to learn how to realize success in building strong and safe relationships in preparation for their permanent return home.

> **Relevant** (developmentally matched to the individual): Residential interventions provide environmental structure and routines that set the stage for new learning in the program and at home. In essence, youth and families are more likely to be able to manage novel situations when things around them are predictable and structured. On the other hand, when things are chaotic, a person's attention is directed toward assessing and monitoring the safety of the novel situation. In order for interventions to be effective, they must balance structure and predictability and be matched to the youth and/or family member's individual developmental needs. In one situation at Hull Services, a youth had significant challenges being with his peers in the morning hours. Instead of insisting that this young person follow the rules of the program, he was provided with his breakfast and invited to engage with the group at his will rather than as part of the program routine. Ensuring that expectations are developmentally matched to the youth while still maintaining as much structure as possible is an essential part of success.

> **Repetitive** (patterned): First, repetition builds neuronal connections that decrease the brain's need to pay attention to distractions and increase the brain's capacity to manage novelty. Managing novelty is made possible when other parts of one's life are predictable. Repetition occurs through the careful planning of day-to-day structure and processes, including time at home and in the community. Second, when there is a significant amount of repetition as an individual is exposed to novel situations, i.e., in the case of learning new skills, the repetition increases one's capacity to understand and integrate into the individual's long-term memory,

thus developing the new skills (e.g., social emotional skills, addition and subtraction, physical abilities, etc.). As an example, at Hull and Cutchins, with both agencies focusing on improving family and youth capacity for relationships, positive relational interactions are provided repetitively, which then increases the capacity for engaging more successfully in relationships.

Rhythmic (resonant with neural patterns): Rhythmic movement improves a person's capacity to regulate and to feel more organized. Calming through rhythm occurs in utero and is visible from the time a baby is born, when caregivers holding the baby rock, sway, and pat to keep the baby calm and/or comforted. Rhythm is offered through bottom-up strategies, such as exercise and dance. Rhythm also occurs through conversations that have a "serve and return," back and forth quality. At Hull, staff are encouraged to inquire about youth's and family's perspectives and engage in rhythmic dialogue rather than simply (re)directing, instructing, or informing; families are supported to build more capacity in such dialogue with their youth as well. A music therapist described using the consistent rhythm of a buffalo drum to help a youth with a brain injury re-learn to walk. The rhythm of the drum was used to indicate each step forward and provided grounding for the youth. Individual and group drumming opportunities at Cutchins integrate rhythmic input into the programming; youth can choose to learn to play an instrument and foster both sensory and motor development (timing, bilateral coordination, modulation of the use of force) and relational skill development by attuning to others while drumming and/or singing together.

Rewarding (pleasurable): Finding pleasure is an important aspect to consider in the work with young people and families. For an adolescent who has trouble with academics and has little opportunity to see friends outside of the program, building more opportunities for pleasurable or rewarding activities in the community impacts the reward center of the brain, develops neural pathways, and increases capacity for success. Providing the youth with more opportunity to "connect" with their family and friends will also impact their reward neurobiology, which in turn will increase the youth's ability to feel regulated.

Respectful (of the youth, family, and culture): Understanding each youth and family's unique set of values is key to providing them with what they need. One family may cherish and value the adolescent stage of development while another may have some anxieties around that stage. By affording family members decision-making opportunities in designing the plan, a deeper understanding of the needs of the youth

222 Robert E. Lieberman et al.

and family is obtained, leading to greater capacity for intervention. In particular, understanding the youth's and family's connection to culture is a significant piece of providing appropriate interventions and creating opportunities for healing.

Application of the Science to the BBI Framework

As has been discussed throughout this chapter, understanding neurodevelopment is critical for youth and family members with sensitized stress response systems who may suffer from developmental trauma; youth with these challenges are commonly referred for residential interventions. Yet the interventions often used are operant in nature—some version of reward and consequence, incentive and sanction. Such interventions often create a level of stress that generates hyper-aroused (explosive) or dissociated (implosive) responses (Perry & Ablon, 2019). Clearly, a different response capacity is needed. The responsibility for the child- and family-serving field in general—and most especially residential interventions—is to move past simplistic behaviorally oriented, conventional wisdom explanations of and responses to behavior toward approaches that contribute to experiences of skill development and healing for youth and families.

The BBI framework has key practices that align with and help facilitate this neurodevelopmental transformation and provide an overall context within which the strategies and interventions emerging from the neuroscience can be implemented. The connections between this framework and key principles of the neuroscience, as identified earlier, are discussed in the following.

Youth-Guided

Youth-guided care involves the youth in decision-making regarding their own treatment as well as agency matters. In short, youth are empowered with voice and choice. This recruits the neural networks that are responsible for development of several neurocognitive skills, including expressing thought, needs, and concerns in words, considering multiple options in response to a situation they are facing, anticipating the likely outcomes of their actions, perspective taking, empathy, and others. Learning these skills in situations related to the youth's immediate life, whether in the program, home, or community and practicing in patterned and repetitive ways helps generate new neural pathways and self-regulatory abilities (Perry & Ablon, 2019).

The process of youth-guided care entails collaboration between youth, families, and staff. It occurs in a patterned, predictable manner, in the various individual, group, committee, and child and family team meetings in which the youth participates. The repetitive and patterned opportunities to dialogue with authority figures and the experience of collaboration—sharing thoughts and concerns safely—strengthen emotional and self-regulation skills (Ablon & Pollastri, 2018) and facilitate relationship development. The youth comes to believe that the adult (whether staff or family member) has their best interest in mind.

The changes in the relationship pattern that can emerge from engaging and empowering youth voice and choice can also empower parent voice and change the fundamental interactive patterns in the home. The skills involved will be necessary for relationship development throughout the life span. Thus, youth-guided practice engages the young person's cognitive resources and allows family members and professionals alike to recognize that it is biologically respectful to "do with" rather than "do to," while providing the youth opportunity to develop and control their capacity for self-identity, interpersonal relationships, and intimacy. Importantly, consider the alternative. When youth opinion, voice, and choice are not systematically engaged, it takes any semblance of control away and is experienced as a slap in the face that sometimes occurs throughout the day, each day, increasing the stress responses that impede learning and growth.

An additional aspect of youth-guided care is the hiring of individuals with lived experience as youth peer support specialists, discussed in detail in Chapter 3. While these individuals are working in a paid, "official" capacity, their training is to use their lived experience as a source of empathic understanding and support. This reduces the perceived and actual power differential that typically occurs with professional staff. Having a conversation with someone with a reduced power differential, to whom empathy may come a bit easier, facilitates the patterned, rhythmic type of interaction that is regulating. It also potentially offers a positive view of the future, in experiencing and empathizing with someone who has been in a similar situation in the past and has converted that into gainful employment and helping others.

At Hull and Cutchins the youth play a central role in the interventions and treatment, guiding family members and professionals in understanding what is and isn't effective. Youth explore and identify sensory and body-based (bottom-up) interventions that they find both regulating and rewarding. Additionally, youth guide their engagement in the community. Recognizing that the goal is to use residential as an intervention rather than a placement, the focus is on providing as many repetitions of time at home and of community building opportunities for the youth as possible. This means maintaining the youth's connection to home and community from the onset of and throughout the residential intervention and concurrently building the capacity to find opportunities to create more support for themselves. For example, a youth can be exposed to yoga, music lessons, or drumming within the context of the residential program or in the community with prosocial peers.

> ## VOICE OF LIVED EXPERIENCE
>
> Youth-guided really means not using point and level systems, as stated previously. If a youth finds playing guitar therapeutic, this should not be only available at such and such level—this can cause that stress that generates the explosive and implosive responses. Family contact should also never be a part of any behavioral level/point system. It is important to also note that youth-guided isn't just youth being involved in their own plans, treatments, etc. but rather that youth voices are heard and asked about in every aspect of the residential intervention—every committee, group, process, or change that occurs in the agency has youth involved—and/or peer support specialists who can represent the youth in these areas.

Family-Driven

Similar principles from the brain science apply to the relevance of family-driven care. When family members are supported in articulating their thoughts, perceptions, and decisions, they develop cognitive flexibility and new ways of coping, relating, and thinking. These enhanced neurocognitive abilities are critical in the rapidly changing cultural environment surrounding young people. Such skills are practiced in all interactions between the youth and family members including child and family team meetings, youth time at home and in the community, or when family spend time at the residential program. Patterned repetition leads to development of new neural pathways, potentially yielding sustainable change in the family system. The improved relationship between family members that can accrue as a result of family-driven practice leads to a stronger sense of attachment and belonging, as well as greater connection with community. Similar benefits as those identified previously for youth can be expected from hiring family (peer) support specialists, discussed in Chapter 2. The empathy available to family members from family support specialists helps move family members down the arousal continuum, facilitating learning and skill development. The experience of not being blamed for their child's problems in an organization that implements family-driven care generates the opportunity for greater attention to the learning potential inherent in the collaborative efforts.

Hull and Cutchins Programs focus on ensuring that staff is skilled in providing interventions that are family-driven. Parents guide the process and assist professionals in better understanding the needs, values, and cultural traditions of the family, including siblings. The goal of the professionals is to support the family and youth. Cutchins Programs trains all staff to support youth and family skills in this way and added Building Bridges managers to provide the supervision needed to foster the development of this staff and organizational skill set. All of Hull's residential programs have Family

Intervention Workers who support families with the intention of increasing parental skill and providing as many opportunities as possible for youth to be involved and engaged with their families. Scheduling of activities is focused on empowering the families to make decisions and support their children. Doses of positive relational interactions are directed toward family members so that they can support the youth's capacity for regulation as much as possible. The more positive interactions the youth has with their parent and siblings, the more the parent will be able to provide support and co-regulate. At both Hull and Cutchins, in home support is provided, with opportunities to both coach and build capacity of parents and youth in their home and community, through repetitive experiences of regulation, relationship, reason, and reward.

Culturally and Linguistically Competent

A significant amount of stress is generated by practices and interactions that are not culturally or linguistically sensitive. Such practices diminish the essential humanity of the recipient and accentuate a power differential they experience consistently simply as a result of their skin color, cultural manifestation, gender identity, language, etc. With a culturally and linguistically competent focus, treatment can be geared toward family values and cultural beliefs. Cultural beliefs will likely shape the specifics of the experiences that parents structure and create for their children; as a result, it is essential for professionals to better understand them.

Implementing culturally and linguistically informed practices, discussed in Chapter 4, involves organizational cultural change. In encountering this challenge, it is important to utilize the same key neuroscientific principles. Interactions throughout the day that honor youth and family voice and are attuned to their culture can mitigate the stress response. Structural elements can assist, for example: Hiring staff—including peer and family support specialists—of similar cultural backgrounds to the individuals served; developing plans that reflect the youth and family ethnicity, culture, and spiritual life; and honoring family and youth choice for culture and language in staff assignments. Practices such as these can help staff gain a deeper awareness of the importance of diversity, equity, and inclusion in the organization and help skill development at the individual level, for both staff and youth/family. Finding the source of empathy for individuals of diverse backgrounds and orientations helps promote the skill of empathy more broadly.

Linkage With Community

One of the consistent indicators of positive sustained post-discharge outcome is the degree to which the residential intervention links and is seamless with community (Blau, Caldwell, & Lieberman, 2014). This is logical, as whatever gains the youth and family members have generated through a residential intervention must generalize to the home and community if gains are to be sustained. That is why integration of program and community services and supports in residential interventions is a pillar of BBI.

The resilience research points to this as well. The key components of resilience (Masten, 2001) are: Connection to community, culture, spirituality; attachment and belonging; and personal capabilities. While all of these can occur within a residential program, the specificity principle of the neuroscience informs us that learnings in one setting won't necessarily generalize to another (Gaskill & Perry, 2017)); thus the learning needs to occur in the real-life settings of home and community for the new neural networks to develop.

The community offers a relational web supporting change and growth for the individuals involved (Campbell, 2018). This can take the form of a child and family team, wraparound team, the more traditional treatment teams, or simply informal relationships and friendships. Important in the structure and function of established teams is that they are relational in nature and regulating in structure and function. Careful attention to the design and facilitation of the meetings is necessary to moderate the degree to which the stress response system is activated for the youth and family so that dialogue and sharing of thoughts and concerns can occur.

Incorporating the importance of the less formal aspect of the therapeutic web will support existing pro-social relationships and the development of new ones. By way of contrast, planning and decision making in silos can threaten the social and relational needs of the individuals by disregarding the importance of the multiple relationships potentially available or new opportunities to develop them. This can lead to a situation in which youth interpret that their social needs are not being addressed (Teicher et al., 2010).

Although community plays a significant role in the well-being of youth and families, community partners, professionals, and lay citizens alike may be threatened by increased community involvement of youth who have previously presented seriously challenging behavior. Thus, approaching individuals reluctant to embrace community presence for these youth requires acknowledgement of the seriousness of their concerns, empathy, co-regulation, and partnership development (discussed in Chapter 8). Nurturing these relationships over time can help facilitate coordinated and collaborative response to issues that may arise.

Trauma-Informed Transformational Change

The BBI practice framework emanated in part from the emerging knowledge about TIC, building on the Six Core Strategies ™ (Huckshorn, 2006) for preventing aggression and coercive interventions and promoting trauma-informed care. This evidence-based approach has often been a foundational framework for organizations implementing BBI. Becoming trauma-informed involves organizational transformation—the learning and embracing of a different mindset for understanding and responding to the impact of adversity, toxic stress, and trauma and for resisting re-traumatization.

Implementing the BBI pillars goes far toward facilitating this transformation. The patterned, repetitive practice of new "habits" (e.g., family-driven, youth-guided, culturally and linguistically competent, strong community partnerships, child and family team planning, etc.) helps build new socioneural pathways in the organization. A direct care staff of one organization commented on the 95% reduction of restraint that occurred as a result of this transformative process, "We used to come in wondering who we might have to restrain. Now when an episode at that level occurs, which is rarely, it's an anomaly—we wonder what went wrong."

When staff understand their work through the lens of the science and evidence and have direct experiences of doing things differently with positive results, new ways of thinking, relating, and coping emerge. In essence, the culture of the organization changes and transformation at both the organizational and the individual levels becomes possible. While this is the promise inherent in the latest science and evidence, it is also the challenge. Transformation requires leadership that is committed and understands that an organization, like individuals, will move up and down the arousal continuum. This means developing trauma-informed staff support structures and policies; providing ongoing applied training; promoting staff self-care; establishing clear, predictable, and consistent communication systems; and gauging decisions through a neurodevelopmentally informed lens by listening to youth, families, and one another, and using new insights toward ongoing improvement. Where attention is placed is critical in order to sustain organizational transformation.

VOICE OF LIVED EXPERIENCE

As a youth with lived experience in the mental health and foster care system, along with out-of-home placement, this chapter provides the most important information to understand when thinking about achieving positive outcomes for the youth in your residential interventions. As a young person in care, I felt alone, hopeless, and like my every decision was forever made for me. I know now that beyond this not being youth-guided, it was not what this chapter calls neurodevelopmentally-informed. I eventually joined a peer advocacy group. While it wasn't very youth-guided, it was a place I could relate to other youth and a place we could talk and voice the way we felt . . . even if at the time our voices weren't valued enough. After finding my voice and using it, I was able to have a choice in my medication—empowering me to keep advocating for myself and eventually leading me to a career of advocating for other youth.

As a professional in this field now, I realize that I did experience some of the practices described in this chapter, and they had positive lasting impact on my adult life and overall recovery journey. I also realized that I, along with many other peers I knew, didn't experience some of the "newer" practices. While we had youth voice in our organization, it wasn't truly youth-guided. We had point and level systems, sometimes our punishments were to miss "visits" with our families, and although some of us had great experience with SOME staff and workers, we weren't able to really identify our own supports. Having a peer advocate is something that I always wanted and then wanted to be. My agency had never offered one, and when I had brought up the idea of one later, it was not seriously considered. Overall, this practice and others described in this chapter can be so beneficial for a youth's recovery, their adult life, the family, and even the program itself. Hard as it may seem, all practices must be used together; you cannot be youth-guided if you are not family-driven, culturally competent, etc. as well—it will not have the same positive effect on all involved. Using a "neurodevelopmentally-informed lens" can help you get there.

Conclusion

In the earlier days of residential treatment, focusing on respectful relational interactions was seen as an alternative to operant behavioral approaches, and it was supported by psychodynamic theories and philosophical frameworks. The family was secondary, if involved at all, and youth voice was nice to have, not a necessity. Now with new knowledge that has emerged from the neuroscience and trauma research, we have compelling science that informs us about why supporting neurodevelopment is a critical precondition for change and why careful and thoughtful implementation of neurodevelopmental approaches including sensory, body-based, and relational strategies within a framework of diversity, equity, and inclusion; youth and family voice; and integration with community is a precondition for organizational transformation. This chapter has connected this science with practical implications, provided examples of two organizations that have initiated this journey, and offered a voice of lived experience. We invite the reader to consider this path. All youth and families deserve this level of relational, rhythmic, repetitive, rewarding, relevant, and respectful attention.

Resources

- Adverse Childhood Experiences Study: www.acestudy.org/
- Beacon House UK Resources: https://beaconhouse.org.uk/useful-resources/

- Building Bridges Initiative: www.buildingbridges4youth.org/index.html
- Center for the Study of Traumatic Stress: centerforthestudyoftraumaticstress.org
- Child Trauma Academy: http://childtrauma.org/
- Eight Dimensions of Wellness (video): www.youtube.com/watch?v=tDzQdRvLAfM&feature=youtu.be
- Every Moment Counts: www.everymomentcounts.org/
- International Society for the Study of Trauma and Dissociative Disorders: www.isst-d.org/
- National Child Traumatic Stress Network: www.NCTSN.org
- MA State Department of Mental Health Seclusion and Restraint Reduction Initiative: www.mass.gov/eohhs/gov/departments/dmh/restraintseclusion-reduction-initiative.html
- OT Innovations: www.ot-innovations.com
- SAMHSA Trauma-informed Care & Alternatives to Seclusion and Restraint: www.samhsa.gov/nctic/trauma-interventions
- Te Pou & Sensory Modulation: www.tepou.co.nz/initiatives/sensory-modulation/103

Notes

1. Between the ages of 0 and 18, sexual abuse, physical abuse, emotional abuse, physical neglect, emotional neglect, and in the household: Incarceration of a parent, domestic violence, substance abuse, mental illness, divorce.
2. Language and communication skills, attention and working memory skills, emotion and self-regulation skills, sensory and motor skills, cognitive flexibility, social thinking skills.

References

Ablon, S., & Pollastri, A. (2018). *The school discipline fix*. New York, NY: W. W. Norton & Company.

Anda, R. F., Felitti, V. J., Bremner, J. D., Walker, J. D., Whitfield, C., Perry, B. D., . . . Giles, W. H. (2006). The enduring effects of abuse and related adverse experiences of childhood. A convergence of evidence from neurobiology and epidemiology. *European Archives of Psychiatry and Clinical Neuroscience, 256*(3), 174–186.

Ayres, A. J. (2005). *Sensory integration and the child: Understanding hidden sensory challenges* (Rev. ed.). Los Angeles, CA: Western Psychological Services.

Blau, G. M., Caldwell, B., & Lieberman, R. E. (Eds.). (2014). *Residential interventions for children, adolescents, and families: A best practice guide*. New York, NY: Routledge.

Blodgett, C. (2015). Personal communication, Grants Pass, Oregon.

Bloom, S. (2005). *Creating sanctuary for children*. Presentation at the Annual Conference of the American Association of Children's Residential Centers, Pasadena, CA, October 20.

Bipartisan Budget Agreement Act of 2018, Public Law 115–123, Family First Prevention Services Act, Division E, Title VII, 132 Stat. 64, 2018.

Bobler, C., Boon, T., Downward, M., Loomes, B., Mountfors, H., & Swadi, H. (2015). Pilot investigation of the use and usefulness of a sensory modulation room in a child and adolescent psychiatric unit. *Occupational Therapy in Mental Health, 31*(4), 1–4.

Bowlby, J. (1988). *A secure base: Parent-child attachment and healthy human development*. London: Routledge and New York, NY: Basic Books.

Boyd, J. E., Lanius, R. A., & McKinnon, M. C. (2018). Mindfulness-based treatments for posttraumatic stress disorder: A review of the treatment literature and neurobiological evidence. *Journal of Psychiatry & Neuroscience, 43*(1), 7–25.

Campbell, K. (2018, June). Personal communication.

Cannon, W. (1932). *Wisdom of the body*. US: W. W. Norton & Company.

Carter, C. S., Ahnert, L., Grossmann, S. B., Hrdy, S. B., Lamb, M. E., Porges, S. W., & Sachser, N. (2005). *Attachment and bonding: A new synthesis*. Cambridge, MA: MIT Press.

Champagne, T. (2011). *Sensory modulation & environment: Essential elements of occupation* (3rd ed. Rev.). Sydney, Australia: Pearson Assessment.

Champagne, T. (2017). *Activities for dynamic living: Workbook companion for the sensory modulation program*. Northampton, MA: Champagne Conferences & Consultation.

Champagne, T., & Stromberg, N. (2004). Sensory approaches in inpatient psychiatric settings: Innovative alternatives to seclusion and restraint. *Journal of Psychosocial Nursing and Mental Health Services, 42*(9), 34–44.

Child Trauma Academy (CTA). (2013a, September 17). *Seven slide series: Sensitization and tolerance*. Retrieved from www.youtube.com/watch?v=qv8dRfgZXV4

Child Trauma Academy (CTA). (2013b, September 6). *Seven slide series: The human brain*. Retrieved from www.youtube.com/watch?v=uOsgDkeH52o

Doidge, N. (2007). *The brain that changes itself*. New York, NY: Penguin Group.

Engel-Yeger, B., Palgy-Levin, D., & Lev-Wiesel, R. (2013). The relationship between post traumatic stress disorder and sensory processing patterns. *Occupational Therapy in Mental Health, 29*, 266–278.

The Family First Prevention Services Act, Division E, Title VII of the Bipartisan Budget Act of 2018, Public Law 115–123. February 9, 2018.

Felitti, V. J., Anda, R. F., Nordenberg, D., Williamson, D. F., Spitz, A. M., Edwards, V., . . . Marks, J. S. (1998). Relationship of childhood abuse and household dysfunction to many of the leading causes of death in adults: The adverse childhood experiences (ACE) study. *American Journal of Preventive Medicine, 14*, 245–258.

Gaskill, R. L., & Perry, B. D. (2017). A neurosequential therapeutics approach to guided play, play therapy, and activities for children who won't talk. In C. A. Malchiodi & D. A. Crenshaw (Eds.), *What to do when children clam up in psychotherapy: Interventions to facilitate communication* (pp. 38–66). New York, NY: Guilford Press.

Hambrick, E. P., Brawner, T. W., Perry, B. D., Wang, E., . . . O'Malley, D. (2018). Restraint and critical incident reduction following introduction of the neurosequential model of therapeutics (NMT). *Residential Treatment for Children and Youth*, 1–22.

Hebb, D. O. (1949). *The organization of behavior*. New York, NY: John Wiley & Sons.

Huckshorn, K. A. (2006). *Six core strategies for reducing seclusion and restraint use©*. Alexandria, VA: National Association for State Mental Health Program Directors.

Jackson, A., Frederico, M., Cox, A., & Black, C. (2019). The treatment of trauma The Neurosequential Model and "Take Two" In B. Huppertz (Ed.), *Approaches to psychic trauma: Theory and practice* (pp. 423–456). London: Rowman and Littlefield.

Jaffee, S. R., Bowes, L., Ouellet-Morin, I., Fisher, H., Moffitt, T. E., Merrick, M., & Arseneault, L. (2013). Safe, stable, nurturing relationships break the intergenerational cycle of abuse: A prospective nationally representative cohort of children in the United Kingdom. *Journal of Adolescent Health, 53*, S4–S10.

Journal of Biological Regulators and Homeostatic Agents, 24, 545–554.

Kelly, P. A., Viding, E., Wallace, G. L., Schaer, M., De Brito, S. A., Robustelli, B., & McCrory, E. J. (2013). Cortical thickness, surface area, and gyrification abnormalities in children exposed to maltreatment: Neural markers of vulnerability? *Biological Psychiatry, 74*, 845–852.

Kuypers, L., & Sautter, E. (2012). Promoting social regulation: Identifying emotional states and utilizing strategies to achieve social emotional success. *Autism Bay Area Magazine*, 8–10.

LeBel, J., & Champagne, T. (2010). Integrating sensory and trauma-informed interventions: A Massachusetts state initiative, part 2. *Mental Health Special Interest Section Quarterly, 33*(2), 1–4.

LeBel, J., Champagne, T., Stromberg, N., & Coyle, R. (2010). Integrating sensory and trauma-informed interventions: A Massachusetts state initiative, part 1. *Mental Health Special Interest Section Quarterly, 33*(1), 1–4.

Lee, S. J., Cox, A., Whitecross, F., Williams, P., & Hollander, Y. (2010). Sensory assessment and therapy to reduce restraint and seclusion use with service users needing psychiatric intensive care. *Journal of Psychiatric Intensive Care, 6*(2), 83–90.

Ludy-Dobson, C. R., & Perry, B. D. (2010). The role of healthy relational interactions in buffering the impact of childhood trauma. In E. Gil (Ed.), *Working with children to heal interpersonal trauma: The power of play* (pp. 26–43). New York, NY: The Guilford Press.

Luxenberg, T., Spinazzola, J., Hidalgo, J., Hunt, C., & van der Kolk, B. (2001). Complex trauma and disorders of extreme stress (DESNOS) diagnosis, part two: Treatment. *Directions in Psychiatry, 21*, 373–392.

Martin, B., & Suane, S. (2012). Effect of training on sensory room and cart usage. *Occupational Therapy in Mental Health, 28*, 118–128.

Massachusetts Department of Mental Health. (2013). *Resource guide: Creating positive cultures of care*. Retrieved May 31, 2018, from www.mass.gov/files/documents/2016/07/vq/restraint-resources.pdf

Masten, A. S. (2001). Ordinary magic: Resilience processes in development. *American Psychologist, 56*(3), 227–238.

McDonnell, C. G., & Valentino, K. (2016). Intergenerational effects of childhood trauma Evaluating pathways among maternal ACEs, perinatal depressive symptoms, and infant outcomes. *Child Maltreatment.* Retrieved August 1, 2016 from, http://cmx.sagepub.com/content/early/2016/07/22/1077559516659556. abstract

Merrick, M., Leeb, R., & Lee, R. (2013). Examining the role of safe, stable, and nurturing relationships in the intergenerational continuity of child maltreatment—Introduction to the special issue. *Journal of Adolescent Health, 53,* S1–S3.

Miller, G. E., Chen, E., & Parker, K. J. (2011). Psychological stress in childhood and susceptibility to the chronic diseases of aging: Moving toward a model of behavioral and biological mechanisms. *Psychological Bulletin, 137,* 959–997.

Miller, L. J., Coll, J. R., & Schoen, S. A. (2007). A randomized controlled pilot study of the effectiveness of occupational therapy for children with sensory modulation disorder. *American Journal of Occupational Therapy, 61,* 228–238.

Murrough, J. W., Huang, Y., Hu, J., Henry, S., Williams, W., Gallezot, J. D., . . . Neumeister, A. (2011). Reduced amygdala serotonin transporter binding in posttraumatic stress disorder. *Biological Psychiatry, 170,* 1033–1038.

National Association for State Mental Health Program Directors (NASMHPD). (2003). *Trauma informed care module: Training curriculum for the reduction of seclusion and restraint* (1st ed.). Alexandria, VA: NASMHPD.

National Association for State Mental Health Program Directors. (2018). *National executive training institute curriculum for the creation of violence-free and coercion-free treatment settings and the reduction of seclusion and restraint* (12th ed.). Alexandria, VA: NASMHPD.

Novak, T., Scanlan, J., McCaul, D., MacDonald, N., & Clarke, T. (2012). Pilot study of a sensory room in an acute inpatient psychiatric unit. *Australian Psychiatry, 20*(5), 401–406.

Perry, B. D. (2001). The neuroarcheology of childhood maltreatment: The neurodevelopmental costs of adverse childhood events. In K. Franey, R. Geffen, & R. Falconer (Eds.), *The cost of maltreatment: Who pays? We all do* (pp. 15–37). San Diego, CA: Family Violence and Sexual Assault Institute.

Perry, B. D. (2002). Childhood experience and the expression of genetic potential: What childhood neglect tells us about nature and nurture. *Brain and Mind, 3,* 79–100.

Perry, B. D. (2004a). *The fear response: The effects of trauma on children.* Retrieved from The Child Trauma Academy, The Core Concepts Video Training Series [online resource] www.childtrauma.org

Perry, B. D. (2004b). *Understanding traumatized and maltreated children: Living and working with maltreated children.* Retrieved from The Child Trauma Academy, The Core Concepts Video Training Series [online resource] www.childtrauma.org

Perry, B. D. (2006). The neurosequential model of therapeutics: Applying principles of neuroscience to clinical work with traumatized and maltreated children. In N. Boyd Webb (Ed.), *Working with traumatized youth in child welfare* (pp. 22–52). New York, NY: The Guilford Press.

Perry, B. D. (2009). Examining child maltreatment through a neurodevelopmental lens: Clinical applications of the neurosequential model of therapeutics. *Journal of Loss and Trauma, 14,* 240–255.

Perry, B. D. (2013). The neurosequential model of therapeutics: Application of a developmentally sensitive and neurobiology-informed approach to clinical problem solving in maltreated children. In K. Brandt, B. D. Perry, S. Seigleman, & E. Tronick (Eds.), *Infant and early childhood mental health: Core concepts and clinical practice* (pp. 21–47). Washington, DC: American Psychiatric Association Publishing.

Perry, B. D., & Ablon, J. S. (2019). CPS as a neurodevelopmentally sensitive and trauma-informed approach. In A. Pollastri, J. Ablon, & M. Hone (Eds.), *Collaborative problem-solving: An evidence-based approach to implementation and practice* (pp. 15–32). Cham, Switzerland: Springer Nature.

Perry, B. D., & Dobson, C. L. (2013). The neurosequential model of therapeutics. In J. Ford (Ed.), *Treating complex traumatic stress disorders in children and adolescents: Scientific foundations and therapeutic models* (pp. 249–260). New York, NY: The Guilford Press.

Perry, B. D., & Pate, J. E. (1994). Neurodevelopment and the psychobiological roots of post-traumatic stress disorders. In L. Kozoil & C. Stout (Eds.), *The neuropsychology of mental Illness: A practical guide*. Springfield, IL: Charles C. Thomas Publishing.

Perry, B. D., & Pollard, R. A. (1998). Homeostasis, stress, trauma, and adaptation: A neurodevelopmental view of childhood trauma. *Child and Adolescent Psychiatric Clinics of North America, 7*(1), 33–51.

Perry, B. D., Pollard, R. A., Blakely, T. L., Baker, W. L., & Vigilante, D. (1995). Childhood trauma, the neurobiology of adaptation, and "use-dependent" development of the brain: How "states" become "traits". *Infant Mental Health Journal, 16*(4), 271–291.

Porges, S. W. (2001). The polyvagal theory: Phylogenetic substrates of a social nervous system. *International Journal of Psychophysiology, 42*, 123–146.

Porges, S. W. (2003). Social engagement and attachment: A phylogenetic perspective. Roots of mental illness in children. *Annals of the New York Academy of Sciences, 1008*, 31–47.

Porges, S. W. (2007). They polyvagal perspective. *Biological psychology, 72*, 116–143.

Public Health Management Corporation. (2013). Findings from the Philadelphia Urban ACE Survey.

Siegel, D. J. (2012). *The developing mind: How relationships and the brain interact to shape who we are* (2nd ed.). New York, NY: The Guilford Press.

Stein, P., & Kendall, J. (2014). *Psychological trauma and the development of the brain: Neurologically based interventions for troubled children*. New York, NY: Routledge.

Substance Abuse Mental Health Services Administration (SAMHSA). (2014a). Guiding principles of trauma informed care. *SAMHSA News, 22*(2), 1.

Substance Abuse Mental Health Services Administration (SAMHSA). (2014b). *Trauma informed care in behavioral health services*. Treatment Improvement Protocol (TIP) Series. Rockville, MD: Author.

Supin, J. (2016, November). The long shadow: Bruce Perry on the lingering effects of childhood trauma [online periodical]. *The Sun*, pp. 4–13

Teicher, M. H., Rabi, K., Sheu, Y., Saraphin, S. B., Andersen, S. I., Anderson, C. M., . . . Tomada, A. (2010). Neurobiology of childhood trauma and adversity. In R. A. Lanius, E. Vermetten, & C. Pain (Eds.), *The impact of early life trauma on health and disease: The hidden epidemic* (pp. 112–120). Cambridge, UK: Cambridge University Press.

van der Kolk, B. (2005). Developmental trauma disorder. *Psychiatric Annals*, 401–408.

van der Kolk, B. (2014). *The body keeps score: Mind, brain, and body in the healing of trauma*. New York, NY: Penguin Group LLC.

Wang, E. (2018). *What does it mean to be trauma informed?* From Theory to Practice: Residential Care for Children and Youth, Align Special Edition #3.

Warner, E., Koomar, J., Lary, B., & Cook, A. (2013). Can the body change score? Application of sensory modulation principles in the treatment of traumatized adolescents in residential settings. *Journal of Family Violence, 2*(7), 729–738.

West, M., Melvin, G., McNamara, F., & Gordon, M. (2017). An evaluation of the use and efficacy of a sensory room within an adolescent psychiatric inpatient unit. *Australian Occupational Therapy Journal, 64*, 253–263.

Wilbarger, P. (1984). Planning a sensory diet: Activity programs based on sensory processing theory. In *Sensory integration special interest section newsletter* (Vol. 18, No. 2, pp. 1–4). Rockville, MD: American Occupational Therapy Association.

Zelechoski, A. D., Sharma, R., Beserra, K., Miguel, J. L., DeMarco, M., & Spinazzola, J. (2013). Traumatized youth in residential treatment settings: Prevalence, clinical presentation, treatment, and policy implications. *Journal of Family Violence, 28*(7), 639–652.

11

MEASURING THE IMPACT OF RESIDENTIAL INTERVENTIONS

A New Frontier

Dana Weiner, Ronald Thompson, and Marvin Cain Alexander

Introduction

For over a decade, youth, families, advocates, policymakers, researchers, and others have called for more systematic efforts to review outcomes of residential interventions (Dougherty, Strod, Fisher, Broderick, & Lieberman, 2014). As the field embraces landmark changes to regulatory expectations regarding the way children and adolescents (hereafter referred to as youth) and families are served by residential interventions (i.e., Family First Prevention Services Act), it is incumbent upon residential providers to reach common ground on the conceptualization and measurement of outcomes.

Ideally, residential interventions help build skills for youth and families to promote healthy development, effective coping, and success in life beyond the residential environment (Whittaker, Holmes, del Valle, Thompson, & Zeira, 2016). Although some leaders among residential providers have been measuring long-term outcomes (e.g., three to five years post-discharge) for years, measuring post-discharge outcomes is not yet standard practice by all residential providers, and no consistent approach has been adopted.

Traditionally, residential programs track outcome measures that focus on satisfaction with services, fiscal outcomes (cost of subsequent placements and hospitalizations), or the resolution of mental health problems within the context of the residential setting (Weiner et al., 2018). Alexander (2015) found that although 88% of agencies providing residential interventions assessed the single measure "experience of care" (e.g., opinions about and satisfaction with residential intervention during the intervention), only 63% assessed experience of care at least once after residential discharge.

Although most providers agree on a set of functional measures across life domains (work, home, school, peers, and community), widespread consistent measurement of these types of outcomes has been challenging. However, recent steps signify substantial progress. The Building Bridges Initiative (BBI), through the Joint Resolution and subsequent monographs (www.buildingbirdges4youth.org), outlines principles (e.g., cultural and linguistic competence; family and youth voice, choice, and roles; trauma and evidence-informed/-based practices) and implementation strategies that can be evaluated to assess the degree to which desired outcomes for youth and families who receive residential interventions are reached (Dougherty & Strod, 2014). This framework informs the evolving definitions of long-term residential outcomes and provides a foundation from which to build consensus among providers of residential intervention on outcome measures, including what (e.g., life domains) and when (e.g., at least six months post-discharge) to measure (Dougherty & Strod, 2014).

This progress has set the stage for the field to move toward measurement that will provide greater understanding of the long-term impact of residential interventions. With relevant tools, more providers can track the impact of interventions on youths' ability to maintain employment, achieve success in school, maintain satisfying relationships with family members, engage with pro-social peers, and contribute to their communities. Measuring this type of impact goes beyond traditionally used outcomes/indicators that measure processes and practices or signify the absence of problems. This new approach focuses on strengths, protective factors, and optimal functioning and highlights the importance of evaluating outcomes post-discharge.

Experts advocate for impact measurement strategies that: (1) Consider the variations in problem severity at baseline and (2) can parse the during-services effects of the residential intervention from the post-discharge functional status indicators of resolution or reduction of symptoms and development of coping skills (Weiner et al., 2018). As an initial step toward this goal, Chapin Hall at the University of Chicago, in partnership with the BBI Outcomes Workgroup, demonstrated the feasibility of a follow-up interview strategy to assess post-discharge functioning six months after discharge. Five providers piloted a ten-minute telephone-based measurement tool that surveys functional status in a series of domains including relationships, living situation, school/education, risk factors, community engagement and support, and access to services. The results indicated that, albeit challenging, it is feasible for providers of residential interventions to collect post-discharge outcome data even with limited resources (Weiner et al., 2018).

This chapter will review the impetus for measuring impact, consider the historical context for outcome measurement efforts, identify precursors for measurement, discuss strategies for measuring outcomes and impact, and present a roadmap for providers and systems seeking to promote accountability, transparency, and continuous quality improvement for residential interventions through outcome/impact measurement.

Why Measure Long-Term Impact?

Of the 50,000–70,000 children who receive residential interventions each year, many are in the custody of the state they reside in (U.S. Department of Health and Human Services, 2018).[1] That is, while some parents privately seek treatment for their children in residential programs, many youth in residential interventions have been removed from their parents' custody and "placed" in residential programs. Given the large proportion of those served who are under the oversight of the child welfare system, it is important to note several key shifts in the child welfare policy arena, as well as the overall child-serving policy context, that are currently underway.

First, in the last decade, the trend in the public sector has been toward purchasing services with documented results that are sustainable for 6–24 months post-discharge, with a preference for interventions for which there is validated empirical evidence (Woll & Martone, 2018). Policy makers, as well as public and private funding agencies, are increasingly relying upon multiple registries that catalogue the relative standing of evidence-based practices (EBP's) to make decisions about which programs to implement and which programs to fund.[2] In this context, understanding the foundation for evidence-informed and evidence-based practices (discussed in detail in Chapter 9) and reliably and validly measuring the effectiveness of intervention strategies becomes increasingly important.

The second recent shift occurred with the passage of the Family First Preventive Services Act (FFPSA, 2018). While this law creates unprecedented flexibility for providers to claim Medicaid funds for evidence-based preventive services delivered to children and parents in families to help them remain intact, the legislation also limits use of federal child welfare funds for residential interventions to what are now being called Qualified Residential Treatment Providers (QRTPs). The law imposes restrictions on the lengths of stay, and the population of youth who can be approved to receive residential interventions must have mental health diagnoses (FFPSA, 2018). These requirements acknowledge that while residential interventions may be essential for the treatment of acute problems among youth with behavioral and/or emotional challenges and their families, their inappropriate or overuse among child welfare-involved youth can exacerbate challenges to permanency and threaten well-being. They in effect establish a new federal "bar" for residential programs and are preliminarily being considered by some policymakers and accrediting bodies as broadly applicable (Milliken Institute School of Public Health, 2019). In this context, stakeholders increasingly seek evidence to establish and/or justify the positive effect of residential interventions.

Third, an increasing number of residential providers have adopted the Building Bridges Initiative's (BBI) Joint Resolution (www.buildingbridges4 youth.org/products/joint-resolution) and accepted the challenge to innovate practice and incorporate the BBI principles noted previously. If rigorously and intentionally designed, further intensified efforts by residential providers to measure the impact of this work can help to generate evidence for the effectiveness of residential interventions and help generate improved positive sustained outcomes for youth and families post-discharge.

History and Evolution of Outcome Evaluation Efforts

The measurement of impact is increasingly recognized as a necessary component of delivering quality service. Over the past 30 years there has been a steady increase in the collection and use of outcome data by residential intervention providers in the US, as indicated in a national survey of providers by the Association for Children's Residential Centers (Sternberg et al., 2013). There is much more information available now about effective residential practices as well as the impact of residential intervention in general. However, the field of residential intervention still lacks national aggregate outcome data about the efficacy of this service. In this section, we will summarize selected examples of outcome initiatives in the field of residential interventions by residential provider associations, service providers, and public agencies. We will conclude with a description of a promising effort initiated by the BBI that is currently underway.

Residential Provider Associations

In the 1990s provider associations pursued outcomes measurement projects, one of which has sustained to this day.

- The Indiana Association of Resources and Child Advocacy (IARCA) initiated a state-wide effort to collect, analyze, and report child services outcome data which resulted in an ongoing collaboration between providers, public agencies, and policy makers to decide on consistent outcome measures, aggregate data across state providers, use outcome data for quality improvement, and influence state level policy about child and family services including residential interventions (Wall, Koch, Link, & Graham, 2010). This project continues to support collaboration between service providers, public agencies, families, and policy makers and could be a model for other states to emulate (www.iarca.org);

- The Alliance for Strong Families and Communities also supported a number of efforts to promote the collection and use of outcome data. This effort began with sponsoring a series of outcome evaluation workshops across the country for provider agencies and later also included a national benchmarking initiative for member agencies managed by a private benchmarking company. A broad number of measures relating to management, financial, program, and outcome data were developed, and provider agencies were advised to compare their data to the aggregate to promote quality improvement and advocacy for their programs;
- The Joint Commission's ORYX Initiative in the late 1990s required accredited organizations to identify benchmarked data as part of their quality improvement efforts and spawned a number of "benchmarking" organizations. One was Child and Adolescent Residential Psychiatric Programs (CHARPP), a provider association of accredited organizations in Oregon that designed and implemented a benchmarking system called the CHARPP Improvement and Measurement Project (CHIMP). CHARPP developed a robust set of indicators, including process (restraints, seclusions, medication errors), experience (Youth Satisfaction Survey for youth (YSS-Y) and YSS-F for families), and functional outcomes measures (CAFAS- Child and Adolescent Functional Assessment Scale, ROLES- Restrictiveness of Living Environment Scale). CHIMP gained participation from approximately 85 residential programs across the country, attracted by the low-cost web-based system which tracked data in real time, yielding run and control charts that were readily actionable. CHARPP worked collaboratively with participants to develop data definitions and work out issues related to comparability of populations between organizations. An annual national conference (Real Data, Real Time) featured leaders in measurement and evidence-based practices, and, along with regular newsletters, kept agencies and their QI staff engaged and informed as to the latest. When the Joint Commission eliminated the benchmarking requirement, most participating agencies stayed with the system due to its value;
- The Association for Children's Residential Centers (ACRC) has also promoted outcome evaluation for residential interventions for the past two decades. The association's research committee conducted a national member survey including evaluation of outcomes and use of evidence-based practices in residential interventions (Sternberg et al., 2013). Results of this survey suggested a growing use of outcome evaluation and evidence-based practices in residential interventions across the US. However, results of a follow-up survey suggested struggles with fidelity in implementation of evidence-based practices in residential settings, partially due to the fact that many of these practices were developed and

tested in community-based settings (James, Thompson, & Ringle, 2017; James et al., 2015). During this same time period, ACRC annual meetings also have had an increased emphasis on measurement.

Service Provider Organizations

Individual provider organizations have also developed effective outcomes with data collection and reporting systems. Examples of four provider agencies who have done this work successfully follow:

In 2004, The Children's Village in New York City committed to organizational change focused on the short-term use of the residential intervention for acute need—"like an emergency room, to be used only when necessary" (BBI, 2017). The leadership at the Children's Village made many changes, including reducing the average length of stay, enhancing their long-term aftercare options for youth and families post-discharge, and investing in stabilization programs. In doing so, the Children's Village achieved positive results in their cohorts: Youth either graduated from high school or were still in school (92%), youth were either in school or working at least part-time (93%), youth maintained stable housing (100%), and youth did not return to residential intervention/remained arrest free (85%).

Damar, a provider agency in Indianapolis, also made systematic changes to their residential interventions and used follow-up interviews to test the effectiveness of these program changes. Damar leadership and staff began to implement a more comprehensive family involvement treatment component and shorter lengths of stay in line with BBI principles. To test the effectiveness of these program changes, Damar conducted six-month follow-up interviews with families. The results of this effort suggested that, with an enhanced family treatment component and shorter lengths of stay, residential interventions could be more effective and less costly (Holstead, Dalton, Horne, & Lamond, 2010). This is a great example of using outcome data to evaluate practice changes, a scaffolding upon which the organization has built three–five year post-discharge measurement efforts.

Youth Villages is a provider agency with national reach, providing a range of services to children and their families, including residential interventions. The agency routinely collects and reports outcome data, including 12- and 24-month follow-up data across their service system. These data have been used successfully for quality improvement and advocacy, which has supported both their program implementation efforts and national expansion (Hurley, Thompson, & Howard, 2009).

Boys Town is another provider agency with national reach that has been a leader in provider-driven outcome evaluation for a number of years. The first comprehensive outcome evaluation completed by this agency was a 16-year follow-up study of youth receiving a residential intervention based on the

Teaching-Family Model, which has promising research evidence. The results of this quasi-experimental study indicated significant long-term positive effects for educational achievement as well as decreased child abuse potential in adulthood (Huefner, Ringle, Chmslka, & Ingram, 2007; Ringle, Ingram, & Thompson, 2010; Thompson et al., 1996).

Boys Town began outcome evaluation with the development of a daily reporting system which generated daily, weekly, and monthly reports used by program managers to address treatment issues (aggression, school attendance and grades, psychotropic data use and changes, etc.) and evaluate intervention strategies. This system was later computerized to allow for a number of reports not only for quality improvement initiatives but also for advocacy and policy development. This system was supplemented by pre-post data collection using both standardized and non-standardized measures and follow-up interviews at six, 12, and 24 months post-discharge. Balanced scorecards and dashboards were also developed to inform executive management, mid-level program managers, and immediate supervisors to help guide financial, staffing, contract, and program improvement decisions (e.g., Cash et al., 2012).

Current BBI Outcomes Project

BBI is currently sponsoring an initiative to address the need to help residential service providers collect post-discharge data and eventually produce aggregate national outcome/impact data. This builds upon the previous work by BBI in developing its Self-Assessment Tool (SAT). The BBI tool, initially developed in 2009 and updated in 2019 and available on the BBI website, helps providers to examine services and practices afforded to youth and families in residential programs. The BBI SAT was purposefully designed to be used with an extensive range of both residential programs (i.e., residential intervention, group homes, crisis residences) and community partners that interface with residential programs (i.e., schools, community mental health clinics, child welfare agencies, juvenile justice agencies, day programs, home-based services, family support groups).

Ideally, the BBI SAT is completed by residential staff, youth and families served by the program, involved advocates, and other key stakeholders, working together. It is designed to help programs improve the quality of service for youth and families, rather than to rank or grade programs. Residential programs that have used the BBI SAT have found that the information derived from a process of critical self-assessment is useful and that the most valuable way to use this information is to openly discuss the responses (SAMHSA, 2019). Comparing responses from different groups of youth, families, staff, and community allows residential programs to see how these groups experience the program differently, which can help to promote an understanding of what is working well and what could be changed (BBI, 2019). This offers an opportunity to correlate residential intervention practices with post-discharge outcomes, to assess impact as well as improve quality.

After developing the Self-Assessment Tool, BBI published the report referenced previously: Building Consensus on Residential Measures: Recommendations for Outcome and Performance Measures (Dougherty & Strod, 2014). The follow-up to this report was to use the BBI Outcomes Work Group (OW) to identify domains of post-discharge outcome data collection for residential interventions. After considering outcome domains including relationship stability, housing stability, community engagement, access to resources, and recidivism/readmission, the group developed and tested a practical ten-minute telephone follow-up survey designed for parents or other caregivers. With input from the OW this was used to pilot test the feasibility of provider agency data collection. The survey focuses on the current status of youth six months post-discharge in domains including relationships, living situation, school/education, risk factors, community engagement and support, and access to services.

Provider agencies were recruited as participants to implement the pilot. The study tested their capacity to (1) successfully identify youth and families six months post-discharge, (2) contact families and administer a brief telephone survey regarding youth functioning, and (3) analyze the data to report on the feasibility of collecting post-discharge outcome data. Provider agencies who participated ranged from very small to very large agencies; some had never collected follow-up data and one very large agency had years of experience doing this type of work. The study concluded that it is feasible for provider agencies to collect and analyze follow-up data (Weiner et al., 2018). By demonstrating capacity and developing a tool, the feasibility study provided a promising next step for the development of a national system to support collection, analysis, and reporting of outcome data to evaluate the impact of residential interventions. The survey and a practice brief on the study are available on the BBI website.

The immediate next step has begun. A tool to assess organizational readiness has been developed by Chapin Hall at the University of Chicago in partnership with the BBI Outcomes Workgroup and is being pilot tested. Along with the survey and feasibility study it is expected to create a foundation for longitudinal measurement of the impact of residential intervention.

Where Do We Begin? Precursors to Measurement

Theories of Change

In order to design reliable and effective measurement strategies, researchers and providers need to know what elements to measure and at what intervals

Measuring the Impact of Residential Interventions **243**

to measure them. One of the most important exercises in evaluation design is the articulation of a theory of change. Theories of change ask us to make explicit our tacit intentions and to spell out what we are doing and why (www.theoryofchange.org/what-is-theory-of-change). While many residential providers assume that others understand the reasons behind the selection of interventions, the training of staff, the engagement of families, or the provision of community supports, without articulating how these features work together to produce positive outcomes it is impossible to measure and test our assumptions. For this reason, outcome and impact measurement efforts ideally begin with clear theories of change.

Initially, theories of change consider the root causes of the problems being addressed, as well as the population affected by them. A consideration of root causes drives the specific activities that will be employed to assist children and their families. This may include specific types of engagement or interactions, curriculum or materials, trainings, strategies, or philosophical shifts (www.theoryofchange.org/what-is-theory-of-change/how-does-theory-of-change-work/). Each of these activities is undertaken because it is hypothesized to play a role in improving the lives of youth and families; those activities that don't further this goal (or support other activities that do) have little value. This step, the description of the specific elements of residential interventions, has often been overlooked in evaluation efforts. Unspecified strategies cannot be measured; that is, if something isn't measured, there is no way to know what works or to benefit from lessons learned. In fact, unless strategies are specified, it will not be known whether interventions are implemented as intended (i.e., fidelity) or understood who truly benefits from the intervention and those who did not. Activities are traditionally measured as outputs or indicators—these might include counts of sessions or numbers of contacts.

In addition to problems, populations, and activities, theories of change identify the intended outcomes of intervention. These may include short-term—or proximal—outcomes for youth and/or family members, such as symptom reduction, increase in skills, life satisfaction, behavioral and emotional regulation, and quality of interactions. The proximal outcomes are thought to be pre-requisites for long-term—or distal—outcomes, which often include the types of sustained functional improvement that have been outlined previously (Larzelere, Chmelka, Schmidt, & Jones, 2002).

Theories of change may originate in accumulated experience; prior research; or theories of trauma, child development, or psychotherapeutic improvement. They guide the assessments that providers can/should use to document both the receipt of services and the change among participants and make long-term outcome measurement possible. Figure 11.1 provides an example of a theory of change for residential interventions (Chapin Hall, 2014).

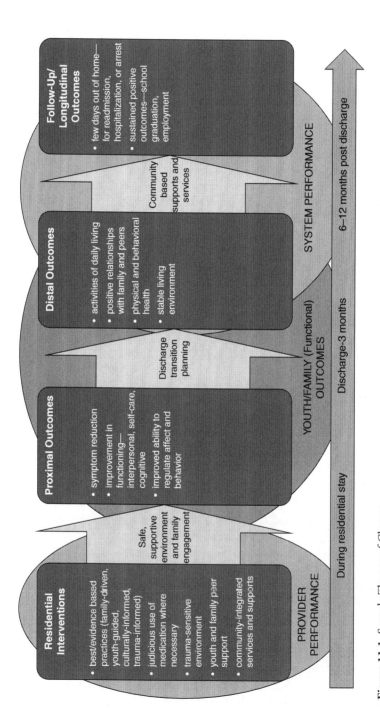

Figure 11.1 Sample Theory of Change

Technical Infrastructure and Capacity

In addition to conceptual framing, outcome measurement requires some technical infrastructure and capacity. Namely, providers need the capacity to collect, manage, store, and analyze data derived from assessments and surveys and the ability to pull from and process administrative data. Providers with robust continuous quality improvement (CQI) infrastructure may be well-versed in tracking performance and outcome data and ready to integrate additional measures to document the elements of outcomes discussed here. Other providers may need to build or fortify CQI infrastructure so that data and evidence can be applied not only to documenting "success" but also to making regular adjustments in the approaches and activities that are used to meet the population's needs.

Technical capacity is further enhanced by implementation supports that provide regular training, supervision, and coaching; organization and system-wide communication pathways to facilitate the collection of reliable and valid data; and analytic capacity for the application of data into evidence for decision making.

Readiness

There are other factors contributing to an organization's readiness to measure impact. As noted previously there is a study underway (in 2019) by Chapin Hall at the University of Chicago and the BBI Outcomes Workgroup—to test a tool for assessing readiness. A sampling of the 30-item draft, to be rated on a four-point Likert scale, offers a snapshot into these factors (Chapin Hall, in progress, 2019):

ORGANIZATIONAL CULTURE: Staff demonstrate commitment to evidence use and performance improvement in everyday practice.

LEADERSHIP SUPPORT: There is a recognized intent by senior leadership to use outcomes data to inform service delivery and program development.

STAFF CAPACITY: Leadership have worked with human resources to update the job requirements of the specific staff positions who will take on responsibilities in the outcomes monitoring process.

PROCESSES: The organization currently has a structure for engaging staff in continuous quality improvement (CQI) activities to address its strategic goals or emergent concerns.

WORKFORCE DEVELOPMENT: Staff training involves demonstration of the new processes and skills by assigned trainers. Skills taught include reliable survey administration and developmentally, culturally, and linguistically competent client engagement.

TECHNOLOGY CAPACITY AND MANAGEMENT: Available software supports statistical analysis and can produce graphical displays of data.

ANALYTIC REPORTING CAPACITY: Staff expertise is available to employ a range of analytical techniques, from simple to sophisticated, to meet organizational data reporting needs.

When complete, anticipated by the end of 2019, the tool and instructions will be available on the BBI website.

Evaluation Components

Model Fidelity

The construct of model fidelity began in experimental research but has been applied to outcome evaluation and practice improvement. Reliable and valid measurement of the impact of residential interventions requires detailed descriptions of program practices as well as measurement of the implementation fidelity of these practices to treatment models or guidelines. It is critical that agencies describe their practices and measure whether they actually adhere to these practices as services are being delivered. There are many different ways to measure model fidelity; some have been developed primarily for research studies, but others have been applied in practice settings to support wide-scale program evaluation and dissemination.

One example from the Teaching-Family Model may be helpful. A critical practice in this model is the 4-to-1 ratio. This means that for every time a staff member has a negative interaction with a youth, there must be four positive interactions. The underlying theory of change, supported by behavioral research, is that positive feedback is more motivating for positive youth growth than negative feedback. In order to test the implementation fidelity of this key practice, staff are observed on a regular basis and observers code positive and negative interactions with youth (Duppong Hurley, Lambert, Gross, Thompson, & Farmer, 2017). Results are used to consult with staff and provide staff development suggestions as needed. To test the implementation fidelity of the 4-to-1 ratio practice on a wide scale, data from 6,000 of these observations were analyzed at one agency. Results indicated a 5-to-1 ratio of positive to negative interactions with youth; the provider's practice met and exceeded the required 4-to-1 criterion (Gross et al., 2015).

A second example of model fidelity assessment is Damar's work to study practice changes. Those being tested included increased family engagement and shorter lengths of stay, which were associated with more positive outcomes for youth. Agency records were used to measure the implementation fidelity of these practices, which indicated an 88% increase in family contacts and a reduction in residential length of stay by 4.6 months (Holstead et al., 2010).

A third example of a more widespread assessment of practice fidelity comes from the State of Rhode Island (RI). For a BBI Quality Improvement Collaboration (QIC) Project, state leaders from the RI Department of Children, Youth and Families, Community Services and Behavioral Health chose metrics for RI residential providers to measure family engagement, as family engagement has been consistently associated with positive youth outcomes. The metrics chosen for residential providers to track and work toward achieving throughout the nine-month BBI QIC included providing support to families in their homes and communities (goal: 50% of families served), providing families a minimum of three communications weekly (goal: 80% of families served), and 100% of agencies completing an action plan to improve the implementation of family-driven care practices. This is a great example of a wide scale practice improvement initiative to support residential programs in improving family engagement practices.

Process and Proximal Outcomes

Other components critical to the identification of outcome measures include process and proximal indicators. Proximal outcome measures can be evaluated using checklists and pre-post comparisons to assess progress during residential interventions. Measures that have been tested with residential interventions include standardized behavioral observations such as the Parent Daily Report (Chamberlain & Reid, 1987), behavior rating scales (e.g., Child Behavior Checklist, Strengths and Difficulties Questionnaire), assessments of cultural and linguistic competency (Cultural and Linguistic Appropriate Services standards), as well as tools that also suggest service needs such as the Child and Adolescent Needs and Strengths (Lyons, 2009). Standardized pre-post measures have shown success while a youth and family are receiving residential interventions; however, improvements may be hard to sustain post-discharge if and when supports are no longer available. Because sustained improvement post-discharge is the most critical outcome measure (as positive functioning with families in homes and communities is the ultimate goal), theories of change must incorporate measures addressing indicators both during the residential intervention and post-discharge. Studies of support to youth and families during the residential intervention could shed light on proximal outcomes and impact, while studies of strategies that provide support to parents and schools after discharge from residential programs, which have shown positive post-discharge results (e.g., Trout, Tyler, Steward, & Epstein, 2012), can also inform both proximal outcomes and impact.

Distal Outcomes and Impact

Model fidelity assessment and evaluation of proximal outcome indicators are both necessary for testing the impact of residential intervention practices and ongoing quality improvement. This alone, however, does not provide the full picture. True evaluation of the impact of residential interventions must also include measurement of longer term or distal outcomes. This type of measurement has been employed in research studies of specific residential intervention models (e.g., Farmer, Seifert, Wagner, Murray, & Burns, 2017), but it is not used on a wide scale by provider agencies for routine data collection. The primary tools used to measure distal impact are surveys of program participants about their well-being. The BBI Outcomes Workgroup initiative described previously established the feasibility of using a long-term outcome survey with parents and caregivers, administered post-discharge to assess distal outcomes on a wider scale. This is a relatively low-cost evaluation process; if a uniform survey approach could be used on a wide scale and aggregated, the impact of residential interventions could also be benchmarked to identify success across providers.

Alternatively, distal outcomes may be measured using examination of public records and administrative data. Examples of these outcome indicators are high school graduation rates, admission to post-graduate education, subsequent out-of-home placements, arrests, and hospitalizations. While these measures can be used to gauge the validity of survey data, indicators for strengths and successes must be added to administrative data to capture dimensions of well-being.

Recommendations

A review of the history of post-residential outcome measurement highlights the challenges that must be addressed to ensure that residential interventions remain available and accountable for improving the lives of youth and families who may need them. This section reviews these challenges and suggests strategies for overcoming/addressing them.

Operationalize Interventions and Activities for Measurement

One of the biggest challenges faced by providers and researchers is the lack of consistency and transparency among the interventions called "residential." Services referred to as residential interventions may include a broad array of strategies, ranging from settings where youth live and receive services together with their families, to small group homes to larger programs with more robust measurement systems. In the absence of a consistent definition of the residential intervention itself, it is paramount that providers articulate the components of the service they deliver in ways that can be measured. This can be facilitated by the development of theories of change, which can provide the "why" to residential interventions' "what." To develop theories of change, providers will need to engage staff and stakeholders in conversations that identify the desired outcomes of the interventions and the activities meant to achieve those outcomes. Definition of the activities will clarify the residential intervention as well as enable the identification of indicators that measure to what degree they occur. The BBI Self-Assessment Tool (SAT) is a helpful resource in the development of a theory of change. Using the BBI SAT residential programs can generate ideas for activities and identification of shared and desired outcomes. Similarly, identification of practices believed or shown to yield positive results can lead to measurement strategies that can provide feedback on the achievement of short- and long-term results that signify meaningful impact.

Incorporate Appropriate Assessment Strategies

Residential providers should shift to using assessments that can (1) parse the effects of context from treatment, (2) measure strengths as well as needs, and (3) provide an accurate source of information that can be used to compare the populations served across a wide range of providers. For example, the CANS tool has been used in the context of residential intervention for each of these purposes. In Illinois, a multi-institutional data-test workgroup set out to utilize the tool to risk-adjust residential providers to facilitate fair comparisons in the context of performance-based contracting (Kearney, McEwen, Bloom-Ellis, & Jordan, 2010). Because the CANS asks raters to consider strengths as well as needs, it provides a foundation for understanding changes in well-being in addition to symptom remission (Lyons, 2009). Because ratings are based on a 30-day window, the instrument can accommodate ratings of the youth and family within and outside of the residential environment. Adopting common assessment strategies across provider agencies may speed the adoption of an overarching impact measurement approach. A survey of providers' current use of assessment strategies may identify other synergies which can be leveraged to build consensus around an appropriate measurement strategy.

Invest in Technological Infrastructure That Can Facilitate Measurement Across Provider Agencies

Providers use a range of technological approaches to capture the data they collect on child and family functioning. Highly variable levels of technological awareness, resources, and capacity have resulted in a system in which some providers capture data on excel spreadsheets and others have centralized databases that can produce meaningful reports that inform internal continuous quality improvement (CQI) processes. Any broad effort to measure residential outcomes across providers will require thoughtful planning and resources to design a system that captures data on child functioning and uses the data to inform providers as well as families, child serving systems, and oversight bodies. In the absence of a single centralized system, articulated standards and dedicated support will be needed to bring all providers to a level of consistency in their data collection and reporting systems.

Develop Designs for Longitudinal Studies and Strategy for Consolidating Findings

With common assessments, data systems, and articulated target outcomes, the network of residential providers who serve youth with behavioral and/ or emotional challenges and their families will be well-positioned to undertake or participate in the type of longitudinal research study that can provide reliable and valid evidence of the impact of residential interventions. This research will take funding, both at the provider level and with national partners who can lead and facilitate such an undertaking. Exploratory studies suggest that with appropriate allocations of staff and infrastructure paired with resources to support assessment and reporting, outcomes measurement is possible and feasible (Weiner et al., 2018). Any such effort should leverage the foundational work of national partners to build consensus among providers about the tools and strategies that will be used to measure activities and outcomes and to facilitate the aggregation of meaningful results.

Conclusion

With support from the Building Bridges Initiative (BBI) Outcomes Workgroup, providers have led transformational efforts to assess the impact of residential interventions beyond discharge. Measuring post-discharge outcomes is feasible and will be a critical next step to demonstrate effectiveness and increase the development and use of best practices. Residential leaders, oversight agencies, managed care companies, and other partners are encouraged to build on this foundational work and implement the recommendations presented in this chapter. In doing so, children, youth, young adults, and families will have the services and supports needed to improve functioning and well-being.

Resources

- Building Bridges Initiative Self-Assessment Tool: www.building bridges4youth.org/sites/default/files/Building%20Bridges%20Ini tiative%20SAT%20-%20Final.pdf

- Building Bridges Initiative Post-Residential Outcomes Pilot Survey: www.buildingbridges4youth.org/sites/default/files/BBI%20Post-Discharge%20Survey%20-%20report%20version%203.23.17_0.pdf
- Building Bridges Initiative Practice Brief The Feasibility of Post Residential Measurement: www.buildingbridges4youth.org/sites/default/files/BBI%20Outcomes%20Measurement%20Practice%20Brief.pdf

Notes

1. Over 50,000 child welfare youth reside in institutional or group home settings at a given point in time (www.childwelfare.gov/pubPDFs/foster.pdf).
2. The California Evidence-based Clearinghouse is the most commonly used repository of evidence-based practices for child welfare.

References

Alexander, M. (2015). Measuring experience of care: Availability and use of satisfaction surveys in residential intervention settings for children and youth. *Residential Treatment for Children & Youth, 32*(2), 134–143. doi:10.1080/0886571X.2015.1043790

Building Bridges Initiative. (2009). *Self-assessment tool*. Retrieved from www.buildingbridges4youth.org/products/tools

Building Bridges Initiative. (2017). *Implementing effective short-term residential interventions*. Retrieved from www.buildingbridges4youth.org/sites/default/files/BBI%20Short%20Term%20esidentiRe%20Intervention%20Guide.pdf

Cash, S. J., Ingram, S. D., Biben, D. S., McKeever, S. J., Thompson, R. W., & Ferrell, J. Z. (2012). Moving forward without looking back: Performance management systems as real-time evidence-based practice tools. *Children and Youth Services Review, 34*, 655–659.

Center for the Theory of Change. (2019). Retrieved from www.theoryofchange.org

Chamberlain, P., & Reid, J. (1987). Parent observation and child symptoms. *Behavioral Assessment, 9*, 97–100.

Chapin Hall Center at the University of Chicago. (2014). *Technical assistance to building bridges initiative: Theory of change*. Unpublished document obtained through professional communication.

Dill, K., & Flynn, R. (Eds.). Special Issue on Educational Interventions, Practices, and Policies to Improve Educational Outcomes Among Children and Youth in Out-of-Home Care.

Dougherty, R. H., & Strod, D. (2014). *Building consensus on residential measures: Recommendations for outcome and performance measures*. BBI Report. Washington, DC: Substance Abuse and Mental Health Services Administration.

Daugherty, R. H., Strod, D., Fisher, S., Broderick, S., & Lieberman, R. E. (2014). Tracking long-term and strength-based outcomes. In G. M. Blau, B. Caldwell, &

R. E. Lieberman (Eds.), *Residential interventions for children, adolescents, and families*. New York: Routledge.

Duppong-Hurley, K., Lambert, M. H., Epstein, M., & Stevens, A. (2015). Convergent validity of the strength-based behavioral and emotional rating scale with youth in a residential setting. *Behavioral Health and Services Research, 42*(3), 346–354.

Duppong-Hurley, K., Lambert, M. H., Gross, T. J., Thompson, R. W., & Farmer, E. M. Z. (2017). The role of therapeutic alliance and fidelity in predicting youth outcomes during therapeutic residential care. *Journal of Emotional and Behavioral Disorders, 25*(1), 37–45.

The Family First Prevention Services Act, Division E, Title VII of the Bipartisan Budget Act of 2018, Public Law 115–123. February 9, 2018.

Farmer, E. M. Z., Seifert, H. P., Wagner, H. R., Murray, M., & Burns, B. J. (2017). Does model matter? Examining change across time for youth in group homes. *Journal of Emotional and Behavioral Disorders, 25*, 119–128.

Gross, T. J., Duppong Hurley, K., Sullivan, J. J., Lambert, M. C., Van Ryzin, M. J., & Thompson, R. W. (2015). Program records as a source for program implementation assessment and youth outcomes predictors during residential care. *Children and Youth Services Review, 58*, 153–162.

Holstead, J., Dalton, J., Horne, A., & Lamond, D. (2010). Modernizing residential treatment centers for children and youth-an informed approach to improve long-term outcomes. *The Damar Pilot, Child Welfare, 89*(2), 115–130.

Huefner, J. C., Ringle, J. L., Chmslka, M. B., & Ingram, S. D. (2007). Breaking the cycle of intergenerational abuse: The long-term impact of a residential care program. *Child Abuse and Neglect, 31*(2), 187–199.

Hurley, S., Thompson, R., & Howard, B. (2009, October). *A smart investment: How outcomes research can help you strengthen and expand your programs*. Paper presented at the Alliance for Children and Families National Conference, Huston, TX.

James, S., Thompson, R., & Ringle, J. (2017). The implementation of evidence-based practices in residential care: Outcomes, processes, and barriers. *Journal of Emotional & Behavioral Disorders, 25*(1), 4–18.

James, S., Thompson, R. W., Sternberg, N., Schnur, E., Ross, J., Butler, L., . . . Muirhead, J. (2015). Attitudes, perceptions, and utilization of evidence-based practices in residential care. *Residential Treatment for Children and Youth, 32*, 144–166.

Kearney, K., McEwen, E., Bloom-Ellis, B., & Jordan, N. (2010). Performance-based contracting in residential care and treatment: Driving policy and practice change through public-private partnership in Illinois. *Child Welfare, 89*(2), 39–55.

Larzelere, R. E., Chmelka, M. B., Schmidt, M. D., & Jones, M. (2002). In C. J. Newman, C. J. Liberton, & K. Friedman (Eds.), *Proceedings of the 14th annual Florida mental health institute research conference: A system of care for children's mental health: Expanding the research base* (pp. 359–362). Tampa: University of South Florida.

Lyons, J. S. (2009). *Communimetrics: A theory of measurement for human service enterprises*. New York, NY: Springer.

Milliken Institute School of Public Health; Sumner M. Redstone Global Center for Prevention and Wellness. (2019, March 28). *Implementing the families first prevention services act: What public health professionals and advocates should know*. Webinar.

Ringle, J. L., Ingram, S. D., & Thompson, R. W. (2010). The association between length of stay in residential care and educational achievement: Results of 5- and 16-year follow-up studies. *Children and Youth Services Review, 32*(7), 974–980.

Sternberg, N., Thompson, R. W., Smith, G., Klee, S., Cubellis, L., & Davidowitz, J . . . Schnur, E. (2013). Outcomes in children's residential treatment centers: A national survey. *Residential Treatment for Children and Youth, 30*, 93–118.

Substance Abuse and Mental Health Services Administration. (2019, May 23). *Assessment tools for residential interventions.* Webinar.

Thompson, R. W., Smith, G. L., Osgood, D. W., Dowd, T. P., Friman, P. C., & Daly, D. L. (1996). Residential dare: A study of short- and long-term educational effects. *Children and Youth Services Review, 18*, 221–242.

Trout, A., Tyler, P., Steward, M., & Epstein, M. (2012). On the way home: Program description and preliminary findings. *Children & Youth Services Review, 34*(6).

U.S. Department of Health and Human Services, Administration on Children Youth and Families (2018). *Child maltreatment 2016.* Retrieved from https://www.acf.hhs.gov/cb/research-data-technology/statistics-research/child-maltreatment.

Wall, J., Koch, S., Link, J., & Graham, C. (2010). Lessons learned from 14 years of outcomes: The need for collaboration, utilization and projection. *Child Welfare, 89*(2), 251–267.

Weiner, D., Lieberman, R., Huefner, J., Thompson, R., McCrae, J., & Blau, G. (2018). Feasibility of long-term outcomes measurement by residential providers. *Residential Treatment for Children & Youth, 35*(3), 175–191.

Whittaker, J. K., Holmes, L., del Valle, J. F., Thompson, R., & Zeira, A. (2016). Therapeutic residential care for children and youth: A consensus statement of the international work group on therapeutic residential care. *Residential Treatment for Children and Youth, 33*(2), 89–106.

Woll, T., & Martone, W. (2018). *10th Annual Trends Report.* Unpublished document obtained from interviews.

12

DEVELOPING FISCAL AND FINANCING STRATEGIES FOR RESIDENTIAL INTERVENTIONS

Julie Collins and Sherry Peters

Introduction

The last few years has seen an increased need to transform residential and community-based services in child welfare, behavioral health and juvenile justice, and to a lesser extent, education. In fact, the federal Substance Abuse and Mental Health Services Administration (SAMHSA) and the Centers for Medicare and Medicaid Services (CMS) are funding transformation efforts as part of the System of Care (SOC) Expansion grants and Medicaid Informational Bulletins and directives. As a result, there has been an increase in the availability of effective funding options for states, counties, and providers to implement the new frontier of transformational practices and the Building Bridges Initiative (BBI) framework. In addition, in February of 2018, the Family First Prevention Services Act (Family First) became law, creating a significant funding tool for the child welfare system. This legislation addresses a number of the challenges that made it difficult for child welfare systems to fund any significant type of residential transformation or to prevent the need for out-of-home intervention altogether. While not yet implemented at the time of this writing, the Family First funding option is referenced in this book and throughout this chapter so that readers will understand which components of the new law will form the basis of the fiscal and financing strategies for the new frontier.

While the chapter on fiscal strategies in the prior Building Bridges Initiative book, "Residential Interventions for Children, Adolescents and Families: A Best Practice Guide," provided high-level information related to the potential funding sources, this chapter provides more in-depth information related to specific funding sources that have and will be key driving forces for the new frontier (Collins, McLaughlin, Peters, & Rauso, 2014). The chapter also

Developing Fiscal and Financing Strategies **255**

provides information on unique fiscal strategies that can help states, counties, cities, and providers understand the options available to them.

What It Takes

When leaders at the state, county, city, and provider (both residential and community-based services) levels are asked how they funded or are funding their residential transformation they all say the same thing: The money does not matter so much as the best practice fiscal strategies laid out in the following checklist. As Jeremy Kohomban, President of The Children's Village (NY), has said, "You can have all the money you want but if you did not do these things—you will not be successful" (Personal communication, n.d.). The following *BBI Best Practice Fiscal Strategies Check List* is a compilation of the actions or strategies that leaders interviewed identified using to implement principles and best practices consistent with BBI. The order in which these actions and strategies are implemented is not intended to be prescriptive. What is most important is that they are used and implemented to realize success.

Table 12.1 BBI Best Practice Fiscal Strategies Checklist

Key Actions for Success

- ☐ Respond to Need for Change
  Ex: Lawsuit; legislation; improved outcomes; right size residential/congregate care; policy change
- ☐ Ensure Strong Leadership to Lead Transformation Effort
- ☐ Adopt a Reframe of Residential Services
  Residential is an intervention and not a destination
- ☐ Research, Review and Analyze Data to Determine Needs and Direction
  Ex: Current performance; fiscal and outcomes data; specific populations; cross-agency and state/regional data trends; visit others with successful residential transformation
- ☐ Identify General System Enhancements Needed to Support the Shift
  Ex: What can be done without any new money, with new money, later with new money
- ☐ Get Expert Help
  Ex: BBI experts; others with documented successful transformations who have improved positive outcomes post-discharge; and developers of evidence-based practices/programs
- ☐ Find Out What Others are Doing
- ☐ Work with Other Child Serving Systems/Agencies
- ☐ Create an Advisory Council/Group of Key Stakeholders
  Ex: Residential and community provider leaders; family and youth peer advocates; families and youth; staff; funders; community stakeholders; and other child and family serving systems reps

(Continued)

Table 12.1 (Continued)

Key Actions for Success

☐ Obtain Input from Key Stakeholders
Ex: Identifying service gaps in the community; overall model design; implementation strategies (for request for proposals, rate setting, training, outcomes, and performance requirements); ongoing evaluation/Continuous Quality Improvement (CQI)

☐ Build on Prior/Other Efforts

☐ Embed New Expectations
Ex: Regulations; licensing requirements; requests for information/requests for proposals; contracts; policy and procedures; job descriptions; supervision and staff evaluation; training programs; data and reporting requirements

☐ Embed BBI/SOC Principles
Ex: Program practices; all program materials; funding; staff skills; etc.

☐ Train/Prepare State/County Staff, Community Stakeholders Including Youth and Families, Funders, and Providers for the New Conceptual Framework/ Redesign
Ex: Expert presentations; use of the BBI Self-Assessment Tool; identify/detail new expectations; train on BBI and best practices; adopt CQI approach

☐ Start Somewhere—act on at least one or two of the best practices and track the outcomes and learn from the results.

Additional State/County/Community Specific Actions

☐ Engage with Other Child and Family Serving Departments to Create Foundation of Trust and Find Workable Solutions for Youth and Families Served by More Than One System
Ex: Create common goals; streamline expectations for providers; address regulatory barriers; pool/braid resources/funds; maintain communication/ information sharing; establish appropriate lead; work together to support the change; create online forum/listserv to have ongoing discussions and information sharing

☐ Commit to a Collaborative Effort with the Providers
Ex: Involvement early and regularly; use data and provide analysis to help them learn

☐ Prepare State/County Staff, Community Stakeholders Including Youth and Families, and Providers for the New Conceptual Framework/Expectations:
Ex: Use data to support provider transformation/performance improvements; create baseline (what they have done to date); establish transition period; provide supports for transformation and learning environment for the change; contract for results/outcomes

Additional Provider Specific Action

☐ Adopt a Reframe
Ex: Do whatever it takes to help youths and families be successful; goal is success of youth and families in the community, focus of work is on skill building for the family and relationship building, and maintaining as much communication and contact between the youth and the family as possible; incorporate research findings and do no harm

Additional Provider Specific Action

- ☐ Get Support of Board of Directors and Staff
- ☐ Work with Funder(s) to Support the Shift
- ☐ Test New Approach(s)/Best Practice(s), Track Outcomes, and Then Go to Funder to Get it Covered
- ☐ Use Data to Support Transformation/Performance Improvements
  Ex: Create baseline; adopt CQI approach; use data to target resources wisely

Funding Options

Funding Sources[1]

- ☐ Use/Maximize Medicaid and SCHIP (State Children's Health Insurance Program)
- ☐ Mental Health Block Grants
- ☐ Substance Abuse Block Grants
- ☐ Child Welfare IV-E, IV-E Waiver or Demonstration Projects
- ☐ Juvenile Justice Title II B Formula Grants, Justice Assistance Grants
- ☐ Education, IDEA (Individuals with Disabilities Education Act)
- ☐ SAMHSA Grants
- ☐ NIMH/NIH Research Grants
- ☐ State/County/City General Funds (Legislative or Executive Allocations)
- ☐ Social Impact Bonds
- ☐ Private Insurance
- ☐ Private Donations

Common Funding Approaches

State/County/City/Managing Entity—Payment Methodologies[2]

- ☐ Realignment of Existing Funds
  Ex: Blended/pooled—use of funds from different systems/programs put together for specific program/approach; braided—funds from different sources remain in same pots but used to support a combined initiative that allows flexibility but also as integrated as possible; flex funding—funds that are used to support families such as concrete supports for families in crisis; provide flexibility in funding to cover transportation and for bed days when youth in residential services visit in their home with family; create Flex funding pool
- ☐ Payment Strategies and Rate Setting to drive practice changes and support transition costs[3]
  Ex: Per Diem rate (for example initially increase then provide a lower rate when LOS extends beyond acceptable limit); case rate—daily, monthly, or yearly or based on severity of need of the child (tiered system); include risk sharing with built in protections as well as performance requirements; payment to providers are front-end loaded, or based on long-term needs of families, or not tied to placement; payments to providers are made very quickly so they have funds as they need to shift/develop community-based services; funding allows front-loading of services and moves to a service rate approach after a certain amount of time

(Continued)

Table 12.1 (Continued)

Common Funding Approaches

☐ Performance-Based Contracting
Contracting for results/outcomes, which can include incentives or penalties
Ex: Fiscal incentives are tied to indicators of achieving goals; payments are based on the level of need of the child; measure improvement over time; providers are rewarded if there are improvements—penalized if not; first year providers are risk free and paid the "earned" reinvestment dollars; agencies are able to transition to the new model and learn as they go without incurring any penalties; outcomes are increased with new contracts as the providers gain experience

State/County/City/Managing Entity Strategies

☐ Examine/Identify What Can be Done Now without New Money, Later without New Money and Later with New Money from Identified Funding Sources
☐ Review Operations/Budget to Identify Potential Areas for Re-direction of Funds
☐ Work with Funding Agency for Special Approvals for Flexibility or Adaptations of Existing Budget
☐ Reinvestment of Savings in Preventative Community Services
☐ Time Limited Transition Funds to Support Shift to New Practice Model or Quality Requirements
☐ Adjust Payments to Ensure Funding Any New Mandates—e.g., Parent Partners and Youth Advocates
☐ Identify Sustainable State, Tribal, and/or Local Match for Medicaid

Provider Strategies

☐ Review Operations/Budget to Identify Potential Areas for Re-direction of Funds
☐ Move Existing Monies from One Part of the Budget to Another on Own without Need for Funding Source Approval
☐ Work with Funding Agency for Special Approvals for Flexibility or Adaptations of Existing Budget
☐ Work with the State/County/City to Establish Rates
☐ Obtain Increase from Current Funder
☐ Create Flex Funding Pool
☐ Obtain Special Funding (i.e., Grant, Foundation, Donation(s), etc.).

1 For additional information about funding peer-to-peer support refer to: http://www.ctacny.org/sites/default/files/trainings-pdf/medicaid_family-youth_peer_support_matrix_chcs_05-121.pdf and http://www.chcs.org/media/ICC-Wraparound-State-and-Community-Profiles1.pdf.
2 Fiscal Strategies that Support the Building Bridges Initiative Principles retrieved March 31, 2019 from http://www.buildingbridges4youth.org/sites/default/files/BBI_Fiscal%20Strategies_FINAL.pdf.
3 There are different ways to manage the various payment approaches. Sometimes, they can be used together. For example, per diem is often the way payment is made to providers either through a fee-for-service or managed care delivery system.

Oversight Agency Strategies

Key Funding Sources

While the funding landscape continues to shift, there are several key funding sources used by oversight entities to drive residential transformation.

Medicaid (Managed Care and Fee for Service)

Medicaid is a major source of health coverage for children and adolescents (herein after referred to as youth), especially those in foster care, and there are many options within Medicaid that oversight agencies have been using to fund their residential transformational efforts. As illustrated later, CMS policies and guidance provide important opportunities for states to use this federal/state partnership to support the BBI framework and best practices that lead to successful outcomes for youth and their family's post-residential involvement. The Early and Periodic Screening, Diagnosis, and Treatment (EPSDT) benefit is a key component of Medicaid, which is being used by oversight entities to fund their transformational efforts. The EPSDT provisions require all states to provide medically necessary services for Medicaid-eligible youth under 21 whether or not they are identified in the Medicaid State Plan. EPSDT establishes the foundation for a comprehensive service array with both community-based and residential interventions.

In recent years, CMS has issued guidance to help states understand how to support a quality service array. Some of these have been issued collaboratively with other federal agencies. Of significance for the funding for the new frontier is the guidance letter[1] collaboratively issued in 2013 by CMS, the Administration for Children and Families (ACF), and the Substance Abuse and Mental Health Services Administration (SAMHSA). In this letter, the federal agencies encouraged the integrated use of trauma-focused screening, functional assessments, and evidence-based practices (EBPs) in child-serving out-of-home interventions such as residential or therapeutic foster care (referred to in the guidance as "settings") for the purpose of improving child well-being.

Another collaborative document was issued by CMS and SAMHSA in 2013[2] and gives practical examples about coverage of community-based behavioral health services for youth that could be used as alternatives to residential, along with the Medicaid authorities that could support the identified community interventions. This guidance drew, in part, from the lessons learned from System of Care grants and the Psychiatric Residential Treatment Facility (PRTF) waiver demonstration project. Some of these services include intensive care coordination using a wraparound approach, parent and youth peer support services, in-home services, trauma-informed systems and evidence-based treatments addressing trauma, mobile crisis response, and stabilization services. These services can be provided in a managed care or a fee-for-service delivery system. Many states have been building capacity for a comprehensive community-based service array including most of the services included in the bulletin, especially parent and youth peer support services, in-home services, and mobile crisis response and stabilization. New Jersey (NJ), Pennsylvania (PA), Virginia (VA), and South Carolina (SC) are good examples of states moving along with building capacity for a comprehensive community-based service array. Some of these interventions can be used in conjunction with flexible short-term residential interventions in inpatient hospital or psychiatric residential treatment facilities when necessary (CMS, 2012, 2018). Oversight entities in VA and PA are in the beginning stages of planning for this approach (personal communication from Brian Campbell, Senior Program Advisor in Virginia's Department of Medical Assistance Services, October 2018 and Kamilah Jackson, MD, Deputy Chief Medical Officer for Children's Services at Community Behavioral Health, November, 2018).

State Medicaid agencies have the opportunity to choose among a variety of Medicaid Authorities for providing the type of services needed by the youth and the families that they serve such as:

A) Home and Community Based Services (HCBS) that first became available in 1983 when Congress added section 1915(c) to the Social Security Act, giving States the option to receive a waiver of Medicaid rules governing institutional care. In 2005, HCBS became a formal Medicaid State plan option. State Medicaid agencies have several HCBS options and the most common ones for youth with behavioral health needs are 1915(c) Home and Community-Based Waivers[3] and 1915(i) State Plan Home and Community-Based Services.[4]

- 1915(c) waivers require the youth to meet the level of care for one of three allowable institutional settings (hospital, nursing facility, or intermediate care facility for individuals with intellectual disabilities), and the services can't cost more than they would have in the institutional setting. In addition to all the services that could otherwise be provided, other services include, for example, respite and flexible supports that may not be available through other authorities. New York (NY), Michigan (MI), and Kansas (KS) all use 1915c Hospital waivers to provide comprehensive home and community-based services;

- 1915(i) state plan authority doesn't require the youth to meet an institutional level of care, and states can use this authority to serve people with specific needs and risk factors such as the elderly, youth who are technology-dependent, people with behavioral health conditions, or persons with intellectual disabilities. Under this authority, states can provide Medicaid to people who would otherwise be eligible only in an institutional setting, often due to the income and resources of a spouse or parent. Services similar to those in a 1915(c) can be provided. Indiana (IN) uses a 1915(i) to provide the following additional services that are not part of their regular Medicaid covered services: Wraparound facilitation, habilitation, respite care, family support, and training for the unpaid caregiver.

State Medicaid agencies can choose to implement a managed care delivery system using three basic types of federal authorities: State plan authority [Section 1932(a)], waiver authority [Section 1915 (a) and (b)], and waiver authority [Section 1115].[5]

Regardless of the authority, states must comply with the federal regulations that govern managed care delivery systems. These regulations include requirements for a managed care plan to provide a quality program, appeal and grievance rights, reasonable access to providers, and the right to change managed care plans, among others.

All three types of authorities give states the flexibility to waive the following requirements of Medicaid law outlined in Section 1902 of the Social Security Act:

A) State-wideness: Allows states to implement a managed care delivery system in specific areas of the state rather than the whole state.
B) Comparability of services: Allows states to provide different benefits to people enrolled in a managed care delivery system.
C) Freedom of Choice: Allows states to require people to receive their Medicaid services from a managed care plan.

Arizona has one of the longest running 1115 waivers that are managed by MCOs. The state has transitioned through a variety of mechanisms and entities with the most recent being the Arizona Health Care Cost Containment System (AHCCCS) that operates under an integrated managed care model. With the prior RHBA model as well as with the AHCCCS Youth Development Institute (YDI), a large residential program in Phoenix, Arizona, has been fortunate in being able to get funding to support a way of providing aftercare services.

Initially, YDI was able to dedicate a budgeted position for their project entitled the Building Bridges (BB) Project; this position is for their BB coordinator. Their BB project is to use the same direct care staff and therapist that worked with the youth in residential as the in-home service providers. They were able to do this as they had a guaranteed $100,000 per year block grant funding stream for billable aftercare services designed to mitigate the funding rule that prohibits charges for in-home services while a youth is in residential.

On May 6, 2016, CMS issued a final rule on managed care in Medicaid and CHIP.[6] The final rule provided guidance on how states that choose to use a managed care delivery system have to implement these plans along with the timeframes to be in compliance. CMS has also issued guidance to communicate special protections for American Indians and Alaska Natives related to this final rule, Indian Provisions in the Final Medicaid and Children's Health Insurance Program Managed Care Regulations.[7] For a summary of the provisions in the previous bulletin related to American Indians and Alaska Natives, CMS also issued a frequently asked questions document.[8]

For information about each state and what kinds of waivers are approved or pending, there is a searchable list with helpful details on the CMS website.[9]

Given how critical Medicaid is as a funding source, whether the youth is receiving services in the behavioral health system or child welfare system, it is critical that the Medicaid Directors be involved in the oversight agency design and delivery of the transformation. While many states include their state Medicaid agency representatives in collaborations to fund their transformation efforts (such as Mississippi (MS), VA, PA, and others), that is not always the case in other states. Those that do are able to have ongoing conversations about research, trends, and any new opportunities from any funding sources, including Medicaid. For state oversight agencies who do not have consistent and regular connections with their Medicaid agency, some strategies that may be helpful are those that provide educational opportunities for the Medicaid director to learn more about the positive fiscal impact of using the BBI framework, SOC principles, and best practices. Including family and youth success stories in these educational opportunities along with information from around the country where there are positive outcomes along with cost effectiveness may be effective in getting them involved in the residential transformational efforts.

Family First Prevention Services Act (Title IV-E)

The Family First Prevention Services Act of 2018[10] (Family First) is aimed at addressing many of the challenges that child welfare oversight agencies, including tribes that administer their own Title IV-E program, have struggled with regarding how they can use various funding sources available to them for serving the youth and families that become involved with the child welfare system. In some instances, Family First added additional funds while in others the new legislation gave much greater flexibility to deliver services. The greatest flexibility is seen with the Title IV-E prevention services option, which states can choose. This is one of the hallmarks of the legislation, and this option allows the child welfare oversight agency to use the IV-E dollars, which heretofore could only be accessed once a child was in out-of-home care, to support the child remaining safely with their family (Administration on Children, Youth and Families, 2018). In addition, there are a number of

Developing Fiscal and Financing Strategies **263**

other groups who are eligible for these funds: An adolescent already in foster care who is pregnant or parenting, parents or kin caregivers where services are needed to prevent the candidate for foster care from entry into care, a child whose adoption or guardianship arrangement is at risk of a disruption or dissolution, and children who need post-reunification services.

The other key hallmark of the Family First legislation that is very relevant to the new frontier is the restrictions on the use of the IV-E funds for any non-foster family living situations. There are limited acceptable non-foster family living situations in licensed private or public childcare institutions (with no more than 25 youth). One that is allowed is the Qualified Residential Treatment Program (QRTP).

The QRTP is a newly defined level of care for placement in a child care institution, while many of the types of congregate care facilities/programs (such as residential shelters and group homes) that currently qualify for the child welfare oversight agency to draw down IV-E funds will no longer qualify under Family First. This has significant implications for the oversight entity as well as their existing congregate care providers and other child serving systems such as behavioral health and juvenile justice. A high degree of collaboration will be required among the various oversight entities across the child and family serving systems to minimize duplication of effort, avoid cost shifting between systems, and maximize resources for a comprehensive continuum of services for youth and families served by and across the various child and family serving systems.

The legislation identifies specific components that focus on quality, family, permanency and oversight/accountability. The components reflect many of the best practices identified through BBI and are consistent with research on sustained outcomes post-residential involvement. The QRTP provider must provide family-based aftercare services for at least six months. Child welfare oversight entities and their residential providers have struggled with funding this critical best practices service, so it is a welcome component of the Family First legislation.[11] The only way for the oversight entity to draw down the Family First IV-E funding for the QRTP is through an assessment by a Qualified Individual that recommends the child or youth requires the services of a QRTP level of care and cannot be in a family or other less restrictive level of care. This assessment must be completed within 30 days of the child or youth being admitted to the QRTP if they are already there. Best practice of course would be to complete the assessment prior to the youth going to the QRTP in order to ensure the appropriateness of the program to deliver the types of treatment services identified in the assessment and assist with meeting the identified short and long-term mental and behavioral health goals for the youth. The other relevant issue for consideration is minimizing the number of disruptions and transitions/moves as possible for the youth. However, ultimately, the court must approve a child or youth being in a QRTP based on the assessment along with other relevant documentation. The court is also responsible for oversight and review of the reassessments and other documentation of progress toward goals provided at status review and permanency hearings. The State/Tribal Child Welfare Agency oversight entity is required to review and provide written approval for a continued stay in a QRTP if the length of stay is longer than 12 consecutive or 18 nonconsecutive months for a youth 13 or over (or more than six consecutive or nonconsecutive months for youth under 13).

The value of the QRTP is that it requires a level of quality in a residential intervention service that has not been required to date. And, the requirements encompass many strategies and approaches consistent with the BBI framework and best practices. Family First also provides the ability to fund the critical aftercare services that has been such a challenge for the child welfare oversight entities and their contracted providers to get funded. Aftercare is a service that helps providers to deliver short-term residential interventions and sustain permanency in the home and community post-residential involvement, so funding of such services is critical and welcomed.

While components of the Family First started October 1st, 2018, such as the background checks for all adults working in child caring institutions, restrictions on the use of IV-E funds for QRTP does not start until October 1st, 2019 unless the state requested a delay of the implementation of the requirement.

Strategies to consider for use of the Family First dollars beyond the QRTP:

- Extend the QRTP Aftercare service beyond the required minimum of six months to one year. This would be consistent with BBI best practice and support a longer period for the family and youth to stabilize and further develop and test their skills so that the youth does not return to out-of-home care. Many providers that provide aftercare, such as Youth Development Institute (AZ) and the Children's Village (NY), an organization that has been committed to residential transformation for many years, find that many of the families need at least a year;
- explore options to use IV-E dollars to support BBI best practices to obtain sustained positive outcomes for youth and families post-residential intervention. Examples include the following:
  - Incorporate parent partner and youth advocate positions in the agency;
  - provide family skill building in the home;
  - cover the cost of the bed day for the provider in a way that encourages and supports the youth being at home with their family as much as possible;
  - and fund effective family treatment and support services such as Functional Family Therapy, Trauma Systems Therapy, and Structural Family Therapy in such a way as to allow the delivery of these in the home and community (BBI, 2017a);

Developing Fiscal and Financing Strategies **265**

- provide services to support foster and kin families following residential intervention (such as Kinship Navigator program or Parent Management Training-Oregon);
- develop and use post adoption/guardianship services;
- include payment for appropriate youth development skills focused on successful transitioning to adulthood programs starting when the youth is age 14.

Other Funding Sources

In addition to Medicaid and Family First, other funding sources are available through behavioral health, juvenile justice, and education systems as well. The following funding sources provide opportunities to implement the BBI framework and best practices. SAMHSA administers several funding programs, including Mental Health or Substance Abuse Block Grants and the Children's Mental Health Initiative (CMHI), which uses the "system of care" framework to provide services and supports. CMHI awards these System of Care grants, which are often used to support capacity-building efforts such as training and coaching for implementation of evidence-based, evidence-informed, and promising practices as well as training in some of the core principles such as cultural and linguistic competence. One example of this comes from the Virginia Department of Behavioral Health (DBH). DBH obtained SOC funding to build capacity for High Fidelity Wraparound. Another example is from the Pennsylvania Office of Mental Health and Substance Abuse. PA is using Block Grant funding to support a yearlong training process for state, county, and managed care staff in cultural and linguistic competence. In New Jersey, the NJ Department of Children and Families Children System of Care (CSOC) used SOC expansion funds to provide training on the evidence-based Six Core Strategies© (Huckshorn, LeBel, & Caldwell, 2019), which include focus on family-driven, youth-guided, cultural, and linguistic competence and trauma-informed care and the Nurtured Heart Approach to all of their residential providers. Funding through the juvenile justice system is sometimes available as well for start-up training and coaching for evidence-based practices (e.g., PA Commission on Crime and Delinquency pays for start-up training for EBPs such as Multi Systemic Therapy and Functional Family Therapy, which is eligible for Medicaid or child welfare funding when providers are certified).

Key Methodologies

While there are shifts in the funding sources available for oversight entities and providers that can help fund their initiatives or efforts for residential transformation, the methodologies used by oversight entities as detailed in the BBI Best Practice Fiscal Strategies Check List, provided earlier in the chapter, continue to be relevant even though the language might be shifting as there is greater emphasis on purchasing outcomes. Value-based contracting is a payment strategy term that is increasingly used in contracting not just in behavioral health but also child welfare.

In the BBI document by Bruce Kamradt, the author highlights additional funding strategies for residential transformation beyond those in the BBI Best Practice Fiscal Strategies Check List based on his 20-year experience running one of the most successful and longstanding SOC projects, Wraparound Milwaukee (Kamradt, 2019). The following are seen as being key funding strategies to be used to help move toward the new frontier of outcome focused residential intervention and transformation.

- Realigning funding streams by pooling new or existing monies—This is an approach that has been effectively used by several system of care communities including NJ CSOC and Wraparound Milwaukee, as well as other state initiatives such as: The California's Residential Reform Project, Massachusetts' Caring Together initiative, and Indiana's DAWN project (Kamradt, 2019; BBI, 2017a);
- funding a care management model to incentivize a short-term outcome-focused residential intervention—The NJ CSOC contracts with Care Management Organizations (CMOs) throughout the state for help managing the behavioral health care for youth and families, but it is the state CSOC that contracts with residential providers with a focus on attaining positive outcomes by aligning with BBI and SOC principles, for example the Child and Family Team assuming a very key role in keeping the focus on what the youth and family need. Maryland (MD) and Georgia (GA) both used a care management model during their involvement with the PRTF Waiver Demonstration. As part of the sustainability plan for the 1915(c) Psychiatric Residential Treatment Facility Waiver and health care reform in MD, the Department of Health successfully amended the MD Medicaid State Plan to allow for youth who met certain eligibility and financial criteria to be served by regional Care Coordination Organizations through Targeted Case Management, a service delivery model similar to those used by the Care Management Entity (CME in GA), which serves youth statewide with significant behavioral health needs and who are at risk for out-of-home placements;[12]
- creating comprehensive service array—VA's Behavioral Health state agency and Medicaid agency are working together with The Farley Health Policy Center[BL1] to move to an EBP-based service system with the right continuum of care. "Virginia Medicaid Continuum of Behavioral Health Services" published in December 2018 can be found at http://farleyhealthpolicycenter.org/wp-content/uploads/2019/02/Continuum-Report.pdf. PA has utilized EPSDT to create a comprehensive service array including intensive home and community-based services such as

Developing Fiscal and Financing Strategies **267**

mobile therapy, therapeutic staff support, psychiatric rehabilitation, and peer support;

- re-investing and re-directing savings—The Tennessee Department of Children Services (TN) contracts (using Title IV-E funds) with providers of residential interventions using a three-level case rate based on the severity of needs of the youth. The contracts are focused on outcomes post-residential involvement, such as remaining in their home and community and doing well in school. The case rate is not reduced if the youth does better and thereby allows the providers the flexibility needed to create the community-based services and supports to allow the youth and family to be successful post involvement. The TN Department of Children Services has created a system that has shifted to having a much more robust community-based service and supports network to better serve the youth and families. One positive outcome is that significantly more youth and families have and are being served by the same ten million dollars, and with each new contracting period they have focused on increasing the quality of the services provided using data (BBI, 2011; Collins et al., 2014). In Wraparound Milwaukee in Wisconsin the reinvestment resulted in an expanded community-based service system with over 70 different services (Kamradt, 2019);

- using managed care strategies such as Utilization Management (UM) and care management along with child and family teams and family advocacy services to encourage alternatives to residential interventions— This is a critical consideration for the management of the Family First prevention and QRTP services (which include mental health and substance abuse prevention and treatment services) as they will be accessed potentially by part of the same population. Such strategies can help with maximizing/using the correct funds, care/service planning, and focusing on outcomes while minimizing any duplication of services and competing goals;

- involving the courts through the use of flex court orders—When a court (juvenile or family) is involved in ordering a placement to a particular residential facility it usually is accompanied by a prescribed period and requires the court to be the authorized party to make any changes to the placement. Wraparound Milwaukee for example has experienced delays in providing the most appropriate level of services for its youth as a result of this type of court involvement and control. To address this, they have worked with the courts to develop "flex orders" whereby the court makes the order to the CME and any decisions related to the treatment (including the residential intervention) and care of the youth are determined by the CME. The court is notified when there is a change in the placement. The court can object prompting a court hearing (Kamradt, 2019). This is an excellent strategy to consider especially for the required court approval process for placement in a QRTP;

- financing a Continuous Quality Improvement (CQI) focus to track and manage utilization, cost, and outcomes—The TN Department of Children Services with the support of staff from Chapin Hall has done an excellent job of working with their residential providers using data to manage utilization, cost, and outcomes as well as make improvements. They uniquely provided training and support using data and monthly calls to help the providers learn how to use data to help them improve practice and to manage within their contract. They held the providers harmless if they did not meet their targeted outcomes (BBI, 2011; Collins et al., 2014);
- financing evidence-informed and evidence-based programs and practices—As described earlier in the chapter there are a number of funding sources that can be used to help providers develop the infrastructure to be able to implement and deliver evidence-informed and evidence-based programs and practices.

In the following, find additional fiscal and program strategies to promote both alternatives to residential treatment and short-term lengths of stays for residential interventions:

- Start somewhere with a best residential practice that does not require any additional funding such as: Ensuring youth and family voice in policies and practices, as well as inclusion in advisory committees; child welfare workers and the residential staff working collaboratively to maintain focus on permanency for the youth; and residential providers using data dashboards as a way of ensuring urgency for achieving permanency;
- embed expectations in RFPs, contracts, licensing, etc.—The TN Department of Children Services contracts for outcomes with its residential providers. With each new contract they have embedded new expectations as they work with their providers to increase the quality of clinical services provided (BBI, 2017a). Massachusetts (MA) embedded the BBI principles in their RFP and contracted expectations with the behavioral health and the child welfare providers. In Delaware, the contracting process was used to help achieve the statewide residential reform efforts by the Department of Services for Children, Youth and their Families, Division of Prevention and Behavioral Health services as part of their "Youth and Family Centered Residential Services Initiative." Utah (UT) has performance expectations in Medicaid contracts for rates of family involvement in treatment, for rates of permanency one year from intake into a program for those in child welfare, and for rates of other (non-treatment) contact with family members and natural supports. Providers in UT engaged in the process of defining the performance measures and identifying other needed changes. When creating contractual expectations, some specific considerations are helpful:

- Effective strategies to consider when having to address licensing and regulatory changes: a) Ensure regulations are broad enough to support transformational practices, especially including youth-guided (including the provision of youth peer supports), family-driven (including the provision of family peer supports), and cultural and linguistic adaptations; b) ensure regulations are broad enough to support community integration in the treatment process either through residential providers also being community-based providers and/or an arrangement that allows for residential and community-based providers to work together; and c) ensure regulations are broad enough to support a flexible plan of care between the community and residential programs as needed;
- effective strategies to consider when having to address payment regulatory changes: a) Ensure payment regulations/guidance support is permitted under licensing; b) ensure payment regulations/guidance support staff providing services in the community both during the residential intervention and after discharge; and c) ensure payment regulations/guidance support the provision of follow-up data collection at six-month intervals following discharge for at least two years;
- effective strategies to consider when contracting with a managed care entity: a) Ensure the managed care organization has the flexibility to initiate value-based purchasing such as case rates that support the flexible movement between residential and community-based settings as needed, b) ensure the managed care organization supports the inclusion of paid family and youth peer support either in the rate setting for the residential provider or in separate payments for the peer providers, and c) ensure a process for follow-up data collection either through the state or county process or through the managed care process.
- Fund creativity of the providers (see provider section) in piloting innovative models—In California (CA) the "Res-Wrap" model was developed by LA County and three residential providers. Based on their work the CA Residentially Based Services (RBS) was created, which included the transformational BBI principles. Based on the documented positive results of both initiatives along with some other efforts, the Department of Children and Families created the CA Continuum of Care Reform (CCR). Magellan, a behavioral health managed care company, has been very receptive to creative approaches to address gaps in services. In Arizona (AZ), where Magellan had the contract as the Maricopa County Regional Behavioral Health Authority (RBHA), the managed care entity funded the creative programs of one of the contracted providers, Youth Development Institute (YDI), and in PA they did so with several

contracted residential providers, including Warwick House. Both agencies developed shorter term residential programs to improve outcomes for the youth, and Magellan provided them with the flexibility in the funding that they needed BBI (2017a). Utah created a funding mechanism to pay for travel for staff traveling to a family home for therapeutic work and expanded the services with which telehealth could be used and are making a telehealth service available to providers free of charge;

- use different methods of funding providers—An example of this is the use of a case rate by the TN Department of Children Services with their residential providers (BBI, 2017a). Another is the use of a case rate that allows the flexible services to be applied when and where needed to meet the needs of the youth and families at Damar Services in Indiana. Both of these were with child welfare Title IV-E funds. Magellan in PA contracted with their providers for a specific rate for a short-term residential intervention model. In the MA Caring Together initiative the clinical team is funded to remain involved while the youth goes back to residential, while the residential provider gets a reduced rate. Utah created an enhanced rate for in-home treatment for youth living at home in rural areas of the state;

- support a process for follow-up data collection either through the rate setting process for the provider or through a separate process in collaboration with the state or county—In the initial stages of Wraparound Milwaukee, if providers had enhancements or additional aspects to their programs, they received an increased rate and providers were paid very quickly. These strategies allowed the providers the flexibility to enhance existing services and create new ones;

- contract for value or performance of clinical and functional outcomes for the child and family post-residential involvement. As described earlier, the TN Department of Children Services contracts with their residential providers for outcomes post-residential involvement, and the providers are penalized if they don't meet their targets and are rewarded by sharing in the cost savings if they do (BBI, 2017a).

Table 12.2 (Kamradt, 2019) highlights the level of difficulty of the methodologies detailed here and in the previous BBI Best Practice Fiscal Strategies Checklist.

Child welfare oversight agencies have already begun using the same steps and actions consistent with the BBI Fiscal Strategies Best Practice Checklist as they prepare themselves and their providers for the significant reform efforts that the Family First legislation requires related to the use of IV-E dollars. While much of the creativity and learning around residential transformation has come from states that have (as of the writing of this chapter)

Developing Fiscal and Financing Strategies   **271**

Table 12.2 Using Fiscal Approaches to Transform Service Delivery: Easier, Moderate, and Difficult Strategies

Easier	Moderate	More Difficult
Expand Service Array	Blend, braid, or pool monies across child serving systems	Re-direct spending from deep-end to home and community-based services
Maximize Title IV-E	Create care management entities	Re-invest savings from reduced institutional care
Maximize Medicaid in lieu of 100% general funds	Finance evidence-based and promising practices	Invest in good data systems to track utilization, quality, costs, outcomes
Finance through EPSDT behavioral health screens	Adopt managed care practices i.e., prior authorization	Modify court orders thru flex orders
Finance an individualized, wraparound approach to service delivery	Utilize and coordinate multiple funding streams	Utilize federal waivers 1915(a), 1915(b), 1915(c), 1915(i) or 1115
Procurement through performance-based contracting	Use of educational advocates, specialized consultants	Providing contract incentives, risk-sharing arrangement

IV-E waivers such as CA, MA, MD, and WI, their continuation is unknown. Although the suggestion in the BBI Fiscal Strategies Best Practice Checklist to use IV-E waivers will no longer be an option, it is included the grid as this option might reemerge at some time in the future. The Family First legislation has been viewed as providing the type of flexibility that the IV-E waivers provided/provide to those oversight agencies (there are currently 27) that have received one.

Provider Level Strategies

While providers of residential interventions are reliant on their funders to outline expectations as part of RFIs and RFPs as well as through contracting, there are many steps that residential leaders can take both with and without their funders that can draw on the BBI framework and best practices and lead to the transformation of their services and organization as a whole. These same strategies are ones that can help them move to the new frontier of residential intervention service delivery. The most common and promising fiscal and funding strategies used by agencies delivering residential interventions that have transformed include:

A. Use the BBI Best Practice Fiscal Strategies Checklist to guide your efforts—Oversight agency and private provider leaders who are working to transform their residential services have indicated that they have found this BBI Checklist very helpful. This practice-based framework draws on the wisdom and experience of those leaders who have successfully transformed.

B. Examine what you can do with no new money—Youth Development Institute (AZ) is a good example of a provider that wanted to do things differently to improve the post-discharge outcomes for the youth and families served. They examined their budget to determine how they might move some money around. They designated one position to do the working with the family in the home and community. As indicated earlier in the chapter, they identified the person as their Building Bridges Project Coordinator. They reduced the number of families that this staff was responsible for to allow the flexibility in their schedule and accommodate the increased intensity needed. They tracked outcomes and when able to produce demonstrable positive results they shared the "model" with their funder with a request for funding. This model program is now part of the behavioral health services paid for through their managed care entity as well as their juvenile justice funder. In another example, leaders from Becket in New Hampshire, which serves youth from child welfare, behavioral health, and education, learned about the BBI framework and best practices and were inspired to go back to their agency to see what they could do without any new money. They too examined their budget to see what they could stop doing in order to have flexibility in their budget to implement the BBI principles. They realized that they were spending a lot of money on transportation for the youth and so bought a number of vans. This increased access to efficient means of transportation, supported their new focus on family time, and facilitated their ability to ensure youth spent time with their family even if they lived hours away from the program.

C. Use evidence-informed and evidence-based programs and practices (EI/EBP's), especially those that help with achieving short-term residential and ensuring sustainable long-term outcomes for the youth and the family post-residential involvement. Use data to look at the needs of the population served and to inform which one(s) would be the most appropriate. Start with one and get some experience with the infrastructure requirements needed and the costs for this as well as the ongoing training, CQI process, and fidelity and outcome tracking. Borrow what you can from others (e.g., attending trainings offered by others).

Developing Fiscal and Financing Strategies **273**

KVC Kansas is an example of an agency that has been using EI/EBPs in their residential program as well as with the family in the home as part of facilitating sustained permanency post-residential involvement. They provide EI/EBPs focused on trauma and parent-child attachment—Trauma Systems Therapy (TST) and Teen CONNECT; Parent Management Training—Oregon (PMTO) for parenting skills; and Seeking Safety and Motivational Interviewing (MI) for substance abuse treatment. They have been able to fund much of this through a federal grant they received from the Children's Bureau ACYF that was focused on permanency. They partnered with the University of Kansas for evaluation support. They use evidence-based approaches that support timely, lasting permanency with a safe and connected framework and flexible, adaptive services such as: a) Intensive to less-intensive service periods that last one-year post permanency, b) 24/7/365 support, c) ongoing adoption support services, d) dedicated staff with specialized training focused on sustained permanency, and e) evidence-based assessments and case planning. Refer to *Implementing Effective Short-Term Residential Interventions: A Building Bridges Initiative Guide* (BBI, 2017b) for additional examples https://www.buildingbridges4youth.org/sites/default/files/BBI%20Short%20Term%20Residential%20Intervention%20Guide.pdf.

D. Talk with funders—test a practice or strategy, prove it works, and then approach a funder to pay for it. In addition to the examples that have already been identified earlier in the chapter, the following are examples of the types of practices to discuss with funders:
   - Support to be able to collect post-discharge outcome data;
   - support for a range of best practices including adaptations for culturally and linguistically appropriate and responsive services;
   - and provision of both family and youth peer support either through employment or through an arrangement with a peer provider.

E. Focus on quality—With the increased involvement of managed care agencies managing Medicaid programs for the state as well as the new Family First legislation that has a focus on quality providers, residential providers will need to incorporate practices that improve the quality of their services. Value-based contracting for achieving positive sustained outcomes post-residential along with greater funder and state expectations to use evidence-informed and evidence-based programs and practices will be key levers in providers' of residential interventions increased focus on quality. The use of the Six Core Strategies© (Huckshorn et al., 2019) framework by agencies such as Youth Development Institute (AZ) to reduce the use of restraint and seclusion or the examination of outcomes such as practiced by The Children's Village (NY) and Damar Services (IN) have helped these agencies improve their quality of services. These strategies have also helped the agencies demonstrate their commitment of "doing whatever it takes" for families to successfully support their youth at home and in the community. In Philadelphia a Learning/Practice Collaborative of residential providers provides a structured forum to share learning about BBI practices as well as successes and lessons learned with each other. This strategy is a way to increase the quality of the programs by creating more consistent and aligned care consistent with BBI across the residential provider network for a specific shared population.

Conclusion

Despite advances in the flexibility of the funding sources that will support the transformations that are being asked for and desired, the challenge still exists for how each oversight agency and its provider partners make the service delivery system effective for the youth and families they serve. The strategies outlined in this chapter will assist oversight agencies, their provider partners, the youth and families, and other key stakeholders in moving toward the new frontier. The vastness of this new frontier will yield many more strategies that have yet to be conceived.

Notes

1. Dear State Director letter found at www.medicaid.gov/Federal-Policy-Guidance/Downloads/SMD-13-07-11.pdf.
2. Coverage of Behavioral Health Services for Children, Youth, and Young Adults with Significant Mental Health Conditions found at www.medicaid.gov/federal-policy-guidance/downloads/cib-05-07-2013.pdf.
3. 1915(c) Home and Community-Based Waivers. Retrieved April 4, 2019, from www.medicaid.gov/medicaid/hcbs/authorities/1915-c/index.html.
4. 1915(i) State Plan Home and Community-Based Services. Retrieved April 4, 2019, from www.medicaid.gov/medicaid/hcbs/authorities/1915-i/index.html.
5. Medicaid Managed Care Authorities. Retrieved March 31, 2019, from www.medicaid.gov/medicaid/managed-care/authorities/index.html.
6. A rule by CMS, Medicaid and Children's Health Insurance Program (CHIP) Programs; Medicaid Managed Care, CHIP Delivered in Managed Care, and Revisions Related to Third Party Liability issued on 5/6/16. Retrieved March 31, 2019, from www.federalregister.gov/documents/2016/05/06/2016-09581/medicaid-and-childrens-health-insurance-program-chip-programs-medicaid-managed-care-chip-delivered.
7. Indian Provisions in the Final Medicaid and Children's Health Insurance Program Managed Care Regulations. Retrieved March 31, 2019, from www.medicaid.gov/federal-policy-guidance/downloads/cib121416.pdf.
8. Frequently-Asked Questions (FAQs), Federal Funding for Services "Received Through" an IHS/Tribal Facility and Furnished to Medicaid Eligible American Indians and Alaska Natives (SHO #16–002), Issued January 18, 2017. Retrieved

Developing Fiscal and Financing Strategies **275**

March 31, 2019, from www.medicaid.gov/federal-policy-guidance/downloads/faq11817.pdf.

9. State Waiver Lists. Retrieved March 31, 2019, from www.medicaid.gov/medicaid/section-1115-demo/demonstration-and-waiver-list/index.html.

10. For the legislative language, use the following link www.cwla.org/wp-content/uploads/2019/01/Senate-Budget-CR_bill-text.pdf (starting on page 172) and for federal guidance use the following link www.acf.hhs.gov/cb/resource-library/search#?keyword%5B0%5D=Family%20First&ajax=1.

11. For additional information about the QRTP requirements, use the following link www.cwla.org/wp-content/uploads/2019/01/Senate-Budget-CR_bill-text.pdf (starting on page 172).

12. For additional information about what MD did, use the following link https://goc.maryland.gov/cme/ and for what GA did use the following link www.myviewpointhealth.org/care-management-entity.da.

References

Administration on Children, Youth and Families. (2018). *ACYF-CB-IM-18–02, information memorandum*. Retrieved from www.acf.hhs.gov/sites/default/files/cb/im1802.pdf

BBI. (2011). *Fiscal strategies that support the building bridges initiative principles*. Retrieved from www.buildingbridges4youth.org/sites/default/files/BBI_Fiscal%20Strategies_FINAL.pdf

BBI. (2017a). *BBI fiscal strategies informational document*. Manuscript in preparation.

BBI. (2017b). *Implementing effective short-term residential interventions: A building bridges initiative guide*. Retrieved from https://www.buildingbridges4youth.org/sites/default/files/BBI%20Short%20Term%20Residential%20Intervention%20Guide.pdf

Centers for Medicare and Medicaid Services. (2012). *CMCS informational bulletin, inpatient psychiatric services for individuals under age 21*. Retrieved from www.medicaid.gov/Federal-Policy-Guidance/downloads/CIB-11-28-12.pdf

Centers for Medicare and Medicaid Services. (2018). *CMCS informational bulletin, requirements of section 12005 of the 21st century cures act*. Retrieved from www.medicaid.gov/federal-policy-guidance/downloads/cib062018.pdf.

Collins, J., McLaughlin, W., Peters, S., & Rauso, M. (2014). Policy & monitoring: Federal, state & county examples of transformation. In *Residential interventions for children, adolescents, and families: A best practice guide*. New York, NY: Routledge.

Huckshorn, K. A., LeBel, J., & Caldwell, B. (Eds.) (2019). *Six Core Strategies©: Preventing violence, conflict and the use of seclusion and restraint in inpatient behavioral health settings. An evidence-based practice curriculum training manual*. Originally developed with the National Association of State Mental Health Program Directors (2002–2009), Alexandria, VA.

Kamradt, B. (2019). *BBI leadership series document innovative fiscal practices employed by wraparound Milwaukee: A 20-year perspective on promoting community-based services and short-term residential interventions that support better long-term outcomes for youth and families*. Retrieved from www.buildingbridges4youth.org/sites/default/files/BBI%20Innovative%20Fiscal%20Practices%20.pdf.

13

RESIDENTIAL TRANSFORMATION

Taking Change to the Next Level

Gary M. Blau, Robert E. Lieberman,
Joe Anne Hust, Janice LeBel, and Beth Caldwell

This book is about transformation: Transforming systems; transforming agencies; transforming services; and, ultimately, transforming the lives of individual youth and families. And, in a purely methodological sense, this book is about transforming outcomes. While there is evidence that residential interventions can positively impact outcomes in the short term (during the residential episode), there is limited data regarding post-discharge outcomes for youth and families and enough readmission to residential program data to raise questions regarding whether the significant emotional, social, and financial cost of this intervention as traditionally practiced is justified.

This is not to say there isn't a need to include residential interventions as part of a comprehensive array of services that comprise a well-functioning system. In fact, the editors and authors of this book strongly believe that youth and families deserve a comprehensive "system of care" that includes all levels of interventions, including the capacity and ability to provide appropriate and effective short-term residential interventions.

Instead of casting aspersions or creating conflict, this book demonstrates that to be an integral component in the overall system of care; residential interventions; community-based services; family and youth partners; managed care companies; and agencies that license, fund, and/or oversee this level of care must all transform and embrace and implement policies and procedures that reflect: The importance of family-driven and youth-guided care; the critical need to be culturally relevant, competent, responsive, and humble; and a focus on outcomes and particularly long-term, post-discharge impact to further develop and incorporate promising, best, evidence-informed, and evidence-based practices. The good news, as evidenced in the 12 previous chapters, is that more and more residential programs, managed care companies, and oversight agencies are transforming, and more and more residential programs, managed care companies, and oversight agencies are interested in transforming.

It is important to note that the process of transformation is not easy and must be ongoing. Transformation is a journey, not a destination. The process is a constant and continual desire and attempt to evaluate and improve the way services are developed, implemented, and measured. Transformation is about never being satisfied or complacent and never accepting mediocrity. As a colleague once decreed, "Mediocrity is not in our vocabulary!"

To ensure a focus on transformation and to create a roadmap for the significant work involved in truly transforming, let's take a moment to look back to the "Transformation Equation," a strategic approach that is more than a simple catchphrase (Blau, 2006). This equation represents a deliberate and planned methodology that can anchor and guide individuals, agencies, and systems as they strive to make an impact—in this situation, to improve the lives of children and youth who may have been impacted by trauma and loss and often have serious emotional and/or behavioral challenges and their families—who also may have been impacted by trauma and loss and a range of serious life challenges.

For all transformation challenges, no matter how big or how small, the Transformation Equation can provide the foundation from which to base decisions and actions. The equation is as follows:

$$T = (V + B + A) \times CQI^2$$

In this equation, "transformation" (the T) is a function of Vision, Beliefs, and Actions multiplied by Continuous Quality Improvement squared. The Vision provides the direction for the work; in this case to improve residential interventions for youth and families so that all young people and their families experience successful permanency, joy, love, health, and hope and grow to reach their full potential and live full and productive lives. Beliefs are the values that guide decision making, rooted in culture, morality, integrity, and spirituality and serve as the guidepost from which actions are derived. As evidenced in this book and as articulated previously, beliefs include the importance and urgency of addressing permanency and of valuing, engaging, and empowering youth and families; a meaningful focus on trauma-informed approaches and cultural indices; and a concerted effort to implement best practices and collect useful data as part of the residential intervention and post-discharge to continually improve practice.

Actions are the actual strategies used to apply the vision and beliefs to create impact and improve outcomes. CQI reflects the importance of obtaining frequent feedback, particularly from youth and families, oversight entities, funders, and researchers and policy makers so that individuals, peer partners, programs, managed care companies, oversight agencies, and systems can continue to grow and develop. CQI is squared to demonstrate the importance of this input and feedback. While perhaps only a metaphor for the transformational journey, the Transformation Equation remains relevant to this conversation as a way to understand, conceptualize, and organize approaches for transformational change.

To facilitate transformation, this book has pointed to new frontiers in the way services are developed, delivered, and described. This is evidenced in chapter names and in the various narratives and examples. And, in reviewing and understanding these new frontiers, a number of cross-cutting themes have emerged. What is interesting and exciting about these themes is that they emerged even though each chapter was written separately and independently. It is also notable that although the term "new frontiers" connotes what is out there and undiscovered, the themes for transformation often spring from going broader and diving deeper with what we already know—as suggested by the equation.

The themes variably involve all elements of the equation—whether expressed in vision, values, strategies, or cycles of improvement individually or in combination. They include:

The Importance of Relationships and Partnerships, Particularly With Families, Youth, and Community

Relationships are central to our work and to the human condition. As noted in the neurodevelopment chapter, the brain is designed to benefit from close relationships and making relationships primary in all things—e.g., family-driven care, youth-guided care, cultural and linguistic competence, and partnerships—resonate with our neurobiological needs and systems. A focus on relationships generates the transformational changes noted throughout the book. It fosters the partnerships highlighted in the chapter on Partnerships and Aftercare and is also described throughout the book as critical in engaging families and youth, designing services and supports, developing measurement systems, working with oversight agencies, crafting effective policies and fiscal strategies, and helping youth achieve permanency. In fact, transformation starts and ends with relationships and partnerships.

The Need to Combine "Ground-Up" With "Top-Down" Strategies

Top-down approaches, typically driven by professionals, have a great deal to offer, and change requires visionary leadership at the top. Ground-up strategies systematically incorporate the voice of lived experience and the "end user" at all levels of the system, whether from youth, families, or staff. Both are needed, though often the default in our systems and interventions is to top-down approaches. The importance—and effectiveness—of what can be called "ground-up" strategies was highlighted throughout this book. For example:

- Starting the change progress with the perspectives and voices of the recipients of services—families and youth—and continually including them and all others involved in ongoing change initiatives, services and supports, and measurement priorities—staff at all levels, oversight agencies, community partners, schools, and the legal system;
- hiring individuals with lived experience to broaden and deepen the understanding of the youth and families being served and supported and what helps;
- and, at the level of the youth and family, remembering that controls from within are more likely to generate enduring change than top-down controls, employing sensory and relational strategies to help youth and families learn skills to help them navigate life at home and in the community.

Throughout the book, the synthesizing of such ground-up with top-down approaches was exemplified by the innovations of many agencies across the country and the importance of doing so reflected in the positive results.

The Pervasive Impact of Trauma and Loss

Stress and trauma is a common and unifying theme—not simply that which emanates from difficult events but also that related to disproportional services, inequities, the stresses of day to day life on families and youth, being away from home and family, and the stresses of the work on all involved. Understanding how this plays out in moment in time interactions, organizational life, and systems affords actionable strategies that can help the stress be moderate, predictable, and controlled, the type of stress that promotes resilience and learning. Again, relationships are key—the quality and continuity of relationships is critical for mitigating the impact of overwhelming stress and trauma, thus emphasizing the importance of serving youth in home and community settings as an essential aspect of residential interventions.

The Critical Role of Equity, Diversity, and Inclusion

Equity, diversity, and inclusion (EDI) and the cultural and linguistic competency that fosters them are indispensable practices for diverse and often marginalized populations but also a cross-cutting necessity for all involved in residential interventions. Treating families, youth, and staff with equity and inclusion and honoring their diversity, such as occurs with family-driven, youth-guided, partnership-oriented practice, reduces the power differential

280 Gary M. Blau et al.

that can generate or recapitulate toxic stress. Cultural humility, defined in the chapter on EDI as having the ability to maintain an interpersonal stance that is other-oriented, is applicable across all settings and levels, foundational to family-driven and youth-guided practice, essential for partnerships, neurodevelopmentally aligned, and vital to the transformation equation.

The Need to Focus on Permanency

While a focus in one specific chapter, the importance of permanency permeates the book. Permanency supports, affirms, discovers, and/or reestablishes long-term familial relationships. It shifts young people from institutional to family and community orientation; potentiates family-driven, youth-guided, and culturally and linguistically competent services and supports; and enriches relationships and partnerships. It is a vision, a set of beliefs and strategies, and an observable and measurable focus for ongoing recursive improvement efforts. It is the work of oversight agencies from all systems, in partnership with residential programs, and with urgency to support all youth in realizing permanency.

A Better Understanding of Neurodevelopment

As explicated in a dedicated chapter though not explicitly referenced in other chapters, neurodevelopmental principles underpin the transformational practices described throughout the book. They afford a grounding in research and science that provides a "why" for the "what's" and "how's" of the transformational actions that are the substance of the work of the many authors and contributors.

The Successful Integration and Use of Evaluation Data

Data and results are a recurring theme, providing the measurement aspects for continuous quality improvement (CQI) and a vision, a set of beliefs, and actionable strategies. This vision is predicated on the idea that outcome measurement must focus on post-discharge functioning. Young people improve during their residential intervention; what is most important is ongoing and long-term connections to home and community and functional improvements for youth and families that are sustained in real world settings. Thus, in order to conduct CQI studies, determine the effectiveness of service delivery, and establish evidence-based and promising practices, more robust measurement systems and sophisticated post-discharge studies as discussed in the Outcomes chapter must be accomplished. There must also be a more concerted effort to create and obtain national aggregate data to better inform policy and practice decisions. Ultimately, it will be the successful integration and use of data that will move the field forward.

A Revitalized Approach to Leadership and Supervision

Evident in the descriptions of transformation work is the importance of leadership. While this moves beyond traditional top-down leadership to leadership at all levels, the importance of leaders to articulate a values-focused transformation vision and to sustain the focus with pragmatic operational strategies and CQI is key. And it is not enough. Cultivating leadership from families, youth, and staff in articulating vision and beliefs, designing initiatives, strategies and programming, and participating as equal partners in quality improvement activities and system change is critical for transformation, as has been demonstrated throughout the book.

Ultimately, A Change of Mindset

All of the chapters come together to describe a transformational change in mindset—in the values, beliefs, and actions we bring to this important work and our ongoing efforts to learn and improve:

- From "treatment/care/placement" to "intervention";
- from "treating" to "partnering" and "empowering";
- from "control" to "collaboration";
- from verbal alone to including sensory and experiential;
- from objective data measurement, to inclusion of subjective data and lived experience.

These transformational themes and mindset changes are readily implemented through use of the BBI framework of research-based values and practices that have shown success, as evaluated qualitatively mostly at the program level but increasingly finding more rigorous research validation. The practice pillars of BBI (family-driven, youth-guided, equity diversity and inclusion, partnerships with community, permanency, trauma-informed care, short-term) offer voice and choice at all levels and stimulate creativity and innovation in the selection of approaches and practices and the design of new ones. BBI provides resources to facilitate practice change, provides guideposts for regulatory advancements across the county, and is a foundation for achieving transformation.

The journey is not easy. The transformational changes identified in this book require significant work. They also require a sense of urgency. Youth and families who could benefit from a residential intervention do not have time to wait for professionals and policy-makers to argue about solutions. They need services and systems to make progress now.

That is why the editors of this volume are calling for the 2020's to become the "**Decade of Residential Best Practice.**" The field is challenged to take change to the next level—to identify, address, and reach a host of big aspirational goals for the new decade. These goals include:

- Residential programs and oversight agencies partners urgently focus on permanency practices that begin even prior to admission;
- youth and families feel engaged and empowered to fully partner in choosing the treatments and supports that they can benefit from;
- youth and families are integrally involved in all aspects of residential interventions, including governance;
- equity, diversity, inclusion, and social justice become the norm and disproportionality a thing of the past;
- workforce capacity is expanded, and all staff are paid a fair wage for providing residential interventions;
- sophisticated systems for training, mentoring, supervising, and evaluating staff are fully embedded within residential program expectations;
- all residential interventions, in conjunction with their community counterparts, provide significant aftercare; collect meaningful, standardized post-discharge outcome data; and use this data to inform practice improvement;
- a national database related to demographics and outcomes is created, maintained, and used for quality improvement purposes;
- licensing and oversight agencies, funders, and managed care companies use flexible and creative fiscal approaches and the most up-to-date information to review practices and not only ensure compliance with quality standards that mirror the best practices outlined in this book—but surpass them;
- and evidence-based practices, which are culturally relevant to individual youth and families, are developed, tested, validated, and implemented.

The editors' goal is that all residential interventions will embrace the values, principles, and practices espoused in this book and the 2014 book and that the field will move from transforming to implementing. In doing so, there will no longer be a need for this type of book. Instead, the next volume can focus more on the needs of youth and families with specific challenges. For example, the next volume (if there is to be one . . .) may include successful practices for working with youth and/or their families with substance use challenges, youth and/or their families on the autism spectrum, youth and/or families with intellectual and/or developmental challenges, sexually trafficked youth, and/or youth and/or families experiencing challenges with aggression.

The next volume may also include specific challenges faced by families formed by adoption and address the unique needs of LGBTQ youth and/or the needs of families worn down by the impact of poverty, gangs, and inadequate community supports in their neighborhoods.

The next volume may include faster and more effective strategies to achieve permanency, to support kinship and foster families, and to ensure success with keeping children in their home schools—even while receiving residential interventions.

The next volume may include providing oversight agencies with tools to ensure that children under the age of 13 can be served in family settings and not in congregate care—and to ensure that youth and families receive residential interventions as close to their home as possible and that, beyond the most extraordinary circumstances, youth are not sent out of state for residential interventions.

The next volume may also highlight how different states have already successfully moved to having youth and families assessed in their homes and communities, not requiring extra time away from home for assessment purposes.

The next volume may focus on research that has moved from process and program outcomes to cross program impact, social justice issues in residential interventions, and successful workforce support and retention strategies.

In short, there are many different areas for all residential stakeholders—from oversight agencies to managed care companies to residential programs to family and youth peer partners—to work on to move to the next level and beyond.

The editors commend the many residential interventions that are already transforming and embracing the new frontier of service delivery. We also continue to encourage those that are skeptical or hesitant to embrace transformational change to start somewhere—and to start now. The youth and families who need residential interventions have shared their sense of urgency, and as a field we must respond with that same sense of urgency. The editors commend the courage and appreciate the wisdom that youth and family with lived experience bring to the field of residential interventions. And, to honor these youth and family, we conclude the volume with a story from a parent partner:

> *"I remember the call like it was yesterday. It had not been long since I had become a parent partner, and when a mother called crying, it got my attention. She asked me if I had read the morning newspaper. I had read the article about how much our county was spending per year for out-of-home placement for youth. The amount was staggering, and a lawsuit had resulted. The mom went on to say that she had pleaded for in-home services and supports for her son, however, she was told the types of services her son needed were only available in a residential placement. She*

noted that it would certainly have cost less for services and supports in her home and that she would have learned how to manage his behaviors while receiving the support she needed. She also thought the outcomes would have been very different and perhaps he would not have spent 19 months away from his family. Her words haunted me and are the same words I have heard from so many parents over the years.

Residential has changed vastly in the years since I first heard that mother's words, especially during the past five years since the first BBI book was published. There is an awareness that didn't exist before about trauma and separating children from their families. Residential lengths of stay have been reduced significantly, the focus on permanency is pervasive, and parent and youth peer support are more common. The Building Bridges Initiative and its many BBI champions have played a big role in helping move the system forward to adapt best practices. Nonetheless, there is one best practice that seems to get in the way for many providers, and maybe it is because the steps cannot be standardized and are different in every situation. This practice requires individualizing the approach and thinking outside of the lines. Simply put, true change and transformation require genuine partnerships with youth and families. Such partnerships are key to transforming residential interventions in the future and have been a consistent theme throughout the chapters of this book.

Transformation cannot happen unless this basic premise is foundational and is practiced from direct care workers, to CEOs, to maintenance workers. If you listen, families will tell you what they need. Imagine the future when all youth and families are engaged and empowered. The possibilities are limitless, and hope is the operative word."

Reference

Blau, G. M. (2006). *Transforming children's mental health in America: The 'transformation equation.'* Presented at the National Association of State Mental Health Program Directors Annual Meeting NASMHPD, San Francisco, CA.

INDEX

Note: Page numbers in *italic* indicate a table.

administrative process 82, 135, 245
admission process: key components of
19, 23–24, 46, 89, 101, 125
adolescents *see* youth
Adverse Childhood Experiences
(ACE's) 198
aftercare: community-based support
systems 77, 79, 89, 105, 143–145,
155, 163; discharge planning
20, 156–159; evidence-based
intervention 144, 161, 168; family:
as core component 7, 9, 159–161,
163; organizational partnerships
146–165
Alexander, Martin 235
Alliance for Strong Families and
Communities, the 239
Anderson, Chad 150, 152, 165
Arizona Health Care Cost Containment
System (AHCCCS) 261
assessment strategies 156, 159, 162, 249
Association of Children's Residential
Centers (ACRC) 239
Author Contact Information 93

Behan, Christopher 115
beliefs and practices 21, 59, 64, 100,
150, 225, 277, 280

Berrick, Ken 77–78
best practice, 4, 13, 64–65, 68, 95, 255
Biopsychosocial Assessments 156–57,
187n3
blame: negativity of 9–10, 12, 66, 115, 224
Blanchard, Dan and Melyssa 19
Blau, Gary M. xv, 3, 5, 8, 11, 49, 54, 96,
121, 170, 225, 277
Blitzman, Jay D. 153, 165
Boys Town 164, 165, 240
Brae, Bonnie 137, 139
brain: development of 201–204,
211–212; neuroplasticity 210; stress
response 204–210, 212–213
Brave Heart, Maria Yellow Horse 57
Breton, Amy 23, 26
Building Bridges Initiative: best
practices 1, 4, 236; best practices
fiscal strategy checklist 255,
265–266, 270, 272; contact
information 26, 87, 116, 128, 236,
238, 250, 258; evidence-based
practice 170, 185–186; innovations
and reform 75–77; outcome data
236, 241–242, 245, 248, 250;
purpose 5; success stories 77, 81, 87;
terminology use 186n
Burk, Lacy Kendrick 186n

286 Index

Caldwell, Beth xii, 88, 182,
California Department of Social
    Services (DSS) 67, 166
California's Continuum of Care Reform
    (CCR) 80, 146, 269
California Residentially-Based Services
    (RBS) 78–80
Cameron, Alex 17, 26
career development 36
Caring Together: challenges faced
    133–134; contact information 139;
    principles of 131–132
Carroll, Brian 166
Casa Pacifica Center for Children and
    Families 33, 39, 41, 44, 45; Alumni
    Association 47
Casciano-McCann, Carlene 87, 93
Casey, Annie E., Foundation 69,
    115, 153
Catholic Community Services 106, 107,
    115, 158
Centers for Medicare and Medicaid
    Services (CMS) 254
Chambers, Ebony 22, 26
change process 75, 77–78, 85, 87,
    92, 452
Child and Family Services Review
    (CFSR) 67
Child Family Teams (CFT) 22, 135
Child Welfare League of America
    (CWLA) 67–68
child welfare systems 67, 134, 182,
    237, 254
children: family driven care and 9–12;
    trauma, effects of 12, 23, 40, 57, 229
Children's Village, the: aftercare
    planning 160–161, 264; contact
    information 26, 166; family
    involvement, shift to 18–19;
    outcome data 240
Children's Village: WAY Home 161
clinical services 4, 144
Co-Incurring Developmental/
    Intellectual and Behavioral Health
    Disabilities (IDD) 64
Coalition for Juvenile Justice (CJJ) 66, 67
Cocoros, David 130, 139, 166
Cocoros, Trish 130, 139, 156, 166
Coercion: reduction/elimination of 40,
    49, 136–137

cognitive competence 39, 64, 181, 199,
    202, 224
Coleman, Kristina 160, 166
collaboration: families and youth 17,
    122, 138, 160, 222; leadership and
    community 18, 22, 34, 37, 152, 238
Collaborative Intensive Bridging
    Services (CIBS) 162–63; see also
    FACTS (Minnesota) 76
Collins, Julie 182
Commission of Accreditation of
    Rehabilitation Facilities (CARF) 68
communication skills, building 62–64
community based providers 1, 156, 269
community based services 79, 122, 135,
    254, 260, 274n1
Community Behavioral Health
    (CBH) 137
community engagement 44–45, 96,
    236, 242
confidence building 43
Contact Information 26, 115, 139, 165
Continuous Quality Improvement
    (CQI) 127, 245, 256, 277, 280
CORE Practice Model 67
Council on Accreditation (COA) 68
cultural and linguistic competence
    (CLC): best practices 68–69;
    definition of 55; improving on
    54–56, 67
cultural change 49, 81, 135, 225
cultural humility 59, 276
culturally and linguistically appropriate
    services (CLAS) 66
Cutchins Programs 23, 202, 214, 216,
    218, 221, 223–25

Dalton, Jim L. 14, 26
Damar Services 14, 26, 240
data collection: aftercare tracking 128,
    157, 160, 241; cultural bias 68, 69;
    fiscal responsibility of 129, 269;
    outcome data 238, 280; real time 128
"Decade of Residential Best Practice" 282
demographics 54, 60, 68, 128, 282
Department of Children and Families
    (DCF) (Massachusetts) 124,
    131, 134
Department of Mental Health (DMH)
    (Massachusetts) 123, 131, 134, 229

Index **287**

direct care staff 16, 23, 25, 83, 99, 113, 227
discharge planning: aftercare as focus 2–3, 8, 14, 89, 96, 158–59, 164; BBI Best Practices *255–258*; Caring Together and 131–135; data collection 241–242, 247–248; pre admission/admission, begins at 64, 79, 156, 160–162
diverse workforce 7, 60
Drake, Jason 16, 26

education: advocates 155; ongoing and community 76, 91, 145, 154, 262; programs for special needs and gifted children 81, 87, 156, 178; trauma informed 5, 65, 81, 159, 241
engaging families 8–9, 11, 22, 26, 116, 278
equity, diversity and inclusion (EDI) 55, 69, 279
evidence based practice (EBP's) 18–26, 171, 174, 237, 239, 251n2
evidence informed practices 2, 168, 170, 174–175, 186, 268, 272

FACTS (Minnesota) 76; *see also* Collaborative Intensive Bridging Services (CIBS) 162–63
families with adolescents: engagements with 23
family driven care: importance of 276; partnership for success 4, 8, 19, 27n1, 90, 178; practices 11, 176, 224; principles 9–10, 14, 25, 108, 177, 179
family engagement: contact information 26; importance of 8, 17, 63, 123–124; improving 21–22, 88, 90, 126, 158, 247; practices and principles of 14–16, 19, 23–25; Pressley Ridge 17
Family First Prevention Services Act (FFPSA) 3, 7n, 8, 76, 143, 177, 187n4, 237, 254, 262
family liaison 89
family partners: caring together service 132; family driven care 9–10, 26n; organizational shift of 13; roll of 8, 12–13 48; titles of 12; youth safety as priority 148
family search 105, 107, 112, 149

family support: contact information 26–27; importance of 13, 24, 41, 110; specialist and counselors, roll of 23, 48, 224–225
Family Systems Trauma (FST) 16
family time 14, 20, 90–91, 105, 272
fiscal and funding strategies: alternatives, promotion of 268–270, 272–274; best practices checklist 255–258; difficulties, levels of addressed *270*, *271*; Family First Prevention Services Act 262–265; funding options 254, 257; funding sources 255, *257*, 259, 262, 265; Medicaid 259–262; value based contracting 266–268
Florida Mental Health Act (Baker Act) 70n
Ford, Joe 114, 146, 165
foster care 46, 48, 76, 81, 148
Friedman, Jeffrey M. 19, 26
funding options 260
funding sources 255, *257*, 259, 262, 265

Galyean, Leticia 77, 93
girls, services for 16, 46, 156
Grimm, Jessica 17, 26

H.R.253 (Family First Prevention Services Act) 2017–2018 69, 72
Hathaway-Sycamores Child and Family Services 115, 146
health: behavioral 66; public, 66
hearing impaired and deaf youth 63
Heintz, Laura 22, 26
Hull Programs 218–221, 223, 225
Hust, Joe Anne 176

identity awareness 63, 68, 182, 223, 225
Indian Child Welfare Act 67
Indiana Association of Resources and Child Advocacy (IARCA) 238
Intellectual and Developmental Disabilities (IDD) 64
Intensive Treatment Foster Care 78, 81

Jackson, Kamilah 139, 260
Jewish Board, the 61
Joint Commission 67
juvenile justice, improved support systems 66–67, 94, 134, 153, 161

288 Index

Kairos, Youth MOVE 44
Kamradt, Bruce 266
Kent, Warren 17, 26, 160, 166
Kohomban, Jeremy 88, 255
Knapp, Angel 14, 26
KVC Health Systems (KVC Kansas) 150, *151*, 273

Lambert, Matthew 164–165
LeBel, Janice xxv, 75, 76, 77,80, 120, 128, 139, 198, 212, 213, 217
length of stay reduction 79, 91, 128, 149, 151, 247
lesbian, gay, bisexual, transgender and questioning, intersex, or two-spirit (LGBTQI2-S) youth 5, 65
Lieberman, Robert E. xiii, 125, 143,
linguistic competence 62
Lister, James 115
lived experience, voice of 212, 218, 224, 227–228, 278
long term outcomes, improving 2–4, 15, 46, 94, 125, 143, 173, 272
Lopez, Luis 156, 166
Lyons, Denise 14, 26

Madera, Vincent 160, 166
Magellan Health Service (MHS) 121, 269–270
Manley, Elizabeth 139
Manners, Debra 115, 146, 165
Martin, Amanda 16, 26
Martin, William R. (Bill) 81, 93
McCloud, Patti 17, 26
Medicaid 129, 237, 254, *257*, 258n1, 259–265, *271*
mental health: care and services for 9, 23, 25, 45, 122, 137; contact information 27, 69–70, 139; peer support 33–35, 37, 46; transitioning and placement assistance 162–63; trauma, impacts on 58, 78
Methodist Children's Home Society (MCHS) 158
mindset change 34, 76, 83, 281
Multi Agency Collaboration for Youth (MACY) 154
Multi-Ethnic Placement Act 67
Murphy, Carol 139

National Federation of Families for Children's Mental Health (FFCMH) 9, 27, 125
National Standards for the Care of Youth Charged with Status Offenses 67
nervous system, fundamentals of 201
neurocognitive abilities 222, 224
neurodevelopment: challenges; adverse childhood experiences and brain development 198, 202, 229n; best practices, implementing 200, 211–212, 218, 222–227; brain structure and development 201–202; lived experience 212, 214–216, 218, 224, 227; regulating stress 202, *203*, 212–213, *214*, *215*, 220–222; sensory diet, as coping strategy 216–217; sensory system functions *205–209*; stress response system and brain development 200–201, 204, 210–211; trauma informed care, implementation of 199, 218–220
Neurosequential Model of Therapeutics (NMT) 219
New Jersey (NJ) Children's System of Care (CSOC) 134
Nickell, Mark 106, 112, 114, 115

Olney-Murphey, Patricia A. 93
On the Way Home (OTWH) 164
organizational: culture 22, 37, 61, 67, 85, 123, 225, 245; leadership 55, 95, 97, 115; transformation 80, 82, 95, 101–102, 227–228
outcome data collection: evaluation of 239, 246, 248; impact measuring 238, 242–243, *244*, 245, 249–250; reporting systems 240–241, 247–248; distal 243, *244*, 248; proximal 243, *244*, 247
outcome data tracking 14, 16, 113, 185, 236, 238–242, 273
Outcomes Workgroup (OW) 236, 242, 245, 248, 250
oversight agencies: Caring Together 131; Community Behavioral Health (CBH) 137; defined as 119; methodology 121–124; New Jersey

Index **289**

(NJ) Children's System of Care (CSOC) 134; policy development 124–126; roll of, 120–121, 127–131

parent peer support 9
parent support partner 9, 14, 89
Participatory Action Research 185
partnerships: developing effective and sustaining 1, 12, 22, 146, 149, 154; family and community 21–22, 144, 150; judicial 153
peer advocates 18, 22, 39–40, 41, 45, 228, 255
peer to peer support 104, 258
Performance Improvement Plans (PIP) 67
permanency: best practices for 95, 100–104, 147–148; defined as 94; key principles of 96–99, 110–115; readiness for 109
Perry, Bruce Dr. 198, 219
Philadelphia (CBH), (DBHIDS) 137
Plummer Home for Boys 97
Plummer Youth Promise: contact information 115; Intervention Model 98, 102; permanency, focus on 95, 97, 111
policymakers 6
Positive Youth Development (PYD) 32, 42–44, 48, 180–181
post discharge: aftercare 158, 163, 236–37, 247; data collection 14, 113, 159, 273–277; outcomes 2–3, 11, 14, 21, 89, 121, 160, 225; planning 8, 40, 45, 80, 101, 160
Post-Traumatic Stress Disorder (PTSD) 199
practice based research 171, 175, 272
Pressley Ridge 17, 26
psychotropic medications, reduction of use 83, 124
punishment 43, 97, 228

Qualified Residential Treatment Programs (QRTP) 3, 237, 263–264
Quality Improvement Collaborative (QIC) 126, 247

racism: cultural humility and 59; definition of 56; refugees and 58; trauma and 57–59
Rieger, Paul 137, 139
request for information (RFI) 271
request for proposal (RFP) 271
residential care: efficacy of 17, 169, 173, 277; family driven care 176; youth guided care 179
residential intervention: aftercare 156–159, 225, 236; community connection 2, 8, 60, 96, 143–146, 151–153; evolution of 2–3, 94, 199, 242–243; impacts and outcomes 197, 235–238, 245–248; neurodevelopmental challenges 197–198, 201, 218–219, 222; organizational readiness 245; permanency as primary focus 91, 95, 111; reliability approach 7; transparency 120, 248; youth engagement 6, 31–32, 44–46, 50, 150
residential programs: evidenced-based practices 170, 174; family involvement 178–179; principles and outcomes of 174–175, 278–279; special needs youth 2, 6, 61; standards of, as lacking 175; youth-guided care 180
residential providers: data collection policy 238, 240, 245, 249; oversight agencies working with 119–120, 125, 134; principles and practices 1, 3, 54, 68, 96, 128; youth and family partners 8, 59, 97, 145
residential treatment: background of 2, 75; successful outcomes 91; transformation methods 76, 78–86, 276
Residentially-Based Services (RBS) 78
resources, as useful for families and professionals 26–27, 50–51, 69–70, 116, 228–229, 250–251
Roach, Kevin 158, 165
Roxbury Youth Advocacy Project 153
Ryan, Jenn 154,

Schleicher, Tina 160
seclusion and restraint: contact information 229; reduction in use 83, 87, 124, 137, 273
Secret Harbor 154
self-advocacy skills 44
Self-Assessment Tool (SAT) 241
self-care 34, 38
self-efficacy 43, 181–182
Seneca Family of Agencies (Seneca) 77–81
Sensory Modulation Program (SMP) 219
sensory system: environmental factors 217; self-regulation 216–217
sensory systems 201, 205; behavioral dysfunction 214; calming strategies 214, 216
sexual abuse, trauma 57, 229
Six Core Strategies© 49, 124, 126, 131, 136, 137, 138, 226, 265, 273
social justice 181, 282
Spiegelhoff, Luke 162, 165
Sprinson, John 78
St. Mary's Home for Children 87
staff training, practices and process 21–22, 24, 58–60, 62, 90, 99, 129, 245
Stanford Youth Solutions 22, 26
Stone-Smith, Mary 106, 107, 115
stress response system 58, 200, 204, 210, 213, 222–223
structural racism, definition of 56; *see also* racism
substance abuse 5, 137
Substance Abuse and Mental Health Services Administration (SAMHSA) 33, 49, 254, 259
Swanson, Mona 17, 26
System of Care (SOC) 122–123, 134, 254, 259, 262, 265, 276

Terreden, Rob, 23, 26
theory of change 243, *244*, 246, 249
therapist: contact information 165; family 21, 89, 163; occupational 133, 163; residential 156, 162, 164, 261
Thompson, Ronald 164, 165
Three Rivers Program 23, 26

Title IV-E *see* Family First Prevention Services Act
Torres, Daphne 160, 166
training: diversity skills 63, 124, 129, 245; for families 147, 164, 178; youth peer support specialists 35–38
transformation equation 277
transition: permanency as goal 80, 107–110; schools, back into 157; success, as back to families 22, 42, 105, 161; success, as to adulthood 36, 265; support and planning 35, 40–42, 44–48, 125, 127, 132
trauma informed care (TIC): complex events, healing from 12, 16, 55–56, 60, 198–199, 227; contact information 229; coping strategies 33; impact of 57–59, 131, 136, 197; implementing 23, 61, 87, 121, 199, *214–215*, 226, 281; peer support 35, 48; six 'R's' of 219–222; staff education in 65, 76–77, 82–83, 112
Trauma-Focused Cognitive Behavior Therapy 60, 79
treatment planning 12, 20–21, 32, 42, 63–64, *84*, 98, 105, 162
treatment teams 163, 226
Treehouse Educational Advocates 155
Trout, Alexandra 164–165

unconditional care model 78
United Nations Children's Rights Conventions 31, 176
Upbring Krause Children's Center 16, 26
Uplift Family Services 61

ValueOptions (VO) 135

Walker, Jane 139
Walker, Shannon Lee 115
Warwick House: contact information 26; discharge and aftercare 20; orientation and assessment 19; treatment and training 19, 20, 270
Waterford Country School (WCS) 81, *86*, 93
WAY Home program 160–161

Index **291**

Weiner, Dana 113
workforce accountability 16, 18, 282
workforce development 21, 38, 60–61, 77–80, 123, 129 245
workforce development, peer supported 31, 33–36, 138
workforce diversity 7, 63
wraparound services: contact information 80, 258n; Continuum 133; defined as 78–80, 134, 138, 156, 226; Hathaway-Sycamore Homeward Bound 149; High Fidelity 138, 265; Milwaukee 266–7
Wright, Takisha 17, 26

young adult lived experience 35
youth: cultural changes, identifying 34, 54, 58–59, 110; engagement, as effective for positive outcomes 31–32, 42–43, 46; leadership 182; neurological development 201; special needs services 63–66, 78, 81; trauma-informed care 23, 57; undocumented 91

Youth Advisory Councils (YAC) 44, 182
Youth Development Institute (YDI): aftercare service 261, 264, 269; contact information 139, 166; innovations in care 45, 130, 182, 261, 269, 272, 273
youth driven care 156
Youth Engagement Specialist 90
youth guided care: engagement strategies 31, 48–49, 90, 108, 222; family role in 47, 179, 213, 224; importance of 276; peer advocates 47, 133, 183, 187n3, n4; resilience, building 95, 180–181, 204, 221, 226, 279; strategies for positive outcomes 42–44; youth advisory boards 182
Youth Peer Support Specialist (YPSS) 33; goals 42, 45; recruitment practices 34–36, 41; trust building advocates 18, 22, 32, 33, 40, 223
Youth Thrive 181
Youth Villages 111, 240
Youth Voice and Choice 90